The University of Law
14 Store Street
London
WC1E 7DE

BSL
LNLD 1
TIT

Buying and Selling Insolvent Companies and Businesses

2nd edition

The University of Law

This book must be returned to the library on or before the last date stamped below. Failure to do so will result in a fine.

Bloomsbury Library
T: 01483 216387
library-bloomsbury@law.ac.uk

Moorgate Library
T: 01483 216371
library-moorgate@law.ac.uk

D1343596

Buying and Selling Insolvent Companies and Businesses

2nd edition

Ken Titchen
Solicitor and Licensed Insolvency Practitioner,
Gateley LLP, www.gateleyuk.com

Susan Singleton
Solicitor, Singletons, www.singlelaw.com

With thanks to Keith Arrowsmith

Bloomsbury Professional

Bloomsbury Professional, Maxwelton House, 41–43 Boltro Road, Haywards Heath, West Sussex, RH16 1BJ

© Bloomsbury Professional 2013

All rights reserved. No part of this publication may be reproduced in any material form (including photocopying or storing it in any medium by electronic means and whether or not transiently or incidentally to some other use of this publication) without the written permission of the copyright owner except in accordance with the provisions of the Copyright, Designs and Patents Act 1988 or under the terms of a licence issued by the Copyright Licensing Agency Ltd, 90 Saffron House, 6–10 Kirby St, London, EC1N 8TS. Applications for the copyright owner's written permission to reproduce any part of this publication should be addressed to the publisher.

E S Singleton and K Titchen assert their right to be identified as authors under the Copyright, Designs and Patent Act 1988.

Warning: The doing of an unauthorised act in relation to a copyright work may result in both a civil claim for damages and criminal prosecution.

Crown copyright material is reproduced with the permission of the Controller of HMSO and the Queen's Printer for Scotland. Any European material in this work which has been reproduced from EUR-lex, the official European Communities legislation website, is European Communities copyright.

A CIP Catalogue record for this book is available from the British Library.

ISBN 978 1 78043 201 4

Whilst every care has been taken to ensure the accuracy of this work, no responsibility for loss or damage occasioned to any person acting or refraining from action as a result of any statement in it can be accepted by the authors, editors or publishers.

Typeset by Phoenix Photosetting, Chatham, Kent
Printed and bound in by CPI Group (UK) Ltd, Croydon, CR0 4YY

Dedication

To my family and friends who have always supported me, and in particular to my mother. Without her tales of life in a solicitors' practice I would never have become a lawyer

Ken Titchen

To my daughters Rachel and Rebecca who qualified as solicitors in 2011 and 2012 – may you have as much fun in law as I do and my sons Ben, Joseph and Sam for being there

To my deceased parents, Dr Peter and Anne Morgan

Susan Singleton

Foreword to second edition

Three years have passed since the first edition of this book was released.... three summers, with the length of three long winters. It has been bleak weather and bleaker economic times. In fact it has been so bleak that even Insolvency Practitioners have been feeling the pinch. Charles Dickens would have loved this era and would have found ample material for a few cold hard novels, with happy endings of course.

When I penned the foreword to the first edition I thought then that the immediate future would bring many administrations of distressed companies and many businesses for sale. In fact, since then Western Europe has seen a period of economic stagnation, high unemployment, low demand and low interest rates. Inhabiting this parched corporate landscape are the charmingly named Zombie Companies, Golem like entities with an existence but little life.

And yet in this grey economic climate Ken's and Susan's *Buying and Selling Insolvent Companies and Businesses* has flown off the shelves. Funding for business purchases and for investment has not been easy and so the skills involved in maximising value when buying and selling insolvent businesses have become more important than ever. It is these very skills that this book has helped to hone for the current generation of restructuring professionals.

The politics of Austerity and of trying to balance the nation's books have translated themselves into new legislation and this book has been updated in order to reflect the changing corporate environment and the new hurdles which need to be cleared when dealing with already distressed businesses. And, of course, it is not all bad news as there are the new provisions to make UK PLC stronger and more adaptable to change. This mercantile adaptability has been the mainstay of the UK, and in particular the City of London, since the Middle Ages.

And so the chapter on Employment covers the halving of the proposed period of consultation when redundancies of over 100 people are being dealt with, thus helping businesses to adapt more quickly to a changing environment. The chapter on Raising Funds covers the emergence of such schemes to lend money to businesses as the Business Finance Partnership, the National Loan Guarantee Scheme and Finance for Lending Scheme. These initiatives are helping to replace the funds which used to come from the high street banks before their appetite for risk collapsed culminating in an enforced starvation diet for some of their clients. The chapter on Leasehold Premises shows us how insolvent businesses are now more likely to survive and to be sold successfully, as pre administration rent is confirmed as an unsecured claim as opposed to a cost of the administration.

As regards balancing the nation's books the chapter on Pension Law introduces us to the new environment of vastly increased employers' workplace pension obligations. The chapter on Pre-Packs reminds us that whilst it is important for the nation to be able to dynamically reprocess its ailing businesses and get them back making a contribution to the country's coffers, it is important that this process inspires confidence and trust in the business community through it being transparently honest and fair. And, on the technical side, Chapter 1 briefs us on the confused state of the case law dealing with the process of putting companies into administration and reminds us of the common sense approach as to who to give legal notice to in such circumstances.......everyone!!

The world and business have become more regulated and complex. There is no place for flabby companies and woolly thinking. Ken's and Susan's book reflects this changing environment and is keenly to the point and focused on briefing its readers as to what they need to know in order to successfully restructure a distressed business, whether they are selling or buying one.

Finbarr O'Connell, Smith & Williamson LLP
http://www.smith.williamson.co.uk/

May 2013

Smith & Williamson is a leading independent provider of investment management, accountancy, tax, corporate and financial advisory services to private clients, corporates, professional practices, and non-profit organisations. With 11 principal offices in the UK and Ireland, 1,500 people and an international capability in over 100 countries, its aim is to provide an innovative global service.

Finbarr O'Connell is a partner in the Restructuring and Recovery Services department at Smith & Williamson. He has 30 years' restructuring and turnaround experience at the highest level. He is a specialist in Fraud and Asset Tracing work and is constantly surprised that nothing surprises him anymore.

Finbarr is a past president of the Insolvency Practitioners' Association and is a Fellow of the Institute of Chartered Accountants in Ireland. He is also a Licensed Insolvency Practitioner.

Preface

In the preface to the First Edition of this book we noted that since the idea was first mooted to write the text, the business and political landscape and the law in which the subject matter sits had developed rapidly. Since July 2010 the economy has struggled to recover, and even now, some 6 years on from the run on Northern Rock and 5 years after the collapse of Lehman Brothers, there continues to be a significant number of companies who are facing enormous financial and market pressures and difficulties on a daily basis. We continue to see a number of high profile insolvencies in the UK, and the rise of the 'zombie companies' limping along with an uncertain future. The financial crisis in the Euro zone rears its head on a regular basis, most recently with the near collapse of the banking system in Cyprus, and the resulting bail out conditions causing shockwaves across Europe and beyond. The global threat of terrorism remains in place, and political uncertainty continues, most latterly in the Korean peninsula.

It is interesting to see that some of the key issues faced by businesses and their suppliers have remained constant throughout the period since July 2010. There is still a great deal of concern about the use of pre-pack administrations, both in the business community and in government, and the Select Committee and the Department of Business, Innovation and Skills continue to review the process alongside the Insolvency Service. The courts have looked further at the balance between a company in administration and a landlord when it comes to the payment of rent. Companies with a large leasehold estate and their landlords continue to grapple with the need to downsize property portfolios, the mechanisms used to achieve downsizing, and the resulting empty sites. The Employment Tribunal continues to be faced with issues relating to responsibility for payment of employee costs when a business has gone into administration.

However as before, where there are difficulties to address there are also opportunities. A number of businesses specialising in restructuring have grown their skill sets and their portfolios. The restructuring community continues to recognise that the pre-pack remains a useful tool, and it has been crucial to maintaining a number of businesses over the course of the last three years. Whilst there will always be some stakeholders who suffer as a result of an insolvency, pre-packs have enabled administrators to preserve many jobs, both directly as a result of keeping a business trading and by ensuring the survival of a key customer for many companies in supply chains. Pre-packs have helped to keep many buildings occupied, when the alternative is yet more empty and desolate high streets and disused industrial parks. They have also helped creditors to achieve a better outcome than would otherwise be the case where failure of the underlying business without restructuring would be inevitable.

Company voluntary arrangements (CVAs) continue to be in the news as far as landlords are concerned, and whilst their use generally has not developed since this book was first published their use in reducing large and cumbersome leasehold estates has progressed.

The role and practice adopted by HM Revenue & Customs and credit insurers remains important as they continue to be key stakeholders in many faltering companies.

The law has also developed over the course of the last three years, and it continues to do so. Some changes have not been helpful to practitioners, such as the confusion that has arisen as a result of two conflicting interpretations by the court of the procedure by which directors appoint administrators. Other changes have been beneficial, such as the modernisation of the Insolvency Rules which has allowed office holders to make far better use of electronic media, making their work more effective and costs more proportionate. Proposed reforms are intended to make insolvencies of European groups less complex. In an uncertain economic world, the law does not stand still.

As with the First Edition, this book is intended to be a practical and legal guide to the sale and purchase of an insolvent business, and is not a definitive explanation of all relevant law and practice. It aims to be comprehensive, and useful to insolvency practitioners and other professionals working in the restructuring and insolvency arena, whether accountants, lawyers, agents or others. It is of use to potential investors and their advisors, and will hopefully inspire students to make this their field of practice in future years.

Between us, Susan Singleton and I have reviewed the different insolvency procedures which you might come across. We have considered specific techniques of dealing with the purchase of an insolvent business, including pre-packs and how they might be used in a positive manner. There are of course a number of areas of concern to be considered on a pre-pack and we have also highlighted those, considering matters such as the re-use of a prohibited name. Notwithstanding that sales of insolvent business often take place within a very tight timescale, it remains extremely important for a purchaser to carry out even limited due diligence, and Susan has focused on that in Chapter 4. We have also looked at funding the transaction, and have highlighted how raising and paying the purchase price may differ from the usual purchase of a business which readers might be more familiar with.

Issues which come up in any corporate transaction are relevant and we have looked at assets which you would normally wish to include in or exclude from the transaction, particularly when the target is insolvent. We have also considered how you deal with employees, pensions and ensuring that the business can continue successfully in a different format after the transaction has completed. Finally, we have considered the specific position of a landlord and how the rights of secured creditors can impact on what a purchaser is trying to achieve.

I continue to find the restructuring and insolvency arena a fascinating one to work in. Although the law relating to insolvency is highly technical and specialised, in practice restructuring and insolvency is one of the most commercial arenas you could wish to operate in. I have been lucky in my career to have met and helped a wide range of businesses in many sectors, to have worked with companies large and small, and to meet a lot of very focused and motivated people. I hope that others people picking up this book will be similarly motivated to continue with, or to make, restructuring and insolvency as their chosen field.

I would personally like to thank my colleagues at Gateley LLP who have assisted me in writing my part of this book, in particular, Chris Davies and Jill Walters. They have provided very constructive and invaluable comment and assistance in dealing with the more specialised areas of employment and pensions.

The law in this book is current as at 1 April 2013. It is that law applicable to England and Wales.

Ken Titchen, Gateley LLP

Foreword to first edition

When invited to write the foreword to *Buying and Selling Insolvent Companies and Businesses* I was sitting on the bottom steppe of a mountain range in central Asia humming a Borodin tune to myself. The invigorating mountain air gave me a crystal-clear understanding of the significance of the arrival of this book at a time in the UK when business insolvencies and the lack of available finance to purchase businesses are, and will continue to be for some time, major issues. Quite simply, the providers of finance do not wish to take any more risks than are absolutely necessary with their funds when they finance the purchase of an insolvent company or business, and this means that business sales and purchases are more highly engineered today than ever before.

In my quarter of a century in a profession which has rebranded itself from *Insolvency* to *Corporate Recovery* to *Restructuring* and which would probably have gone on to rebrand itself as *Corporate Makeover* had the current recession not arrived, I have seen the process for selling insolvent businesses change beyond recognition. Gone are the days of a receiver and later of an administrator learning frantically about how to build nuclear submarines or how to trade financial derivatives having been appointed, out of the blue, to these businesses by a stressed banker late on a Friday afternoon. Nowadays, there are very few, if any, surprise appointments and the process of being appointed administrator over a distressed company is just a stage in a planned sequence of events aimed at removing or at least controlling the risk variables from a business sale.

This highly engineered business-sale environment means that the sellers, purchasers, funders and professionals involved in these sales must be completely up to date with all of the knowledge and skills necessary to ensure that the planned outcome is achieved. This does not mean that the partners in the large firms cannot don their tweeds and go to their country estates on a Friday afternoon – it just means that they must bring their blackberries with them and that their trusted lieutenants must stay in the office.

One major development in this process of de-risking business sales has been the arrival of the pre-packaged administration ('pre-pack'), and Ken's and Susan's book has very properly highlighted the significance of this development. Very simply, the pre-pack process describes a procedure in which the distressed business is confidentially marketed and then, based on the results of that marketing, packaged for sale prior to the appointment of an administrator. The administrator will have been involved in the planning stage of the pre-pack process and, when they are comfortable with it, will execute the sale. Clearly, the creditors will be concerned that the business is being sold at the best price, and the control mechanism to ensure that this is the case is that the sale will be carried out by an independent licensed insolvency practitioner, acting as administrator, whose professional reputation (and PI policy!!) is at risk if they have undersold the business. Ken and Susan's book recognises the importance of this balancing act for the administrator and makes it clear how an administrator should go about getting themselves comfortable with a business sale in a pre-pack situation.

Whilst there are a lot less sales of insolvent companies than businesses I was involved a few years ago in the sale of an insolvent company. The reason why the company was being offered for sale rather than the business was because the company had the non-transferrable right to race a Formula 1 team.

Ken and Susan's book is completely up to the minute and is packed full of all the essential information relating to the important issues which anyone involved in the sale or purchase of an insolvent business needs to know. Whilst there are other books which cover some of the issues relating to this area, their book is the only one which contains all of the relevant issues in one well-referenced volume. The book is a timely arrival in this hothouse environment where knowledge is king and where those who can successfully navigate their way through all of the issues will succeed in maximising value for themselves or for their clients from the sale of insolvent companies or businesses.

Finbarr O'Connell, Managing Partner, Re10
http://re10.org.uk/

June 2010

Re10 is one of the leading independent turnaround specialists in the UK. Its expert team has a wealth of industry experience across many industry sectors, and works with organisations of every size on a local, national and international basis.

Finbarr O'Connell is the Managing Partner of Re10. He has over 25 years' restructuring and turnaround experience at the highest level. Prior to joining Re10, Finbarr spent 10 years with KPMG LLP where he was a Partner in their London Restructuring practice.

Finbarr is a past president of the Insolvency Practitioners' Association and a Fellow of the Institute of Chartered Accountants in Ireland. He is also a Licensed Insolvency Practitioner and Member of the Institute of Credit Management.

About the authors

Ken Titchen has been a solicitor for over 19 years, and he has dealt with almost every aspect of restructuring and insolvency in his career. He joined Gateley LLP in London in 2011, after spending most of his career with another national law firm. Ken carries out mostly non-contentious assignments in the UK and, together with professionals in other jurisdictions, across Europe and the United States. Ken represents lenders and insolvency practitioners, boards of directors, turnaround professionals and other stakeholders in distressed businesses, and he has recently been involved in assisting major clearing banks and insolvency practitioners in several high profile UK restructurings.

Ken has written a number of articles and legal updates, and is a regular speaker on restructuring and insolvency related topics at training seminars and conferences, whether they are local, national or international events. Ken is a member of the Association of Business Recovery Professionals (R3), the Insolvency Lawyers Association and INSOL Europe, and he works closely with colleagues who are members of the Turnaround Management Association (UK) and the Institute for Turnaround. Ken is a Licensed Insolvency Practitioner (non appointment taking).

About Gateley LLP

Gateley is a full service national law firm with a real passion for local delivery. Promoting the commercial and strategic interests of companies, individuals and organisations across the UK and beyond, the firm offers a partner-led, solutions-driven service.

Founded in 1974, Gateley has grown to be a firm of over 140 partners spread across 9 offices. Gateley continues to attract work from a range of clients including SMEs, major UK companies and UK subsidiaries of overseas-owned corporates. The firm is particularly adept in providing legal advice in corporate, banking, employment, real estate, planning, corporate recovery and pension matters. Key sectors include financial services, retail, telecommunications, energy services, social housing and local and central government.

Gateley has been ranked as the leading national firm for service delivery and partner relationships in the 2012 Legal Week Client Satisfaction Report.

Susan Singleton is a solicitor with her own London solicitor's firm, Singletons (www.singlelaw.com) which specialises in commercial law including buying and selling companies, commercial litigation, competition law, intellectual property law and IT/ecommerce law. Trained at Nabarro, she joined Slaughter and May on qualifying, moving to Bristows, where she remained until founding her own law firm in 1994. Since then she had advised over 800 clients In 2002 she acted for the claimant in the first damages action for breach of the EU competition rules to come before the English courts *Arkin v Borchard and*

Others. Her clients range from major plcs and institutions around the world to small start up businesses. She is a frequent speaker at legal courses at home and abroad speaking at about 50 conferences a year.

She is author of over 30 law books on topics such as internet and ecommerce law, competition law, commercial agency law, data protection legislation and intellectual property and writes regularly for the Solicitors Journal. She is author of *Buying and Selling Private Companies and Businesses* (Beswick & Wine, 8th edition, Bloomsbury Publishing). She speaks at about 50 conference a year in the UK and abroad in areas such as contract law, data protection and intellectual property, competition and commercial law fields. In 2010 she acquired the subscription legal journals IT Law Today, Finance and Credit Law, Corporate Briefing and International Trade Finance from Informa.

She is Vice Chairman of the Competition Law Association, is a member of the Licensing Executives Society (EC/Laws Committee) and serves on the Contracts Group of the Chartered Institute of Purchasing and Supply (CIPS). Until 2010 she sat as an independent member/Director on the Direct Marketing Commission. She has five children and lives in London.

Susan Singleton
Singletons
Solicitors
Tel 020 8866 1934
Fax 020 8866 6912
www.singlelaw.com
Email susan@singlelaw.com
Twitter – @Singlelaw

About Singletons, Solicitors

London commercial law firm Singletons was founded in 1994 and provides advice to clients from all over the UK and abroad from large plcs to small start up businesses in the area covered by this report – terms and conditions of sale – retention of title clauses and commercial disputes and litigation as well as the following:

— commercial litigation/disputes

— competition law – advisory and guidance, litigation, OFT, EU

— intellectual property

— IT/ecommerce law

— commercial agency regulations and claims

— agency and distribution agreements

— buying and selling businesses

Contents

Contents

Table of Statutes

Table of Statutory Instruments

Table of EC and International Material

Table of Other Material

Table of Cases

Chapter 1

What is Corporate Insolvency?

Introduction

1.1　There is no officially accepted or formal definition of 'insolvent' or 'insolvency' set out in the legislation relevant to insolvency. As a result the terms can be defined in a number of different ways depending on the context in which they are used.

A company may be insolvent as it cannot meet its debts as they fall due[1] even though it has a positive balance sheet and the value of its assets is greater than the amount of its liabilities. This is often termed 'cash flow' insolvency and is usually the most immediately apparent indicator of an insolvent company. A shortage of cash is usually what brings a company into the realm of an insolvency professional. However a company may also be insolvent at a time when it is able to pay its debts as they fall due. The reason is that it has a negative balance sheet, where the value of its assets is less than the amount of its liabilities[2]. This is often termed 'balance sheet' insolvency. For the purposes of the Insolvency Act 1986 ('IA 1986') liabilities taken into account when considering whether a company is balance sheet insolvent include contingent and prospective liabilities.

Alternatively a company may be said to be insolvent as it has entered into a formal insolvency process, for example where an administrator or liquidator has been appointed to take control of the company's affairs[3]. An insolvency practitioner appointed to a company is generically known as an office-holder, whatever the actual insolvency process might be.

A company may also be said to be insolvent if it has entered into a restructuring process, where a binding agreement is made between the company and its creditors (and possibly other stakeholders) by which the company is able to avoid entering into a formal insolvency procedure. Restructuring may also involve a combination of a contractual arrangement made between the company and its creditors/stakeholders and a formal insolvency procedure, such as a company voluntary arrangement ('CVA') or administration.

---

[1]　　IA 1986, s 123(1)(e).
[2]　　IA 1986, s 123(2).
[3]　　See section 1.4 below.

1

Insolvency law

1.2   The general aim of corporate insolvency law is to regulate and balance the competing interests of those parties affected by a failed business, including not only those with long recognised interests such as creditors and directors (who may bear responsibility for the failure), but also others who suffer as a result of the process, including employees, suppliers and other business partners, and the wider community in which a company operates. Other interested parties particularly benefit by the legal regime promoting a rescue culture. The law regulating insolvency proceedings is located in a number of different sources, with the result that there is no one place to look to for specific guidance in this area.

Insolvency Act 1986

1.3   The principal statute governing the different formal insolvency proceedings is the Insolvency Act 1986. It provides for four formal corporate insolvency procedures: administration; CVA; receivership; and liquidation. A number of important changes were made to the IA 1986 by the Insolvency Act 2000 ('IA 2000'), and the law relating to administration was revised significantly in September 2003 when the corporate insolvency provisions of the Enterprise Act 2002 ('EA 2002') came into force.

Insolvency Rules 1986

1.4   The Insolvency Rules 1986 (SI 1986/1925) ('the Rules') are the product of secondary legislation made pursuant to the IA 1986 and other primary statutes. The Rules are one of a number of pieces of secondary legislation that operate in the insolvency arena, and they are by far the most important. They supplement the provisions of the IA 1986 and in particular specify procedure that is to be followed when a company enters into, or is in, a formal insolvency process.

The Rules have been subject to a number of revisions since they were first introduced in 1986, and wide ranging amendments were made to them with effect from 6 April 2010 to bring the Rules into line with current practice and procedure in some areas, and to promote new practice and procedure in others. Some of the changes brought in are significant, and it is likely that over time a new body of case law will build up to give office-holders assistance to interpret the entirely new Rules introduced by the 2010 revisions.

EC Regulation on Insolvency Proceedings 2000

1.5   Council Regulation 1346/2000/EC ([2000] OJ L160/1) on insolvency proceedings ('EC Regulation') came into effect in the UK on 31 May 2002 and applies to all EU states save for Denmark. The purpose of the EC Regulation was to introduce an orderly scheme for dealing with the affairs of an insolvent company which carried on its business in more than one EU member state. It provides a regime for determining the jurisdiction in which main insolvency proceedings can be initiated, and describes the roles of office-holders in different jurisdictions should it be permissible for more than one insolvency process to be commenced in respect of the same corporate entity. The EC Regulation does not seek to standardise or harmonise insolvency legislation across the EU member states, but rather to provide an overarching framework within which office-holders operate.

Under the EC Regulation a court of a member state only has jurisdiction over a company for insolvency purposes if that company has its Centre of Main Interests ('COMI') or an Establishment in the member state. Main proceedings may only be commenced in the member state where the company has its COMI. If the company has an Establishment within a member state then it may be possible to open 'territorial' or 'secondary' insolvency proceedings. Determining where a company's COMI is situated, or whether it has an Establishment in a different jurisdiction, is an essential prerequisite to commencing those insolvency procedures that are subject to supervision of the court. There is a presumption that a company will have its COMI in the member state where the company has its registered office. However that presumption may be rebutted and issues of COMI have been considered at some length by national courts across the EU[4], and by the European Court itself[5]. In practice COMI is found to be in the place where a company carries out its head office functions (the so called 'head office function test'), providing the factors that enable the presumption of registered office to be rebutted are objective and ascertainable by third parties[6], with greater importance given to the place where the company's central administration is located[7].

The EC Regulation does not apply to voluntary winding up (unless it is confirmed by the court)[8] or receivership[9].

Forum shopping can occur so that a company may take advantage of the insolvency regime that is most favourable to the outcome it is seeking to achieve. There are now a number of instances where COMI has been changed to make use of the UK administration procedure, and appointments of administrators in such circumstances have taken place via the out-of-court route and on administration application. In *In the matter of Hellas Telecommunications*

---

[4]   For example in *Re BRAC Rent-A-Car International Inc* [2003] EWHC 128 (Ch), [2003] 2 All ER 201; *Re Collins & Aikman Europe SA and others* [2006] EWHC 1343 (Ch), [2007] 1 BCLC 182; *Re MPOTEC GmbH* [2006] BCC 681; *Re Lennox Holdings Plc* [2008] EWHC B11 (Ch), [2009] BCC 155.

[5]   *Re Eurofoods IFSC Ltd* (C-341/04) [2006] Ch 508; *Rastelli Davide e C. Snc v Jean-Charles Hidoux* [2011] EUECJ C-191/10; *Interedil Srl (in liquidation) v Fallimento Interedil Srl and another* [2011] EUECJ C-396/09.

[6]   *Re Stanford International Bank Limited and others* [2009] EWHC 1441 (Ch), [2009] BPIR 1157.

[7]   *Interedil Srl (in liquidation) v Fallimento Interedil Srl and another* [2011] EUECJ C-396/09.

[8]   EC Regulation, Annex A.

[9]   EC Regulation, Annex A.

(Luxembourg) II SCA[10] the court considered the 'head office function test' and was satisfied that the company's COMI had been changed to the UK some three months before the administration application was made. Although the company's registered office remained in Luxembourg, for those three months its head office and principal operating address were in London, it had carried out the majority of its banking in London and all creditors had been notified of its move to London. One of the most important features was that all negotiations with creditors had taken place in London. An administration order was made.

The European Commission put the revision of the EC Regulation in its Work Programme for 2012, and launched a public consultation on 31 March 2012, to include the insolvency of groups and the efficiency and effectiveness of cross-border insolvencies. The outcome of the consultation was issued on 12 December 2012[11], in which the Commission proposed a modernisation of European laws on cross-border business insolvencies based on the benefit of 10 years experience of the EC Regulation. The proposed new rules are intended to shift focus away from liquidation and develop a new approach to helping businesses overcome financial difficulties, whilst at the same time protecting creditors' rights to get their money back. It is estimated that the proposed new rules will benefit around 50,000 companies across the EU every year, and they are intended to be the first step towards an EU 'rescue and recovery' culture. The proposals have been passed to the European Parliament and the Council of the EU for negotiation and adoption, but their final format and the timing of implementation are currently uncertain.

Other primary legislation

1.6   Insolvency law is not confined to IA 1986, the Rules and the EC Regulation. Relevant primary legislation is also found in the Company Directors Disqualification Act 1986 ('CDDA 1986'), the Companies Act 2006 ('CA 2006') and in certain specific statutes relating to specific industries.

CDDA 1986 sets out provisions under which a director of an insolvent company may be disqualified from acting as a director if his or her conduct is found by the court, or by agreement, to have been such as to make him or her unfit to act as a director or to be involved in the management of a company. The purpose of CDDA 1986 is to prevent a delinquent director from continuing to carry on business with the benefit of limited liability.

CA 2006 includes provisions dealing with matters such as the creation and registration of effective security in an insolvency situation, and a codification of directors' duties.

---

[10]   [2009] EWHC 3199 (Ch), [2010] BCC 295.
[11]   http://ec.europa.eu/justice/newsroom/civil/news/121212_en.htm.

Other secondary legislation

1.7   There are many other pieces of secondary legislation which have been made pursuant to IA 1986 and other relevant statutes. Examples include rules to deal with insolvent partnerships, the insolvency of limited liability partnerships, the procedure for prosecuting directors under CDDA 1986 and charges over cash or financial instruments[12].

Regulations are also in place to implement internationally agreed insolvency provisions which are designed to enhance co-operation between those courts and professionals practising insolvency globally. Specifically, the Cross-Border Insolvency Regulations 2006 (SI 2006/1030), which came into force on 4 April 2006, have the effect of implementing the UNCITRAL Model Law in the UK. The Model Law, adopted by the UN Commission on International Trade Law on 30 May 1997 and by the UN General Assembly on 15 December 1997, was drafted with a view to harmonising law on cross-border insolvency in different countries by way of the countries enacting legislation based on the Model Law itself.

Judge-made law

1.8   As in any common law jurisdiction, legislation enacted by or under statutes passed by Parliament is subject to interpretation by the courts. Over a period of time a body of case law builds up which supplements primary and secondary legislation, and in many areas it becomes the major source of authority as the courts fill in any gaps in the legislation, or interpret words whose meaning may not be entirely clear. Judges have made a number of highly significant decisions in the field of insolvency which have had a major impact on office-holders and stakeholders (for example the treatment of a purported fixed charge over book debts[13] and the payment of certain rents as an expense of administration[14]), and on how companies carry on their business.

Practice Directions and Practice Statements have also been issued from time to time to supplement court procedure, such as the Practice Direction: Insolvency Proceedings[15] introduced with effect from 23 February 2012, and the Practice Direction: Applications under the Companies Acts and other Related Legislation[16].

---

[12] Financial Collateral Arrangements (No 2) Regulations 2003 (SI 2003/3226).
[13] *National Westminster Bank plc v Spectrum Plus Limited and others* [2005] UKHL 41, [2005] 2 AC 680.
[14] *Goldacre (Offices) Ltd v Nortel Networks UK. Ltd (in administration)* [2009] EWHC 3389 (Ch), [2010] 1 Ch 455.
[15] http://www.justice.gov.uk/courts/procedure-rules/civil/rules/insolvency_pdf.
[16] [2007] BCC 833.

Statements of Insolvency Practice

1.9   Statements of Insolvency Practice ('SIPs') are not law, but are referred to here as they set out standards of practice that an office-holder must maintain, and they are often taken into account by the court as and when relevant as if they were legally binding regulations. SIPs give guidance as to the best practice to be adopted by authorised insolvency practitioners having regard to the relevant legislation. They are adopted by each of the Recognised Professional Bodies ('RPBs') (the bodies that regulate insolvency practitioners) as part of its regulatory regime. SIPS issued after 1 June 1996 follow consultation between representatives of the Department for Business, Innovation and Skills, the RPBs and the Joint Insolvency Committee, and are under regular review.

SIPs set out required practice in a number of specific areas of insolvency. A breach of the standards set out in SIPs may lead to disciplinary action against an office-holder.

The insolvent entity

1.10   This book is principally concerned with buying and selling insolvent companies within the jurisdiction of England and Wales. However it is important to keep in mind that corporate insolvency is not just restricted to companies that are registered under one or more of the various Companies Acts. Many of the principles referred to in the book will also apply to other insolvent entities.

Partnership

1.11   Partnership is 'the relation which subsists between persons carrying on a business in common with a view of profit'[17]. No formal requirements must be satisfied to create a partnership (unlike for a company), and although partnerships are often referred to as if they were a separate legal entity from the individual partners, that is not the case. Individual partners are liable for partnership debts. Nevertheless partnerships may enter into administration, or become subject to a partnership voluntary arrangement, or be wound up by virtue of provisions of The Insolvent Partnerships Order 1994[18] ('IPO'). The IPO modifies the IA 1986 and the Rules so that they have effect in relation to partnerships.

The insolvency of a partnership will generally encompass the assets and liabilities of the partnership, as opposed to the personal assets and liabilities of the individual partners. However it does not preclude creditors from seeking recourse to the individual partners and their personal assets if claims are not paid in full.

---

[17]   Partnership Act 1890, s 1.
[18]   SI 1994/2421.

6

Limited Liability Partnership

1.12   A Limited Liability Partnership ('LLP') is a body formed under the Limited Liability Partnership Act 2000 ('LLPA 2000'), supplemented by the Limited Liability Partnerships Regulations 2001 (SI 2001/1090) ('LLP Regulations'). Unlike a partnership an LLP does have a legal identity of its own, and only the assets of the LLP are available to creditors in an insolvency scenario. The assets of the individual members are not. An LLP has much more in common with a company than a traditional form of partnership.

The LLPA 2000 and the LLP Regulations modify the IA 1986 and the Rules so that they have effect in relation to LLPs. The amended legislation is very similar to that applying to companies.

Unregistered companies

1.13   An unregistered company is a company or association that is not registered under the Joint Stock Companies Acts or under the legislation (past or present) relating to companies in Great Britain[19]. An unregistered company may be wound up by the court under IA 1986[20] if:

(a)   the company is dissolved, or has ceased to carry on business, or is carrying on business only for the purpose of winding up its affairs;

(b)   the company is unable to pay its debts;

(c)   the court is of the opinion that it is just and equitable that the company should be wound up.

There are no provisions enabling unregistered companies to enter into administration, CVA, receivership or voluntary liquidation.

Formal insolvency processes

1.14

Administration

1.15   Administration is the process whereby a company, an LLP or a partnership, is placed under the control of an administrator in one of a number of ways. The method of appointment may be crucial to the sale of the company or its business, as the procedure can be instantaneous or involve an interval of five business days or more between initiation of the appointment process and the appointment of the administrator.

---

[19]   IA 1986, s 220(1)(b).
[20]   IA 1986, s 221.

Commencement

1.16   Administration commences when the appointment of the administrator takes effect, and that can be by way of an order of the court made on an administration application, or on appointment made out of court by:

(a)   the holder of a qualifying floating charge ('QFC'); or

(b)   the company or the directors.

Anything done by the directors in the administration process may be done by a majority of them[21]. However directors' meetings must still be called, and decisions made, in accordance with the company's articles of association or their decisions may be found to be invalid[22].

Administration application

1.17   An administration application may be made by the company, the directors, one or more creditors or the designated officer of a magistrates court in the exercise of certain powers[23]. An administration application is most often used by the company or the directors when a creditor has presented a winding-up petition to the court against the company and the petition has not yet been disposed of. A creditor may in some circumstances make a successful administration application, even when its debt is disputed by the company, if there are good reasons for the court to make an administration order[24].

The court may make an administration order if it is satisfied that the company is unable to pay its debts and that the administration order is reasonably likely to achieve the purpose of administration. There is an exception to this where a creditor who holds a QFC makes an administration application; then the court may make an administration order without being satisfied that the company is unable to pay its debts, but it must be satisfied that the creditor could appoint an administrator by the out-of-court procedure[25] described in section 1.18 below.

An administration application must be served on the company (unless it is making the application itself) at least five days before the hearing. It must be similarly served on:

(a)   the proposed administrator;

(b)   the holder of a QFC;

(c)   any creditor who has presented a petition to wind up the company; and

(d)   other prescribed persons[26].

---

[21]   IA1986, Sch B1, para 105.
[22]   *Minmar (929) Ltd v Khalastchi and another* [2011] EWHC 1159 (Ch), [2011] BCC 485.
[23]   IA 1986, Sch B1, para 12(1).
[24]   *Hammonds (a firm) v Pro-fit USA Ltd* [2007] EWHC 1998 (Ch), [2008] 2 BCLC 159.
[25]   IA 1986, Sch B1, para 14.
[26]   IA 1986, Sch B1, para 12(2) and rule 2.6.

An interim moratorium[27] arises on making an administration application[28], and a moratorium[29] applies when a company is in administration[30].

Appointment by the holder of a qualifying floating charge

1.18   To hold a QFC a creditor must hold a floating charge which either[31]:

(a)   states that IA 1986, Sch B1, para 14(1) applies to the floating charge; or

(b)   purports to empower the holder to appoint an administrator of the company; or

(c)   purports to empower the holder to appoint an administrative receiver within the meaning of IA 1986, s 29(2),

and the floating charge, alone or in combination with other security of which at least one charge is a QFC, relates to the whole or substantially the whole of the company's property.

The holder of a QFC may appoint an administrator to a company by the out-of-court procedure set out in IA 1986, Sch B1, paras 14–21. The holder of the QFC must make a statutory declaration to the effect that its floating charge has become enforceable[32], and if there is a holder of a prior ranking QFC it must file a Notice of intention to appoint an administrator at court, and serve the notice on the holder of the prior ranking QFC. If there is no need to give notice the holder of the QFC may go straight to filing a Notice of appointment of an administrator, and if so the administration commences immediately. If a Notice of intention to appoint is served then the proposed appointer must, in the absence of consent to proceed, wait at least two clear business days after service before filing and serving a Notice of appointment[33].

An interim moratorium restricting the ability of third parties to enforce certain rights against a company arises on filing a Notice of intention to appoint[34], and a moratorium applies when a company is in administration[35]. In an urgent case the holder of a QFC may also appoint an administrator by the out-of-court route outside of usual court opening hours[36].

---

[27]   See section 1.21 below.
[28]   IA 1986, Sch B1, para 44(1).
[29]   See section 1.21 below.
[30]   IA 1986, Sch B1, para 43.
[31]   IA 1986, Sch B1, para 14(2).
[32]   IA 1986, Sch B1, paras 16, 18(2).
[33]   IA 1986, Sch B1, para 15(1).
[34]   IA 1986, Sch B1, para 44(2).
[35]   IA 1986, Sch B1, para 43.
[36]   Rule 2.19.

Appointment by the company or by the directors

1.19   The company or the directors may appoint an administrator to a company by the out-of-court procedure set out in IA 1986, Sch B1, paras 22–30. There are a number of restrictions on use of the out-of-court procedure by the company and the directors:

(a)   the company must be unable, or be likely to become unable, to pay its debts[37];

(b)   there cannot have been a previous administrator appointed under IA 1986, Sch B1, para 22 within the last 12 months[38];

(c)   there cannot have been a moratorium under IA 1986, Sch A1 in place without a CVA being approved or an approved CVA failing[39]; and

(d)   there can be no petition for winding up or administration application that has not been disposed of, and no administrative receiver in office[40].

The company or directors must make a statutory declaration to the effect that none of the restrictions on an out-of-court appointment apply[41]. If there is a creditor or creditors holding a QFC the company or directors must file a Notice of intention to appoint an administrator at court, and serve the notice on the holder or holders of the QFC(s). If there is no creditor holding a QFC the company may proceed straight to filing a Notice of appointment of an administrator, and if so the administration commences immediately. If a Notice of intention to appoint is served then the company or directors must, in the absence of consent to proceed, wait at least five clear business days after service before proceeding with the Notice of appointment[42].

An interim moratorium arises on filing a Notice of intention to appoint[43], and a moratorium applies when a company is in administration[44].

There is no procedure whereby in a case of urgency the company or the directors may appoint an administrator by the out-of-court route outside of usual court opening hours.

If the company is regulated by the Financial Services Authority ('FSA') as an authorised person or an appointed representative, or is carrying on a regulated activity, the company and the directors must obtain the prior written consent of the FSA before appointing an administrator out of court[45]. If the

---

[37]   IA 1986, Sch B1, para 27(2).
[38]   IA 1986, Sch B1, para 23(2).
[39]   IA 1986, Sch B1, para 24.
[40]   IA 1986, Sch B1, para 25.
[41]   IA 1986, Sch B1, para 27(2).
[42]   IA 1986, Sch B1, para 26(1) and see section 1.20 below.
[43]   IA 1986, Sch B1, para 44(4).
[44]   IA 1986, Sch B1, para 43.
[45]   Financial Services and Markets Act 2000, s 362A.

prior written consent of the FSA is not obtained, the purported appointment of an administrator is potentially invalid and incapable of perfection. In *Re MTB Motors Ltd (in administration)*[46] the High Court found that the purported appointment of administrators without the necessary consent of the FSA was invalid and could not be declared effective by the court. However in *Peter Lloyd Bootes and others v Ceart Risk Services Ltd*[47] the High Court found in similar circumstances that although there had been a defect in the administration procedure, the defect could be remedied by the court. The High Court has subsequently preferred the approach taken in *Ceart*[48].

Conflicting authorities

1.20   There are unfortunately two contradictory lines of High Court authority relating to out of court appointments made by directors in situations where there is no holder of a QFC which have not (as at 1 April 2013) been resolved by the Court of Appeal.

Paragraph 26(2) of IA 1986, Schedule B1, provides that a person making an out of court appointment of an administrator shall

'...also give such notice as may be prescribed to such other persons as may be prescribed'.

Rule 2.20(2) provides that

'A copy of the notice of intention to appoint must ... be given to:

(a)   any enforcement officer who ... is charged with execution or other legal process against the company;

(b)   any person who ... has distrained against the company or its property;

(c)   any supervisor of a voluntary arrangement under Part 1 of [IA 1986]; and

(d)   the company, if the company is not intending to make the appointment.'

In *Hill and another v Stokes*[49] the directors of the company failed to notify a landlord who had levied distress against company assets of their intention to appoint an administrator, and the High Court found that there was no obligation to do so. The obligation only arose where there was a QFC holder. In *Re Virtualpurple Professional Services Ltd*[50] the directors failed to give the company notice of intention to appoint an administrator, and again the High

---

[46]   [2010] EWHC 3751 (Ch).
[47]   [2012] EWHC 1178(Ch), [2013] Bus LR 116.
[48]   *Re BXL Services* [2012] EWHC 1877 (Ch).
[49]   [2010] EWHC 3726 (Ch).
[50]   [2011] EWHC 3487 (Ch), [2012] BCC 254.

Court found this did not necessarily invalidate the subsequent administration, and that the court could waive any procedural defect in the appointment process.

However in *Minmar (929) Ltd v Khalastchi and another*[51] the High Court had indicated that failure by the directors to give notice of intention to appoint an administrator to the company would invalidate the subsequent purported appointment. This decision was followed by the High Court in *National Westminster Bank plc v Msaada Group (a firm)*[52], a decision handed down on the same day as the decision in *Virtualpurple Professional Services*. Accordingly directly conflicting decisions of the High Court were handed down at the same time.

In *Msaada* the court suggested that the directors should give notice of intention to appoint an administrator to all prescribed parties, including the company using the prescribed Form 2.8B (even though the Form is drafted on the basis that it will be used to give notice to the holder of a QFC). Further, it suggested that all prescribed parties should be given a minimum of 5 business days notice of the proposed appointment.

In *Re BXL Services*[53], a subsequent decision of the High Court, the court followed the *Virtualpurple Professional Services* line of authority and stated that it was now settled law that any failure by the directors to notify the parties referred to in Rule 2.20(2) of their intention to appoint an administrator would not automatically invalidate the subsequent appointment of administrators. However until the point is decided by the Court of Appeal, the prudent approach is for directors who wish to appoint administrators to follow the guidelines set out in *Msaada*.

Purpose of administration

1.21   The purpose of administration is defined in IA 1986, Sch B1, para 111(1) as an 'objective specified in paragraph 3'. IA 1986 Sch B1, para 3 provides a hierarchy of objectives, and in order of priority, an administrator must perform his functions with the objective of:

(a)   rescuing the company as a going concern; or

(b)   achieving a better result for the company's creditors as a whole than would be likely if the company were wound up (without first being in administration); or

(c)   realising property in order to make a distribution to one or more secured or preferential creditors.

---

[51]   [2011] EWHC 1159 (Ch), [2011] BCC 485.
[52]   [2011] EWHC 3423 (Ch), [2012] BCC 226.
[53]   [2012] EWHC 1877 (Ch).

The administrator must perform his functions in the best interests of the creditors as a whole, even if he has been appointed by the holder of a QFC, and he must do so with the first objective unless he thinks that it is not reasonably practicable to achieve it, or the second objective would achieve a better result for the company's creditors as a whole. He may only perform his functions with the third objective if he thinks that it is not reasonably practicable to achieve either of the first two objectives and he does not unnecessarily harm the interests of the creditors of the company as a whole.

There is an important distinction between the first two objectives. The first is to rescue the company itself as a going concern (i.e. the entity that has gone into administration). To achieve this objective the company would usually be restructured by way of a CVA or a scheme of arrangement. The first objective cannot be achieved by a sale of the entirety of the company's business. However the second objective can. A sale of the business as a going concern often enhances realisations for creditors, for example by way of realising value for goodwill, and by maximising work in progress and debtor recoveries. This achieves the better result for the company's creditors set out in the second objective. In this scenario a different company carries on the insolvent company's business going forward, leaving the shell of the insolvent company behind.

The moratorium

1.22   Often the most useful aspect of the administration process is the moratorium. An interim moratorium arises under IA 1986, Sch B1, para 44 when either an administration application is made or a Notice of intention to appoint an administrator is filed, and a continuing moratorium arises under IA 1986, Sch B1, paras 42 and 43 on commencement of administration. The moratorium provides the company with protection from actions that could otherwise be taken by creditors, with a view to preserving the company's assets and assisting the administrator to achieve one of the three objectives.

The important features of the moratorium are:

(a)   (subject to specific exceptions) no resolution may be passed or order made for the winding up of the company[54];

(b)   without consent of the administrator (once appointed) or permission of the court[55]:

- •   no step may be taken to enforce security over the company's property;

- •   no step may be taken to repossess goods in the company's possession under a hire-purchase agreement (including a conditional sale agreement, chattel leasing agreement and retention of title agreement);

---

[54]   IA 1986, Sch B1, para 42.
[55]   IA 1986, Sch B1, para 43.

- a landlord may not exercise a right of peaceable re-entry in relation to premises let to the company;

- no legal process (including legal proceedings, execution or distress) may be instituted or continued against the company or property of the company;

- an administrative receiver may not be appointed.

The moratorium does not generally have effect outside of the jurisdiction[56], although the High Court has extended the moratorium to give it extra-territorial effect in the case of the administration of a UK bank[57].

On an administration order being made any pending winding-up petition shall be dismissed[58], and if administration commences on appointment by the holder of a QFC any pending winding-up petition is suspended[59]. Any administrative receiver shall vacate office[60], and any receiver over part of the company's property shall vacate office if the administrator requires them to do so[61].

Effect of administration on directors

1.23   When a company goes into administration directors remain in office unless and until they are removed or resign. However they are not entitled to exercise a management power in relation to the company without the consent of the administrator[62]. In practice an administrator will rely on the directors after his or her appointment, particularly if the company continues to trade, and will consent to and authorise the directors to carry out certain functions under his or her control. An administrator may remove and appoint directors to the company[63].

The duties of a director once an administrator is appointed to a company are considered in section 1.37.

Company voluntary arrangement

1.24   A company voluntary arrangement ('CVA') is a mechanism whereby a company enters into a binding agreement with its creditors (either a composition in satisfaction of its debts or a scheme of arrangement[64] ('Scheme')) under

---

[56]   *Harms Offshore Aht 'Taurus' GmbH & Co Kg v Bloom and others* [2009] EWCA Civ 632, [2010] Ch 187.
[57]   *Re Kaupthing Singer & Friedlander Ltd (in administration)* [2012] EWHC 2235 (Ch).
[58]   IA 1986, Sch B1, para 40(1)(a).
[59]   IA 1986, Sch B1, para 40(1)(b).
[60]   IA 1986, Sch B1, para 41(1).
[61]   IA 1986, Sch B1, para 41(2).
[62]   IA 1986, Sch B1, para 64(1).
[63]   IA 1986, Sch B1, para 61.
[64]   IA 1986, s 1(1).

the supervision of an office-holder in order to compromise its debts. A 'composition' is an agreement between a debtor and creditor that the debtor will pay a sum of money in lieu of a larger amount due, or an agreement by the creditor to accept less than the full amount due from the debtor in full satisfaction of its claim[65]. A Scheme[66] may also be a composition but it may not include a compromise or release of claims. It could, for example, simply provide for a moratorium[67]. Typically a CVA involves a composition in which creditors agree to accept a part payment of their claims over a period of time. The company pays regular amounts to the Supervisor of the arrangement out of future profits. Alternatively the company may agree to sell certain assets over time, or a benevolent third party may pay the Supervisor an amount equal to the value of the company's assets. The Supervisor then agrees creditors' claims and makes distributions to creditors out of the fund in his or her hands, and in accordance with the terms of the proposal.

The benefit of a CVA to creditors is that they can expect to recover more for their claims than on a winding up of the company, and the benefits to the company and the directors are that the directors retain control of the company, and they avoid some of the major disadvantages (in a director's eyes) of the more intrusive insolvency procedures such as administration and liquidation. In particular the directors' conduct is not made subject to a report to the Department for Business, Innovation and Skills under CDDA 1986.

CVAs have become the procedure of first choice for retailers or other businesses with multiple leasehold sites who wish to downsize their property portfolio as part of a restructuring process.

Commencement

1.25 A proposal for a CVA is made by the directors of a company (or its administrator or liquidator). The proposal will usually be prepared by the directors with the assistance of the proposed Supervisor, who at that stage will be acting as Nominee. The proposal is submitted to the court together with a report from the Nominee, who will suggest dates for holding meetings of the creditors and shareholders of the company. The Nominee will then convene the meetings on the suggested dates, and the proposal plus notice of the meetings is distributed to all known creditors and shareholders. The proposal is then put to the meetings and voted on, with or without modifications.

The key factor to approval of a CVA is the creditors' vote. Providing:

(a)   a majority of three-quarters or more in value of the creditors voting on the resolution in person or by proxy approve the proposal[68], and

---

[65]   *IRC v Adam & Partners* [2000] BPIR 986.
[66]   See section 1.31 below.
[67]   *March Estates plc v Gunmark* [1996] 2 BCLC 1.
[68]   Rule 1.19(2).

(b)   those voting against it are not more in value than one-half of those creditors who are not connected[69],

the CVA will be binding on all creditors who were entitled to vote at the meeting. It is irrelevant whether or not a creditor voted against the proposal; or did not attend the meeting; or did not vote; or was not aware of the meeting. Although a meeting of members of the company is also called to consider the proposal, if the creditors vote in favour of approval and the members vote against, it is the creditors' vote that will prevail[70].

The proposal

1.26   The contents of a proposal for a CVA must comply with the Rules[71], and the directors will usually rely on the assistance of the Nominee in the drafting. However it is the directors' proposal, and they will commit an offence if they make any false representations or fraudulently do anything to obtain approval by the creditors. The proposal is delivered by the directors to the Nominee, and he or she must prepare a report to the court stating his or her opinion as to whether or not the proposal has a reasonable prospect of being approved and implemented, and whether meetings of creditors and members should be called[72]. The Nominee must be satisfied that the proposal is serious and viable[73].

Consideration of the proposal

1.27   The meetings of creditors and members will consider the proposal as put to them by the directors, and may suggest modifications, providing they would not invalidate the proposal. The chairman of the meetings will usually be the Nominee, who decides whether a person claiming to be a creditor of a company is entitled to vote, and if so the value of the vote[74]. A dissatisfied creditor has a right of appeal to the court[75], and as a result a body of case law has built up on voting rights[76]. As stated earlier a proposal, as modified (if that is the case), will be approved and will bind all creditors, providing:

(a)   a majority of three-quarters or more in value of the creditors voting on the resolution in person or by proxy approve the proposal[77], and

(b)   those voting against it are not more in value than one-half of those creditors who are not connected.

---

[69]   Rule 1.19(4).
[70]   Rule 1.21(5).
[71]   Rule 1.3.
[72]   IA 1986, s 2(2).
[73]   *Greystoke v Hamilton-Smith* [1997] BPIR 24.
[74]   Rules 1.17, 1.17A and 1.18.
[75]   Rule 1.17A(3).
[76]   For example *Re Cranley Mansions Ltd* [1994] BCC 576; *Doorbar v Alltime Securities Ltd* [1994] BCC 994; *Re Newlands (Seaford) Educational Trust* [2007] BCC 195.
[77]   Rule 1.19(2).

Approval of the members is obtained by a majority of more than one-half in value of those members present in person or by proxy who vote on the resolution[78].

The creditors' meeting may not approve a proposal which affects the rights of a secured creditor without the secured creditor's agreement[79].

Once a proposal is approved a Supervisor is appointed and the proposal is implemented in accordance with its terms, as they may have been modified.

Any person who was entitled to vote at the meetings, or would have been entitled to vote had they had notice of the meetings, or the Nominee, or an administrator or liquidator of the company, may make an application to the court to challenge the decision of the meetings of creditors and members, but only on one of the following grounds[80]:

- that the arrangement as approved unfairly prejudices the interests of a creditor, member or contributory of the company[81]; or

- that there has been some material irregularity at or in relation to either of the meetings[82].

Any such challenge must be within 28 days of the date on which the Nominee reports to the court on the outcome of the meetings, or (if a person was not notified of the creditors' meeting) within 28 days of the date on which he or she became aware that the meeting had taken place[83].

Moratorium

1.28   Small companies are entitled to seek a moratorium similar to that which arises in administration before a proposal for a CVA is put to the meetings of creditors and members. If a moratorium is required by any other company, for example if creditors are taking action against it whilst a proposal is prepared and considered, a company will have to go into administration to obtain protection. The administrator will then propose the CVA to creditors, relying on the first of the objectives of administration considered at 1.21. If the CVA is approved the administration will usually come to an end and the administrator will hand control of the company back to the directors. The administrator would typically then act simply as Supervisor of the arrangement.

In order to enable a company to gain the benefit of a moratorium without incurring the cost of administration, the IA 2000 introduced a scheme whereby small companies could seek a moratorium whilst the directors prepared a

---

[78]   Rule 1.20(1).
[79]   IA 1986, s 4(3).
[80]   IA 1986, s 6(1), (2).
[81]   For an example see *Mourant & Co Trustees Ltd and another v Sixty UK Ltd and others* [2010] EWHC 1890 (Ch), [2010] BCC 882.
[82]   For an example see *Re Newlands (Seaford) Educational Trust* [2007] BCC 195.
[83]   IA 1986, s 6(3).

proposal for a CVA. IA 2000 introduced a new Schedule A1 ('Schedule A1') into IA 1986 with effect from 1 January 2003, and Schedule A1 governs the small companies moratorium regime. A small company is one which satisfies two or more of the requirements for being a small company specified for the time being in CA 2006, s 382(3)[84]. Those requirements are:

- turnover of not more than £6.5m;

- a balance sheet total of not more than £3.26m;

- the number of employees not to be more than 50.

A moratorium is obtained by filing the requisite documents at court[85]. No hearing is required. It generally lasts until the date on which the latter of the creditors' and members' meetings takes place, or if no such meetings are called, for 28 days[86]. During a moratorium the affairs of the company must be monitored by the Nominee[87], and this can be an onerous task. Moratoriums under IA 1986, Sch AI are not commonly used.

Effect of CVA on directors

1.29   The directors remain in office on approval of a CVA and continue to manage the business and affairs of the company. They are subject to the role of the Supervisor in so far as implementation of the CVA is concerned.

Advantages and disadvantages of a CVA

1.30   CVAs offer great flexibility to a company to effect a restructuring plan.[88] It can be problematic that CVAs do not generally have the benefit of a moratorium whilst they are being agreed, but subject to the exceptions highlighted above, there is no restriction on the nature of the proposal that can be put to creditors so the procedure is very flexible. The company stays under the control of the directors and the role of the office-holder is limited to supervising compliance with the terms of the arrangement, and implementing the terms in so far as they relate to agreeing the claims of creditors and making distributions to them. This helps to keep professional costs down.

Directors and creditors need to be aware of tax issues when considering a proposal for a CVA. There may be both advantages and disadvantages.

For directors, a CVA avoids any risk of being disqualified as a director under CDDA 1986. For creditors, there are no provisions enabling a Supervisor to apply to the court to overturn voidable antecedent transactions as there are in

---

[84]   IA 1986, Sch A1, para 3.
[85]   IA 1986, Sch A1, para 7(1).
[86]   IA 1986, Sch A1, para 8.
[87]   IA 1986, Sch A1, para 24(1).
[88]   See section 13.6 as an example. The CVA procedure has been commonly used to achieve a reduction in size of a company's leasehold portfolio.

administration and liquidation, and no claims may be made against directors for misfeasance or wrongful trading.

Scheme of arrangement

1.31   A Scheme is a compromise or arrangement made by a company with its creditors or members, or any class of them, under CA 2006, Pt 26. The court is much more involved in a Scheme than it is when the directors propose a composition of debts. It is the court that gives directions to the company to call meetings of creditors and members to vote on the proposal, and to set out the procedure for doing so, and the court which ultimately sanctions the Scheme.

If a majority in number representing 75 per cent in value of the creditors, or each class of creditors or members (as the case may be), present and voting either in person or by proxy at the meetings agree the proposed Scheme, the court may sanction the compromise or arrangement[89]. On an application for sanction the court will consider if the Scheme is fair, and once sanction is given and the court order giving sanction is filed at Companies House[90], the Scheme will become binding on all those within the respective classes of creditors or members affected by the Scheme (whether they voted or not)[91]. The ability to bind dissenting creditors in this manner can be a significant benefit over other potential routes to a restructuring.

Schemes have historically been less common than CVAs as a way for an insolvent company to deal with its liabilities. However they are useful in situations where a company has a complex capital structure which makes consensual arrangements difficult to achieve, and where the court may sanction proposals that would otherwise enable creditors to challenge a CVA as being unfairly prejudicial[92].

In *Re Bluebrook Limited*[93] (otherwise known as *IMO Carwash*) the court sanctioned a Scheme in which junior creditors, who under the provisions of the Scheme would recover nothing, were put in the same class as senior creditors who would make a recovery. If the junior and senior creditors formed one class the junior creditors would comprise less than 25 per cent of the votes and would be bound by the vote of the senior creditors. The court considered the wider context of the restructuring in considering whether the Scheme represented a genuine compromise or arrangement, and rejected the junior creditors' argument that they should comprise a separate class apart from the senior creditors. The court denied them the opportunity to reject the Scheme at their own meeting. The junior creditors also argued that the company's assets

---

[89]   CA 2006, s 896(1).
[90]   CA 2006, s 896(4).
[91]   CA 2006, s 896(3).
[92]   See *Re Bluebrook Ltd: Re IMO (UK) Ltd: Re Spirecove Ltd* [2009] EWHC 2114 (Ch), [2010] 1 BCLC 338; compare with *Re Lehman Brothers International (Europe) (in administration)* [2009] EWCA Civ 1161, [2010] BCC 272.
[93]   [2009] EWHC 2114 (Ch), [2010] 1 BCLC 338.

should be valued on the basis of future potential after the proposed restructuring rather than at current market values. The alternative basis of valuation they proposed would mean that they did have an interest in the outcome of the Scheme. The court rejected that argument too. It was appropriate to use current valuations based on actual market conditions rather than a proposed valuation based on potential future conditions, and the court would rely on the judgement of those experts carrying out the valuation exercise. This decision, and the ability to cram down creditors with no economic interest in the outcome of the restructuring, continues to attract interest.

The court has since confirmed that it will consider the wider terms of a restructuring in determining whether a Scheme does constitute a fair compromise for a class of creditors[94].

Receivership

1.32   Prior to the coming into force of the corporate insolvency provisions of EA 2002 on 15 September 2003, administrative receivership was the primary route by which a secured creditor with the benefit of a floating charge ('Debentureholder') over the undertaking and property of a company would enforce its security. An administrative receiver is a receiver or manager of the whole (or substantially the whole) of a company's property appointed by or on behalf of the holder(s) of a floating charge[95]. Since 15 September 2003, an administrative receiver may not be appointed under a QFC created since that date[96] save for in relation to certain specific 'City' exceptions[97], and the principal insolvency procedure available to a Debentureholder (who will invariably have the benefit of a QFC) is now administration. Accordingly administrative receivership is less and less relevant as time moves on. However an administrative receiver satisfying IA 1986, s 29(2) may still be appointed in relation to a floating charge created before 15 September 2003.

A secured creditor may still appoint a receiver over assets that are subject to an effective fixed charge, and a receiver appointed under a fixed charge or under the Law of Property Act 1925 may still be appointed over land. However the role of a fixed charge or Law of Property Act receiver is limited to dealing with the specific asset over which he or she has been appointed.

In view of the now lesser importance of receivership when it comes to buying and selling insolvent companies, receivership will not be considered in detail in this book.

---

[94]   *Re Uniq plc* [2011] EWHC 749 (Ch), [2012] Bus LR D18.
[95]   IA 1986, s 29(2).
[96]   IA 1986, s 72A.
[97]   IA 1986, ss 72B–72H.

Liquidation

1.33   Liquidation, or winding up, is the process whereby a company's affairs are taken out of the control of the directors and put into the hands of a liquidator, who realises the company's assets, pays its debts and liabilities, and then returns any surplus to the members. Liquidation is appropriate when a company cannot continue as a going concern.

There are two methods of winding up a company, namely voluntary and compulsory liquidation. Voluntary liquidation occurs when the members of a company resolve to wind it up, and compulsory liquidation occurs when the court makes a winding-up order against a company. Voluntary winding up may be either members' voluntary liquidation ('MVL'), which occurs when the directors make a statutory declaration that in their opinion the company will be able to pay its debts in full within 12 months of the commencement of the winding up[98], or creditors' voluntary liquidation ('CVL'). Any voluntary liquidation in which no such statutory declaration has been made is a CVL. This book will be concerned with CVL and not MVL, save that it is relevant to note that a winding up that starts out as an MVL may be converted to a CVL if the liquidator forms the opinion that creditors will not be paid in full as anticipated[99].

Both CVL and compulsory liquidation are collective procedures, in that they are processes carried out for the benefit of all unsecured creditors. Those creditors in the same class are treated equally.

Commencement of CVL

1.34   CVL is most likely to be commenced by the members of a company when the directors have come to the opinion that the company is insolvent and there is no value in the company's business which might be preserved by way of a sale as a going concern. In the latter situation administration is more likely to be the appropriate insolvency procedure. CVL is a quicker way to put a company into liquidation than compulsory winding up, and the directors and members retain control as to the timing of the process. Once the liquidation is in place CVL is also a more cost-effective alternative to compulsory winding up, as the costs of the Official Receiver are avoided, and realisations do not have to be paid into the Insolvency Services Account, where significant fees and charges have to be paid. However the directors or members may have to fund the liquidator if the company has no assets with a realisable value.

The directors of the company will call a meeting of the members, at which they will be asked to pass a resolution that the company be wound up. Alternatively the directors may propose a written resolution. If there is a secured creditor with the benefit of a QFC over the assets of the company, it must be given

---

[98]   IA 1986, s 90.
[99]   IA 1986, s 95.

not less than five business days' notice in writing of the proposed resolution before it is passed, or the secured creditor must give its written consent to the resolution[100]. At the meeting the shareholders will pass a special resolution to put the company into liquidation[101] and to appoint a nominated liquidator. The winding-up commences at the time the resolution is passed[102].

In a CVL there must also be a meeting of the company's creditors, held within 14 days of the date on which the resolution to wind up is passed. In practice the creditors' meeting is usually held on the same day as, and immediately after, the members' meeting. The creditors' meeting will either confirm the appointment of the liquidator or propose a different insolvency practitioner to act as liquidator, and it may also pass a limited number of other resolutions[103]. If creditors propose a different liquidator to the person chosen by the members, the creditors' choice will prevail[104]. The creditors may also appoint a creditors' committee.

CVL may also be used as an exit route for administration where the administrator has realised assets and has funds to distribute to unsecured creditors. Providing the administrator thinks that:

(a)   the total amount that each secured creditor of the company is likely to receive has been paid or set aside for them, and

(b)   a distribution will be made to the unsecured creditors of the company,

he or she may file a prescribed notice with the Registrar of Companies[105]. On the Registrar registering the notice the appointment of the administrator ceases to have effect and the company is wound up (goes into liquidation) as if a resolution to wind it up had been passed on the day the notice is registered[106].

Commencement of compulsory liquidation

1.35   Compulsory liquidation is usually initiated by a creditor of the company, who presents a petition to the court when there is a debt owed to him or her. The ground of the creditor's petition will be that the company is unable to pay its debts[107]. A petition may also be presented by prescribed people on a number of specific grounds[108], perhaps most commonly seen where winding up is stated to be in the public interest.

---

[100]   IA 1986, s 84(2A), (2B).
[101]   IA 1986, s 84(1)(b).
[102]   IA 1986, s 86.
[103]   Rule 4.53.
[104]   IA 1986, s 100(2).
[105]   IA 1986, Sch B1, para 83.
[106]   IA 1986, Sch B1, para 83(6); *Re Globespan Airways Ltd (in liquidation)* also called *Cartwright & Anor v The Registrar of Companies* [2012] EWCA Civ 1159.
[107]   IA 1986, s 123(1)(f).
[108]   IA 1986, s 122(1), ss 124, 124A.

When a winding-up petition is presented to the court it is endorsed with a hearing date and returned to the petitioner. It is his or her obligation to serve the petition on the company[109] (unless the company itself is the petitioner), usually at its registered office, and to advertise it in the *London Gazette* in accordance with the statutory requirements[110]. At the hearing of the petition the court may make a winding-up order, or it may dismiss or adjourn the petition, or make an interim order or any order it thinks fit[111]. The court may also make a winding-up order at the hearing of an administration application[112]. If a winding-up order is made the date of commencement of the liquidation is the date of presentation of the petition[113] or the date on which the order on the administration application is made[114].

On the making of a winding-up order the Official Receiver becomes liquidator of the company[115]. He or she has a duty to decide as soon as practicable and within 12 weeks of the date of the winding-up order whether to call a meeting of the company's creditors and contributories for the purpose of choosing a liquidator to be appointed to the company in his or her place[116]. One-quarter in value of the company's creditors can require the Official Receiver to hold a meeting of creditors to appoint an alternative liquidator[117]. Otherwise a liquidator other than the Official Receiver may be appointed by the Secretary of State[118], or may be appointed by the court if the winding-up petition was presented by the administrator of a company or by the supervisor of the company's CVA[119].

Consequences of liquidation

1.36   There are certain consequences of winding-up proceedings and liquidation which are designed to protect the assets of the company for the benefit of creditors. However no moratorium arises as in administration.

Under IA 1986, s 126 any creditor or contributory of the company may apply to the court at any time after presentation of a winding-up petition and before a winding-up order is made to stay proceedings against it. Once a winding-up order is made no proceedings against the company or its property may be commenced or proceeded with except by leave of the court[120]. Any attachment, distress or execution put in force against the company's estate or effects after the commencement of the winding up is void[121]. Goods or their proceeds of sale

---

[109]   Rules 4.8–4.10.
[110]   Rule 4.11.
[111]   IA 1986, s 125.
[112]   IA 1986, Sch B1, para 13(1)(e).
[113]   IA 1986, s 129(2).
[114]   IA 1986, s 129(1A).
[115]   IA 1986, s 136(2).
[116]   IA 1986, s 136(5)(a).
[117]   IA 1986, s 136(5)(c).
[118]   IA 1986, s 137.
[119]   IA 1986, s 140.
[120]   IA 1986, s 130(2).
[121]   IA 1986, s 128(1).

which have been made subject to distraint ending with the date three months prior to the winding-up order are charged with the company's preferential debts to the extent that the company's assets are insufficient to meet them[122]. Any disposition of the company's property after the commencement of the winding up is also void, unless the court otherwise orders[123].

There is no similar automatic stay of proceedings or avoidance of dispositions of property in CVL, although a liquidator may apply to the court to apply similar provisions under their general power to apply to determine any question arising in the winding up in IA 1986, s 112(1).

Effect of liquidation on directors

1.37   In CVL the powers of directors cease when the liquidator is appointed, save to the extent that the creditors' committee or (in the absence of a committee) the creditors sanction their continuance[124]. If there is no liquidator appointed by the company after a winding-up resolution is passed, the directors may not exercise their powers save with the sanction of the court[125] other than to dispose of perishable goods or other goods whose value is likely to diminish if not immediately disposed of, or as may be necessary for the protection of the company's assets[126].

IA 1986 does not state the effect of compulsory winding up on the powers of directors. However the liquidator takes control of the company's affairs and exercises his or her powers in relation to the company, and the usual view is that the directors' powers cease on a winding-up order being made.

In liquidation and administration directors still have a number of duties, notwithstanding that their powers have come to an end. For example they must make a statement of affairs of the company[127], and they have a duty to co-operate with the office-holder[128], enforceable by way of an application to court if they fail to comply. A director may also be required to attend an initial creditors meeting in administration[129]. Further, a director's obligations under CA 2006 to prepare annual accounts, lay them before a general meeting of the company, and to file accounts still continue, although in practice the Registrar does not take action in default of compliance once a company is in liquidation or administration.

---

[122]   IA 1986, s 176(2).
[123]   IA 1986, s 127(1).
[124]   IA 1986, s 103.
[125]   IA 1986, s 114(2).
[126]   IA 1986, s 114(3).
[127]   IA 1986, ss 99, 131 and Sch B1, para 47(1).
[128]   IA 1986, s 235.
[129]   Rule 2.34(2).

Informal arrangements

Introduction

1.38   In many instances it will be beneficial to the relevant stakeholders to seek to agree a consensual rescue of a business outside of a formal insolvency process. Whether or not this can be achieved will often depend on whether or not the interested parties can work together as a body, with similar and aligned interests, or if they are a disparate and fragmented group with different and competing interests. An agreed rescue plan, or workout, can vary from a formalised arrangement involving complex debt restructuring entered into with sophisticated commercial lenders, to a series of debt repayment plans made with individual trade creditors.

A consensual arrangement may not require full and widespread disclosure of a company's financial difficulties to all stakeholders, and this can be a significant benefit where the interested parties are a disparate group who might act independently and solely in their own interests on learning of a potential problem. Informal arrangements are flexible and confidential. For the company, benefits of a workout include the fact that the directors retain control of the company, and there is no risk to them of an insolvency office-holder making claims against them personally, or of an office-holder submitting an adverse report as to their conduct as directors under CDDA 1986. For creditors advantages are that they can take the opportunity to improve their position as against an immediate formal insolvency, such as by taking additional security and avoiding crystallising a loss. Also the costs of a formal insolvency proceeding are avoided, and in the long term there may be a better prospect of recovery.

As against that, it may be seen as a disadvantage to the significant creditors (banks and other commercial lenders) that the same directors who have led the company into financial difficulty retain control, and the very fact that any informal arrangement or workout is consensual means that dissenting stakeholders cannot be bound in against their wishes. There is no moratorium to stop creditor claims and enforcement action against the company whilst arrangements are put in place, and should the arrangements fail any insolvency office-holder who is appointed will review transactions that took place as part of the rescue plan to see if they constitute voidable transactions that may be set aside by the court as a transaction at an undervalue[130] or a preference[131]. Any informal arrangement may not represent the final position for stakeholders if the arrangement fails and the agreements that are put in place are unravelled. For directors, there are risks of subsequent personal claims for misfeasance[132] if an administrator or liquidator is subsequently appointed to the company, and wrongful trading[133] if the company goes into liquidation.

---

[130]   IA 1986, s 238.
[131]   IA 1986, s 239.
[132]   IA 1986, s 212.
[133]   IA 1986, s 214.

An informal workout can be the only process a company is engaged in to turn it around. Alternatively it can be used as a precursor to a formal insolvency, for example by way of a group of stakeholders working together to help the company into an improved financial position whereby a formal insolvency proceeding involving all stakeholders (such as a CVA) can be successfully implemented.

The process

1.39   All informal arrangements are based on contract. Generally the company will approach its bankers, other funders, and major creditors and suppliers with the initial aim of negotiating a standstill whilst more long-term arrangements are put in place. Major customers may also be involved even at this early stage, as they have an interest in continuity of supply. That gives the company time to carry out a full investigation of its financial position in conjunction with its advisors and stakeholders, and for the future viability of the company in whatever format might be necessary to ensure survival to be assessed.

Depending on the size of the enterprise there may typically be a detailed analysis of the business carried out:

- an investigation into the causes of its financial difficulties;

- a review of its viability and future prospects;

- consideration of a number of proposed solutions; and

- an action plan agreed upon.

If there is inherent value in the business and it has a viable and attractive medium-to-long-term business plan it may be worthy of support with a view to creditors maximising their recovery and minimising their risk, and other stakeholders preserving their own business and/or employment. Potential solutions may include:

- a restructuring of debt and equity;

- a sale of the business, or part of it;

- the introduction of a turnaround professional to assist management;

- replacing management;

- any other potential solutions that appear to be workable to the stakeholders; or

- a combination of any of the above.

Lenders will need to consider funding during and after the standstill and workout period, and how their existing and new exposure can be secured or restructured, whether by way of new security, new priority arrangements, debt rescheduling, debt for equity swaps or other means. Creditors will need to think about repayment plans, whether they can take security for their debt, writing off or restructuring debt or part of it and their future exposure. Supply contracts may need to be rewritten. Customers will need to ensure continuity of supply and may face pressure to renegotiate pricing structures and delivery schedules.

If the company's only significant creditor is its bank, this whole process may take place in the context of control of the company's account passing from the usual relationship manager to the bank's 'intensive care' team. All major lenders have teams who are used to dealing with customers in financial difficulty. Banks do not use their 'intensive care' processes solely as a precursor to formal insolvency. The bank may well instruct accountants and insolvency practitioners to carry out a detailed review of the company, but that is usually with a view to agreeing a way to assist the directors to manage the company back to financial health so that the bank can either return control of the account to the usual relationship manager or get the company to a position where it can rebank with a different clearer. Institutional lenders will usually see a formal insolvency proceeding as a last resort. There is a clear benefit to the banks in engaging in this process, providing they do not assume the role of a shadow director, upon whose directions or instructions the directors are accustomed to act[134]. A shadow director may be personally liable for any misfeasance or wrongful trading[135] that occurs should the company go into administration or liquidation in due course, and banks will be very careful to take all necessary steps to avoid this possible consequence. However there may be disadvantages for other interested parties. Whilst the bank will usually be aiming to avoid a formal insolvency process for the company, it will not necessarily act in the best interests of other creditors in exercising control over the supply of cash and credit to the company to improve its own position, and in view of its usual status as a secured creditor who can appoint an administrator, the bank often has a significant advantage over other stakeholders in terms of the information available to it and the level of control it can exert.

Common features of a workout

1.40   Once a structure for the workout has been agreed, whether it be trading out of the difficulty with or without the sale of the company's business or a part of it, a standstill pending a refinancing or with a view to entering into a formal insolvency proceeding in due course, there will usually be an agreement or agreements made between the company and certain of its stakeholders, and a separate agreement between the stakeholders themselves.

The agreement with the company would usually include some, if not all, of the following features:

• the terms of any standstill arrangement;

---

[134]   IA 1986, s 251.
[135]   IA 1986, s 214(7).

- a waiver of existing defaults;

- the terms of and extent of any new lending or credit made available to the company during any standstill period;

- the purpose to which such new lending or credit may be put;

- how existing debt and any new lending or credit is to be secured;

- restrictions on the company during the standstill period and workout period, such as a prohibition on carrying on trade other than in the ordinary course of the company's business without prior written consent; a prohibition on entering into new significant contracts; limits on the level of trade credit obtained, on capital expenditure, on the declaration of dividends; and terms in relation to a potential range of other agreed matters;

- the provision of regular financial information to all stakeholders;

- how the costs of the process are to be paid.

The agreement or agreements between the stakeholders or different classes of them would usually include some, if not all, of the following features:

- if there is a syndicate, who is to take the lead role;

- how decisions are to be made by the syndicate;

- who and in what proportion is to make any new lending or credit available to the company;

- the basis and terms on which any new lending or credit is to be made available to the company and the purpose it can be put to;

- revised priority arrangements/the basis for sharing recoveries on administration or liquidation of the company;

- how the costs of the process are to be apportioned;

- how any enforcement action is to be agreed upon and taken.

The process should provide for all stakeholders in the same class to share the risk and rewards equally, and no one creditor will usually be permitted to improve its position at the expense of others. The only common exception to this is that anyone who provides new finance during a standstill or restructuring period may demand and be given priority in the event that the company ultimately fails.

Once it becomes common knowledge that a company is going through a restructuring via a workout there may well be trading of its debt at discounted prices. Specialist investors will buy claims at a discount and take a position as part of the restructuring process. This can create opportunities for the distressed debt trader and difficulties for the company and the remaining stakeholders, who might find that the parties they began negotiations with are now entirely different, not only in identity but also in approach. Debt traders are much more likely to be interested in short-term gain rather than the company's medium-to-long-term prospects.

Causes of company failure

Statistics

1.41   To put this book into context, corporate insolvency statistics (not seasonally adjusted) issued on 1 February 2013 (the most recently available data at the time of writing) for the period since 1 January 2009 were as follows[136]:

	Administration	CVA	Liquidation	Compulsory	Voluntary
Q1 2009	1,311	156	5,110	1,555	3,555
Q2 2009	1,027	157	5,059	1,520	3,539
Q3 2009	974	194	4,536	1,253	3,283
Q4 2009	849	219	4,372	1,315	3,057
Q1 2010	783	204	4,196	1,330	2,866
Q2 2010	777	232	4,094	1,185	2,909
Q3 2010	633	159	3,881	1,082	2,799
Q4 2010	642	170	3,874	1,195	2,679
Q1 2011	782	183	4,297	1,111	3,186
Q2 2011	695	187	4,268	1,317	2,951
Q3 2011	673	206	4,152	1,149	3,003
Q4 2011	658	191	4,169	1,426	2,743
Q1 2012	779	175	4,482	1,233	3,249
Q2 2012	625	352*	4,107	1,028	3,079
Q3 2012	548	161	3,860	1,033	2,827
Q4 2012	580	151	3,689	949	2,740

* This figure included 156 companies within the Southern Cross Healthcare Group.

Looking at the figures for Q4 2012 as against those for Q4 2011: administrations were down 11.9%, CVAs were down 20.9%; total liquidations were down 10.7%; compulsory liquidations were down 33.8%; and voluntary liquidations were up 0.4%. As against Q3 2012, total liquidations were down 3.3%, with compulsory liquidations down 15.2% and voluntary liquidations up 1.2%.

Approximately 1 in 144 of active registered companies (0.7%) went into liquidation in the year ending Q4 2012, which is down from the figure of 1 in 138 for the year ending Q3 2012. The liquidation rate remains low compared to a peak of 2.6% in 1993 and the average of 1.2% seen over the last 25 years. This is against a backdrop of the number of active registered companies increasing from some 900,000 to some 2,500,000 over the same 25 year period.

[136] Source: Insolvency Service. http://www.insolvencydirect.bis.gov.uk/otherinformation/statistics/201302/index.htm.

Nevertheless the figures reflect the view held within the corporate recovery industry and across the business sector generally, that despite the continuing financial pressures facing UK plc there is not an upturn in insolvencies.

There are a number of potential causes of the insolvency of a company, and circumstances will change from time to time. However, particular features commonly encountered are:

(a)   loss of or changes to a company's market place;

(b)   failure to deal with tax affairs; and

(c)   failure of management.

Loss of market

1.42   Loss of or changes to a company's market place is often cited by directors as a 'no fault' cause of failure, and insolvency professionals have seen this ground repeated in various guises over the years. In some instances there is no doubt that external factors are the primary cause of failure. For example the impact of the financial crisis from 2007, and the global recession since 2008/2009, has forced many companies into insolvency or severe financial difficulty. There have been huge pressures on companies in a wide range of sectors, particularly seen in those relying directly or indirectly on consumer spending. However the number of companies entering into formal insolvency processes has declined over the same period, despite the pressures on businesses, largely as a result of the unprecedented period of very low interest rates that has followed the financial crisis and the reluctance of financial institutions to enforce their rights under security interests.

Loss of market may be due to a reduction in customers, disputes with customers or suppliers, increased competition and increased costs. It is a more common cause of failure for companies that have traded for a long period, and perhaps have become complacent, too reliant on a small number of customers and/or suppliers, or subject to attack by competitors.

Failure to deal with tax affairs

1.43   Failure to deal with tax affairs results in a significant number of companies facing winding-up petitions. The Crown departments are an involuntary creditor and often the last creditor to be paid when a company suffers a decline in cash flow. A significant liability to the Crown can accrue in a short space of time, and despite a recent more lenient period and genuine attempts to make 'time to pay arrangements' with debtors, Her Majesty's Revenue and Customs ('HMRC') is active in recovering debts due to it, particularly where there have been persistent arrears or a history of non-compliance.

Failure of management

1.44   Failure of management can encompass a number of areas. Common problems seen are under-capitalisation, unwarranted confidence, bad planning, excessive/uncontrolled costs and failure to manage debtors and collect debts. It is a more common cause of failure in companies which have traded for a short period of time, as bad management may mean the business never really got off the ground.

General trends

1.45   It is generally the case that failures are more likely to arise as a result of failure to manage tax affairs or mismanagement in smaller, owner-managed businesses. The failure of larger companies is more likely to arise when there are external pressures in place.

In many instances directors seek advice on restructuring and insolvency options at a late stage in the process. It is invariably the case that by addressing the situation earlier rather than later a company maximises its options for restructuring and preserving stakeholder value, whether by way of a sale of the insolvent business outside or as part of a formal insolvency process. Early recognition of a potential problem is vital, and it must then be addressed. Immediate liquidation can often be avoided if action is taken early on, and this book will set out some of the options that enable liquidation to be avoided.

The concern that usually drives a company to seek advice on insolvency matters is cash flow and liquidity. Well known pressure points come at the end of each month when employee wages are due, or at the end of each quarter when rent is due. Potential buyers and sellers of an insolvent business should be aware of these pressure points as they will impact on timing, price and the need for immediate working capital and readily available cash post completion.

For those seeking to buy an insolvent company or business the reason for the company's failure will often be less relevant than other factors, such as whether or not the company is in a formal insolvency procedure, and if so which type of insolvency procedure it is. However the reason or reasons for failure can be relevant. If there was a loss of market the new business going forward may have to focus its attention on a narrower or more specific customer base, or conversely widen its customer and supplier base. If there is a history in the insolvent company of failure to pay tax, or default in filing tax returns, HMRC may be more likely to seek a deposit to secure payment of future VAT under Value Added Tax Act 1994, Sch 11, para 4(2)(a). This is particularly so if the directors of the insolvent company are involved in the 'new' business going forward, and the business was acquired out of administration. If the major cause of the insolvency was management failure then the buyer has to consider carefully the future role (if any) of the previous management. They are all matters for consideration.

Warning signs

1.46   There are a number of typical warning signs of a company that is in financial difficulty which can be identified by outside parties who might be interested in acquiring a business. These can include:

- A decline in reputation and market perception. If a company loses its identity, and the confidence and support of its customers and suppliers, it may fall into rapid decline. It can be useful to evaluate the performance of a business against its competitors over time.

- Falling gross profit. A decline in reported gross profit suggests that a company is generating less revenue from either falling sales or increased costs. Falling revenue may indicate a loss in market share due to a loss in confidence amongst customers, or it may be due to incorrect pricing. Rising costs suggests a weakness in bargaining position with suppliers or an inflexible business model in the face of an increase in the cost of raw materials.

- Relaunches and rebranding. Whilst this can be a perfectly valid process for a company to go through if new lines complement and enhance the existing business, a company may also be rebranding itself and its business as a way to try and extend the life of an out-of-sorts offering. If the relaunch offers nothing new, that may indicate declining performance.

- New projects. If a company suddenly and unexpectedly looks to move into new areas of business, that may be because its existing business model is failing, and it is making a desperate attempt to find turnover and profit elsewhere. It may also be a sign that management time and resource has been focused on areas other than running the existing business. Any new area of operation can also take valuable time and resource away from the core business, affecting key personnel, IT systems, and resources for advertising and marketing.

- A change in management involvement in the business. Senior managers, or new senior personnel, becoming involved in day to day matters might be a sign of financial difficulties.

- A fall in staff morale, high turnover of staff, redundancies or failure to replace those that leave by natural wastage.

- Factoring or discounting invoices. This may be a sign that the company needed to find a new source of funding or generate immediate cash flow.

- A change in company policy on collecting debts. For example offering discounts for early payment might be a sign of a need to generate cash quickly.

- The company taking longer to pay its debts, or adopting a confrontational position with creditors. Payments becoming erratic when they used to be consistently made on time.

- Unexpectedly raising disputes on invoices or about performance.

- Suppliers being unable to obtain credit insurance, and/or putting the company on stop.

- Sub-contractors leaving worksites.

- The company seeking to renegotiate or find a way out of contracts.

- Creditors taking steps to recover debts. County Court judgments registered against the company, or statutory demands and/or winding-up petitions.

Any or all of the above warning signs may exist, and may be evident from either a potential acquirer's own records or by keeping an ear to the ground. A competitor may speak with company staff from time to time, and may be aware of news circulating in the market place or the local press. A supplier's own records will show if a company's payment profile has changed. Also, publicly available sources might be helpful, such as Companies House, the register of county court judgments and the *London Gazette*. Companies House will provide copies of filed accounts (although these are an out-of-date snapshot by the time they are filed). It will also show the creation of new security, the appointment of an administrator, liquidator or receiver, any changes in the directors of a company, and any new companies acquired by the existing directors. The *London Gazette* shows details of winding-up petitions presented against a company, and meetings to place a company into creditors' voluntary liquidation. Insolvency appointments, including the appointment of an administrator or a liquidator to a company, are also noted in the *London Gazette*.

There are a number of signs that a company is under financial pressure, any one of which could be the trigger to a potential sale and purchase.

Chapter 2

Pre-pack Administrations

Introduction

2.1   There is no formal or legal definition of the term 'pre-pack', but it is a commonly used description of a situation where a sale of the business of an insolvent company is agreed with a buyer before the company goes into an insolvency procedure (usually administration). The buyer is identified prior to the insolvency, and is often a vehicle owned by the incumbent directors or management. The entire sale contract is negotiated with the proposed office-holder before the insolvency appointment is made, including details of the assets to be transferred to the buyer and the price to be paid. The office-holder then completes the sale soon after his appointment.

A pre-pack is defined in Statement of Insolvency Practice 16 ('SIP 16')[1] as:

> 'An arrangement under which the sale of all or part of a company's business and assets is negotiated with a purchaser prior to the appointment of an administrator, and the administrator effects the sale immediately on, or shortly after, his appointment.'

Pre-packs are not new, and they are not confined to administration. However a number of factors make administration the ideal process for pre-packs:

(a)   a specified person may be appointed as administrator with immediate effect out of court;

(b)   the appointment takes place at a time controlled by the appointor;

(c)   an administrator takes immediate control of the entire business and assets of a company on appointment, with the protection of the moratorium[2]; and

(d)   an administrator can deal with the company's assets on appointment without prior reference to creditors.

Pre-packs are frequently in the public domain due to a perceived increase in their use in administration in recent times, and they have attracted a degree of media attention, public concern and criticism. One reason for the increase in the number of pre-packs has undoubtedly been the rise of administration as

---

[1]   See section 2.5.
[2]   See section 1.21.

the insolvency procedure of choice following the corporate insolvency reforms introduced by the Enterprise Act 2002 ('EA 2002'). Statistics published by the Insolvency Service do not distinguish between pre-pack administrations and others, in which the company may have traded in administration, or the business was not for other reasons subject to an immediate sale. They do, however, show that between 2004 and 2009 the number of administrations increased from 1,602 in 2004 to 4,161 in 2009. The numbers have since reduced, such that in 2010 there were 2,817 administrations, in 2011 there were 2,808 administrations and in 2012 there were 2,532 administrations.

SIP 16 requires an administrator to report to creditors on their actions following a pre-pack, and a copy of the SIP report must be sent to the Insolvency Service. In its *Report on the Operation of Statement of Insolvency Practice 16 1 January to 31 December 2010* the Insolvency Service reported that it received SIP 16 reports relating to 769 companies, indicating that some 27% of all administrations that year involved pre-pack sales. For the same period in 2011 the Insolvency Service received SIP 16 reports relating to 723 companies, indicating that some 25% of all administrations in 2011 involved pre-pack sales[3]. In 2010, 72% of pre-pack sales were to parties connected with the insolvent company[4] and in 2011, 79% of sales were to connected parties[5].

As at 1 February 2013 the Insolvency Service report on the operation of SIP 16 for the year ending 31 December 2012 has not been published.

Benefits of pre-packs

2.2   The key benefit to pre-packs is speed. The manner in which the sale of the business is effected immediately on the appointment of an administrator preserves goodwill and maintains value in a business which might otherwise erode rapidly on insolvency. Key employees, suppliers and customers are often retained, whereas there can be a period of uncertainty and apprehension if a company trades in administration for a time whilst a buyer is found. During that period employees, suppliers and customers are often lost. If the company's business can be transferred immediately on the appointment of an administrator, a positive message of 'business as usual' can be disseminated from the outset to deflect from the fact that there has been an insolvency event.

The risk and cost of trading the business passes immediately to the buyer, and avoids the problem of funding in a trading administration. It is often a shortage of cash that triggers an insolvency appointment, and unless there is a (usually existing) secured lender who is willing to support and fund ongoing trading,

---

[3]   Insolvency Service Report on the Operation of Statement of Insolvency Practice 16 1 January to 31 December 2011.
[4]   Insolvency Service Report on the Operation of Statement of Insolvency Practice 16 1 January to 31 December 2010.
[5]   Insolvency Service Report on the Operation of Statement of Insolvency Practice 16 1 January to 31 December 2011.

the cash shortage continues into administration. An administrator may also find it impossible to trade a business because of other practical factors, such as:

• the risk of incurring liabilities relating to employees;

• the need to pay rent[6] and rates as expenses of the administration;

• key suppliers making demands for ransom payments;

• the risk of trading at a loss; and

• the risk that no buyer will be found.

All of these matters disappear in a pre-pack. In the absence of a pre-pack a company may have to cease trading in administration, with the result that the value of the goodwill of the business is lost to creditors, whereas in a trading situation it may well attract a premium. It is invariably the case that valuations of assets on a going-concern basis are greater than in a close-down scenario where the business and assets are simply liquidated.

There is also evidence that pre-packs are beneficial in preserving employment, and result in a better return to secured creditors[7]. The speed of the process helps to minimise the costs of the administration.

A sale by an administrator, as opposed to a pre-insolvency transaction, is also attractive to the directors of the company as the administrator then takes on the risks of the sale process itself. The directors avoid the possibility of a subsequently appointed office-holder scrutinising their conduct in relation to the sale for the purposes of considering a personal claim against them for misfeasance[8], and of the sale being reported to the Secretary of State for the purposes of possible disqualification under the Company Directors Disqualification Act 1986 ('CDDA 1986').

Notwithstanding the criticism that has been made of pre-packs[9] they are a very valuable tool in many circumstances, and may be the only mechanism by which an administrator can achieve the purpose of administration.

Criticism of pre-packs

2.3   Despite their clear benefits in some circumstances, pre-packs have come in for a considerable amount of criticism from a variety of sources, including Members of Parliament, the media and the general public:

---

[6] *Goldacre (Offices) Limited v Nortel Networks UK Limited (in administration)* [2009] EWHC 3389 (Ch), [2010] 1 Ch 455.

[7] Dr Sandra Frisby's report dated August 2007 entitled *A preliminary analysis of pre-packaged administrations*; and see section 2.3.

[8] IA 1986, s 112.

[9] See section 2.3.

- Unsecured creditors complain that as they only find out about a pre-pack after the event they have no opportunity to vote on or approve the proposed sale.

- The statutory framework within which administrators operate[10] does not provide for pre-packs. Indeed the opposite might be said:

  — The statutory purpose of administration (see section 1.4.1.5) provides a hierarchy of objectives[11], the first of which is to rescue the company as a going concern. It is only if the administrator thinks that it is not reasonably practicable to rescue the company[12] or that the second objective would achieve a better result for creditors as a whole, that he or she can move on to the second ranking objective of achieving a better result for the company's creditors as a whole than would be likely if the company were wound up (without first being in administration). As a pre-pack involves a sale of the company's business it will not result in a rescue of the company as a going concern. Has an administrator really considered the purpose of administration when he or she signs a sale contract immediately on his or her appointment?

  — An administrator is obliged to make a statement of his or her proposals for achieving the purpose of administration[13] and to send a copy of the proposals to every creditor of the company of whose claim and address he or she is aware[14] as soon as is reasonably practicable after the company enters administration and in any event within eight weeks of his or her appointment[15]. At the same time, unless specific exceptions apply[16], the administrator must invite creditors to a meeting[17] at which they are given the opportunity to vote on and approve his or her proposals[18]. A pre-pack disenfranchises creditors from that process as the administrator will have already effectively made the proposals and put them into operation before creditors get the opportunity to see what they are, consider them and vote.

- Creditors do not know if the sale was in their best interests. If the business is never exposed to the market (or only limited marketing takes place), the administrator cannot know that the price paid for it was the true market value. He or she may be able to rely on evidence from attempts that the directors made to sell the business before the administrator became involved in the process, and he or she ought to obtain their own

---

10 IA 1986, and Insolvency Rules 1986 (SI 1986/1925) ('the Rules').
11 IA 1986, Sch B1, para 3.
12 IA 1986, Sch B1, para 3(3).
13 IA 1986, Sch B1, para 49(1).
14 IA 1986, Sch B1, para 49(4)(b).
15 IA 1986, Sch B1, para 49(5).
16 IA 1986, Sch B1, para 52(1).
17 IA 1986, Sch B1, para 51(1).
18 IA 1986, Sch B1, para 53(1).

professional valuation of the business and assets. However the only true test of market value is to expose the business to the market.

• The process lacks transparency and accountability. As the transaction is negotiated in secret before the administrator is appointed, and may have long since completed by the time the creditors find out what has happened, it can be difficult to find out what did happen. This concern is even more prevalent when the business has been sold back to the existing directors or management. Creditors may then believe that the administration process has been abused to leave them with claims against an insolvent shell whilst the directors who mismanaged the company can continue to trade profitably and to their own benefit free of the burden of debt.

• The business itself is not restructured, and the new company may fail just as the old one did.

Aware of the criticism of pre-packs, the Association of Business Recovery Professionals ('R3') funded Dr Sandra Frisby[19] to carry out research into pre-pack administrations, leading to a report dated August 2007 entitled *A preliminary analysis of pre-packaged administrations*[20] ('Dr Frisby's Report'). Dr Frisby produced a summary of her findings as follows:

• Pre-packs were increasing sharply in number over time, most notably in administrations.

• A wide range of firms carried out pre-packs, ranging from the big four accountancy practices to the small and sole-practitioner practices.

• It may be that pre-packs were being used in predominantly 'small' cases.

• There were grounds for a more rigorous disclosure regime, particularly in relation to practitioners' statements of proposals and other reports to creditors. However overall pre-pack reports tended to be more informative than reports on more traditional administrations resulting in a business sale.

• Whilst pre-packs gave creditors no chance to vote on the sale of the business, that was also true of the majority of cases where the business was sold other than through a pre-pack.

• Proportionately more pre-pack sales were to connected parties than are other business sales, and that trend was accelerating in post EA 2002 pre-pack administration cases.

• There was some evidence to suggest that pre-packs resulted in lower overall returns for unsecured creditors.

• There was clear evidence that pre-packs performed better than other business sales in preserving employment.

---

[19] Associate Professor in Company and Commercial Law, University of Nottingham.
[20] Source: R3.

2.3 Pre-pack Administrations

- Pre-packs may have failed slightly more often than other business sales but this was inconclusively demonstrated. There was clear evidence that where a business was sold to a connected party it was more likely to fail.

Whilst some of the criticisms of pre-packs were borne out in Dr Frisby's Report, she also found that some of them were perhaps not justified when compared to the effect of the administration process generally, and there were some benefits of pre-packs. Nevertheless her report was one of the factors which led to the introduction of SIP 16[21].

The Business and Enterprise Select Committee ('Select Committee') has also considered pre-packs, reporting firstly on 6 May 2009[22] and again on 6 February 2013[23]. In May 2009 the Select Committee reported in the context of a number of high-profile retail insolvencies at the time[24]. It noted that there was controversy over the balance between the benefits and drawbacks of pre-packs, including their susceptibility to abuse. It accepted the logic that more value would be recovered from the sale of a company's business and assets where it continued to trade than where it was broken up. However it also noted evidence that creditors fared worse during a pre-pack[25], and that pre-packs also adversely affected competitors who continued to carry costs which the so called phoenix company had shed. Criticism of pre-packs was sharpest where the existing management bought the business back after negotiating with the proposed administrator, and the same management then continued the business clear of trade debts.

The Select Committee noted that the concerns they voiced had led to the introduction of SIP 16, and that its introduction was welcomed by some. However there was general agreement that its impact must be monitored closely. The Insolvency Service had committed to check each pre-pack administration to ensure compliance with both the letter and the spirit of SIP 16.

The Select Committee concluded on pre-packs that public confidence in the insolvency regime was being damaged and that prompt, robust and effective action was needed to ensure that pre-pack administrations were transparent and free from abuse. The interests of unsecured trade creditors must take a higher priority, especially in 'phoenix' pre-packs. Where there were good reasons for an insolvency practitioner to agree to a pre-pack, which there often could be, this must be explained fully and clearly. The introduction of SIP 16 was welcomed, as was the Insolvency Service's commitment to monitor implementation. If SIP 16 did not prove effective it would be necessary to take more radical action, possibly by giving stronger powers to creditors or the court. Anyone who suspected abuse of the process was urged to contact the

---

21 See section 2.5.
22 http://www.parliament.the-stationery-office.co.uk/pa/cm200809/cmselect/cmberr/198/19806.htm.
23 http://www.publications.parliament.uk/pa/cm201213/cmselect/cmbis/675/67502.htm.
24 Including The Officers Club, Whittards of Chelsea and MFI.
25 R3: *Pre-packaged sales ('pre-packs')* Briefing Note.

Insolvency Service, or the body that licences the administrator concerned. The Select Committee also encouraged large creditors, in particular Her Majesty's Revenue and Customs ('HMRC'), to take an active role in exposing abuse.

In March 2010 the Insolvency Service launched a consultation on improving the transparency of, and confidence in, pre-pack sales in administrations[26], and outlined 5 options for consideration:

1.   No change.

2.   Giving statutory force to the disclosure requirements in SIP 16, and providing penalties for non-compliance.

3.   Following a pre-pack sale, restricting the exit to compulsory liquidation in order to achieve scrutiny of the directors and the administrators by the Official Receiver.

4.   Require different insolvency practitioners to undertake pre and post administration appointment work.

5.   Require the approval of the court or creditors, or both, for all pre-pack business sales to connected parties.

A summary of the responses was published in March 2011[27], and the main findings were as follows:

- The current pre-pack framework did not provide a sufficient level of confidence that pre-packs were being used appropriately.

- A majority of those responding believed pre-packs were subject to some form of abuse.

- The main cause of concern related to connected party sales, and that any measures introduced should focus on this.

- The greatest support was for making no substantive change to the current regime, broadly reflecting the views of insolvency practitioners, lawyers and regulators.

- There was some support for introducing statutory force to SIP 16 disclosure requirements.

- There was very little support for the requirement to use separate insolvency practitioners to conduct pre and post appointment work.

- Some respondents, primarily insolvency practitioners and regulators, indicated that an approval mechanism for pre-pack sales involving creditors of the court would be unworkable, and obviate the benefits of pre-packs.

---

[26]   http://webarchive.nationalarchives.gov.uk/+/http://www.insolvency.gov.uk/insolvency
       professionandlegislation/con_doc_register/Pre-pack%20consultation%2031march%2010.pdf.
[27]   http://webarchive.nationalarchives.gov.uk/+/http://www.insolvency.gov.uk/insolvency
       professionandlegislation/con_doc_register/FINAL%20Pre-packs%20summary%20of%20
       responses.pdf.

2.3 *Pre-pack Administrations*

The Government response to the consultation[28] was to announce measures intended to improve the transparency of, and confidence in, pre-pack sales in administration, including:

- Requiring administrators to give notice to creditors where they proposed to sell a significant proportion of the assets of a company or business to a connected party in circumstances where there had been no open marketing of the assets.

- Requiring administrators to file at Companies House a detailed explanation of why a pre-pack sale was undertaken as part of their administration proposals.

- Requiring administrators to confirm that the sale price represented best value for creditors.

A draft statutory instrument was issued by the Insolvency Service on 16 June 2011[29] to make amendments to the Insolvency Rules 1986 in order to give effect to the proposed changes. However following further consultation with a range of interested parties including secured and unsecured creditors, insolvency practitioners and business representatives the Government announced on 26 January 2012[30] that it would no longer seek to introduce the proposed new legislative controls on pre-packs at that time.

The Select Committee subsequently decided to return to the issues it had reported on in 2009, and it invited interested parties to submit written evidence on the role and function of the Insolvency Service, including its role in pre-pack administrations, and particularly on the questions of transparency and their link to phoenix companies. It held oral evidence sessions in early 2012 and October 2012, in the context of continued public mistrust of the use of pre-packs. The Select Committee made a number of recommendations:

- Noting that the only research carried out into pre-packs was that undertaken in 2007 by Dr Frisby, it recommended that BIS and The Insolvency Service commission research to renew the evidential basis for pre-packs.

- Stronger penalties by way of larger fines for breaches of SIP 16 and stronger measures of enforcement were needed to make monitoring of SIP 16 compliance by the Insolvency Service more effective.

- The Insolvency Service should amend its monitoring process to include feedback to each insolvency practitioner and their regulatory body where SIP 16 reports are non-compliant.

---

[28] Written Ministerial Statement 31 March 2011 http://www.publications.parliament.uk/pa/cm201011/cmhansrd/cm110331/wmstext/110331m0001.htm.

[29] http://webarchive.nationalarchives.gov.uk/+/http://www.insolvency.gov.uk/insolvency professionandlegislation/con_doc_register/PPresponse/Pre-packs%20-%20note%20for%20 internet%20150611.doc.

[30] Written Ministerial Statement 26 January 2012 http://www.publications.parliament.uk/pa/cm201212/cmhansrd/cm120126/wmstext/120126m0001.htm.

- The criteria by which SIP 16 reports are judged should be published alongside the guidance.

The Select Committee also made a further recommendation when considering the issue of suppliers demanding ransom payments from a business on or after insolvency. Research suggested that up to 2,000 additional businesses a year could be saved from liquidation if suppliers were obligated to continue to supply, and the number of pre-packs would be likely to decrease[31]. Insolvency practitioners claimed that more than one in five of the administrations they were involved in were managed as pre-packs due to fear of such unreasonable actions by suppliers. The recommendation was that BIS should undertake a consultation as a matter of urgency on the rules relating to the continuation of supply to businesses on insolvency to assess if liquidations could be avoided if supplies were better protected.

In conclusion the Select Committee stated that there were a number of concerns about pre-pack administrations which still needed to be addressed. Greater transparency, higher levels of compliance with SIP 16 and a stricter regime of sanctions were needed. Equally more attention needed to be given to educating creditors of their rights. Pre-pack administrations continue to be in the news,[32] and the government has announced that an independent review of pre-packs will take place, with a launch date of late spring 2013.[33]

Case law

2.4   The court has considered the question of pre-packs both before and after the corporate insolvency reforms introduced by the EA 2002:

Re T&D Industries plc[34]

In *Re T&D Industries plc* the court was asked to consider whether an administrator could dispose of the assets of a company before his or her proposals had been approved by creditors without a direction from the court. At the time it was common practice for administrators to apply to court for a direction approving a sale. The court found that no direction was necessary, noting that:

(a)   administration was meant to be a more flexible, cheaper and less destructive process than liquidation;

---

[31]   Ev 83, BIS Committee: Evidence.
[32]   For example, in February 2013 in relation to law firm Cobbetts, and in March 2013 in relation to bed retailer Dreams.
[33]   http://www.bis.gov.uk/insolvency/news/news-stories/2013/Mar/PrePackStatement.
[34]   [2000] 1 WLR 646.

(b)   it was not desirable for the court to have to deal with numerous applications for a direction in such circumstances, particularly given the delay that would involve; and

(c)   a sale was normally an administrative or commercial decision for the administrator to take.

Re Transbus International Limited[35]

In *Re Transbus International Limited* the same question was asked of the court following the introduction of the EA 2002 reforms. The court concluded that the difference in wording between the old provisions of IA 1986 providing for administration, and the new provisions of IA 1986, Sch B1 did not prevent administrators from acting before their proposals were approved or without obtaining a direction from the court. If administrators were prevented from acting without the direction of the court this would be against the policy of the EA 2002 to reduce court involvement, and that could not be right.

DKLL Solicitors v Her Majesty's Revenue and Customs[36]

In this case the partners of DKLL applied to the court for an administration order, and proposed that if an order was made the administrators would immediately sell the business to a newly incorporated partnership. HMRC was the majority creditor of the partnership and it opposed the administration application. It argued that as the majority creditor it could defeat the administrators' proposals at a creditors' meeting if one were held. It opposed a pre-pack sale, and if the sale was permitted to go ahead despite its opposition it would be disenfranchised.

The court rejected HMRC's argument. Even if HMRC did not approve the administrators' proposals, that did not amount to an absolute veto on them. The administrators could seek directions from the court, and on the evidence before it the court found that the proposal to effect a pre-pack sale was reasonably likely to achieve the purpose of administration. It took HMRC's position into account, but also considered the impact of the administration on other stakeholders. There was evidence that administration would enhance realisations by some £300,000 and reduce creditor claims by some £44,000. It would also preserve 50 jobs and ensure a minimum of disruption for the firm's clients. Accordingly the administration order was made and the pre-pack sale went ahead.

This was the first reported acknowledgement of the pre-pack process.

---

[35]   [2004] EWHC 932 (Ch), [2004] 1 WLR 2654.
[36]   [2007] EWHC 2067 (Ch), [2008] 1 BCLC 112.

Re Kayley Vending Limited[37]

This was an unremarkable administration application, but the court took the opportunity to give guidance on the subject of pre-packs and SIP 16. The court said that when an administration application was made, it was primarily a matter for the applicant to identify what information was likely to assist the court in deciding whether to make an administration order[38]. If a pre-pack was proposed that would be appropriate information to include as part of the evidence in support. Whilst relevant matters to include might not be limited to those in SIP 16, it seemed likely that in most cases the information required by SIP 16, in so far as it was known or ascertainable at the date of the administration application, should be included.

The decision confirms that the court must have all relevant facts before it when a pre-pack is proposed.

Re Hellas Telecommunications (Luxembourg) II SCA[39]

An administration application was made to the court in respect of Hellas Telecommunications, in which it was proposed that if appointed the administrators would carry out a pre-pack sale of shares registered in the company's name to another member of the same group of companies.

On considering the application the court found that it was not easy to see where in the statutory structure it was concerned with the merits of a pre-pack sale. That was a matter for the administrator to deal with. If creditors were sufficiently aggrieved they had a remedy in the course of the administration to challenge an administrator's decision. The court might refuse to make an administration order if it was obvious that a pre-pack would be an abuse of the administrator's powers, or it could direct the administrator not to carry out the proposed sale. On the other hand it may be obvious that a pre-pack was the only real way forward, in which case the court could give the administrator liberty to proceed. But in the majority of cases the making of an administration order should not be taken as the court's blessing on the pre-pack sale.

Clydesdale Financial Services Limited and others v Smailes and others[40]

An LLP (a firm of solicitors) was funded by Clydesdale and others. It fell into financial difficulty and sought the advice of an insolvency practitioner as to its financial position, and how the LLP members should proceed. The insolvency

---

[37] [2009] EWHC 904 (Ch), [2009] BCC 578.
[38] Rule 2.4.
[39] [2009] EWHC 3199 (Ch), [2010] BCC 295.
[40] [2009] EWHC 1745 (Ch), [2009] BCC 810.

practitioner concluded that the LLP should enter into a pre-pack administration under which it sold its work in progress ledger to another firm at a price based on a valuation of the ledger. The insolvency practitioner was involved in a review of the ledger, the negotiations for the sale and in due course became administrator of the LLP. He concluded the sale on appointment. The bank objected to the terms of the sale alleging that the valuation of the work in progress had not been properly carried out, and as the office-holder had been so closely involved in negotiating the contract and in the circumstances leading to the administration he should be removed from office so that an independent investigation could be carried out. The court found that the terms of the sale contract and the circumstances leading up to it did warrant investigation, and that as the office-holder had been so closely involved with the negotiations it would be difficult for him to carry out an independent review. It also noted that most of the creditors supported the application. The court also rejected the office-holder's submission that the court could not grant the application sought as most of the acts complained of took place before he was appointed as administrator. The facts of the case were sufficiently obscure to make it difficult to divorce the office-holder's actions before appointment from his actions afterwards. In the circumstances it was appropriate to remove the administrator from office.

The position of the court seems to be that it has at most a minor role to play in determining whether or not a pre-pack should be put into effect. The court will not generally endorse a pre-pack on the hearing of an administration notwithstanding that it will be aware that an immediate sale of the business is proposed. That is a matter for the administrator alone. If a creditor does not like the process his remedy is to come to the court after the event to challenge the administrator's decision, and the court has shown that it will take steps to remove an administrator if it finds it appropriate for there to be an independent review of his actions.

Statement of Insolvency Practice 16

2.5   Statements of Insolvency Practice were considered in section 1.9. SIPs are guidance notes issued by R3 and which set out required practice in a number of specific areas of insolvency. They set out standards of practice that an office-holder must maintain, and they are often taken into account by the court as and when relevant as if they were legally binding regulations.

SIP 16 was specifically introduced with effect from 1 January 2009 to address pre-packs. It reminds office-holders that they must be clear about their role in the pre-appointment period. If their role is to advise the company, the directors should take independent advice, particularly if they are to buy the assets of the company in a pre-pack sale.

The main thrust of SIP 16 is disclosure. As unsecured creditors are not given the opportunity to consider the sale of the business and assets of the company before the sale takes place, they must be provided with a detailed explanation and justification of why the pre-pack was carried out so they can be satisfied that the administrator acted in the best interests of the creditors of the company as a whole. The following information must be disclosed to creditors in all cases where there is a pre-pack sale:

- the source of the administrator's initial introduction;

- the extent of the administrator's involvement prior to appointment;

- any marketing activities conducted by the company and/or the administrator;

- any valuations obtained of the business or the underlying assets;

- the alternative courses of action that were considered by the administrator, with an explanation of possible financial outcomes;

- why it was not appropriate to trade the business, and offer it for sale as a going concern during the administration;

- details of requests made to potential funders to fund working capital requirements;

- whether efforts were made to consult with major creditors;

- the date of the transaction;

- details of the assets involved and the nature of the transaction;

- the consideration for the transaction, terms of payment, and any condition of the contract that could materially affect the consideration;

- if the sale is part of a wider transaction, a description of the other aspects of the transaction;

- the identity of the purchaser;

- any connection between the purchaser and the directors, shareholders or secured creditors of the company;

- the names of any directors, or former directors, of the company who are involved in the management or ownership of the purchaser, or of any other entity into which any of the assets are transferred;

- whether any directors had given guarantees for amounts due from the company to a prior financier, and whether that financier is financing the new business;

- any options, buy-back arrangements or similar conditions attached to the contract of sale.

SIP 16 states that the information above should be provided to creditors in all cases unless there are exceptional circumstances. If the sale is to a connected party it is unlikely that considerations of commercial confidentiality would outweigh the need to provide information to creditors. Information should be provided with the first notification of the administration, and in any case where there has been a pre-pack sale the initial creditors' meeting should take place as soon as possible after the administrator's appointment.

2.5 *Pre-pack Administrations*

When an administrator sends SIP 16 information to creditors he or she is also obliged to send a copy to the Insolvency Service[41]. The Insolvency Service has a strategy to evidence compliance with the letter and spirit of SIP 16 to ensure the desired transparency of pre-packs is achieved. It monitors the timing of the provision of information to creditors, and explanations given as to why any information is withheld. The Insolvency Service also monitors the conduct of directors who are involved in pre-packs to ensure that no misconduct on their part has occurred. It also works with the RPBs to follow up any non-compliance on the part of administrators.

It is this obligation on the part of administrators which enables the Insolvency Service to review the operation of SIP 16. In its report on the First Six Months' Operation of SIP 16[42], issued in July 2009, the main findings of the Insolvency Service were as follows:

- Office-holders were generally positive in their approach to SIP 16. However a significant number of reports fell short of full compliance, often due to a failure to supply sufficient detail.

- Only limited data was available regarding directors' misconduct in SIP 16 cases. However misconduct did not seem to be significantly more prevalent in pre-packs than in other administrations.

- SIP 16 resulted in better information for creditors at an early stage and a greater degree of transparency in pre-packs. The Insolvency Service believes its continued operation will increase confidence in the process.

- There remained significant room for improvement in the information provided in a good proportion of cases. In particular:

  — In a minority of cases administrators were not sending out information in a timely manner.

  — Failure to provide full details of valuations or any marketing exercise was a common weakness. Without details of values placed on assets it was usually very difficult for creditors to determine whether the pre-pack was in their interests.

  — It was highly important that any connection between the company in administration and the buyer was fully disclosed in order to maintain confidence in the integrity of the sale and the insolvency regime as a whole.

- A number of areas were identified where SIP 16 might be refined and improved. These include:

  — Making what is required more explicit and clear.

  — Giving additional information that would be beneficial to creditors.

---

[41] See section 2.3 in relation to the Select Committee.
[42] http://www.bis.gov.uk/assets/insolvency/docs/insolvency%20profession/sip%2016%20 reports/sip16-first%20six%20months%202009.pdf.

— Setting out an explicit timescale for administrators to provide SIP 16 information.

— A requirement to provide the Secretary of State with a copy.

— Giving details of any security to which the assets were subject.

— Ensuring valuations and the directors' financial interests are fully disclosed.

• The regime to deal with misconduct by directors was already sufficiently robust to deal with any misconduct issues arising out of pre-packs.

• SIP 16 did improve transparency for creditors, and properly applied will ensure they receive the information they need to decide whether a pre-pack was in their best interests.

In October 2009 the Insolvency Service issued further guidance to office-holders in the light of its experience gained in monitoring SIP 16 reports[43]. The guidance made a number of points, and in doing so highlighted the deficiencies in reporting in the first months of operation of SIP 16:

• A short response to the bullet-point disclosure requirements listed in paragraph 9 of SIP 16 would not provide the required detailed explanation and justification of why a pre-pack sale took place.

• Creditors should be provided with sufficient information so that they do not need to ask further questions.

• Sufficient information should be provided to enable creditors to ascertain:

— What the company did.

— What financial pressures the company was under and the primary cause of insolvency.

— Why the company was insolvent.

— If applicable, why a pre-pack was used for some form of corporate restructuring.

— Any issues which necessitated speedy sale of the business.

• SIP 16 information should be sent within 14 days of the sale and not with the administrator's statement of proposals some weeks after his or her appointment.

• The convenience of the administrator was not a factor in determining when the report was to be sent.

• Creditors should be able to understand the extent of the work undertaken by the administrator before he or she was appointed.

• The name of any introducer and the circumstances leading to the referral must be disclosed.

---

[43] *Dear IP*, Issue 42.

- Details of any marketing activities carried out by the company or the administrator should be provided.

- Valuations of assets, including the basis on which the business was valued and the name of the valuer, should be disclosed.

- Details of those assets included in the sale and those excluded should be provided.

- The consideration paid should be broken down so it can be compared to asset values.

- The structure and timescale of payment of any deferred consideration should be made clear and details of any security obtained should be provided (or the fact that there is no security).

Further reports have since been issued by the Insolvency Service, for the periods July – December 2009[44], January – December 2010[45] and January to December 2011[46]. In its most recent review of SIP 16 the Insolvency Service reported that:

- 68% of reports reviewed were fully compliant with SIP 16.

- 7% of reports reviewed, equivalent to 4% of reports submitted, were sufficiently non-compliant to be referred to the insolvency practitioner's authorising body for it to consider the matter from a regulatory and disciplinary perspective.

- The main areas of concern continued to be issues with timeliness, background information, valuations, marketing, asset details and apportionment of sale consideration.

- There had been improvement in explanations given for the pre-pack sale, the timing of disclosures made and reasons for not marketing the business for sale.

- There was no evidence of any definitive link between directors' misconduct and pre-pack administration.

Statement of Insolvency Practice 13

2.6 SIP 13 is also relevant to pre-packs where the business and assets of the insolvent company are sold back to the directors. It gives guidance to office-holders to ensure that they:

- are familiar with the legal obligations of directors in relation to the acquisition of assets of companies by them or persons connected with the insolvent company;

---

[44] http://www.bis.gov.uk/assets/insolvency/docs/insolvency%20profession/sip%2016%20 reports/sip16%20report%20dec%202009.pdf.

[45] http://www.bis.gov.uk/assets/insolvency/docs/insolvency%20profession/sip%2016%20 reports/final%20sip%2016%20report%202010.pdf.

[46] Available at http://www.bis.gov.uk/insolvency/insolvency-profession/Regulation/statements-of-insolvency-practice/SIP-16-Reports-pre-packs.

- are aware of their legal obligations as office holders in relation to the disposal of assets to directors;
- apply best practice with regard to the disposal of assets to, and their acquisition by, directors;
- apply best practice with regard to the disclosure of such transactions.

Many of the matters set out in SIP 13 are covered by SIP 16 in relation to pre-packs and it will not be considered further.

Other matters

The appointment process

2.7   One of the essential elements to a pre-pack administration is the ability to appoint administrators quickly under the out-of-court route. However as noted in Chapter 1[47] there are unfortunately two contradictory lines of High Court authority relating to out-of-court appointments made by directors in situations where there is no holder of a QFC which have not, as at 1 February 2013, been resolved by the Court of Appeal.

Paragraph 26(2) of IA 1986, Schedule B1, provides that a person making an out of court appointment of an administrator shall

'…also give such notice as may be prescribed to such other persons as may be prescribed'.

Rule 2.20(2) provides that

'A copy of the notice of intention to appoint must … be given to:

(a)   any enforcement officer who … is charged with execution or other legal process against the company;

(b)   any person who … has distrained against the company or its property;

(c)   any supervisor of a voluntary arrangement under Part 1 of [IA 1986]; and

(d)   the company, if the company is not intending to make the appointment.'

In *Hill and another v Stokes*[48] the directors of the company failed to notify a landlord who had levied distress against company assets of their intention to appoint an administrator, and the High Court found that there was no obligation to do so. The obligation only arose where there was a QFC holder. In *Re Virtualpurple Professional Services Ltd*[49] the director failed to give the company

---

[47]   Section 1.20.
[48]   [2010] EWHC 3726 (Ch).
[49]   [2011] EWHC 3487 (Ch), [2012] BCC 254.

notice of intention to appoint an administrator, and again the High Court found this did not necessarily invalidate the subsequent administration, and that the court could waive any procedural defect in the appointment process.

However in *Minmar (929) Ltd v Khalastchi and another*[50] the High Court had indicated that failure by the directors to give notice of intention to appoint an administrator to the company would invalidate the subsequent purported appointment. This decision was followed by the High Court in *National Westminster Bank plc v Msaada Group (a firm)*[51], a decision handed down on the same day as the decision in *Virtualpurple Professional Services*. Accordingly directly conflicting decisions of the High Court were handed down at the same time.

In *Msaada* the Court suggested that the directors should give notice of intention to appoint an administrator to all prescribed parties, including the company using Form 2.8B (even though the Form is drafted on the basis that it will be used to give Notice to the holder of a QFC). Further, it suggested that all prescribed parties should be given a minimum of 5 business days notice of the proposed appointment.

In *Re BXL Services*[52], a subsequent decision of the High Court, the Court followed the *Virtualpurple Professional Services* line of authority and stated that it was now settled law that any failure by the directors to notify the parties referred to in Rule 2.20(2) of their intention to appoint an administrator would not automatically invalidate the subsequent appointment of administrators. However until the point is decided by the Court of Appeal, the prudent approach is for directors who wish to appoint administrators to follow the guidelines set out in *Msaada*.

The risks arising on a defective appointment apply even more in a pre-pack situation, where the assets of the company will already have been disposed of if the administration is successfully challenged on the basis that the appointment of the administrators is invalid. In order to achieve the necessary speed and certainty an appointment by the holder of a QFC is preferable where possible. Otherwise a court application for an administration order can be considered, or if there is no alternative to an appointment by the directors, all relevant parties must be served with a Notice of intention to appoint, and all necessary consents must be obtained before the appointment takes place.

Employees

2.8   In *DKLL Solicitors v Her Majesty's Revenue and Customs*[53] the court made reference to the interests of all stakeholders, including employees.

---

[50]   [2011] EWHC 1159 (Ch), [2011] BCC 485.
[51]   [2011] EWHC 3423 (Ch), [2012] BCC 226.
[52]   [2012] EWHC 1877.
[53]   [2007] EWHC 2067 (Ch), [2008] 1 BCLC 112.

In its *Dear IP* letter to insolvency practitioners dated 28 January 2009 the Insolvency Service stated that it was:

> 'of the opinion that pre-packs are a useful tool for practitioners, and one that can ultimately save jobs and rescue businesses that would otherwise not survive a company's insolvency'.

However the position of employees is not referred to as a consideration in IA 1986, Sch B1, which states that an administrator must perform his functions in the interests of the company's creditors as a whole[54]. Whilst the position of employees may be a factor which influences the court in exercising its discretion whether or not to make an administration order in a pre-pack situation, or indeed in any other administration, it appears that the interests of the creditors should take priority.

The Transfer of Undertakings (Protection of Employment) Regulations 2006 ('TUPE')[55]

2.9   Regulation 8(7) of TUPE states that its provisions providing for the transfer of contracts of employment on a relevant transfer of a business, and protecting an employee from dismissal, do not apply when a company is the subject of:

> 'bankruptcy proceedings or any analogous insolvency proceedings which have been instituted with a view to the liquidation of the assets of the transferor and are under the supervision of an insolvency practitioner'.

The insolvency proceedings which fall within regulation 8(7) are not identified, and the argument had been put forward that a pre-pack sale, where it was always the intention to liquidate the assets of the insolvent company, was an analogous insolvency proceeding within regulation 8(7). In *Oakland v Wellswood (Yorkshire) Limited*[56] the Employment Appeal Tribunal ('EAT') found that the question of whether an administration fell within regulation 8(7) was a question of fact to be determined by the employment tribunal. On appeal to the Court of Appeal the court reached its decision on other grounds, and no finding was made as to whether or not regulation 8(7) applied to administration. However the point soon came back before the EAT in *OTG Ltd v Barke & others*[57]. In a judgment delivered on 16 February 2011 the EAT considered both the 'absolute' approach, which would mean administrations could never fall within regulation 8(7), and the 'fact based' approach, whereby administration could fall within regulation 8(7) if it was found as a matter of fact to have been instituted with a view to liquidating the assets of the transferor, such as on a pre-pack sale. The EAT came to the conclusion that the 'absolute' approach was the correct one, and that administration would never fall with the

---

[54]   IA 1986, Sch B1, para 3(2).
[55]   SI 2006/246.
[56]   [2009] IRLR 250.
[57]   [2011] ICR 781.

exception set out in regulation 8(7). TUPE would operate to transfer relevant contracts of employment on the pre-pack sale of a business. The EAT gave 5 inter-related reasons for its decision:

1.   The distinction between bankruptcy proceedings and analogous insolvency proceedings is more likely to be intended to depend on the legal character of the procedure, not the objective of those operating it.

2.   When he takes an appointment as administrator every insolvency practitioner has an obligation to consider first of all whether he can rescue the company as a going concern.

3.   There is no requirement for an administrator to state at the outset which of the objectives of administration he is pursuing.

4.   A fact based approach would increase the likelihood of disputes.

5.   The purpose of TUPE was to protect employees in the event of a transfer and particular to ensure that their rights are safeguarded. The 'absolute' approach results in that outcome.

The Court of Appeal has since confirmed[58] that the 'absolute' approach is correct, and that administration (whether or not encompassing a pre-pack sale) is not an analogous insolvency proceeding within TUPE regulation 8(7), and that administration will never fall with the exception set out in regulation 8(7).

Landlords

2.10   In many instances an administrator will permit a buyer to occupy leasehold premises under the terms of a licence to occupy after a business sale has completed. This will invariably be agreed between the company in administration and the buyer without the landlord's consent, particularly so following a pre-pack where there has been no opportunity to negotiate with the landlord. Allowing an unauthorised occupier into leasehold premises will invariably be a breach of the lease. The usual remedy for the landlord would be to take steps to forfeit the lease, but he or she cannot follow that course of action without either consent of the administrator or permission of the court as a result of the moratorium that arises on administration[59].

In *Sunberry Properties Limited v Innovate Logistics Limited (in administration)*[60] the administrator allowed an unauthorised occupier into leasehold premises, and the landlord made an application for permission to enforce the terms of the lease by way of seeking an injunction order. The Court of Appeal held that in order to reach its decision the court should carry out a balancing exercise between the interests of the landlord and the interests of the creditors generally in accordance

---

[58]   *Key2Law (Surrey) LLP v De'Antiquis* [2011] EWCA Civ 1567, [2012] ICR 881.
[59]   IA 1986, Sch B1, para 43; and see section 1.20.
[60]   [2008] EWCA Civ 1321, [2009] 1 BCLC 145.

with the guidance set out in *Re Atlantic Computer Systems plc*[61]. There was evidence that the company needed to allow the buyer into occupation of the premises in order to achieve the purpose of administration. The occupier would pay a monthly licence fee equal to the passing rent and that would be handed over to the landlord. The potential loss to the landlord of denying forfeiture was outweighed by the potential loss to creditors generally if the company was required to deliver up possession of the property, and accordingly permission to forfeit would be denied.

In *Goldacre (Offices) Limited v Nortel Networks UK Limited (in administration)*[62] the circumstances were different, in that it was the company in administration itself that continued to occupy the premises after administration. There was no pre-pack and no unauthorised occupier. The landlord applied to the court for an order that rent be paid as an expense of the administration as it fell due, quarterly in advance. The court applied the same principles as in liquidation[63] and found that whilst the company made use of the premises for the purpose of the administration, rent that fell due for payment after the administrators had been appointed was payable in full as an expense or as a necessary disbursement under the Insolvency Rules 1986 (SI 1986/1925) ('the Rules')[64]. This reasoning could apply on a pre-pack where it might be argued that the company itself continues to benefit from the use of the premises, for the purpose of the administration, by allowing the buyer to enter into occupation.

It is however clear that rent payable in advance which fell due prior to the commencement of administration is not payable as an expense[65]. Any risk of a landlord claiming rent as an expense in a pre-pack administration can therefore be mitigated from the administrators' point of view if the appointment of administrators is made shortly after a rent payment date.

VAT

2.11   Under Value Added Tax Act 1994, Sch 11, para 4(2):

> 'where it appears to the Commissioners requisite to do so for the protection of the revenue they may require a taxable person, as a condition of his supplying goods or services under a taxable supply, to give security, or further security, of such amount and in such manner as they may determine, for the payment of any VAT which is or may become due from him'.

HMRC may rely on this provision in pre-packs to require the buyer to pay a deposit of up to six months' anticipated VAT as security for future payment.

---

[61]   [1992] Ch 505, CA (Civ Div).
[62]   [2009] EWHC 3389 (Ch), [2010] 1 Ch 455.
[63]   *Re Lundy Granite Co* (1870–71) LR 6 Ch App 462, CA.
[64]   Rule 2.67(1).
[65]   *Leisure Norwich (2) Ltd & Others v Luminar Lava Ignite Limited & Others* – [2012] EWHC 951(Ch), [2012] BCC 497.

This is particularly so where it is the previous directors or management who have acquired the business from the administrator in the pre-pack. This additional expense will have a significant impact on the immediate working capital requirements of the ongoing business.

Challenging a pre-pack

2.12   IA 1986, Sch B1 provides the remedies available to a creditor who wishes to challenge a pre-pack:

Paragraph 74

2.13   Paragraph 74 includes the following:

'74(1) A creditor or member of a company in administration may apply to the court claiming that–

(a)   the administrator is acting or has acted so as unfairly to harm the interests of the applicant (whether alone or in common with some or all other members or creditors), or

(b)   the administrator proposes to act in a way which would unfairly harm the interests of the applicant (whether alone or in common with some or all other members or creditors).'

'74(4) In particular, an order under this paragraph may–

(a)   regulate the administrator's exercise of his functions;

(b)   require the administrator to do or not do a specified thing;

(c)   require a creditors' meeting to be held for a specified purpose;

(d)   provide for the appointment of the administrator to cease to have effect;

(e)   make consequential provision.'

By the time a creditor is aware of a pre-pack it will be too late for him or her to prevent the administrator from acting in the manner he or she complains of. Paragraph 74 may still be relevant, but as the court has noted that entering into a sale of the business is a commercial matter for the administrator[66], it may be reluctant to interfere in his or her commercial decision-making and to provide an adequate remedy in relation to a transaction that has already taken place.

The court has indicated that it may prefer to rely on paragraph 88 to remove an administrator if that is the appropriate course of action[67].

---

[66]   *Re T&D Industries plc* [2000] 1 WLR 646; *Re Transbus International Limited* [2004] EWHC 932 (Ch), [2004] 1 WLR 2654; *Re Hellas Telecommunications (Luxembourg) II SCA* [2009] EWHC 3199 (Ch), [2010] BCC 295.

[67]   *Clydesdale Financial Services Limited and others v Smailes and others* [2009] EWHC 1745 (Ch), [2009] BCC 810.

Paragraph 75

2.14 Paragraph 75 provides for an administrator, liquidator or creditor to make an application to the court alleging that an administrator has breached a fiduciary or other duty in relation to the company, or has been guilty of misfeasance[68]. It provides a simple mechanism to seek a remedy for any breach of duty, such as a sale of the business and assets for less than their true market value. The court may be invited to order the administrator to contribute a sum to the company's property by way of compensation for any breach of duty or misfeasance that is proven[69].

Paragraph 88

2.15 Paragraph 88 states as follows:

'88 The court may by order remove an administrator from office.'

It is likely that the applicant in any such case would have to show cause as to why the administrator should be removed[70].

Clydesdale Financial Services Limited and others v Smailes and others[71]

2.16 In *Clydesdale Financial Services Limited and others v Smailes and others* a creditor of the LLP in administration applied to remove the administrator from office under paragraphs 74(4)(d) and 88, and the administrator cross-applied to strike out a claim made against him for compensation and/or damages under paragraph 75. The business of the LLP had been sold in a pre-pack, and the administrator had been intimately involved in the negotiations before his appointment. The creditor objected to the terms of the sale and sought to remove the administrator from office so that his conduct could be made subject to independent review. The creditor also brought a claim for compensation under paragraph 75. The administrator applied to strike out the compensation claim on the basis that the allegations made referred to events prior to his appointment as administrator.

The court found that the fact and terms of the sale contract were a legitimate matter for consideration and investigation by an office-holder acting in the interests of creditors. The administrator and his firm were so closely involved in the negotiations for the sale that he could not be expected to conduct an independent review. As a result the court found that there was a proper basis on which it could exercise its discretion to remove the administrator, but in doing so it did not intend to impugn his integrity.

---

[68] IA 1986, Sch B1, para 75(3)(d).
[69] IA 1986, Sch B1, para 75(4)(c).
[70] *Sisu Capital Fund Limited and others v Tucker and others* [2005] EWHC 2170 (Ch), [2006] BCC 463.
[71] [2009] EWHC 1745 (Ch), [2009] BCC 810.

Turning to the application under paragraph 75, the court did not accept the administrator's argument that the claim could not be maintained as the acts or omissions complained of occurred before his appointment. The facts were sufficiently obscure to make it difficult to divorce the administrator's actions before appointment from his capacity as administrator. The claim was not struck out.

The case shows that there is a potential remedy for creditors who are dissatisfied with a pre-pack. It perhaps also demonstrates the importance of consulting with major creditors before a pre-pack is carried out. The matters reported so far are the results of the preliminary skirmishes only and do not confirm the final remedy that the court might be willing to offer creditors; it remains to be seen if creditors use this case as an impetus to ask the court to remove and replace administrators in further pre-pack cases.

The Insolvency Service

2.17   The Insolvency Service operates a pre-pack complaints 'hotline', which provides interested parties with a telephone number, email address and post address at which they can register a complaint[72].

Future developments

2.18   On 12 November 2009 the Office of Fair Trading ('OFT') announced a market study into corporate insolvency, and its report was issued on 24 June 2010 ('OFT Report'[73]). The study considered the structure of the insolvency market, the appointment process for insolvency practitioners and any features in the market which could result in harm and restrict firms and practitioners from competing freely. As the OFT also announced that the final scope of the study would depend on the result of the initial phase, it was thought that it could well be extended to specifically include pre-packs. However that was not the case. The OFT concluded that as long as banks did not recover their assets in full, the market worked reasonably well. However where the secured creditor was paid in full, the remaining unsecured creditors found it hard to control or influence the process, and were harmed as a result[74]. The OFT proposed a number of remedies to increase the efficiency and effectiveness of the regulatory regime and the regulations it enforces to address the harm to the market:

- an independent complaint body with the ability to assess fees;

---

[72]   http://www.bis.gov.uk/insolvency/insolvency-profession/Professional%20conduct/how-complain-against-an-IP/pre-packs-complaints-process.

[73]   Office of Fair Trading, *The market for corporate insolvency practitioners – A market study*, June 2010 (http://www.oft.gov.uk/shared_oft/reports/Insolvency/oft1245).

[74]   OFT Report, paras 1.6 and 1.7.

- setting clear objectives for the regulatory regime, and increasing its ability to deliver them;

- amending some of the regulations.

The OFT reported that problems associated with pre-packs were symptomatic of the problems it found in the market as a whole, and that its recommendations went some way to resolving the issues. However it did not discuss pre-packs extensively outside its discussion of administrations generally[75].

The Insolvency Service and the Secretary of State will continue to monitor compliance with SIP 16, and if it is not seen as successful in providing creditors with further information, improving transparency and increasing confidence in the insolvency process, further regulation and perhaps law reform may be expected. The Government indicated that further review would take place when it abandoned the proposed changes to the Insolvency Rules in January 2012 and that will leave to a revised SIP 16 in due course. A draft of the revised SIP 16 was considered by the Joint Insolvency Committee in November 2012, and it was then to be considered by each of the regulatory bodies for insolvency practitioners. It is currently anticipated that the new SIP 16 will be put in place during 2013.

No specific review of SIP 13 has been undertaken, but all SIPs are currently under review to identify those which should be revised, and it is likely that SIP 13 will fall into that category.

---

[75]   OFT Report, para 3.25.

Chapter 3

Purchasing Vehicles and Insolvency Act 1986, s 216

Introduction

3.1　As with any sale and purchase of a company or business there are two processes by which the buyer might make the acquisition. The buyer might acquire the shares of the insolvent company as part of a plan to restructure the business and turn it around. The same legal entity will retain ownership of the business. Alternatively the buyer might acquire the business and assets of the insolvent company, transferring ownership of the business to a different legal entity. The insolvent company itself will remain in the ownership of the original shareholders and its affairs, in so far as they have not been transferred to the new owner, will usually be dealt with by an insolvency practitioner. In the latter scenario the buyer acquires only those assets and liabilities that it agrees to buy and the seller agrees to sell, whereas in the acquisition of shares the buyer takes ownership of all of the insolvent company's assets and liabilities.

If the seller is in a formal insolvency proceeding the office-holder will usually sell the insolvent company's business and assets, as he or she has no control over its shares and cannot himself agree to transfer them. That does not of course apply to any subsidiary of the company over which he or she is appointed. In that situation the shares of the subsidiary will be an asset of the company, like any other, over which the office-holder does have control. He or she will sell the company's assets without warranties, which may make the purchase of the subsidiary's shares unattractive to a buyer, subject to the price reflecting the risk. In relation to the company over which he or she is appointed, an administrator or receiver will usually sell the company's business after approval of the terms of the transaction by the company's bankers and any other party who has security over the property or undertaking of the company. The buyer will want to ensure that the assets are sold free of any fixed or floating charge (which will by this time have crystallised), and it will invariably be a term of the transaction that any security over the assets is released on completion.

Although the first objective of administration is to rescue the company as a going concern[1], an administrator will usually satisfy his or her obligation to achieve the statutory purpose of administration when he or she sells the business of an insolvent company by relying on the second objective, achieving a better result

---

[1]　IA 1986, Sch B1, para 3(1)(a).

for the company's creditors as a whole than would be likely if the company were wound up (without first being in administration)[2]. A sale of a business as a going concern by an administrator, even an insolvent business, will tend to generate a greater return for creditors than a simple break-up of the assets, as the value of goodwill is preserved and realised. Additionally, as customers of the insolvent company will see a seamless continuation of the business, and the service it offers or goods it supplies, they are less likely to assert claims for breach of contract or failure to fulfil warranties than they would on a cessation of trade. Such claims often arise when a business ceases to trade or continuity is interrupted, and they are invariably set off against debts due to the company by customers. The collection of receivables by the office-holder is therefore enhanced on a sale of the business, as are other recoveries such as retentions. The realisation of goodwill and increased recovery of debtors will usually be the major contributors to achieving the second objective of administration on a sale of the business.

Shares or assets?

3.2   Those behind the acquiring entity will need to consider the same issues as arise on any corporate transaction when they acquire an insolvent business, plus they then need to take into account the insolvent nature of the seller. When determining whether to acquire shares or assets the buyer will want to investigate precisely what assets the insolvent company owns, how it holds them, and what liabilities might attach to them (see Chapter 4, Due Diligence). As with any corporate transaction, tax planning will also be a major part of the initial planning process (see 4.26, 4.37, and 4.54 at '11. Taxation').

Aside from taxation the buyer will have to consider the following matters when deciding whether it is in their best interests to acquire the shares or assets of the insolvent company:

- In a share purchase the buyer will acquire all of the assets and liabilities of the seller whereas in an asset purchase they will only acquire those assets and liabilities they agree to take on or assume by operation of law.[3] This is often the most relevant factor when the seller is insolvent. Buying assets protects the buyer from unknown issues and liabilities, and from having to rely on warranties, which in many instances will not be available if the seller is in an insolvency process.

- A purchase of shares requires the co-operation of all shareholders, whereas assets can be sold by the company itself. This is subject to the company having power to sell its property and undertaking, such power to be exercised by the directors, in its Memorandum and Articles. An office-holder appointed over a company relies on Schedule 1 of the Insolvency Act 1986, which includes a power in favour of an

---

[2]   IA 1986, Sch B1, para 3(1)(b).
[3]   See Chapter 9 (Employees).

administrator or administrative receiver to sell or dispose of the property of the company by public auction, private auction or private contract[4]. An office-holder does not have the power to sell the shares of the company in respect of which he or she is appointed.

- A share purchase may be quicker, simpler and less disruptive if there are few shareholders. There is no need to identify specific assets to be transferred; or to document individual transfers; or to seek third-party consents.

- If the buyer is acquiring a division only of the insolvent seller rather than the whole of the business, they will have to acquire assets, limited to those that relate to that particular division only. The only exception would be if the assets were first hived down into a separate subsidiary company.

- As the seller is insolvent, there will invariably have to be further restructuring carried out after a purchase of shares in order to restore the company to solvency free of its historic liabilities. This might involve a formal insolvency proceeding such as a company voluntary arrangement or a scheme of arrangement to enable the company itself to continue to operate. It might also involve administration at the instigation of the buyer, followed by an asset purchase from the administrator, perhaps as a pre-pack transaction. A combination of a share purchase followed by an asset purchase can be a useful tool.

- A purchase of assets may give the buyer the opportunity to apportion the consideration to its advantage, relying on tax advantages for the acquisition of certain classes of asset. However there may be competing interests if the seller is in an insolvency proceeding, as an administrator or liquidator must apportion the price in accordance to his or her valuation evidence. It is relevant to the company's creditors as a whole that the consideration is apportioned correctly to those assets that are subject to a fixed charge and those that are subject to a floating charge. Subject to the costs of realisation, the net proceeds of sale of a fixed-charge asset will be paid in their entirety to the charge-holder. However where a debenture was created after 15 September 2003 the office-holder has to retain a prescribed part out of net proceeds of sale that would otherwise be available to the holder of a floating charge, and he or she must distribute those retained moneys to unsecured creditors[5].

The prescribed part is an amount equal to 50 per cent of the first £10,000 that would otherwise be paid to the floating charge holder, and then 20 per cent of further sums that would otherwise be available up to a maximum prescribed part of £600,000[6].

- A purchase of assets may provide the buyer with a simpler mechanism to fund the acquisition by charging the assets it acquires to secure loans. However this may not now be so relevant as a factor in deciding whether

---

[4] IA 1986, Sch 1, para 2.
[5] IA 1986, s 176A.
[6] Insolvency Act 1986 (Prescribed Part) Order 2003 (SI 2003/2097).

to enter into a share purchase or asset purchase since it is no longer unlawful for a private company to provide financial assistance for the purchase of its own shares[7].

- If a sale of assets takes place before the seller is in a formal insolvency proceeding the buyer will need to consider whether any administrator or liquidator subsequently appointed to the seller could attack the acquisition as a transaction at an undervalue[8].

A transaction at an undervalue occurs when:

— a company has gone into administration or liquidation[9];

— it has made a gift to a person or otherwise entered into a transaction on terms that provide for no consideration, or for a consideration the value of which, in money or money's worth, is significantly less than the value, in money or money's worth, of the consideration provided by the company[10];

— the transaction occurred at a relevant time[11].

A transaction takes place at a relevant time for the purpose of IA 1986, s 238 if it is entered into during the period of two years ending with the onset of insolvency[12] and at the time the company is unable to pay its debts within the meaning of IA 1986, s 123 or becomes unable to pay its debts as a result of the transaction[13].

If an administrator or liquidator subsequently appointed to the seller believes that there may have been a transaction at an undervalue, he or she has powers to investigate the transaction and may call for relevant information and documents from the seller and the buyer[14]. Anyone who fails to co-operate with the office-holder's enquiries may be brought before the court and required to provide information and documents to the office holder. The administrator or liquidator can make an application to the court to set aside a transaction at an undervalue[15], and the court may make such order as it sees fit for restoring the position to what it would have been if the company had not entered into the transaction[16]. That may include an order that the buyer transfer the assets back to the seller. Or the court may require the buyer to pay the seller the difference between what it did pay and the true monetary value of the assets at the time.

---

[7]   CA 2006, s 678.
[8]   IA 1986, s 238.
[9]   IA 1986, s 238(1).
[10] IA 1986, s 238(4).
[11] IA 1986, s 238(2).
[12] IA 1986, s 240(1)(a).
[13] IA 1986, s 240(2).
[14] IA 1986, ss 234, 235, 236.
[15] IA 1986, s 238(2).
[16] IA 1986, s 238(3).

The key to avoiding this potential problem in a purchase of assets from an insolvent seller before any formal insolvency proceeding is to take relevant professional advice. The parties must ensure that the assets are valued at the time of the transaction by a reputable agent or agents. Then any subsequent allegations of a transaction at an undervalue can be refuted with reliable contemporaneous evidence.

• In a share purchase the buyer will automatically acquire title to the assets in so far as title was vested in the company, as there is no transfer of ownership of the assets. In an asset sale an office-holder will only sell such right title and interest as the company can transfer and he or she will give no warranty as to title. Various consents may be required from third parties to complete the transfer of title or rights, and these may not be readily available. For example finance companies may not be willing to transfer the benefit of finance agreements, a landlord may not be willing to assign rights of occupation, or in each case not until all arrears have been paid by the buyer.

• Existing contracts and trading arrangements may terminate on a change of ownership of shares, but not necessarily so. Contracts must be reviewed for any such terms. On a transfer of assets, contracts and trading arrangements will remain legally with the seller, and may need to be novated to the buyer in order for the agreements to continue. This gives the other contracting party an opportunity to renegotiate terms or look for an alternative contractor to deal with. This can be a significant risk to the buyer if key contracts may be lost.

• In either scenario employee rights and liabilities will remain to be dealt with by the buyer, whether as a result of contracts of employment remaining with the insolvent company on a share sale, or by them transferring to the buyer of assets under the Transfer of Undertakings (Protection of Employment) Regulations 2006 (SI 2006/246) ('TUPE'). A transfer of assets as opposed to a share transfer may involve an obligation to inform and consult with employee representatives before the transaction is completed.

Method of sale

3.3 The sale of the business may be achieved by auction or private treaty. For an insolvent company it is more usual for the business to be subject to marketing (however limited) and then sold by private treaty after negotiations with a preferred bidder.

Marketing an insolvent business must be handled carefully as it can destroy value. Once the market knows that a company is in financial difficulty, potential acquirers and competitors may seek to take advantage of the situation. This could manifest itself in a potential bidder making low offers; a competitor approaching key customers and clients with a view to taking over contracts with the company; and competitors poaching key staff. When an office-holder has been appointed to the seller he or she will be under an obligation to act in the best interests of the creditors of the company, which will include realising assets for their true market value. That is usually best demonstrated by a well-planned and executed marketing campaign leading to rival bids, and the office-holder selecting the preferred offer based on price and other relevant factors, including consideration of additional terms proposed, the availability of funding to the proposed buyer and/or deferred payment terms, timing of the transaction, the buyer's ability to move quickly where necessary, and any regulatory issues that might arise. However extensive marketing is not always possible for the very reason that it can destroy value, and on many occasions speed is of the essence. It is issues such as a lack of marketing and the speed of the transaction that make pre-pack administrations a contentious topic.

Timing of a sale is a crucial matter to take into account. From the buyer's point of view, if an insolvent business is to survive in the hands of a new owner then the transaction may need to be delayed to the start of a critical part of the business cycle, to give the insolvent business the best prospects of success going forward. For example in a seasonal business the buyer will want to acquire the company shortly before the high season starts, and not at the end. At the same time the seller may want to take advantage of the optimum trading period. Alternatively the seller may want to complete the acquisition at the earliest possible time before the business deteriorates further. From the seller's point of view, the longer an insolvent company continues to trade the greater the risk of the company's funders taking matters into its own hands and enforcing security. Any sale would then be put into the hands of (usually) an administrator and taken out of the control of the directors. Also, the longer a company trades in a distressed situation the greater the risk to the directors of a claim for wrongful trading from a subsequently appointed liquidator[17].

A director may be made liable for wrongful trading on an application to the court by a liquidator if the court is satisfied that at some time before the commencement of the winding up the director knew or ought to have concluded that there was no reasonable prospect that the company would avoid going into insolvent liquidation[18], and that the director failed to take every step with a view to minimising the potential loss to the company's creditors that he or she ought to have taken[19]. The court will apply an objective standard to the director's conduct based on the general knowledge, skill and experience that may be reasonably expected of a person carrying out the functions of the director, and a subjective standard based on the general knowledge, skill and experience that the director has[20]. If the court is satisfied that there has been wrongful trading it can make a declaration that the director is liable to make such contribution to the company's assets as the court thinks proper[21]. The usual order would be in terms that a director in breach of IA 1986, s 214 must pay the liquidator an amount equal to the additional loss caused to the company's creditors by the

---

[17]   IA 1986, s 214.
[18]   IA 1986, s 214(2)(b).
[19]   IA 1986, s 214(3).
[20]   IA 1986, s 214(4).
[21]   IA 1986, s 214(1).

breach. In other words, the amount of the payment will be determined by the increase in the deficiency to creditors that occurred from the date the director knew or ought to have concluded that there was no reasonable prospect that the company would avoid insolvent liquidation, and the actual date of the winding up. Personal liability arising from wrongful trading is a real concern for directors of an insolvent business.

A delay in timing of a sale can also increase the risk of subsequent disqualification from acting as a director under the Company Directors Disqualification Act 1986. Wrongful trading is a ground which the court can rely on when making a disqualification order.

These are all competing factors to be brought into the negotiations.

The sale process

3.4   The sale process itself will be much as for any sale of a corporate entity, but subject to a number of constraints that may take some issues out of the parties' hands. It would be usual to see the process involve the matters set out below to some extent:

• Planning. Acquisitions of insolvent companies may be well planned, with strong businesses looking for opportunities to increase their market share, turnover and profit in a difficult market. However much of the corporate activity in this arena will be opportunistic, as the buyer will simply not know that the potential target business is or may be available until the prospect presents itself. A predator in this situation has to be ready to move quickly in all aspects of the process, and particularly to have ready access to appropriate funding.

• Funding. The usual sources of money may be available to support acquisitions of insolvent companies. However mainstream sources may not be keen to lend into a distressed situation, where due diligence and warranties are not available or are limited, and the lender has to move quickly and at short notice. However there are funders in the marketplace which specialise in purchases of distressed businesses. They are used to investing with limited due diligence and warranties and can move quickly, understanding the greater potential risk, but also recognising the greater potential rewards available to them.

   If an office-holder is appointed to the seller he or she will invariably want to see proof of funding before taking any offer for the business seriously.

• Information. There may well be an information memorandum prepared. Those advising a distressed company or a proposed administrator may carry out limited advertising to seek out interested bidders, or make use of their own contacts, or seek to revive interest from parties who have previously expressed an interest to acquire the company. Care also has to be taken so as not to destroy the value of the seller by making its financial difficulties widely known. Available information may therefore be limited.

In a formal insolvency proceeding, particularly where the appointment was hostile, the office-holder may simply not have access to documents or people with relevant information.

• Confidentiality agreements would be used. There may be wide restrictions placed on the proposed buyer as to non-solicitation of key employees and staff, and restrictions on trading in the seller's debt, particularly if the proposed buyer is a competitor. The early stages of the sales process will often involve disclosure of commercially sensitive information.

• A data room may be prepared for larger, planned transactions. However information may be limited, particularly if the seller is in a formal insolvency proceeding. A prospective buyer may have a substantial advantage over other bidders if they have assistance from the seller's directors (or if they are the seller's directors). Whatever information is supplied to a prospective buyer, they will be required to rely on their own enquiries about the business. The sale agreement will exclude all representations made by the seller or any office-holder, and no warranties as to the accuracy or completeness of information will be provided.

Not only will a lack of information be relevant, but also cost. An office-holder will not incur a disproportionate cost in setting up a data room in many sale processes.

• Negotiation on price and structure of the transaction:

— Outside factors such as the need to complete a sale with speed; the position of a secured lender who might enforce security; the requirements of a relevant regulator, such as CQC[22] or the Environment Agency; the potential loss of key customers, suppliers and employees in an insolvency proceeding; and a lack of cash to fund ongoing trading, are some of the matters which may take an unexpected priority in the transaction.

— It would be usual to see a lower consideration in a distressed or insolvency sale than might otherwise be the case, but with reduced or no warranties to protect the buyer.

— The company or an office-holder may be willing to negotiate with a number of prospective bidders, and a short period of exclusivity may be made available. Alternatively there may be a process of sealed bids or a straightforward auction of the business. The seller will choose whatever method is likely to produce the best possible outcome for itself, and even when a preferred bid has been identified an office-holder may want to be able to take advantage of any better offers made before an agreement is concluded. An office-holder in an insolvency proceeding may be obliged to consider higher offers before completion.

---

[22] Care Quality Commission.

— The parties may consider the potential benefits of an office-holder hiving the insolvent business down into a new subsidiary of the seller, which the buyer then acquires. This structure may have beneficial tax or other consequences for the buyer.

— The parties will recognise that it may not be possible to satisfy all the requirements of TUPE as to consultation with employees or their representatives on the sale of an insolvent business. However the well-advised seller and buyer will take all such steps as they can to consult in order to minimise the risk of successful employee claims in the future. Buyers might wish to insure against the TUPE risk, in which case the requirements of the insurer may also have to be taken into account.

— The buyer will need to consider any pension arrangements put in place by the seller for its employees, and pension provisions that may need to be put in place for transferring employees after completion. If there is a defined benefit scheme the buyer will want to ensure that any deficit does not transfer to it. The position and potential involvement of the Pensions Regulator will also need to be considered.

— Any parties will also need to consider tax issues arising on the transfer of the business. A sale of the business as a going concern will usually qualify for an exemption from VAT, but the buyer will be required to pay any VAT that is subsequently charged on the transaction or any part of it, and it will be required to indemnify the seller and any office-holder in relation to any such charge to VAT. The seller will need to consider any charges to capital gains tax that may arise on a sale, preserving any unused tax losses that may be of benefit to a special purchaser. The buyer will need to consider matters such as stamp duty, Stamp Duty Land Tax and any 'option to tax' in relation to land.

— Approvals and consents to the transaction, or parts of it, may have to be obtained after completion rather than be put in place beforehand. These can relate to key components of the arrangements, such as the assignment of a lease; novations of contracts with third-party suppliers; agreeing claims with retention of title creditors; novations of funding agreements with financiers of key plant and machinery or other equipment; and obtaining the assignment of a licence to use intellectual property. Obtaining all such approvals and consents will usually be at the buyer's risk.

• Sale contract:

— Once heads of terms have been agreed the legal contract will usually be prepared, negotiated, agreed and signed with all due haste.

— If the seller is in an insolvency proceeding the office-holder will authorise the sale and be a party to the contract in order to take advantage of the exclusions and indemnities within it. The buyer should check that the appointment is valid and effective, and the office-holder will expect to be asked to supply documentation to that effect.

The buyer will not need to be concerned that the sale is taking place before the creditors of a seller in administration have approved the administrator's proposals[23] for achieving the purpose of administration[24]. An administrator's actions can be challenged by creditors who can claim on an application to the court that the administrator has acted so as to unfairly harm their interests[25] or has misapplied property of the company, or has breached a fiduciary duty in relation to the company, or is guilty of misfeasance[26]. However the court is reluctant to interfere with an administrator's exercise of commercial judgment[27].

— The buyer must ensure that where assets are subject to a fixed charge, there is an obligation in the sale contract on the part of the seller to deliver a release from the security on completion. Alternatively an administrator will need to provide a relevant court order on completion[28].

— The buyer should not expect to see the usual form of a share purchase or asset sale agreement. Warranties will be absent, there will be exclusions of liability, and if the seller is in a formal insolvency proceeding the office-holder will seek indemnities from the buyer. This will be vital to the seller where the buyer will carry on the business in the seller's name prior to any formal novation or assignment of contracts. The office-holder will not warranty information and will exclude liability on the basis that he or she has no actual knowledge of the seller, having been appointed to it for only a short period of time before the sale, and that he or she must protect the interests of the creditors.

The price paid will usually reflect the additional risk to the buyer.

— The parties should ensure that the sale contract identifies the assets to be sold as clearly as possible, ideally by way of schedules. This may, however, be difficult where information is limited.

In particular the seller will want to ensure that certain assets do not transfer to the buyer (for example cash at bank, claims, specific books and records) and the buyer will want to ensure that those assets that are vital to the business do transfer (for example key contracts and equipment). Provision also needs to be made

---

[23] Made under IA 1986, Sch B1, para 49(1).
[24] *Re Transbus International Limited* [2004] EWHC 932 (Ch), [2004] 2 All ER 911.
[25] IA 1986, Sch B1, para 74(1)(a).
[26] IA 1986, Sch B1, para 75.
[27] *DKLL Solicitors v Revenue and Customs Commissioners* [2007] EWHC 2067 (Ch), [2008] 1 BCLC 112.
[28] IA 1986, Sch B1, para 71.

for assets which may or may not transfer, such as cash floats and book debts, and for third party assets such as those items subject to retention of title claims, or lease or hire purchase agreements.

— Where the seller operates out of leasehold premises the buyer may need to ensure that the contract includes a licence to occupy the premises pending negotiations with the landlord as to the terms of a formal assignment of the lease.

— Where the directors of the insolvent company are seeking to acquire the business back from administrators or liquidators, the sale contract does not need to provide for delivery by the seller of a resolution of the members of the seller under section 190 Companies Act 2006 ('CA 2006'), Substantial Property Transactions, approving the arrangements. An exception is provided by CA 2006, s 193 where the seller is being wound up (unless the winding up is a members' voluntary winding up) or is in administration.

— There may be little if any time between exchange and completion. The parties will usually want to complete the transaction as quickly as possible. However this may not be possible where regulatory licences are vital to the business, such as those relating to the provision of care, or recycling or waste services. In that event negotiations may have to take place with the relevant regulatory body after exchange and prior to completion.

— If the seller is in a formal insolvency proceeding the contract will be signed by an office-holder rather than the directors. The office holder will exclude all personal liability as a term of the contract.

• Post-completion the buyer may be left to deal with matters arising within the business with little assistance and little information:

— If directors and other senior members of staff are not retained as part of the transfer of the business a key source of knowledge may be unavailable.

— The business still has to be turned around, which can be time-consuming and costly. For example key customers and suppliers will watch the situation with keen interest; competitors will be trying to take advantage of the disruption to the business to poach key contracts; ransom payments may have to be made to a landlord, vital suppliers, subcontractors, utilities etc; employees will be concerned as to their job security; HM Revenue & Customs may require a deposit in relation to the future VAT liability of the ongoing business.

— Any office-holder may agree to provide such further information and assistance as the buyer may reasonably request, at the buyer's expense. However the office-holder, particularly if he or she is administrator, will be under an obligation to conclude the insolvency proceedings as quickly as possible, to make a distribution to creditors, and to close the case. His or her assistance can only be relied upon for a short time, if at all.

— Negotiations will invariably have to take place with third parties such as landlords, key suppliers, finance companies and owners of intellectual property. Ideally negotiations would take place before completion such that all necessary documentation can be signed on closing. However that may not be possible in the short timescales that often apply to a distressed sale.

— Contracts with key suppliers and customers may have to be novated, resumed, brought back within agreed timescales, or renegotiated in order to ensure they can be completed successfully and profitably. The buyer may have to deal with retention of title creditors quickly in order to make use of stock and other goods supplied to the seller that it needs to carry on the business.

Buyers should not necessarily expect the smooth integration of an insolvent business into their operation as they might expect with a well-thought-out, planned and executed acquisition outside of a distressed situation.

Hive-down

Introduction

3.5 Structuring a sale by way of a hive-down may create a tax advantage in that unrealised tax losses may be carried forward against future profit[29]. The business, including the benefit of the losses, is transferred from the insolvent parent company to a new company formed as a subsidiary. The new subsidiary will have the assets of the insolvent parent but not the liabilities, and it may then be transferred by a simple share sale. However anti-avoidance provisions can make it difficult to preserve and make use of the benefit of trading losses carried forward. Further, the amount of transferable losses will be limited by the extent to which liabilities left in the parent company exceed the value of relevant assets remaining in the parent company (including the value of the consideration 'paid' by the subsidiary). As the hive-down is intended to create a clean subsidiary without the liabilities of the parent company, these provisions make the use of hive-downs rare, and specialist tax advice is needed if this structure is considered.

Hive-down agreement

3.6 If a hive-down is used it will be documented by a hive-down agreement made between:

---

[29] Income and Corporation Taxes Act 1988, s 343; Corporation Tax Act 2010, Pt 22, Ch 1.

(a)   the insolvent parent company;

(b)   a new subsidiary of the insolvent parent company; and

(c)   the office-holder.

There will then be a subsequent share sale agreement made between:

(i)   the insolvent parent company;

(ii)   the subsidiary company;

(iii)   the buyer; and

(iv)   the office-holder.

The buyer will usually be involved in negotiating the terms of the hive-down agreement notwithstanding that it is not a party to it, as the terms will impact on the subsequent share sale agreement and the benefit of the transaction to the buyer. It will be important to the buyer that the hive-down company is a newly formed company and not an existing dormant subsidiary, to ensure that the buyer does not acquire any unexpected liabilities alongside the business of the insolvent company. The new subsidiary will have to be separately registered for VAT and the new company must enter into its own insurance and licensing arrangements. Any restrictions on the transfer of assets between members of a group will also need to be considered, together with stamp duty and Stamp Duty Land Tax charges that may arise.

The consideration for the transfer of the business from the parent company (seller) to the subsidiary will be left outstanding on a loan account. When the parent company sells the shares in its subsidiary to the buyer, the consideration for the shares will be their par value, and as a separate agreement the buyer will agree to discharge the amount due from the subsidiary to the parent company under the loan account.

Insolvency Act 1986, ss 216 and 217

Introduction

3.7   IA 1986, ss 216 and 217 will be relevant if the directors of the seller are or will become directors of the buyer, and the buyer wishes to carry on the insolvent business using the same corporate or business name.

The predecessors of IA 1986, ss 216 and 217[30] were introduced in response to events where the activities of a failed company were continued by the same people who had been responsible for the business failure. The original directors would often use a new company to trade, frequently under the same or a similar name to the failed one, using the old company's assets and goodwill.

---

[30]   Insolvency Act 1985, ss 17 and 18.

The new company would essentially carry on the old business but without the burden of its debt, leaving the creditors of the old company to prove their claims against an empty shell. People dealing with the new company would generally not know of the past failure. Whilst it was recognised that it was right for an insolvent company to go into liquidation, and that if the insolvency had arisen through misfortune or in good faith it might be appropriate for the same directors and their employees to carry on what was once a viable business through a new company, it was not always the case that a phoenix occurred in such circumstances. IA 1986, ss 216 and 217 do not distinguish between a 'good' phoenix, where the company has failed through no fault of the directors, and a 'bad' one, where the directors have acted unscrupulously, and their effect is not limited to a situation where the new company has exploited the old company's assets and goodwill.

IA 1986, s 216 applies to a person where a company has gone into insolvent liquidation and that person was a director or a shadow director of the company at any time within the 12 months ending with the day before the company went into liquidation[31]. It provides that except with leave of the court or in other prescribed circumstances, a person to whom the section applies shall not:

- be a director of any other company known by a prohibited name;

- in any way, whether directly or indirectly, be concerned or take part in the promotion, formation or management of any such company; or

- in any way, whether directly or indirectly, be concerned or take part in the carrying on of a business carried on (otherwise than by a company) under a prohibited name

at any time in the period of five years beginning with the day on which the first company went into insolvent liquidation[32].

A prohibited name is one by which the first company was known at any time in the period of 12 months ending with the day before the company went into liquidation, or is a name so similar as to suggest an association with that company[33]. It applies to both the name a company bears at Companies House and any name under which the company carries on business[34].

A person acting in breach of IA 1986, s 216 is liable to imprisonment or a fine or both[35].

Further, under IA 1986, s 217 a person who acts as a director of, is concerned in or takes part in the management of a company in breach of IA 1986, s 216, or acts or is willing to act on instructions given by a person he or she knows to

---

[31] IA 1986, s 216(1).
[32] IA 1986, s 216(3).
[33] See n 28 above.
[34] IA 1986, s 216(6).
[35] IA 1986, s 216(4).

be in breach of section 216, is personally responsible for the relevant debts of the new company[36]. Liability is joint and several with the new company[37], and relevant debts are those incurred by the new company at the time the person acted in breach of section 216, or knowingly acted or was willing to act on instructions given by someone in breach[38].

A finding that a person has acted in breach of section 216 may also be taken into account by the court when it determines the appropriate period of disqualification to apply under the Company Directors Disqualification Act 1986[39].

Thus it can be seen that the provisions of IA 1986, s 216 are very wide-ranging. They do not apply to an employee who merely has a managerial role. Nor do they apply to the name itself. If none of the directors of the old company have an involvement in the new business then section 216 is not relevant. However the provisions do operate so as to prevent a director who is caught by them trading for a five-year period as a director, in partnership or as a sole trader under a prohibited name.

Sections 216 and 217 apply if the prohibited name was only one name under which the company traded rather than the only name, and if the prohibited name was only used for part of its business[40]. They also apply if the new company only carries on part of its business under the prohibited name. In that event civil liability only applies in relation to the debts in incurred by the new company in relation to that part of the business operating under the prohibited name[41]. Ss 216 and 217 also apply if a new company which originally had a different name later changes its name to one that is prohibited under section 216[42].

What is a prohibited name?

3.8   Whether a name is caught by section 216 is a question of fact to be determined in each instance. The following are examples of names that have been found to be so similar as to suggest an association within the meaning of IA 1986, s 216:

- 'Mike Spence Classic Cars Limited' was found to be sufficiently similar to 'Mike Spence (Reading) Limited' and 'Mike Spence (Motorsport) Limited'[43];

---

[36]   IA 1986, s 217(1).
[37]   IA 1986, s 217(2).
[38]   IA 1986, s 217(3).
[39]   *Re Migration Services International Limited* [2000] BCC 1095.
[40]   *ESS Production Limited v Sully* [2005] EWCA Civ 554, [2005] BCC 85.
[41]   *Glasgow City Council v Craig* [2010] BCC 235.
[42]   See n 36 above.
[43]   *Thorne v Silverleaf* [1994] 1 BCLC 637.

- 'MPJ Contracts Limited' and 'MPJ Construction Limited'[44]. It was irrelevant that the new company used different stationery and styles when promoting its name;

- 'Air Equipment Co Limited' and 'The Air Component Co Ltd'[45]; and

- the shortened informal name 'ESS' and 'ESS Solutions Limited'[46].

The Court of Appeal has stated[47] that when considering whether a name suggests an association which falls within IA 1986, s 216(3), an assessment has to be made of the likely impact of the name on a reasonable person in the relevant commercial context. Matters such as the types of product being dealt with; the location of the businesses; the types of customers concerned; the people involved in the business; and the context in which the name was used might all be important.

Criminal liability

3.9   A person acting in breach of IA 1986, s 216 is liable on indictment to imprisonment for up to two years, or to an unlimited fine or both. In the magistrates court a person is liable to imprisonment for up to six months and a fine of up to £5,000 or both[48].

The offence is one of strict liability[49], and the facts are to be determined objectively.

Civil liability

3.10   It is to be noted that civil liability has a wider basis than the criminal sanction, in that it applies not only to those who, in contravention of section 216 are involved in the management of the new company, but also to those who are involved in the management of the new company and act or are willing to act on the instructions of a person who is known to them to be subject to IA 1986, s 216[50]. In other words civil liability will be imposed on a person who allows himself or herself to act as a nominee in order for a director of the old company to try and avoid section 216.

A person is involved in the management of a company for the purposes of section 217 if he is a director of the company or if he is concerned, directly or indirectly, or takes part in, the management of the company.

---

[44]   *Archer Structures Limited v Griffiths* [2003] EWHC 957 (Ch), [2004] 1 BCLC 201.
[45]   *Rickets v Ad Valorum Factors Limited* [2003] EWCA Civ 1706, [2004] 1 BCLC 1.
[46]   *ESS Production Limited v Sully* [2005] EWCA Civ 554, [2005] BCC 85.
[47]   *Rickets v Ad Valorum Factors Limited* [2003] EWCA Civ 1706, [2004] 1 BCLC 1.
[48]   IA 1986, ss 216(4), 430 and Sch 10.
[49]   *R v Doring* [2002] EWCA Crim 1695.
[50]   IA 1986, s 217(1)(b).

A person can make a claim against a director under section 217 even if he or she is found to have aided and abetted the director to breach section 216 and to have known of all the relevant facts and circumstances[51].

The question of set-off has also been considered by the court. When a company goes into insolvent liquidation a statutory mechanism of set-off applies as between the company and a debtor where there are mutual credits and debits[52]. In *Archer Structures Limited v Griffiths*[53] the court decided that although set-off applied in relation to the company, the director who had acted in breach of section 216 still remained personally liable for the whole of the original debt, and not just the reduced amount that remained owing by the company after set-off. There was no statutory mechanism to reduce the claim in so far as the director was concerned.

Liability under section 217 is automatic and does not require a prior application to the court, or the prior conviction of a director[54]. Nor can the court absolve a director under CA 2006, s 1157 on the ground that the director acted honestly and reasonably and ought fairly to be excused from liability[55].

Permission of the court

3.11   The court has a discretion to allow the use of what would otherwise be a prohibited name under section 216(3)[56], and it is likely to exercise that discretion in favour of a director who can show that his or her conduct was not to blame for the liquidation of the old company.

The court has held that the object of section 216 is to prevent phoenix operations, and it should consider whether there is any risk to creditors of the new company beyond that usually arising where there is limited liability, and whether there is any substantial risk that people would be confused by the similar name[57]. It is wrong to treat an applicant for permission as someone who has been found to be unfit to be a director unless there is evidence of misconduct[58]. The court may grant permission to use a prohibited name in a company that was previously dormant or has been incorporated for the purpose of carrying on the business providing the company in question is specified[59]. It will not, however, give permission for a name to be used in future generally[60].

---

[51]   *Thorne v Silverleaf* [1994] BCC 109.
[52]   Rule 4.90.
[53]   [2003] EWHC 957 (Ch), [2004] 1 BCLC 201.
[54]   *First Independent Factors & Finance Limited v Mountford* [2008] EWHC 835 (Ch), [2008] 2 BCLC 297.
[55]   See n 49 above.
[56]   See section 3.14.
[57]   *Penrose v Official Receiver* [1996] 1 WLR 482; *Re Lightning Electrical Contractors Limited* [1996] BCC 950.
[58]   *Penrose v Official Receiver* [1996] 1 WLR 482.
[59]   *Re Lightning Electrical Contractors Limited* [1996] BCC 950.
[60]   See n 53 above.

The court may require appropriate undertakings to be given on granting permission[61], or it may require additional, new directors to be appointed to the board, and it will often require the applicant to give notice to all creditors of the old company that permission has been granted, and to advertise the terms of the order in the *London Gazette*.

The court cannot grant retrospective permission to use a prohibited name as that would have the effect of decriminalising the breach. Permission to use the name only applies for the future.

Any application for permission is made on notice to the Secretary of State for Business, Innovation and Skills, who may appear at the hearing and, whether he appears or not, may make representations to the court[62]. The court may call on the liquidator or former liquidator of the old company to report on the circumstances in which the company became insolvent and the extent (if any) of the applicant's apparent responsibility for the winding up[63]. The Secretary of State or the Official Receiver may appear at the hearing and bring to the court's attention to any matters which seem to him or her to be relevant[64]. In practice an applicant would seek to agree the terms of an order giving leave to use a prohibited name with the Insolvency Service prior to the hearing, and then invite the court to make an order by consent.

Excepted cases

3.12   Having created a prohibition on the use of prohibited names in section 216, IA 1986 goes on to provide three exceptions to the prohibition over and above obtaining leave of the court[65]:

First Excepted Case[66]

3.13   Rule 4.228 was amended with effect from 6 August 2007[67] following the decision of the Court of Appeal in *Churchill v First Independent Factors and Finance Limited[68]*, and the narrative below refers to the law as it now stands. Prior to the amendment to rule 4.228 it was almost impossible for a director to make use of the First Excepted Case.

Rule 4.228 applies where a person has been a director of a company that has gone into insolvent liquidation, and he or she carries on or proposes to carry on

---

[61]   *Re Bonus Breaks Limited* [1991] BCC 546, where undertakings were given to the court to ensure that the company's capital was maintained at a certain level.
[62]   Rule 4.227A(1).
[63]   Rule 4.227A(2).
[64]   IA 1986, s 216(5).
[65]   Rule 4.226.
[66]   Rule 4.228.
[67]   Insolvency (Amendment) Rules 2007 (SI 2007/1974).
[68]   [2006] EWCA Civ 1623, [2007] Bus LR 676.

the whole or substantially the whole of the business of the insolvent company in a manner that would otherwise be caught by IA 1986, s 216. In order to bring himself within the exception:

- the director or his new trading vehicle must acquire the business or substantially the whole of it from the insolvent company, under arrangements made by its liquidator or an office-holder acting as administrator, administrative receiver or supervisor of a company voluntary arrangement before the company went into liquidation[69]; and

- the director must:

    — give notice in the prescribed form[70] to every creditor of the insolvent company whose name and address is known to him or her or could be found out on him or her making reasonable enquiries; and

    — publish a notice in the *London Gazette*[71].

Notice may be given and published before the business of the old company has been acquired from the liquidator or other office-holder, and must be given and published no later than 28 days after completion of the acquisition[72]. The notice must state:

- the name and registered number of the insolvent company;

- the name of the person;

- that he or she intends to act, or to continue to act, as a director of a company known by a prohibited name; or be concerned or take part in the promotion, formation or management of a company known by a prohibited name; or be concerned or take part in the carrying on of a business carried on other than by a company under a prohibited name, for the purpose of carrying on the whole or substantially the whole of the business of the insolvent company;

- the prohibited name[73].

The notice procedure provides a very useful mechanism for a director to carry on using what would otherwise be a prohibited name without having to make an application to court for permission. It allows a director to trade either through a new limited company, or in a partnership or as a sole trader. It also enables him or her to give notice before the company goes into liquidation, for example if he or she has bought the business from an administrator[74]. In that event it is vital for the director to give notice within 28 days of acquiring the business from an administrator even though the company may not go into liquidation for many months. The time limit of 28 days runs from the date on

---

[69]   Rule 4.228(1).
[70]   Rule 4.228(3)(c).
[71]   Rule 4.228(2).
[72]   Rule 4.228(3)(a).
[73]   Rule 4.228(3)(b).
[74]   Rule 4.228(4)(a).

which the whole or substantially the whole of the business is acquired, not the date of liquidation. If the director waits until the company goes into liquidation it will be too late to use the notice procedure to avoid the effects of section 216, and if a director then wants to act in a manner that would breach section 216 he or she must apply to the court for permission.

However the procedure is not without its limitations. It cannot be used where there has already been a breach of section 216. A director will not have contravened section 216 if notice is given before the director acts in a manner that would otherwise be a breach of the section. Giving notice does not act retrospectively to 'cure' a breach that has already occurred. Nor can it be used when the business or substantially the whole of the business of the insolvent company is acquired from a liquidator, unless the prohibited name is only used after the notice has been given[75]. Therefore the relevant person cannot be a director of the company acquiring the business from the liquidator using a prohibited name (or otherwise act in a manner that would be a breach of section 216) until such time as notice has been given. The acquiring company must not use the prohibited name at all until after the notice has been given, and that may be difficult to demonstrate if the goodwill of the insolvent company including the name has been acquired as part of the transaction. Otherwise the person cannot be a director or shadow director of the acquiring company or otherwise be involved in the business in breach of section 216 until notice has been sent to creditors and published. Nor can a nominee act for him or her as the nominee will then be in breach and become personally liable for the relevant debts of the new company[76].

The limitation of the use of the notice procedure makes it much more suitable to a situation where a business has been acquired out of administration. However with careful planning it can still be useful where a business is acquired from a liquidator.

Second Excepted Case[77]

3.14   Rule 4.229 applies where a director makes an application to the court for permission to use a prohibited name. Providing he or she makes the application not later than seven business days from the date on which the company went into liquidation[78], the director may act in a manner that would otherwise be in breach of section 216 for the period beginning with the day on which the company went into liquidation and ending either on the day falling six weeks after the date of liquidation, or on the day on which the court disposes of the application for permission under section 216, whichever of those days occurs first[79].

---

[75]   Rule 4.228(4).
[76]   IA 1986, s 217(1)(b).
[77]   Rule 4.229.
[78]   Rule 4.229(1).
[79]   Rule 4.229(2).

The time allowed under Rule 4.229(2) allows a director to use a prohibited name whilst he or she makes an application for permission under Rule 4.229(1) without breaching section 216 in the interim period until the hearing takes place. The time limits are short, and if a hearing date for the substantive application cannot be obtained within the 6 week period it may be necessary to ask the court, within that short time, for permission to be granted until the final disposal of the application.

Third Excepted Case[80]

3.15   The third case relates to the situation where the business of the insolvent company is carried on by a successor company which has an established history of using what would otherwise be a prohibited name, and it allows the insolvent business to be carried on by another 'group' company.

Rule 4.230 provides that permission of the court under IA 1986, s 216(3) to use a prohibited name is not required when there would otherwise be a breach of section 216 where:

- the company in relation to which the relevant person acts has been known by the prohibited name for the whole of the period of 12 months ending with the day before the insolvent company went into liquidation; and

- it has not at any time in those 12 months been dormant within the meaning of CA 2006, section 1169(1), (2) and (3)(a).

CA 2006, ss 1169(1), (2) and (3)(a) read as follows:

'1169 Dormant Companies

(1)   For the purposes of the Companies Acts a company is "dormant" during any period in which it has no significant accounting transaction.

(2)   A "significant accounting transaction" means a transaction which is required by [CA 2006] section 386 to be entered in the company's accounting records.

(3)   In determining whether a company is dormant, there shall be disregarded –

    (a)   any transaction arising from the taking of shares in the company by a subscriber to the memorandum as a result of an undertaking of his in connection with the formation of the company;'

CA 2006 section 386 provides that every company must keep adequate accounting records.

If the Third Excepted Case applies, where the company has an established name which it has used for more than 12 months before the liquidation, then the

---

[80]   Rule 4.230.

director can continue to be a director of the business with the established name without seeking permission of the court. This includes where the established name includes the same word, words or otherwise suggests an association with the insolvent company[81].

Conclusion

3.16   When a director is acquiring an insolvent business he or she must give due consideration to section 216 of the Insolvency Act 1986. It can be disregarded if:

- he or she was not a director or shadow director of the insolvent company at any time within the period of 12 months ending with the day before it went into liquidation;

- he or she will not:

  — be a director of any other company known by a prohibited name;

  — in any way, whether directly or indirectly, be concerned or take part in the promotion, formation or management of any such company;

  — in any way, whether directly or indirectly, be concerned or take part in the carrying on of a business carried on other than by a company under a prohibited name;

- the ongoing business will not be incorporated under or trade using a prohibited name.

Otherwise section 216 will be relevant, and if it is breached the penalties, both criminal and civil, can be significant. Section 216 is firmly in the sights of certain creditors, including HM Revenue & Customs and those who take assignments of claims in a liquidation solely with a view to bringing actions against directors who are in breach of section 216. Section 216 is highly relevant in a pre-pack situation and must be kept in mind in all cases where a director is involved in acquiring his or her own insolvent business back, whether the old company is in liquidation or not. If it goes into liquidation at any point within 12 months of a person being a director or shadow director, section 216 will apply.

---

[81]   *ESS Production Limited v Sully* [2005] EWCA Civ 554, [2005] BCC 85.

Chapter 4

Due Diligence

'Due diligence' is the term used to describe the process of checking the business to be purchased. It is part of the 'belt and braces' of business purchase – on the one hand a buyer has the benefit of warranties or promises about the business and on the other and in addition it checks the property first. This is because a business purchase is such an important transaction. However buying from administrators rarely gives the buyer:

(a)   good warranties; and

(b)   much opportunity to engage in thorough due diligence.

Some of the due diligence described in this chapter administrators will simply not permit, and the buyer who may well be paying a 'bargain basement price' does so taking on risks that buyers in other situations would not do. If advising on such a situation make sure that the solicitor explains that issue clearly to the client.

Buyers of insolvent companies and businesses have less opportunity to engage in thorough due diligence than in other business purchases. Indeed, as seen in Chapter 2, in pre-pack administrations there can be very little time at all to engage in meaningful due diligence and even issues such as any lease of premises can end up not being properly formalised until after the sale, with the court having to balance the landlord's interests against those of the creditors in an administration. However some due diligence can be done and some purchases of ailing businesses are not purchases which are as time-critical as others. At the end of this chapter there is an Appendix containing a short-form Due Diligence Checklist.

Essential due diligence

4.1   Where the directors and shareholders of the company buy its assets from the administrator they may know the company and not need much due diligence. However in other cases at least some must be done no matter how quickly the deal has to proceed because of the financial difficulties of the business. Check:

•   How many employees there are and their costs.

•   What debts are owed to employees.

•   Financial records, costs, losses and expenses.

- Contracts – look at principal suppliers and customers, and contracts with subcontractors and others as well as those with employees; are there any particularly onerous contracts?

- Check what litigation is currently in prospect or has taken place.

- In insolvent businesses debts are very important – how much is owed to whom and which debts would be 'left behind' with the previous business if a purchase of assets is contemplated. Where instead shares are purchased, which is rare with insolvency companies, liabilities may be taken over.

Visit the premises. Interview appropriate people, such as the accountants and key members of staff. Look at original documents as much as possible. In particular check if the position presented to potential buyers about the company's debt position is accurate. In some cases where the business is being purchased principally because of a large customer to whom the seller supplies products it may even make sense to visit that customer confidentially with the seller to see if the buyer might secure its business after a sale. In some sales such future business is the principal asset acquired and yet there may be no assurance that the customer would transfer its business after the sale.

Let the buyer beware

4.2   Whatever the type of business purchase, the basic common law legal principal is 'let the buyer beware' – caveat emptor. Common law does not help buyers if they make a bad business decision.

Due diligence, where there is time and money, will usually consist of a combination of reports on the business or specific parts of it by professional advisers (including accountants, lawyers, environmental consultants, surveyors, pension advisers and insurance brokers) and searches of publicly available information, enquiries of the seller and a physical inspection of tangible assets. Normally professionals are not instructed until it is clear a deal is possible, otherwise the fees paid to them may be wasted.

The objective of a typical due diligence exercise is to provide the purchaser with the maximum amount of independently verified information regarding the target as soon as possible so as to enable the purchaser to make an informed investment decision and to assess whether the assumptions and basis upon which it agreed in principle to purchase the target at the agreed purchase price are correct. If the due diligence exercise reveals unknown liabilities, problems or other information not known when striking the deal in principle, it provides the purchaser with an opportunity to renegotiate terms.

In determining the extent and nature of the due diligence exercise, the purchaser should be aware that enquiries of third-party sources are, in general terms, inconclusive in that they offer no formal protection if the information provided as a result of the enquiry proves to be inaccurate. They do, however, provide the purchaser with comfort and are a means of verifying the information given to it by the seller.

Where a purchaser is acquiring assets and liabilities rather than the target company itself, the investigations tend to be less burdensome as they need only relate to the specific assets and liabilities to be taken over. This is the case with purchases of most businesses from an administrator and indeed there will be much less due diligence all round because the administrator will simply not permit it. There is neither time nor money for much of the usual due diligence in these situations.

What to investigate

4.3   Investigate as much as possible. The list below will not often be possible in all its parts in an insolvency situation but is worth considering in any event. Assumptions relied upon by the purchaser in striking the purchase price probably merit the most keen investigation by the purchaser. For example, if the purchase price has been agreed to reflect a multiple of the previous year's earnings, the purchaser will want to ensure that those earnings have not been distorted in any way, whether by overstating sales, understating costs or otherwise.

Title to the target's shares

4.4   A due diligence review relating to a proposed acquisition of shares should establish whether the seller has good title to the target company. Of course if assets are being purchased this is not relevant.

The starting place is a review of the target's statutory register of members since a person does not become a member (shareholder) until his or her name has been entered into the register of members. Although this review will reveal legal ownership of the target's shares, it will not disclose beneficial ownership (if different). Without notice of beneficial ownership being transferred to another party, the members entitled to legal ownership will be those entitled to sell the target. Where beneficial ownership is held by somebody else and the purchaser is aware of this, that party should be included as a party to the acquisition agreement but only for the purposes of transferring beneficial ownership.

Having checked that the seller is the registered owner of the target's shares, the purchaser will want to investigate the seller's title to those shares. That is to say, the purchaser must investigate the transfer to the seller of the shares in question and each preceding transfer as far back as the original allotment of the shares by the target company. If on any such occasion the transfer or allotment required, for example, some resolution of the directors, the purchaser must satisfy itself that the persons who purported to pass the necessary resolutions were indeed the properly appointed directors of the target company at the relevant time.

In addition, the purchaser will need to consider the application of CA 2006, s 549 and any restrictions in the Articles about allotment of shares. Since 1 October 2009, CA 2006, s 550 'Power of directors to allot shares etc: private company with only one class of shares' provides that where a private company has only one class of shares, the directors may exercise any power of the company:

(a)   to allot shares of that class; or

(b)   to grant rights to subscribe for or to convert any security into such shares, except to the extent that they are prohibited from doing so by the company's articles.

However it is still necessary to check the Articles for any restrictions; and public companies and private companies not within section 550 still need authorisation (see section 551). However many companies have Articles of Association which require authority to allot shares to be obtained.

Title to the target's assets

4.5   When acquiring a company the purchaser will assume and expect the target to own or hold a valid lease of or licence to use the underlying assets so that the business of the target can be operated from completion without interruption. When acquiring a business the same considerations will apply.

As part of the purchaser's due diligence review, it is important to ensure that title to the key assets used in the business is held by the target or seller (as the case may be) free from encumbrances. It is quite possible, for example, that another group company owns certain assets used in the target's business.

Except for certain property and certain intellectual property assets (such as registered patents), title to business assets cannot be established conclusively by, for example, reference to a register. Accordingly, due diligence investigations can only aim to establish whether the target acquired (or received a licence to use) the assets in question, the nature of the interest acquired, that no competing claims to title have been made and that the assets have not been sold, charged, leased or otherwise disposed of.

Property

4.6   Chapter 2 looked at the issue of an administrator granting the buyer a licence to occupy property under a lease granted to the company. The Landlord may not agree but unlike in situations where there is no administration, the Landlord may be required to accept the situation because of the strict power given to administrators.

If the purchase is not from an administrator, however, and the company is simply in financial difficulties, the usual position applies and the situation of any lease must be sorted out before the sale. It is difficult to envisage a transaction that does not require at least some investigation of the property assets. The type and extent of investigations will depend upon the type of property asset and whether the transaction is a share or asset purchase. The importance of the property to the business will be a key factor on approach: if the location of the property is fundamental to the business a claim in damages for breach of warranty will never be sufficient to remedy the situation. It must always be remembered that where shares are to be acquired the ownership of the property remains the same, whereas when assets are acquired the ownership of the property changes and transfer documentation will be needed to effect this.

Either the purchaser's solicitors can carry out an investigation of title (which may be full, or more limited, dependent upon the circumstances of the deal) or the seller's solicitors can provide the purchaser with a certificate of title.

In choosing its method of investigation, a purchaser should consider the following factors:

- costs – rather than carrying out an investigation of title it may be more cost-effective to accept a basic certificate of title when considering the value of the transaction; it is also usually considered that certificates are a less expensive route for a purchaser, if the process is run efficiently;

- the timing and convenience of each method if there is a tight timescale: investigation by the purchaser's solicitors is usually a more effective route to meeting a short deadline, as less liaison is required and the purchaser's solicitors have greater control over the receipt of title and search information;

- the relative bargaining power of the seller and the purchaser;

- the purchaser's existing knowledge of the property: if the vendor has recently purchased the property, its solicitors will usually provide a certificate;

- the relative remedies and protection each method provides;

- the volume and the respective importance of the properties in the portfolio;

- whether the transfer of any property is unregistered and its transfer will trigger first registration: in these circumstances the title will need to be reviewed for submission for first registration to HM Land Registry, so it is more cost-effective for the purchaser's solicitor to investigate the title as a pre-test to submitting the first registration;

- the identity of the firm of solicitors acting for the seller giving the certificates; both the type of firm and the level of its intellectual property ('IP') cover will be relevant.

(i) Investigation

4.7   Investigation of title will involve a review of the target's title to the property and the carrying out of all the usual conveyancing searches, preliminary enquiries and other enquiries of the seller and third parties as if the transaction were a normal conveyancing matter. Investigation of title may not, however, be practicable in the timescale allowed. In such a case warranty cover will be the only feasible route.

Title to the property assets should be deduced by the seller's solicitors in the usual way depending on whether it has registered or unregistered title. In the case of registered titles, office-copy entries and filed documents (if any) will be obtained from the Land Registry. In the case of registered leasehold property, an office copy or a certified copy of the lease should be inspected. In the case of unregistered land, certified copies of the title deeds should be reviewed. As in most transactions where exchange of contracts and completion occur simultaneously, all usual pre-contract and pre-completion searches should be carried out. These will include searches of the relevant Local Authority, the Land Charges Registry, the Local Land Charges Registry and the Land Registry and/or Companies Registry. Depending upon the location of the property, additional searches (for example, Commons Registry, coal mining, brine, clay or rail) may be necessary.

An often forgotten enquiry is whether the property requires, and if so, whether it has had done, a fire safety risk assessment. These by the Regulatory Reform (Fire Safety) Order 2005 replaced the earlier requirement for a fire certificate. See https://www.gov.uk/workplace-fire-safety-your-responsibilities.

Additional enquiries will be needed for particular categories of properties, for example licensing for leisure property.

(ii) Certificate of title

4.8 A certificate of title should be the easiest and least time-consuming method of investigation, especially if the seller's solicitors have recently acquired the property. The form of certificate, however, can give rise to lengthy negotiations as solicitors acting for sellers rarely provide certificates of title in the form required by the purchaser's solicitors. This means that on occasion, the factual element of the certificate is not provided to the purchaser's solicitors until later in the transaction, which can be problematic where title defects are revealed.

(iii) Preferred choice

4.9 In general, purchasers tend to investigate title rather than rely on certificates of title, as they are often qualified. When opting to investigate title a purchaser should take care to ensure that its investigation and the seller's disclosure against warranties does not cancel out the effectiveness of the warranties, although the level of warranty cover will automatically reduce where the purchaser undertakes title investigation.

Even where the purchaser undertakes full due diligence on title, some warranty cover will always be required, whether the acquisition is a share or an asset purchase. In the case of an asset purchase, at the very least, replies to enquiries provided by the sellers should be warranted. Additional warranty cover may be sought where replies to enquiries provided by the vendor prove inadequate.

In the case of a share acquisition, the same level of warranty cover as required for an asset purchase is needed, but in addition details of the properties owned/occupied must be warranted as being all of the property liabilities affecting the company. Additionally, warranty cover to deal with contingent liabilities, usually arising from assets previously owned, or properties in respect of which guarantees have been given, will be needed.

As the level of due diligence undertaken diminishes, a greater level of warranty cover will be sought, unless the company's interest in the relevant property and the liability relating to it are viewed as negligible.

Capacity of the seller

4.10   Clearly, when buying from an administrator, check that that person is indeed the administrator. A typical sale agreement will give the name of the seller. This will usually be the name of the company selling the assets, such as ABC Limited, Company No ...., Registered office address ...., Acting by [name the administrators] joint administrators of the Seller and both of [name administrator's firm]. Check the register at Companies House as to the status of the seller, for example whether it is in administration. The administrators themselves will have details of their own appointment too.

If the seller is not in administration the usual checks should be made, ie that the seller has power to sell. In the case of a corporate seller, its Memorandum and Articles of Association will need to be considered to check who has the power to sell its investment (usually the board of directors) and whether there are any restrictions on that power of sale. If it is the board of directors that has power then the purchaser will be concerned to ensure that a board meeting is convened in accordance with the company's Articles of Association, that a requisite quorum is present, that any directors interested in the sale declare their interest, that the sale is approved and one or more directors are empowered to execute the agreement on behalf of the corporate seller (CA 2006, s 40).

(i)   Receivers

Administrative receivers

4.11   Administrative receivers are appointed under a power in debentures which usually grants fixed charges over most known assets and a floating charge over the remainder. Such a receiver has all the powers within the debenture and Schedule 1 of IA 1986. These powers include the power to sell (Sch 1, para 2). It will, however, be necessary, as with all non-court-appointed receivers, to check whether there is any security which has priority over the appointor's security or inter-creditor agreements which alter the usual rules of priority. In addition, it will need to be ascertained whether the appointment of the receiver was performed in accordance with the provisions of the debenture and that the debenture itself is valid. IA 1986, s 232 provides that the acts of an administrative receiver (and administrator, liquidator or provisional liquidator) but not any other sort of receiver 'are valid notwithstanding any defect in his appointment, nomination or qualifications'. However, this would not operate to protect acts done where there is no power to appoint at all. With the appointment of a receiver, whether pursuant to a court order or otherwise, this must be notified to the Registrar of Companies within seven days of the appointment (CA 1985, s 405(1)). It is important to note that with a debenture created after 4 February 1991 any defects in the target company's constitutional documents will not affect the validity of the security as, provided it acted in good faith, the charge-holder will be protected by the provisions of CA 2006, s 40 (previously CA 1985, s 35(A)).

Fixed charge Law of Property Act receivers

4.12   Receivers are also appointed under fixed charges which usually also grant powers under the Law of Property Act 1925. Special care needs to be taken where powers under the Act are not included within the charge because the power to appoint under section 101 only arises in limited circumstances (subject to Commonhold and Leasehold Reform Act 2002, s 21 (no disposition of part-units)). It is also necessary to check that the receiver was appointed in accordance with the charge and that the charge itself is valid. In addition, it is necessary for the purchaser to verify whether the assets subject to the sale are included within the security documentation, such as goodwill.

Court-appointed receivers

4.13   Section 37 of the Senior Courts Act 1981 provides for the appointment of receivers where 'just and convenient'. This sort of appointment is rare and usually arises where there is either a deadlock in management, no power of appointment elsewhere or in circumstances where assets of a company are in jeopardy. The powers of a court-appointed receiver are contained in the court order and are often restricted to safeguarding assets of the target company rather than realising them. If the order is limited, it will be necessary for the receiver to seek a further order from the court permitting a sale of company assets. The purchaser should seek a sealed or certified copy of the relevant court order.

(ii)   Administrators

4.14   Administration is a process which involves the appointment of an administrator. This used to have to be by court order, but from 15 September 2003 this requirement was removed by the Enterprise Act 2002. The court may still appoint an administrator, but most administrations are now commenced either by the holder of a Qualifying Floating Charge filing a Notice of Appointment of an Administrator at court, or by the company itself or the directors doing so. Notice of intention to appoint an administrator has to be given in some circumstances before an appointment can take place. The application for an administration order is made either by the company, the directors, or by a creditor (or creditors) where the court route is used.

Following commencement of administration, whether by filing a Notice of Appointment or the making of an administration order, a moratorium freezing action from most creditors applies. An interim moratorium applies when Notice of Intention to Appoint an Administrator is filed or an administration application is made but has not yet been heard (see IA 1986, Sch B1, paras 43 and 44, as introduced by the Enterprise Act 2002).

Administration – grounds

4.15   IA 1986, Sch B1, para 3(1) replaced the previous four statutory purposes of administration with a single purpose made up of three objectives, which the administrator should consider in turn. The administrator must perform his or her functions with the objective of:

(a)   Rescuing the company as a going concern, which should be taken to mean retaining as much as possible of its business.

(b)   Achieving a better result for the creditors as a whole than would be likely in an immediate winding up, for example by sale of the business(es) or its(their) assets. This objective can only be pursued where rescue is not reasonably practicable, or where it would give a better outcome for creditors than objective (a).

(c)   Realising the company's property so as to make a distribution to one or more secured or preferential creditors. This objective can only be pursued where it is not reasonably practicable to achieve either of objectives (a) or (b).

Administration is not an alternative to liquidation in cases where properly the affairs of the company should simply be wound up and there is no benefit to the creditors from trading on under the protection of the administration moratorium.

For further information about the administration process see http://www.insolvency.gov.uk/faq/eactfaq.htm.

In order to go into administration the target company must be insolvent and the proposed administrator must be satisfied that there is a reasonable prospect of achieving the single purpose mentioned above made up of the three objectives.

Administrators have the same powers as an administrative receiver under IA 1986, Sch 1, which include the power of sale, but there are also requirements that an administrator's proposals should be approved by creditors. This can lead to difficulties where there is a possible early sale of the target company before a meeting of creditors under IA 1986, Sch B1, para 51. *Re T&D Industries plc and another* [2000] 1 BCLC 471 held that leave of the court is not required for an administrator to sell. Specific advice on this issue should be obtained by the purchaser where appropriate. Chapter 2 examines the case law in this area.

(iii)   Liquidators

4.16   Liquidators have the power to sell any of the company's property without sanction (IA 1986, Sch 4, Pt III, para 6).

There are two types of insolvent liquidation: compulsory (usually instituted by a creditor through the courts); and creditors' voluntary liquidation ('CVL'), which is instituted by the company itself and does not involve the court.

A purchaser should be aware that after a winding-up petition is presented against a company, dispositions of a company's property and shares are void unless the court orders otherwise. There is a similar restriction in a CVL on the transfer of shares (IA 1986, ss 88, 127).

In a CVL, the winding-up resolution passed by members must be filed with the Registrar of Companies within 15 days, and care needs to be taken as this may be inadequate for a purchaser to receive notice of the same. In relation to compulsory winding-up petitions, a register of pending petitions (liquidation and administration) is maintained at the Royal Courts of Justice in the Strand, who can be contacted by telephone to check whether there are any relevant pending winding-up or administration petitions. In order to minimise the risks of the target company/assets being in liquidation, company searches should therefore be carried out on a regular basis and prior to completion to check if any notices of resolutions or appointments are shown at the Register of Companies.

The old section 320 of CA 1985 could have applied to the sale of assets by a receiver and possibly an administrator, but not a liquidation following the decision in *Demite Limited v Protec Health Limited* [1998] BCC 638. CA 2006, s 190 replaced and made some changes to CA 1985, s 320. Under section 190, 'Substantial property transactions: requirement of members' approval', a company may not enter into an arrangement under which:

(a)   a director of the company or of its holding company, or a person connected with such a director, acquires or is to acquire from the company (directly or indirectly) a substantial non-cash asset; or

(b)   the company acquires or is to acquire a substantial non-cash asset (directly or indirectly) from such a director or a person so connected,

unless the arrangement has been approved by a resolution of the members of the company or is conditional on such approval being obtained.

The meaning of 'substantial non-cash asset' is given in section 191.

If the director or connected person is a director of the company's holding company or a person connected with such a director, the arrangement must also have been approved by a resolution of the members of the holding company or be conditional on such approval being obtained. A company shall not be subject to any liability by reason of a failure to obtain approval required by the section. No approval is required under this section on the part of the members of a body corporate that:

(a)   is not a UK-registered company; or

(b)   is a wholly owned subsidiary of another body corporate.

An arrangement involving more than one non-cash asset, or an arrangement that is one of a series involving non-cash assets, is treated as if it involved a non-cash asset of a value equal to the aggregate value of all the non-cash assets involved in the arrangement or, as the case may be, the series. Section 190 does not apply to a transaction so far as it relates:

(a)   to anything to which a director of a company is entitled under his service contract; or

(b)   to payment for loss of office as defined in section 215 (payments requiring members' approval).

Section 191 defines 'substantial' non-cash asset:

'(2)   An asset is a substantial asset in relation to a company if its value–

  (a)   exceeds 10% of the company's asset value and is more than £5,000, or

  (b)   exceeds £100,000.

(3)   For this purpose a company's "asset value" at any time is–

  (a)   the value of the company's net assets determined by reference to its most recent statutory accounts, or

  (b)   if no statutory accounts have been prepared, the amount of the company's called-up share capital.

(4)   A company's "statutory accounts" means its annual accounts prepared in accordance with Part 15, and its "most recent" statutory accounts means those in relation to which the time for sending them out to members (see section 424) is most recent.

(5)   Whether an asset is a substantial asset shall be determined as at the time the arrangement is entered into.'

If the target is a business, in addition to the investigations referred to above, the purchaser will need to establish who has the right to sell each individual asset used in the business. With a few exceptions (for example, patents and other registered forms of intellectual property) there is no statutory register of ownership of the various assets comprised in the business. As a result, however detailed the purchaser's due diligence investigations are, they will not be able to establish an absolute right to ownership and the purchaser will need to rely on warranties for that protection, but such warranties are generally unavailable when purchasing a business from an insolvency office-holder.

Consents/approvals required

4.17   The due diligence review should establish whether the seller and/or the target require any consents or approvals to enable the proposed acquisition to proceed. At the same time the purchaser will also need to give consideration to the consents and approvals it may require to approve the acquisition and to authorise it to enter into the acquisition agreement. Where an approval and/or consent is required it is usual practice for the approval/consent to be obtained between the exchange of contracts and completion and for completion to be conditional upon such approval/consent being obtained.

In an insolvency situation there is not much time to obtain consents. Even with bank collapses, however, there may be later divestment. The EU state aids rules for example have required the bail-out of Northern Rock and other banks to be notified to the EU for approval, and indeed banks have been obliged to sell off branches in consequence – see http://ec.europa.eu/eu_law/state_aids/state_aids_en.htm. Also under competition law, divestment post-purchase where the purchase led to a substantial lessening of competition is also a risk in some, but not most, cases.

The consents and approvals required will differ depending upon whether the sale is structured as a sale of shares or assets and the identity of the seller(s). The following is an outline of those most commonly required.

Shareholders

4.18   The approval of the seller's shareholders may be necessary where:

- the seller is a listed public company and the sale represents a significant disposal;

- within the previous ten years the target's shares have been listed or advertised on a regular basis or the target has issued a prospectus;

- the seller's Articles of Association and any agreements between the shareholders (commonly called a shareholders' agreement) relating to the conduct and management of the target require such approval; and

- one or more of the directors of the seller are connected with the purchaser.

Most purchases of insolvent companies are of assets, not shares, so share issues are not considered in detail here.

The provisions of the target's Articles of Association, or any shareholders' agreement regulating the conduct and management of the target, may contain restrictions (for example, on the transfer of the shares in the target without first offering the shares proposed to be transferred to existing shareholders on a pro rata basis) or require prior approval to certain transactions (for example, class consent rights in the Articles or institutional/minority shareholder protection provisions in a shareholders' agreement). Although this is more likely to be the case with a management buy-out vehicle, joint-venture company, a company owned by a large number of shareholders or a company financed partly by venture capital, the Articles of Association and, where relevant, shareholders' agreement of all target companies should be checked to ensure no such restrictions apply.

If the purchaser is a director of the seller (or its holding company) or a person connected with such a director, then, depending upon the value of the transaction, the sale may require shareholder approval pursuant to CA 2006, s 190 (previously CA 1985, s 320). It is important to note that section 190 prohibits a company from entering into 'an arrangement' unless 'the arrangement is first approved' by the company in general meeting. Therefore, it seems that conditional contracts are of no help and the resolution should be passed before the contract is entered into. 'Connected persons' are defined in CA 2006, s 252:

(a)   members of the director's family (defined in section 253);

(b)   a body corporate with which the director is connected (as defined in section 254);

(c)   a person acting in his capacity as trustee of a trust:

   (i)   the beneficiaries of which include the director or a person who by virtue of paragraph (a) or (b) is connected with him; or

   (ii)   the terms of which confer a power on the trustees that may be exercised for the benefit of the director or any such person,

   other than a trust for the purposes of an employees' share scheme or a pension scheme;

(d)   a person acting in his capacity as partner:

   (i)   of the director; or

   (ii)   of a person who, by virtue of paragraph (a), (b) or (c), is connected with that director;

(e)   a firm that is a legal person under the law by which it is governed and in which:

   (i)   the director is a partner;

   (ii)   a partner is a person who, by virtue of paragraph (a), (b) or (c) is connected with the director; or

   (iii) a partner is a firm in which the director is a partner or in which there is a partner who, by virtue of paragraph (a), (b) or (c), is connected with the director.

References to a person connected with a director of a company do not include a person who is himself or herself a director of the company.

In the case of a share purchase it will be necessary to investigate the share-transfer provisions of the target's Articles of Association to ascertain the share-transfer process, which may either require shareholder or board approval. The purchase of assets, on the other hand, will almost invariably require approval by the target's board of directors. This will involve the convening of a board meeting to approve the proposed transaction, where practicable the prior circulation of a copy of the proposed sale agreements, and a vote of the directors to approve the sale in principle and to authorise any one or more of the directors to sign the sale contract on behalf of the seller company.

In deciding whether to approve the proposed transaction, each director must act in good faith in what he or she considers to be the best interests of the company of which he or she is a director. If any director is personally interested in the proposed transaction (for example, because he or she is a director of the purchaser), under CA 2006, s 182 (which some will remember as CA 1985, s 317), the director is required to declare his or her interest at the meeting of the board to discuss the transaction. In addition, the seller's Articles will need to be further checked to ascertain whether, having declared his or her interest, the interested director can vote or be counted in the quorum.

Section 182, 'Declaration of interest in existing transaction or arrangement' provides that where a director of a company is in any way:

> 'directly or indirectly, interested in a transaction or arrangement that has been entered into by the company, he must declare the nature and extent of the interest to the other directors in accordance with this section. This section does not apply if or to the extent that the interest has been declared under section 177 (duty to declare interest in proposed transaction or arrangement)'.

The declaration must be made:

(a)   at a meeting of the directors; or

(b)   by notice in writing (see section 184); or

(c)   by general notice (see section 185).

A director need not declare an interest:

(a)   if it cannot reasonably be regarded as likely to give rise to a conflict of interest;

(b)   if, or to the extent that, the other directors are already aware of it (and for this purpose the other directors are treated as aware of anything of which they ought reasonably to be aware); or

(c)   if, or to the extent that, it concerns terms of his or her service contract that have been or are to be considered:

    (i)   by a meeting of the directors; or

    (ii)   by a committee of the directors appointed for the purpose under the company's constitution.

Landlord

4.19   Most commercial leases have provisions for the landlord's consent to be obtained for any assignment of the lease. The position for insolvent companies was looked at in Chapter 2 and earlier in this chapter. Some leases may have an absolute prohibition against assignment. If there is no purchase from an administrator and there is time, then the usual investigations should take place.

The purchase of assets will involve the transfer of customer and supplier arrangements to the purchaser. Unless the existing arrangement with the target contains a free right of assignment the transfer of the arrangement will require the approval of the relevant customer or supplier.

Regulatory approvals

4.20   To carry on business in certain market sectors requires a licence from the governing body. Accordingly, a target engaged in any of the following businesses should be investigated to ascertain whether any prior consents (and the industry requirements relating to the transfer of their operating licence) are necessary:

- banking and building societies;

- insurance;

- Ministry of Defence contractors;

- newspapers;

- restaurants, bars and other establishments selling liquor; and

- telecommunications.

Banks/finance

4.21   Almost all purchasers will require the target's assets to be transferred to it free from any encumbrances and will have agreed to purchase the target on that basis. Where, therefore, the target's assets are charged to its bankers as security for outstanding indebtedness, the consent of the target's bankers will be required to ensure the charges are released on completion. This can, however, result in timing problems because the bank will be reluctant to release the charges until its debt is repaid and, typically, the seller/target will not be in a position to repay the debt until the sale proceeds are received. This impasse can normally be resolved in one of two ways: either by the bank's solicitors undertaking to discharge the charges upon receipt of the outstanding indebtedness together with a mechanism for paying the outstanding amount direct to the bank, or by the bank supplying a release of the charges to the target's lawyers on an undertaking to the bank only to supply the release when funds sufficient to repay the indebtedness are released to them.

Further consent/approval may be required under the terms of any loan or other finance agreements and, accordingly, such terms should be investigated.

Competition regulations

4.22   When reviewing a potential acquisition it is important to consider whether the transaction could be delayed or even thwarted by competition regulators. These are the European Commission; the Office of Fair Trading, and Competition Commission ('CC') (in the UK); and national competition authorities in the other countries in which the target operates. They all have power to block mergers which fall within their jurisdiction and which they consider might have serious anti-competitive effects.

Forthcoming changes

In 2013 it was proposed that the OFT and CC be merged into the Competition and Markets Authority (CMA) whose Chief Executive was appointed with effect from March 2013, in addition to a one stage UK merger approval process being effected in place of the previous OFT then CC examination of some mergers. In the current stage of transition of the law both references are given below. In February 2013 the Enterprise and Regulatory Reform Bill which effects these changes was due before the House of Lords. See http://discuss. bis.gov.uk/enterprise-bill/. The reforms are due to come into effect in April 2014 and do not change the fundamentals of UK merger law, although they will change the nature of the merger investigation and replace the current dual stage investigation by OFT, and then if there were competition concerns the CC, to one investigation by the CMA.

A merger will not be considered by the EC and UK competition authorities at the same time. If the EC has jurisdiction, the UK OFT/Competition Commission/ CMA will not. For either authority to have jurisdiction the transaction must exceed certain thresholds, and so many smaller, private company/business mergers and acquisitions escape scrutiny altogether.

If the EC Merger Regulation (Council Regulation 139/2004/EC ([2004] OJ L24/1) on the control of concentrations between undertakings) does not apply and either the target or a purchaser/investor who acquires control of the target carries on business in the UK or under the control of a company incorporated in the UK and either:

- the gross world-wide assets of the target taken over are £70m or more; or

- the purchaser/investor and the target are competitors in the UK and together their UK (or a substantial part thereof) market share is 25 per cent or more,

the OFT has jurisdiction to investigate the transaction under the Enterprise Act 2002 (formerly mergers were assessed under the Fair Trading Act 1973) for up to four months after the transaction takes place. Where within those criteria above, the OFT must refer any merger which it believes has resulted, or may be expected to result, in a substantial lessening of competition ('SLC') in a UK market. It would then be referred to the Competition Commission (formerly the Monopolies and Mergers Commission) for a more detailed investigation. From April 2014 it is expected this process will be replaced by a one stage examination by a new merged body – the Competition and Markets Authority. Although notification of a merger falling within the tests set out in the legislation is not mandatory, it may nevertheless be advisable to do so in certain circumstances. After 2014 it will also remain a non mandatory system with the same criteria – see below.

As in the case of the EC merger rules, 'control' is not limited to the acquisition of outright voting control but can simply be an ability materially to influence the policy of the target. Such influence is usually conferred by the acquisition of 25 per cent shareholding, but occasionally shareholdings of less than 15 per cent can attract scrutiny given the particular circumstances.

Some transactions may give rise to concerns about loss of competition because of an overlap which creates a significant market share but involves only part of the activities of the merged company. In that case binding undertakings may be accepted for the divestment of part of the merged company's business as an alternative to a reference. There are also powers to accept behavioural undertakings regarding the future conduct of the merged entity in relation to any adverse effects on competition of the merged enterprise.

If the transaction is referred to the Competition Commission and it decides that there is a SLC present it may recommend remedies to counter the concerns that it has identified. The OFT may then order a transaction to be blocked, require parties to divest shares or limit voting powers, order the break-up of a company or control the conduct of the merged entity by, for example, regulating the new company's prices. Any transaction which is investigated by the OFT and in respect of which a decision is made on whether or not to refer the matter to the Competition Commission attracts a fee (even if ultimately it is concluded that the transaction does not operate against the public interest). The level of fee is determined by the size of the transaction .

UK Merger Notification Fees Table from October 2012

Charge band: value of the UK turnover of the enterprise(s) being acquired	Fee on or after 1 October 2012
£20 million or less	£40,000 (an increase of £10,000)
Over £20 million but not over £70 million	£80,000 (an increase of £20,000)
Over £70 million but does not exceed £120 million	£120,000 (an increase of £30,000)
Exceeds £120 million	£160,000 (an increase of £70,000)

Smaller companies (turnover under about £11m) are exempt from the fees.

It is possible to seek prior guidance on whether the OFT consider that they have jurisdiction to investigate a transaction and whether they are likely to refer it to the Competition Commission under what has been known as 'confidential guidance' and is now called informal advice, for which there is no fee; but any view of the OFT is not binding, in particular because third parties have not been consulted.

In April 2008, the Competition Commission and the OFT launched a joint review of their respective guidelines for the assessment and analysis of mergers. New joint guidelines were then issued numbered OFT 1254.

See also the Quick Guide to Merger Assessment – OFT 1313

http://www.competition-commission.org.uk/assets/competitioncommission/docs/pdf/non-inquiry/rep_pub/rules_and_guide/pdf/11_03_25_a_quick_guide_to_uk_merger_assessmentpdf.pdf.

Confidential guidance/informal advice

4.23 At the date of writing it is still possible to obtain interim or confidential guidance from the OFT on prospective mergers, but this is under review. In 2014 when the CMA takes over from the OFT and CC this is likely to be revised.

De minimis

4.24 Some mergers are too small to be caught by the rules. In November 2007 the OFT issued *Revision to mergers – substantive assessment guidance – exception to the duty to refer: markets of insufficient importance* (OFT516b).

The guidance introduces a significant increase of the threshold for a market to be considered of insufficient importance, from £400,000 to £10m, although some mergers under £10m may still be caught.

The guidance makes clear that, subject to some caveats, the OFT will generally consider affected markets worth less than £10m in aggregate to be of insufficient importance to justify reference.

There are two categories of cases, however, in which the use of the de minimis exclusion was 'less likely' to be appropriate despite the market(s) falling within the relevant threshold size figure:

(a)   mergers in very highly concentrated markets where the prospect of entry is low; and

(b)   mergers in markets where there is evidence of co-ordination between competitors.

If merging parties and their advisers are in doubt as to the exercise of its discretion for mergers below the £1m mark, the OFT (via the Mergers Group) offers informal advice. It states that:

'seeking proper advice at the transaction planning stage, supplemented where necessary by informal advice from the OFT, will be preferable to proceeding with a merger on misplaced expectations as to the OFT's likely decision. This is especially true with respect to this exception to the duty to refer, as the proposed transaction at issue will often be small, and the cost of a CC inquiry to the parties, relative to the size of the transaction, will be substantial'.

The OFT mergers internet page and information on the Enterprise Act 2002 and mergers is at http://www.oft.gov.uk/advice_and_resources/resource_base/Mergers_home.

Practical guidance

4.25   Most small mergers fall outside the £70m turnover/25 per cent market-share test so merger control law is not an issue on an acquisition. It is the buyer who is concerned about these issues because the buy may be required after a sale to sell off the assets if the merger is referred. Therefore it would normally be a buyer which makes the sale agreement subject to a condition of prior clearance under the formal merger notice procedure under the legislation. Where the assets are under £70m but the market share is high there is always an issue as to whether to apply for confidential (now interim) guidance and/ or formal clearance. Most small-value merges are not examined and many will pass unnoticed by competition authorities. However even in very small markets, after a sale there is a risk that a competitor or customer might object, and an ex post facto reference could be made. The de minimis £10m threshold is helpful although it is not an absolute assurance.

Where more than 25 per cent of the market is involved and assets are under £10m it is unlikely a reference will be made. Over £10m and below £70m it is still fairly unlikely in most cases, but with high market shares the buyer will have to spend some time considering the risks and the pros and cons of a clearance.

Unknown or understated liabilities

4.26   Whether liabilities are of concern to the purchaser will depend upon how the acquisition is structured. In the case of a business transfer, pre-contract liabilities will usually remain with the seller, thereby reducing the need to investigate them.

Financial advisers often take responsibility for the tax review but this should be clearly ascertained by the legal advisers at the outset to ensure the relevant advisers cover all relevant tax due diligence.

Other than tax (see 4.37, and 4.54 at '11. Taxation'), there are four main areas of investigation:

(a)   property (see 4.50);

(b)   environment (see 4.51);

(c)   employees (see 4.27); and

(d)   pensions (see 4.29).

Where the purchaser is acquiring the target by means of share purchase, all that will change is the ownership of the target company. Chapter 9 deals with employment issues in general, to which reference should be made.

Employees

4.27   So far as the employees are concerned, their contracts with the target company remain unaltered as a consequence of the sale, notwithstanding the change in ownership and the fact that the character and aims of the new controlling shareholder may be radically different to those of the old. No question of redundancy or dismissal will automatically arise on the sale of the target company's shares, and the mutual obligations of the company and the employee continue. Of course, once the sale is concluded, then the requirements of the new controlling shareholder may give rise to changes within the workforce.

In the case of a business transfer, the Transfer of Undertakings (Protection of Employment) Regulations 2006 (SI 2006/246) ('TUPE') will almost certainly apply. TUPE operates to transfer the employees of the business automatically to the purchaser, so that on completion the contracts of employment take effect as if they had originally been made between the employee and the purchaser. Therefore, where there has been a business transfer the identity of the employer changes. However, the purchaser, being the new employer, inherits virtually all rights, duties, powers and liabilities in respect of this new workforce (there are certain exceptions, the most important of which is pensions – see Chapter 10).

While the acquisition of the target's business involves a change in the employer's identity, the share acquisition of the target does not, the status quo essentially continuing. However, in both scenarios the purchaser needs to know what it is taking on. Therefore the purpose of investigating the target's employees will involve broadly the same objectives whether there is share acquisition or a business transfer. The investigation will identify their contractual terms of employment, any outstanding contractual liabilities (such as accrued holiday or sick pay) and statutory employment rights such as maternity pay, equal pay or compensation for sex or race discrimination.

Therefore, prior to the acquisition the purchaser will be concerned to have full details of the target's workforce and their terms of employment. The seller should be asked to provide a copy of all standard terms of employment and state to which employees such terms apply. These details can be incorporated into the acquisition agreement by the seller warranting a schedule of employees containing relevant information, which will include their names, dates of birth, dates of commencement of continuous employment, job titles, duties, remuneration, proposed increments and review dates, frequency of payment and places of work. Where the employees have individual service contracts, copies of these may be annexed to the agreement. Details of any trade union recognition agreement will also be required.

The purchaser should obtain information from the seller concerning any outstanding claims that have been, or may be, made by former employees who have been dismissed. They should also discover if any decisions have been taken or implemented which may result in a claim; for example, an employee may have been given notice of dismissal which will not take place until after completion; or an employee could be in dispute in circumstances which could give rise to a claim after completion, perhaps of sexual or racial discrimination; or a resignation which could be constructive dismissal may have occurred before completion.

Where there has been a share transfer, the mere fact of a change in the target company's ownership will not affect its liability to meet such claims. Similarly, where the purchaser has become the employer following a business transfer, even though it was not involved in these events it will frequently have to face the consequences of such disputes. It may even inherit liability in situations where the seller has dismissed employees prior to completion. The purchaser should therefore seek the appropriate warranty, indemnity or a reduction in the purchase price, depending upon the possible value of such claims.

All this information will enable the purchaser to assess the full extent of employee liabilities of the target company or its business, and, perhaps more importantly, any possible difficulties or liabilities it may encounter should it have plans to change the workforce post-completion. Whenever a company or business is acquired, a key consideration for the purchaser will be to establish what are its rights and liabilities in relation to the existing employees of that company or business. In certain circumstances this may not present a problem. If the purchaser is acquiring a successful company or business, it may wish to retain the existing board, management and workforce and continue 'business as normal'. However, it is frequently the case that following the acquisition of a company or business, the purchaser may wish to make certain changes in the workforce and/or implement a programme of redundancies from the target's workforce, and possibly from its own.

The identity of the workforce is one important piece of information which the purchaser should check. Where the target or its business forms part of a larger group, its day-to-day operation may involve, or even be dependent upon, individuals who work for the target (either exclusively or in part), but whose contracts are with, for example, its holding company. Because a share sale will have no effect on any contract of employment, the purchaser may suddenly find that it lacks key employees required to run the business. If they do not work for the company it has acquired they will be left behind. Similar problems might arise where employees are working in the business to be transferred, but the seller of that business is not their employer or, if it is, the individuals are not allocated to the business or are ones the seller wishes to retain. In such circumstances appropriate arrangements may have to be negotiated with the seller to secure their future services.

Changes under TUPE 2006

4.28   The TUPE regulations made the following changes:

(a)   A new requirement that the transferor provides the transferee with 'employee liability information'. This has to include details of all the rights, powers, duties and liabilities in connection with the contracts of employment of transferring employees.

(b)   A very limited new right was given to change terms and conditions of employment after a transfer where there is an economic, technical or organisational reason ('ETO') entailing changes in the workforce. This right is not as far-reaching as it may at first appear, because case law has held that an ETO will only *entail changes in the workforce* where there is a change in the number or functions of the workforce. The ability to change terms and conditions is therefore still restricted to a limited number of very specific situations. The basic rule remains that in most cases no changes are allowed.

(c)   The transferor and transferee share liability for failure to consult with employees in advance.

In relation to all TUPE transfers note that special rules apply where a public-sector body is involved.

Pensions

4.29   Many an acquisition has foundered on pensions issues. Chapter 10 considers pensions in detail. If a pension is being taken over, detailed advice should be taken. The purchaser will need to know whether any of the target's employees are entitled to pension benefits and, if so, the nature of the vendor's present pension arrangements for the employees of the company or business being sold. Is it final salary or money purchase, insured or self-administered, contracted in or contracted out of State Earnings Related Pension Scheme ('SERPS')? The purchaser will also need to know the levels of benefits provided and the ongoing costs. It needs to know if a scheme is underfunded and may need to approach the Pensions Regulator. It is important to seek up-to-date copies of all the arrangements governing documentation (including, where relevant, the latest Trust Deed and Rules and all amending deeds, documents and resolutions), a copy of the latest actuarial valuation of any final salary scheme, a list of the scheme's existing members and those who are likely to become members during the course of the next few months on completing service or age qualifications, a copy of the latest scheme booklet, copies of any deeds of appointment of trustees, any deed of adherence by which the company to be sold adhered to the scheme, evidence of the scheme's exempt approved tax status and, if appropriate, a copy of the contracting-out certificate covering the employer. Buying shares means taking on more pensions obligations. On a business sale, however, the obligations of the employer under the contracts of employment will normally transfer to the purchaser under TUPE, which excludes from this transfer:

- that part of the contract of employment (or collective agreement) which relates to an occupational pension scheme; and

- any rights, powers, duties or liabilities under or in connection with any such contract or subsisting by virtue of any such agreement and relating to such a scheme or otherwise arising in connection with the person's employment and relating to such a scheme.

The validity of regulation 7 under the older TUPE 1981 regulations has in the past been challenged on the grounds that it is not consistent with the EC Directive which TUPE 1981 were adopted to comply with. Although these challenges had some success, it does now appear safe to assume that because of regulation 7, the purchaser will be under no legal obligation (in the absence of any requirement in the business sale agreement) to make any pension provision for the transferring employees after completion or assume any liability for pensions rights accrued prior to completion. It is therefore open for the purchaser to decide what pension arrangements post-completion are appropriate to its circumstances and whether it wishes to negotiate any special transfer terms from the seller's scheme for employees who wish to transfer the value of accrued rights to the purchaser's new arrangements.

It should be noted that the exclusion in regulation 7 only applied to occupational pension schemes. Therefore, any obligation of the seller to pay contributions to a personal pension plan of an employee (or to a group personal pension plan) will transfer to the purchaser on completion.

TUPE 2006 exclude most pension rights as long as those rights do not transfer (although sometimes courts have held that early-retirement benefits will transfer). Under the Pensions Act 2004 buyers are obliged to provide specified pension arrangements for transferring employees who were, prior to the transfer, members of, or eligible to be members of, an occupational pension scheme to which the seller made contributions. There is a requirement that the buyer must make matching contributions of up to at least 6 per cent of salary to the pension arrangements provided for eligible transferring employees. The Pensions Act 2004 gave occupational pension scheme members rights to pension benefits after TUPE transfers for the first time.

In 2012 for larger companies the new compulsory employer second pension came into force with all employees opted in unless they choose to opt out. If there is no existing pension scheme employers use NEST (National Employment Savings Trust) set up by the Personal Accounts Delivery Authority. The plan to roll out the scheme to companies with fewer than 250 staff has not yet begun at the date of writing.

What to look out for when carrying out pensions due diligence

4.30   The depth to which the purchaser will need to investigate a seller's or the target's occupational pension scheme will depend on whether the purchaser intends to acquire that scheme as part of the deal or wants to negotiate the payment of a bulk transfer payment from the seller's scheme to its own new or existing arrangements.

If the purchaser is acquiring the seller's or the target's occupational scheme, the purchaser will need to:

- Check whether the scheme is established under interim or definitive documentation. If a scheme is established only under interim documentation, it will still be operating under interim approval from HMRC and definitive documentation will have to be executed in due course.

- Check it is sufficiently funded and in some cases obtain prior clearance from the Pensions Regulator.

- Check that it has received copies of all subsequent deeds of amendment, amending resolutions, announcements to members and booklets together with copies of the latest scheme accounts and actuarial valuations or reports.

- Ascertain whether the scheme is an exempt approved scheme approved by HMRC or, if not, whether an application for approval is pending. This is important to ensure that the scheme is obtaining the full benefit of the tax advantages available to approved pension schemes. Obtain a copy of the letter of approval or application for approval.

- Establish whether the scheme is contracted in or out of SERPS and, if the scheme is contracted out, on what basis it is contracted out. Obtain a copy of any relevant contracting-out certificate.

- Establish whether the scheme is a final salary scheme or a money purchase scheme.

- Establish the benefits provided to members/categories of members.

- Establish the current level of employer and employee contributions and the recommended rates if different, and confirm that all contributions due have been paid.

- Establish whether lump-sum benefits payable on death are insured and, if so, on what terms and at what cost. The purchaser should establish whether these costs are in addition to the disclosed employer's contribution rate or included within that rate.

- Confirm that all expenses of the scheme incurred prior to completion have been or will be paid prior to completion.

- Check that men and women are treated equally both in respect of the benefits provided and in relation to access to the scheme or arrangement. The existence of unequalised benefits or benefits that have not been properly equalised could result in claims being made against the scheme. If the scheme is a final salary scheme that contains guaranteed minimum pensions ('GMPs'), it should be borne in mind that these are unlikely to have been equalised due to the complexity of the calculations required to do so. Notwithstanding this, it is the authors' view that GMP equalisation is something that is likely to be required at some point in the future. In reality, however, the cost of equalising GMPs is unlikely to be substantial for most schemes and is likely to be outweighed in any event by the administration costs of making the changes.

- Ensure the scheme provides access to part-timers. This is particularly important if the target company has employed a considerable number of part-timers in the past, the majority of whom are of one particular sex, since a member may argue that exclusion of part-timers amounts to indirect sex discrimination. Successful claims could, if brought within the relevant time periods, lead to claims for retrospective membership of the pension scheme as far back as April 1976.

- Check whether any augmentations/increases in benefits have been granted which have not been specifically funded.

- Check that no discrepancy exists between the scheme rules and any scheme booklet or announcement to members which could result in the scheme booklet being relied on by members as providing more generous (and therefore more expensive) benefits.

- Ascertain whether any litigation or Pensions Ombudsman claims relating to the scheme have been instigated or are being considered which may result in the liabilities of the scheme increasing.

- Check that the scheme has not accepted any transfer values from schemes whose benefits were not equalised as between men and women, since the liability to equalise will have passed to the receiving scheme. It is advisable to seek confirmation that transfers made into the scheme since 16 May 1990 have been from schemes that were at the relevant time properly equalised.

- Check if there is a stakeholder pension where there ought to be one.

- Check that there are no outstanding transfer values due to be paid to or by the scheme.

- Occupational pension schemes are subject to and must comply with the requirements of pensions legislation, although there are specific exemptions from some requirements for particular types of schemes (eg SSASs). It is therefore important to ensure that any occupational scheme is Pensions Act compliant. The main items to consider are:

    — Have member nominated trustees/directors been appointed? If not, is a valid employer opt-out in place? What are the terms of the opt-out? Obtain copies of the relevant notices.

    — Has a statement of investment principles been adopted? If so, obtain a copy.

    — Is a schedule of contributions (final salary scheme) or a payment schedule (money purchase scheme) in place? If so, obtain a copy.

    — Have professional advisers (ie auditors, actuary and fund managers) been appointed in accordance with Pensions Act 1995, s 47? If so, obtain copies of letters of appointment.

— Have audited accounts been produced within seven months of the end of each scheme year?

— Have payments to trustees been made by the target in accordance with the prescribed time limits? Perhaps most importantly, have deductions made from members' pay been paid to the trustees of the scheme within 19 days of the end of the month in which the deductions were made?

— Have the relevant aspects of the disclosure regulations been complied with, ie providing members with basic scheme information?

— Has an internal disputes resolution procedure been established? If so, obtain a copy.

— Have breaches of the Pensions Act 1995 (as amended by the Pensions Act 2004) been reported to the Pensions Regulator (which replaced the Occupational Pensions Regulatory Authority ('OPRA')). Ask for details of any reports that have been made to the Regulator or OPRA and any correspondence with the Regulator/OPRA and any adviser.

— Have all amendments to the scheme since 5 April 1997 been made in accordance with Pensions Act 1995, s 67?

• For those companies with more than 250 staff check if they comply with the new compulsory employee second pension scheme – either through NEST or their own scheme with auto enrolment.

• Establish how the assets of the scheme are invested. Obtain copies of any relevant investment management and custody agreements. Confirm that any self-investment does not exceed permitted levels.

• Establish the identities of the trustees and administrator and check that they have been properly appointed.

• Establish whether the power to amend the scheme is exercisable by the employer or the trustees and whether the consent of any other party is required.

Additional matters to look out for in relation to final salary schemes

4.31 Where the seller's scheme is a final salary scheme the purchaser will also need:

• To check whether the scheme is funded or unfunded. If the scheme is unfunded, this means that liabilities have been accruing without any assets being put aside to meet those liabilities in due course. This could have serious implications for a purchaser who takes on the obligation to meet those liabilities.

• If the scheme is funded, to establish the latest funding position and whether the current funding is adequate to meet the liabilities on an ongoing and MFR basis. Obtain the most recent funding information available on the scheme (such as the last actuarial valuation or report).

This is particularly important if the scheme operates on a balance of cost basis. If the scheme's liabilities exceeded the value of its assets on an MFR basis, this could result in the purchaser having to make up the deficiency.

• To consider getting an actuary to check that the assumptions on which the most recent valuation was based are realistic and that the funding position is not materially worse (or better) than is represented in that valuation.

• If a transfer value from the seller's scheme is contemplated, to check that there is an appropriate bulk transfer out clause in the relevant scheme documents and whether any basis of calculation is specified. Given the complexities of valuing a pension fund's assets and liabilities where the transaction involves the transfer or assumption of pension liabilities, actuaries should be instructed to advise on the funding and financial implications of the transfer of pension rights involved in the transaction for the parties and their pension schemes.

Additional matters to look out for in relation to money purchase schemes

4.32 When the seller's scheme is a money purchase scheme the purchaser will also need:

• to ensure the contributions payable by employees and employers have been made and have been made on time and that all expenses of the scheme incurred prior to completion will be paid before completion; and

• to ascertain whether there is any guarantee or targeting of the level of benefits to be provided by the member's account. If there is, establish the likelihood of this guarantee requiring the target company to inject additional sums into the scheme in the future.

Stakeholder pensions

4.33 Stakeholder pensions represent the previous government's attempt to ensure that medium-income individuals have sufficient savings to fund a pension on retirement. Stakeholder pensions are a government-designed financial product which private-sector financial institutions apply. They are low-cost, flexible, money purchase pension schemes into which individuals (and their employers) can make contributions throughout their life, and are able to convert the terminal fund at retirement into an annuity, which will form the pension.

Stakeholder pensions are listed on a register at http://www.thepensionsregulator. gov.uk/stakeholderPensions/theRegister/registerSearch/index.aspx.

Arrangements infringing competition law

4.34 As well as investigating whether the proposed transaction requires notification to UK or EC merger-control regulators, the purchaser will need to investigate whether the target is party to arrangements that infringe UK or EC competition law regulations, otherwise it may find itself liable to fines of up to 10 per cent of turnover and damages from actions by the victims of such practices. This may be so even if all infringements took place prior to the acquisition and have been terminated. The EU rules are contained in Articles 101 and 102 of the Treaty on the Functioning of the European Union ('TFEU'), and in the UK in the Competition Act 1998 and Enterprise Act 2002.

Provisions in contracts that infringe competition rules will also be void and unenforceable and third parties who suffer loss as a result of the infringement may be in a position to bring proceedings for an injunction or damages. In order to protect itself against such risk, the purchaser should review the main agreements and arrangements to which the target is party to ensure that it does not infringe competition rules.

As both UK and EC competition rules apply to informal arrangements as well as formal agreements, the purchaser should also investigate any 'understandings' the target may have which may give rise to competition law concerns.

Connected party transactions

4.35   Transactions between related parties are not always carried out on an arm's length basis because at the time of the transaction it may have suited them to load the benefit or burden of the transaction in favour of one party rather than the other. This is particularly significant as the rules relating to the ability of liquidators and administrators to attack certain transactions are weakened in the case of transactions involving 'connected' parties (see IA 1986, ss 249 and 435 for definitions).

There have rarely been so many breaches of these and related rules, allegations of sales of assets at an undervalue, transfers before a sale to family members of directors and other malpractices as in the current recession. An investigation of transactions between the target and related parties should help the purchaser establish:

- Whether the financial position or trading performance of the target has been distorted. For example, if the target was a member of a group of companies it may have suited the ultimate holding company to reduce the target's cost of sales by selling its stock from another group company at cost, thereby distorting the target's gross profit and increasing its attractiveness to potential purchasers.

- The likelihood of the target being ordered to return to the original transferor assets previously transferred to it on the basis that they were acquired at an undervalue. Under IA 1986, s 238 a liquidator or administrator has power to set aside transactions and wide discretion to grant other relief prior to the onset of the transferor's insolvency (see IA 1986, s 240(3) for definition). For the purposes of the IA 1986, the transaction is at an undervalue if it constitutes a gift or if the value of the consideration received by the transferor is significantly less than the consideration provided by the transferee. The important words are 'significantly less'. At the time of the transfer it is presumed (although this can be rebutted) that the transferor was unable to pay its debts within the meaning of IA 1986, s 123 or became unable to pay its debts as a result of the transaction.

- Liquidators or administrators also have the power under IA 1986, s 239 to seek relief where a creditor, surety or guarantor of the target company has been given a preference. A preference can include anything which has the effect of putting the recipient into a position which, in the event of liquidation, will be better than the position he or she would have been in if that thing had not been done. It is generally difficult to show a preference, but it is easier in respect of connected parties because a key ingredient that the person giving the preference is influenced by a 'desire' to produce the effect is presumed, although this can be rebutted. In the case of connected parties, the connected provisions apply for a period of two years (six months otherwise) from the onset of insolvency and insolvency of the target company is also presumed.

Because of the undervalue and preference provisions of IA 1986, any transfers or other relevant actions to the target company within two years prior to the date of the proposed acquisition should be investigated.

In the case of a sale and purchase of business assets, if the seller and purchaser are members of the same group of companies it is important to ensure that the assets are transferred at their market value. Following the case of *Aveling Barford v Perion Ltd* [1989] BCLC 626, if the transferor did not have sufficient distributable reserves the undervalue element of any transfer would be treated as an unauthorised return of capital. From the purchaser's point of view, if it knew or had reasonable grounds for believing the transfer was at an undervalue it would be liable to repay the distribution to the seller.

Forms of due diligence

4.36   Due diligence is usually carried out by the purchaser's own personnel and professional advisers engaged for the purpose of the acquisition (lawyers and accountants and, where appropriate, surveyors and environmental specialists). The most common forms of due diligence investigation are as follows (in an insolvency situation these often have to be truncated):

Accountants' report

4.37   The key element of most due diligence exercises is the accountants' report on the financial aspects of the target's business. The purpose of the accountants' report is to provide the purchaser with comfort on the past trading record of the target, the current net asset and taxation position of the business, taxation implications of the acquisition and the achievability of the target's financial projections. The report will usually include an analysis of:

- historic trading results;
- current trading position and comparison to budget;
- trends as regards profitability and margins;
- forecast trading results;
- the assets and liabilities to be acquired and their relative values;
- capital investment;
- the target's accounting systems and financial controls;
- suppliers and customers;
- competitors;
- product development;
- management structure;
- the target's taxation affairs; and
- potential synergies.

It would be unnecessary for the accountants' report to cover the historic financial performance of the target if the purchaser could rely upon the audited accounts of the target, so that if the profits of the target were overstated or its liabilities understated the purchaser could pursue the target's auditors. Unfortunately for purchasers the tortious liability of auditors to third parties has been restricted by a number of court decisions, commencing with *Caparo Industries v Dickman* [1990] 2 AC 605, [1990] 1 All ER 568. In this case the House of Lords made it clear that a company's auditors do not owe a duty of care to third parties unless the auditor knew at the time that the third party was placing reliance on the audited accounts for a particular purpose, and that the third party would act on those accounts. The exception to the principle that auditors do not owe a duty of care to third parties laid down by the House of Lords was illustrated in the case of *ADT Ltd v BDO Binder Hamlyn* [1996] BCC 808) when the High Court held that BDO was liable to ADT when an audit partner told ADT that he stood by the accounts (which were found to be negligently audited) of a target company ADT went on to purchase.

Notwithstanding the exception to the general principle that auditors do not owe a duty of care to third parties, because most accounts are not audited in the knowledge that a prospective purchaser is in the wings and will be placing reliance on them, it is still commonplace for accountants' reports to review historic accounts. This practice may, however, alter in the future if the previous government's proposed changes to the laws relating to auditors' liability become law. The then Department of Trade and Industry (DTI) proposed passing legislation to reverse the *Caparo* decision in its March 2000 consultation on company law (*Modern company law for a competitive economy: developing the framework*) and in a further consultation paper in November 2000 (*Modern company law for a competitive economy: completing the structure*). The Companies Act 2006 included provisions which allow companies to agree to limit an auditor's liability arising from an audit for the financial year specified in the agreement. The agreement cannot apply to more than one year's audit. The shareholders must authorise these terms and have rights to cancel this. Shareholders in private companies may also pass a resolution removing the need for that approval. However any limit on liability must be limited to an amount which is 'fair and reasonable' (section 537) and there are powers in regulations for the Government to set out rules for disclosure of an agreement. Part 16 (Audit) of the Companies Act 2006 (section 534 et seq) (liability limitation agreements) came into force on 1 April 2008.

Because of the cost implications, it is unusual for a purchaser to instruct its accountants to prepare a report until the principal terms of the acquisition and the scope and timescale for the investigation have been agreed. Such agreement should also cover issues such as the accountants' access to the target and to its auditors' working papers. It should also deal with the question of confidentiality and set clear deadlines. When agreed, the purchaser should define the areas which it wishes the accountants to investigate to avoid the waste of time and expense involved in the duplication of investigations.

An accountants' report typically takes between three and six weeks to prepare and is traditionally prepared in draft and issued to various parties for comment prior to being finalised. Unless prohibited by the seller, in preparing their report the accountants will establish contact with the management to obtain an overview of the business and more detailed information regarding the specific areas to be covered by their report. The accountants will usually distribute a draft of the report to the management of the target for their comments, and to other professional advisers carrying out investigations (for example, the purchaser's solicitors), prior to release to the prospective purchaser.

In its conclusions, the report will often review the proposed price for the target in the light of the information discovered.

A copy of the accountant's report should be given to the purchaser's solicitors for drafting purposes as it is likely to contain information of relevance which will have an impact on some of the terms of the purchase agreement and the warranties/indemnities required.

Legal due diligence report

4.38   There may not be time in insolvency situations to prepare a legal due diligence report, but in other circumstances they can be useful. Although normally of secondary importance to the accountants' report on the basis that if the financial performance doesn't stack up there will be no deal for the lawyers to concern themselves about, legal due diligence reports have become an important aspect of most transactions.

To reduce exposure to unnecessary costs, and if the timescale allows, it is usually advisable to delay commencement of the legal due diligence until at least a draft accountants' report is in circulation and the prospective purchaser is comfortable that that draft doesn't raise fundamental issues which may jeopardise the transaction.

Legal due diligence reports are usually based upon the answers provided to enquiries of the target's management and the results of third party enquiries, and usually include an analysis of:

- ownership of the target/target business;

- restrictions/impediments on the power to sell the target/target business;

- the target's properties;

- the employees engaged in the target business and their employment terms;

- any intellectual property rights used in the target business or necessary to carry on the target business (see Chapter 7);

- key customers/suppliers, the contractual terms entered into with customers/suppliers and disputes with them;

- any litigation the target business may be engaged in and contingent liabilities;

- health and safety issues relating to the carrying on of the target business;

- environmental and other consents necessary to carry on the target business; and

- competition issues.

Enquiries of management

4.39   Enquiries are normally raised in writing in the form of a legal due diligence request. The due diligence request relating to the purchase of assets is similar to that relating to a purchase of shares except that it focuses more on the individual assets to be acquired and liabilities to be assumed and less on the corporate information regarding the target and its subsidiaries. The precedents should always be tailored to the particular circumstances of the transaction and the type of business being acquired. For example, the importance of employment terms is far more significant in the acquisition of a service business than in one of a manufacturing business.

The value of such enquiries depends almost entirely upon the attitude of the seller in answering them and the relevant terms of the acquisition documentation, or the lack of them. When faced with voluminous enquiries, sellers are often slow to reply and rarely do they provide all the information requested. It is, therefore, important for the purchaser to avoid unnecessary enquiries and duplication and to set a clear and reasonable timetable for the replies to be given. Before drafting the due diligence request, the purchaser's solicitors should enquire of the purchaser the information given to it and whether or not its accountants have been instructed to prepare a report on the target and, if so, the extent of their investigation. Nothing infuriates a seller or its advisers more than duplicate requests for information.

If the purchaser places importance on the replies to the due diligence request, the replies should be the subject of a specific warranty in the sale and purchase agreement.

Searches and enquiries of public registers

4.40 Common sources of third-party enquiries are the various public registers.

(i) Companies Register

4.41 A search of the target's register at Companies House will reveal details of the company's ownership, management, historic financial position, charges and other matters relevant to the purchaser's review (for example the Memorandum and Articles of Association). The accuracy of a company search is not guaranteed because it is compiled by the target itself and therefore the results should be compared with the outcome of the purchaser's review of the target's statutory books.

(ii) Land Registry

4.42 A search at HM Land Registry against the title number to the land owned or leased by the target will reveal the registered proprietor of the land and any charges or encumbrances registered against it. Even if the title number is not known a search of the Index map at the Land Registry with a plan of the target's property will reveal whether or not the property is registered and, if so, the title number or numbers.

(iii) Central land charges

4.43 Where title is unregistered, a central land charges search will reveal any encumbrances registered against the estate owners specified in the search in respect of its period of ownership. The purchaser can immediately search against the target, but to do so the purchaser will need to have received full details of the unregistered title to enable it to search against predecessors in title.

(iv) Local land charges

4.44 A local land charges search of the local authority in which the property is located will reveal details of development plans, road schemes, planning decisions, resolutions made under a compulsory purchase order, breaches of planning decisions and building regulations and other matters under the control or supervision of a local authority.

(v)   Environmental registers

4.45   The following list is comprised of the main environmental registers held by the Environment Agency, water companies or Local Authorities which may currently be consulted by the public and which may provide useful information not only in relation to the terms of any relevant authorisation, licence or consent but also in respect of any past prosecutions:

- registers of authorisations relating to processes prescribed for the purposes of integrated pollution control and local authority air pollution control under Part I of the Environmental Protection Act 1990 and the Pollution Prevention and Control Act 1999;

- registers relating to waste under Part II of the Environmental Protection Act 1990;

- trade effluent register under Part VII of the Water Industry Act 1991;

- pollution control registers under Part VIII of the Water Resources Act 1991;

- registers of remediation notices, declarations and statements under Part IIA of the Environmental Protection Act 1990;

- registers of abstraction licences under Part II of the Water Resources Act 1991; and

- registers under the Producer Responsibility Obligations (Packaging Waste) Regulations 1997 (SI 1997/648).

Defra has created a central register showing where statutory and other environmental registers can be found, as required in Article 3(5)(c) of Directive 2003/4/EC ([2003] OJ L41/26) on public access to environmental information and repealing Council Directive 90/313/EEC – see also Regulation 4 of the Environmental Information Regulations 2004 (SI 2004/3391). The register initially held details of Defra and Defra Agency registers and is being expanded to contain as many UK environmental registers as possible.

It is accessible at http://www.defra.gov.uk/corporate/opengov/eir/pdf/register. pdf and runs to 13 pages (2008 version).

(vi)   Intellectual Property Office and domain names

4.46   A search of the Intellectual Property Office in the UK (www.ipo.gov. uk) of registered UK patents, registered designs and registered trademarks (and indeed international registered intellectual property rights) can be undertaken, as can searches of relevant internet domain name registrations.

Chapter 7 looks at intellectual property issues.

Statutory books

4.47   By law a company must keep registers of directors and secretaries (CA 2006, s 162), members (CA 2006, s 113), directors' interests and charges.

These registers, together with registers of share allotments and transfers and a minute book, are commonly referred to as a company's statutory books.

All inspection of the target's statutory books should reveal the actual position in these areas rather than the 'filed' position, which is often misleading due to the failure by the target to register changes. In the case of members and establishing who has the right to sell the target's shares, this review is extremely important because a person does not become a shareholder until his or her name is registered in the register of members.

Credit agency searches

4.48   Searches may be obtained from reputable credit agency companies such as Equifax and Experian to obtain information about a company's creditworthiness. This information is nearly always more up to date than that obtainable from a search at the Companies Registry.

Many different searches are available from credit agencies. A typical full search against a company will reveal the following information concerning the company, and may also provide a comparison of this information to the industry average:

- profit margin;

- current ratio;

- liquidity ratio;

- debt collection period;

- creditor payment period;

- return on shareholders' funds; and

- suggested credit limit.

Physical inspection

4.49   Far too frequently transactions proceed without any form of physical inspection of the business assets by either the purchaser or, more importantly, independent experts. For confidentiality reasons the seller may be reluctant to allow an inspection. However, if it takes place outside of normal working hours the seller may have no objection.

The two most common forms of physical inspection are:

- property survey; and

- environmental survey.

Property survey

4.50   Physical inspection of the business premises by a professional surveyor is the most recognised and common form of inspection. It should be normal practice where the purchaser is proposing to accept an assignment of a lease under which it will be responsible for repair of the property. In such cases, the survey can provide an assessment of the cost of repairing the dilapidations.

Environmental survey

4.51   As purchasers become increasingly more aware of the potential environmental liabilities in the properties they acquire, and given the natural reluctance of sellers to give indemnities, environmental surveys are becoming commonplace when there is a risk of the purchaser inheriting contaminated land. Not only will an environmental land survey provide the purchaser with an assessment of whether the site on which the business property is located is or is likely to be contaminated, it will also provide an assessment of the likely clean-up costs. Environmental surveys will also give information on compliance with environmental and health and safety legislation.

Seller's disclosure letter and documents

4.52   There are usually few warranties on a purchase from an administrator. In that case a disclosure letter which is virtually always supplied by the buyer in ordinary business purchases disclosing matters 'against' the warranties is not therefore common, so is not discussed here, in the context of insolvencies.

Summary

4.53   This chapter has looked at the principal areas of investigation on an acquisition. In practice there may be only a few days available before the company is sold by flatpack administration (see Chapter 2), but it can do a buyer no harm to be aware of the areas it might investigate and to be aware of the areas of risk if it fails to undertake what in other situations might be regarded as essential checks when buying a business. At the least the inability to undertake such checks should be reflected in the final sale price the buyer pays and how it structures its purchase so as to minimise liabilities if matters go wrong later.

Appendix

4.54

Due Diligence Checklist

SALE AND PURCHASE OF _____ **LIMITED**

PRELIMINARY DUE DILIGENCE QUESTIONNAIRE (short form)

Please supply as soon as possible to Singletons, The Ridge, South View Road, Pinner, Middlesex HA5 3YD, UK (susan@singlelaw.com) the following information and documentation relating to _____ Limited ('the Company').

For the purposes of this questionnaire references to the Company also include its subsidiaries (if any) as defined in Companies Act 2006.

1.   CORPORATE MATTERS

1.1   Copy up-to-date Memorandum and Articles of Association of the Company including copy Certificate of Incorporation of the Company and any Certificates on Change of Name.

1.2   The registered office and principal place of business of the Company.

1.3   Name and address of the auditors of the Company.

1.4   The name and address of the Company Secretary, if any.

1.5   Details of the share capital of the Company including:

(a)   the authorised and issued share capital of the Company;

(b)   the names and addresses of all shareholders in the Company, together with details of the number and class of shares held and of the beneficial ownership of such shares;

(c)   details of any uncompleted or unexercised contracts or options for the issue of further shares in the Company.

1.6   Details of the amount and description of shares and other investments held by the Company and the terms on which such investments are held.

1.7   Copies (or, in the case of unwritten agreements, details) of any shareholders agreements in respect of shares in the Company.

2.   FINANCIAL INFORMATION

2.1   Copies of the audited accounts of the Company for its last three financial periods, together with a copy of the latest management accounts and any other accountants' or other reports on the business or activities of the Company since the last audited accounts.

2.2   Name and address of the bankers of the Company.

2.3   Copies of all bank mandates, details of any [group] banking arrangements and overdraft and other facilities, copies of any agreements or documents evidencing the same and a statement of the amounts currently borrowed under such facilities.

2.4   Copies of all outstanding mortgages, charges and other security of any kind over any property, assets or rights of the Company.

2.5   Details of all loans made to or by the Company and copies of any agreements or documents evidencing the same.

2.6   Details of all guarantees, indemnities and other assurances given by or in respect of the Company and copies of any agreements or documents evidencing the same.

2.7   Details of all derivatives and other capital market transactions entered into by or in respect of the Company (including, without limitation, any interest or currency rate transactions of any kind) and copies of any agreements or documents evidencing the same.

2.8   Details of any dividends declared since the last accounts date.

3.   FREEHOLD AND LEASEHOLD PROPERTIES

3.1   A schedule of all freehold properties owned by the Company, giving address, description, approximate area and particulars of any restrictive covenants affecting the property and copies of all documents of title.

3.2   A schedule of all leasehold properties owned by the Company, including address, approximate area, term, rent, rent review and user provisions, together with copies of all leases.

   Equivalent details of any leases or licences granted by the Company in respect of any of its property, whether freehold or leasehold, together with copies of any such leases and licences.

3.3   Details and copies of any planning applications made in respect of the properties and the result of such applications.

3.4   Copies of all valuation or survey reports of the properties in the last three years.

4.   OTHER ASSETS

4.1   A schedule of all plant and machinery and motor vehicles (giving make and registration number) owned by the Company.

4.2   Details of all computer systems (including hardware and software) owned or used by the Company with details of the ownership of rights in such systems and details and copies of all agreements relating to the use or operation of them.

5.   DIRECTORS AND EMPLOYEES

5.1   The names and addresses of all directors of the Company, together with job title and details of any other directorships and business interests held.

5.2 Details (including pension arrangements, fringe benefits, periods of notice and bonus schemes, etc) of all service agreements or terms of employment of directors and of other senior employees [with salaries in excess of [ ] a year]. Also copies of these agreements and of any relevant board resolutions.

5.3 A list of all the employees of the Company, giving their full name, sex, age, date of commencement of employment, job title and salary and fringe benefits, together with a copy of any standard conditions of employment, staff handbook and other similar documents.

5.4 Details of any trade union or other labour agreements or arrangements and of the employees participating in such arrangements. Also details of any industrial relations problems in the last three years.

5.5 Details of all profit sharing, bonus, share option, share incentive and other special benefits enjoyed by any employees.

5.6 Details of all pension and life assurance schemes affecting any of the employees. Also copies of relevant trust deeds and rules, any information circulated to employees, details of latest actuarial valuations and of employer's and employees' contributions. Also a copy of any contracting out certificate and a list of those employees not participating in any scheme.

6. CONTRACTS

6.1 Copies of the Company's standard terms and conditions of business.

6.2 Copies of all hire purchase, credit sale, rental or leasing agreements entered into by the Company (other than those supplied in response to 4.1 or 4.2) and details of each such agreement which is not in writing.

6.3 A list of those customers of the Company who in any of the last three financial years have accounted for 5% or more of the turnover of the Company and the value of sales to such customers in each of the last three financial years.

6.4 A list of those suppliers of the Company who in any of the last three financial years have accounted for 5% or more of the goods supplied to the Company and the value of supplies from such suppliers in each of the last three financial years.

6.5 A copy of each subsisting long-term contract, incorporating unusual terms and details of any subsisting material capital commitments made by the Company and details of each such contract which is not in writing.

6.6 A copy of each agency, distributorship, franchise, factoring or licence agreement to which the Company is a party (and details of any such agreements which are not in writing), together with any rules to which the Company may be subject as a member or participator in any trade association.

6.7 A copy of each agreement which is capable of being terminated or varied on a change of ownership of the Company.

6.8 Copies of any contracts or details of any arrangements now, or within the last three years, entered into by the Company with any party otherwise than by way of bargain at arm's length or on other than market terms.

6.9 Copies of all contracts relating to the acquisition or disposal of companies, businesses or fixed assets by the Company during the last six years.

7. INTELLECTUAL PROPERTY GENERALLY

7.1 Details of all patents, trade marks and registered designs in which the Company has any interest plus details of all registrations distinguishing between IP rights used by the Company and whether owned or not owned by it.

7.2 Details of any proceedings threatened or commenced alleging that any part of the Company's business infringes patents, trade marks, registered designs, design rights or copyright ('IP rights') of third parties.

7.3 Details of any subsisting claims on the part of the Company that any other person has infringed any of the IP rights owned by or licensed to the Company.

7.4 Confirmation that no present or former employee owns or claims to own any IP rights.

7.5 Confirmation that all IP rights owned by the Company or which it is entitled to use, which are licensed or sub-licensed by the Company to third parties, are fully documented in formal licence agreements.

7.6 Details of the names under which the Company carries on business and sells its products.

7.7 Confirmation that the Company has paid all registration/renewal fees in respect of its IP rights.

7.8 Details of any licences or other rights necessary for the manufacture of any of the Company's products or as an ingredient of any of its service provision and of any agreements entered into by the Company for the licensing or use of any IP rights belonging to third parties.

8. LICENSED SOFTWARE

Confirmation that:

(a) the Company is free to use all software currently or contemplated to be in use by it ('Software') without restriction;

(b) licences granted to third parties to use Software have not been sold or exercised on terms wider than those under which the Company itself was licensed;

(c) Software licensed or made available by the Company to any third party

(i) performs in accordance with its specification;

(ii) is properly documented;

(iii) is properly maintained, has clear notices on it and includes all related manuals;

(iv) is not the subject of any limitation imposed by the supplier as to its use including any limitation upon its location or the number of concurrent users;

(v) has no significant current technical problems;

(vi) is free of virus infection; and

(vii) the Company has full maintenance and updating support in place and has arrangements for full access to all source codes on any breach of ongoing commitments.

9. COMPUTERS AND COMPUTER SYSTEMS OWNED AND USED BY THE COMPANY

9.1 Please confirm that all computers and computer systems owned or operated by or for the Company:

(a) are fully operational and free of virus infection;

(b) are not obsolete and are not likely to require replacement within 2 years;

(c) are owned and controlled by the Company;

(d) have sufficient capacity for the Company's needs;

(e) have security, back-ups and disaster recovery arrangements in place and maintenance staff;

(f) have full written technical descriptions and manuals;

(g) have been operated and used in accordance with manufacturers' recommendations; and

(h) which are in use (indicating which models and when they were purchased).

9.2 All software used or stored on any computer owned or operated by or for the Company:

(a) performs its functions in accordance with any relevant specification;

(b) is the subject of a maintenance agreement (copy to be appended) the provisions of which are to be confirmed as being fulfilled;

(c) is lawfully held and used on the computer system and does not infringe third party IP rights;

(d) being packaged software, has either been purchased outright by the Company or is licensed to the Company with no right on the part of the supplier to terminate such licence (please provide copies);

(e) and which is not owned by the Company, is licensed to the Company under a written licence subject to the payment of a fixed annual fee and no other payment and is not terminable by the licensor except on breach by the Company.

9.3 Please confirm that:

    (a)   all information stored by the Company in electronic form is readily accessible through the present computer systems of the Company;

    (b)   no third party has access to the computer system or can demand any payment other than the current licence fee and reasonable remuneration for services rendered;

    (c)   all appropriate employees are properly trained so that they are able to use and operate the computer systems owned or used by the Company to the full extent;

    (d)   the Company has taken proper precautions to preserve the integrity of its computer systems which are reviewed regularly by independent experts in the field; and

    (e)   the Company's computer systems:

        (i)   perform in accordance with their respective specifications;

        (ii)   are the subject of suitable maintenance arrangements as well as operating manuals;

        (iii)   are not the subject of any limitation imposed by the supplier as to their use including any limitation upon location or the number of concurrent users; and

        (iv)   there are no significant current technical problems.

9.4 The Company has complied with all requirements of Data Protection Act 1998 and has registered as a user under the Act.

10. LITIGATION

Details of any litigation or other disputes or proceedings (including industrial tribunal actions) in which the Company is or may become involved, together with details or copies of all pleadings, statements of case and material documentation, the basis and amount of any claims made, advice received as to likely settlement levels and estimated costs of the dispute or proceedings.

11. TAXATION

11.1 A statement as to whether the Company is a close company and, if so, details of any statutory apportionments.

11.2 Copies of tax computations for the last three concluded financial years of the Company.

11.3 Copies of last three years of VAT returns.

11.4 Details of any subsisting disputes or otherwise unresolved matters with HMRC.

11.5 Details of all loss relief claimed.

11.6 Details of any stamp duty relief obtained by the Company.

12. INSURANCE

Details of all insurances taken out by the Company.

13. REGULATING LICENCES

Please supply details and (where applicable) copies of all licences, consents, permits, approvals and permissions necessary or desirable for the Company to carry on its business in accordance with applicable laws, regulations and requirements.

14. ENVIRONMENT

14.1 Details of all properties at which the Company currently has operating facilities ('Facilities') and confirmation of the date on which the Company first undertook operations at each Facility.

14.2 Details of all other facilities which the Company has previously owned, occupied or used and in each case specify:

(a) the dates of ownership, occupation or use;

(b) the precise nature of the processes and operations undertaken at each of those facilities;

(c) whether the Company is aware of any (actual or anticipated) environmental or pollution problems at any of those facilities or any neighbouring properties;

(d) what happened to the relevant facility once it ceased to be so owned, occupied or used (eg sold to a third party, demolished, redeveloped, etc).

14.3 Details of all previous owners, occupiers and/or operators of the Facilities and, to the extent possible, describe the operations that each conducted at the Facilities.

14.4 Details of all current manufacturing and other operations at the Facilities, specifying process inputs and all outputs, including waste.

14.5 Details of any part of any Facility which has been used for the disposal of hazardous materials and details of any underground storage tanks.

14.6 Copies of all permits, authorisations, licences, consents or registrations required for the operation of the processes at the relevant Facility ('Permits').

14.7 Copies of all actual or pending Permit applications and any correspondence or other documents which relate to the variation, modification, suspension, termination, renewal or transfer of an existing Permit.

14.8 Details of any new or proposed environmental laws and regulations which will or may apply to any of the business undertaken by the Company and the effect on the Company that they are likely to have.

14.9 Details of any outstanding or pending complaint, action, investigation or notice alleging that any Facility has failed to operate in compliance with the requirements of any applicable environmental laws and/or Permits.

14.10 Copies of any reports or other documents relating to the compliance of any Facility with any environmental laws or Permits.

14.11 Details of any spills, leaks, emissions, releases, or other discharges of any toxic, hazardous or other substance from any Facility to the environment.

14.12 Details of any contamination of soil or groundwater at any Facility. Please provide copies of all reports, audits, soil surveys or assessments relating to such contamination and of any health and safety audits carried out in the last five years.

14.13 Details of any known surface waters or abstraction wells near any Facility.

14.14 Copies of all environmental and health and safety policies, procedures, training manuals, emergency response materials, spill control plans, risk management reports and insurance and indemnity policies.

14.15 Details of workers' compensation claims and annual summaries of injuries and illnesses for the last five years.

14.16 Details of any planned or anticipated expenses or investments for the next three years relating to environmental or health and safety matters at any of the Facilities.

15. MISCELLANEOUS

Any other information or documents which may be relevant to the Purchaser [including:

(a), (b) etc – to be completed in each case with additional queries].

Dated

Chapter 5

Raising Funds

The price

5.1　　When the company or business to be sold is insolvent the negotiation process between the seller and buyer will differ in some regards from the position when the company or business is solvent. In a solvent situation each party to the negotiations will know which assets or which part of the business they are willing to sell or buy, and each will know what they are prepared to sell for or pay. However in an insolvent scenario the seller may not know which assets it can sell, and the usual parameters by which a business or assets are available and are valued will be subject to the impact of the restructuring or insolvency process.

There are a number of objective methods of valuation employed when a business or company is sold, including the following:

- *Price/earnings*. The seller's current or historic earnings (pre- or post-tax) are multiplied by a price/earnings ratio.

- *Net assets*. The value of the seller's net assets is determined by taking the book value of those assets and adjusting it to determine their true market value. The value of certain assets may be further adjusted to reflect their future earning potential to the buyer, especially in relation to goodwill.

    Net asset value is the most common basis of valuation employed in distressed or insolvency situations, where the buyer knows that the asset value in the seller's mind is based on the price the business or administrator might achieve on a break-up of the seller if it is forced into liquidation and assets are sold at auction. That scenario is likely to result in the lowest of all prices achievable on a realisation of the assets of any company.

    There are a number of specialist valuers who are highly experienced at valuing assets in a distressed or insolvency situation, and any administrator or other insolvency office-holder who is engaged in relation to the seller will employ such an agent to advise him or her on values. In that way the office-holder can demonstrate to creditors at a later date that in the valuer's opinion the assets were sold for their true market value in the circumstances. This is especially important to the office-holder in a pre-pack administration where the sale of the assets will not have been made subject to any competitive bidding. The disclosure requirements placed on the administrator in a pre-pack sale mean he or she has to reveal valuations that he or she obtained prior to the sale.

The value placed on assets by a secured lender may also be relevant in determining the price paid. An administrator can sell assets subject to a floating charge as if it were not subject to the security[1], although in practical terms the buyer is inevitably going to ask for a deed of release to confirm that the assets are sold free of all security. The co-operation of a secured lender or an order of the court[2] is always required in order to ensure that assets are sold free of fixed-charge security. The buyer will insist that the lender release its fixed-charge security on completion. If the lender does not agree the valuation placed on the fixed-charge assets it may be unwilling to provide a release, meaning that the only way for the seller to transfer the fixed-charge assets free of security is for its administrator to make a costly and time-consuming application to court[3].

Similar considerations apply to assets sold by an administrator that are subject to a hire-purchase agreement, conditional sale agreement, chattel-leasing agreement or a retention-of-title agreement[4].

The buyer will always look to discount the net asset value placed on the items he or she is willing to buy, and will rely on factors such as the following to seek to negotiate a further discount:

— Loss of goodwill; loss of confidence in the marketplace; loss of credibility in the marketplace; loss of key people arising as a result of the insolvency.

— The seller (if in administration or any other insolvency proceeding) will not provide him or her with any warranties as to title, and will seek indemnities in respect of any future liabilities that accrue.

— Uncertainty as to whether third parties will co-operate with the transfer of the business to the seller. This could include concerns as to the transfer of a lease of property, where the landlord has to give his or her consent to the assignment; leases of equipment, where the owner may be unwilling to permit the buyer to take over the seller's responsibilities under the finance contract; regulatory or other licences necessary to operate the business; and the novation of key contracts with suppliers and customers.

— The cost of obtaining third-party co-operation. This could include paying arrears that have accrued under leases before the landlord or equipment-owner will give consent to an assignment or novation; ransom payments that have to be made to ensure continued support from a supplier or customer; or renegotiation of prices by key suppliers and customers, who might seek to claw back losses arising on the insolvency of the seller.

— TUPE costs, as relevant employees will transfer to the buyer on the sale of a going concern. Any associated redundancy or other restructuring costs will have to be met by the buyer.

---

[1] IA 1986, Sch B1, para 70(1).
[2] IA 1986, Sch B1, para 71(1).
[3] IA 1986, Sch B1, para 71(1).
[4] IA 1986, Sch B1, paras 72(1), 111(1).

- *Cashflow*. A value based on discounted cashflow is less relevant in a sale of a distressed business. It involves placing a current value on the business purchase based on its projected future cashflow following the sale, discounted to reflect the cost of capital required to fund the business.

Once one of the above objective methods of valuation has been applied to the business or assets, there is a subjective element to be applied to the valuation which will vary from one situation to another. The proposed buyer may be a special purchaser which is uniquely placed to benefit from the synergies between its current business and the seller, and so can benefit by maximising future earnings and profit. Or it may wish to take a competitor out of the market. That may tend to drive up the price it is willing to pay. On the other hand the proposed buyer may be the only purchaser which can realise the benefit of the assets if, for example, key suppliers and customers indicate that they will not co-operate with any other potential buyer, or the proposed buyer itself is a key customer or supplier. That means the power in the negotiations on price will shift to the buyer and will tend to drive the price down, whatever figures the valuer provides to the seller or its administrator.

There are yet further considerations that will come into play:

- Tax planning. A charge to capital gains tax will arise on the realisation of an asset by the seller, and a base price fixed for the buyer. This will need to be considered.

- The amount the buyer can afford to pay. If it is a situation where, for example, the previous directors are the only people who can realise any value from an insolvent business, or the seller does not have a range of bidders to negotiate with for any other reasons, then the price agreed may well be limited to what the buyer can afford to pay. It may be severely restricted in its ability to raise funds.

- The buyer may find that if the price is prohibitive it can achieve its business objectives by other means, such as cherry-picking key staff, and contacting key suppliers and customers directly. It may be able to rely on the fact that if it does not buy the business it will remain unsold. The seller will cease to operate on any level and go into liquidation, leaving the proposed buyer with free reign to effectively 'acquire' the business by default and at no cost.

- The manner in which the sale is effected. A proposed buyer may not be willing to be drawn into a competitive bidding situation.

- The manner in which the buyer proposes to pay the agreed purchase price. In a distressed situation most sellers would rather have cash on completion than a promise of a greater sum to be paid over a period of time. Most would also prefer certainty of the sum to be paid rather than an earn-out based on future performance. Therefore the seller or its administrator may be willing to accept a bid that is not the highest in its cash amount, but which offers more favourable payment terms.

Payment terms

5.2   As noted above, the terms on which payment for an insolvent company or business is to be made can be as important as the amount to be paid. If the seller needs funding to continue operating as a going concern, say it is selling a division or a subsidiary to gain a much-needed injection of actual cash, deferred payment terms may not be of interest to it. The same need for cash may apply to an administrator or other insolvency office-holder, but for different reasons. An administration should ordinarily last for no more than one year and payment terms over a period of time may not be appropriate where the insolvency proceeding would otherwise come to an end quickly. Creditors look for and expect certainty and an early distribution of funds in administration. However where there is a longer term insolvency proceeding in place or proposed, such as liquidation or a company voluntary arrangement, creditors may prefer an option that maximises their return even if it is less certain and takes longer to result in a distribution to them. Payment over time, and perhaps based on future performance of the ongoing business, may then be appropriate for the seller.

The buyer's position and needs are also relevant. The ongoing business it acquires will have to be funded if it is to be a success. There may be restructuring costs to pay. The immediate need for working capital and resource for other needs may dictate that the buyer cannot pay in cash for the business on completion, and deferred terms are all that it can afford. Or a mixture of both. If there is no other buyer available to it the seller may have to accept deferred terms whether that suits it or not, perhaps subject to the buyer providing suitable security by way of retention of title; or a debenture over the assets that the seller transfers; or guarantees from other group companies or the directors of the buyer.

For both the seller and the buyer tax planning and future accounting considerations will also be relevant when the manner of payment is determined. In all transactions the most appropriate mechanism for payment will vary from one situation to another, and the method and timing of payment will always form part of the negotiations.

Fixed-cash terms

5.3   A fixed price, to be paid in cash on completion, is the preferred payment term in most situations. It provides clarity, simplicity and certainty for all parties and avoids future disputes.

If the whole of the agreed price cannot be paid in cash on completion then the seller or its administrator will usually require that at least part of the consideration is paid in cash on completion, if nothing more to ensure that the costs of the transaction can be paid. The position of secured creditors also needs to be considered. It is likely that sufficient cash to pay fixed-charge creditors will have to be raised on completion or it is unlikely that fixed-charge security will be released.

Variable-cash terms

5.4   The price to be paid may be determined by reference to completion accounts that are not available on completion, and/or to the future performance of the business that is transferred. An earn-out will incentivise the seller if it is to have some involvement in managing the business under new ownership, although it is not an ideal scenario for the seller if it retains no involvement in the business going forward. Performance will be entirely out of its hands and hence so will the amount of the consideration to be paid. If the seller is in administration then it is unlikely to be involved in the business after completion.

The problems with variable-cash terms may be overcome by including minimum payment terms based on draft completion accounts or expected future performance figures, agreed prior to completion. That at least gives some certainty to the seller as to what it will receive.

In any scenario where the consideration is subject to future performance the buyer will need to prepare and provide regular accounting information to the seller so that it can monitor performance, usually against expectations, and the whole process is ripe for dispute. It is usually preferable wherever possible to agree a fixed price during the negotiations, where seller and buyer are keen to work with each other and resolve any disagreements between them quickly and amicably rather than allowing them to become full-blown disputes. That incentive has gone after completion.

Deferred consideration

5.5   An agreement that the buyer pay part or all of the consideration on a deferred basis is much less attractive to the seller than payment in full on completion.

Any office-holder appointed to the seller has duties and obligations to satisfy, and will want the certainty of cash on completion to enable him or her to get on with the insolvency proceeding. The seller's creditors will want to see the consideration paid in full on completion so the earliest possible distribution can be made to them.

However deferred terms may be the only option in circumstances where the buyer's access to cash on completion is limited and it needs to utilise money it has raised to fund operation of the ongoing business and avoid it failing once again. The buyer will have working capital requirements plus, potentially, ransom payments to make and/or restructuring costs to meet on day one. All of these have to be met from somewhere. Where funds are limited that will mean meeting the costs out of funding that might otherwise pay for the business and assets. The amount of any deferred consideration might be fixed by way of agreed cash payments, or linked to completion accounts, or determined on an earn-out basis subject to future performance of the business. In most instances it is preferable to avoid uncertainty and for any deferred consideration to be agreed and paid on fixed terms. Otherwise there is further uncertainty and possible delay for any office-holder, further uncertainty and delay for the seller's creditors, and potential adverse tax consequences.

Where there is deferred consideration the seller will usually want some form of security for payment, and that can be provided in a number of different ways. Whether or not any security is offered, or demanded, or agreed will depend on the bargaining strength of each of the parties. If the buyer has the upper hand the seller may have to agree to deferred consideration without security. Otherwise the most appropriate form of security will vary from one situation to another.

Retention of title (ROT)

5.6   This may be appropriate where assets transferred are largely physical in nature. The seller can retain title to them until all of the deferred consideration is paid.

The ROT clause should be drafted carefully to make sure that:

- the buyer is obliged to keep ROT assets separate from its other assets or those belonging to other third parties;

- they are clearly identified as belonging to the seller; and

- the seller has the right to enter onto the buyer's premises to inspect its goods and to recover them in the event of default.

There are, however, limitations on the benefit of an ROT clause:

- The buyer would usually be entitled to sell ROT goods in the ordinary course of its business prior to default, and an ROT clause may seek to extend the seller's interest into the proceeds of sale of its goods. That may create a charge over the goods which will be void as against an office-holder if not registered at Companies House. Any ROT clause must provide that if any part of it is declared to be invalid that does not invalidate the entire clause.

- The buyer might mix the goods with other items, or attach them to other goods or include them in a manufacturing process. If such goods retain their individual identity, title may remain with the seller, but if goods lose their identity and cannot readily be returned to the seller, title will be lost. Again, any attempt to extend the seller's rights into any new product is likely to create a charge which may be void for lack of registration.

- If the buyer goes into administration, enforcement of an ROT clause is prohibited without the consent of the administrator or permission of the court as a result of the moratorium that arises.[5]

---

[5]   IA 1986, Sch B1, para 43.

A debenture over the assets of the buyer

5.7   This option gives title to the assets sold to the buyer on completion, but then puts the seller in the position of a secured creditor which can appoint an administrator if the buyer defaults on payment terms. The buyer will have to make sure on a share transfer that it does not fall foul of the provisions on financial assistance in CA 2006. As they only apply to a public company, the financial assistance provisions will not be considered further here.

The main difficulty in the buyer granting the seller a debenture is often that the buyer will need to charge the assets it acquires to its bank or other lender in order to raise money to fund the acquisition and/or to satisfy its working capital/restructuring cost requirements. The buyer may not be permitted to grant a debenture to the seller by any prior ranking charge-holder, or it may only be able to create a second-ranking debenture which may be subject to a deed of priority with the buyer's principal lender. That may restrict the seller's ability to enforce its security, so diminishing the effective value of the security.

A typical debenture will create a number of fixed charges over specific assets of a company, and a floating charge over the property and undertaking of the company. A clause in a debenture which purports to create a fixed charge, but where the security fails to take effect as such, will create a floating charge only. This may particularly apply to a purported fixed charge over book debts and over other assets which the buyer rather than the seller has control of.

A guarantee

5.8   A guarantee and indemnity may be provided by a parent or other group company, or by the directors of the buyer themselves. A guarantee is a promise to satisfy the obligations of the buyer if it fails to meet them, whereas an indemnity is a promise to be responsible for any losses arising as a result of the buyer failing to meet its obligations. The obligations of a guarantor are dependant on and cannot be greater than those of the buyer, whereas the obligations under an indemnity are separate from those of the buyer and not dependant on them. An indemnity can therefore survive any failure of the underlying transaction. Most documents purporting to be a guarantee are a guarantee and indemnity.

A guarantee, save to the extent that such rights are excluded by the guarantee document itself, provides the guarantor with a right of subrogation which arises once the guarantor has fulfilled all of the obligations of the buyer. This entitles the guarantor to step into the shoes of the seller and take over all of the rights that the seller had against the buyer, including the benefit of any other security. A guarantee is subject to Statute of Frauds Act 1677, s 4 which states that a guarantee must be in writing and signed by or on behalf of the guarantor in order to be effective. A guarantee is also subject to the usual requirements of a contract, so there must be an offer and acceptance, and consideration for the guarantee unless it is signed as a deed.

An indemnity is a primary obligation from the indemnifier to the seller and hence more robust than a guarantee. It is not dependant on the underlying transaction and can be relied upon even if the contract of sale made between the seller and buyer is declared to be void. An indemnity is not subject to Statute of Frauds Act 1677, s 4. Nor does it cease to be effective if there are any changes or variations made to the underlying contract. For example unless the guarantor agrees otherwise, if the seller granted further time to the buyer to pay deferred consideration that could have the effect of releasing the guarantor from its obligations. Most guarantees will protect the seller from any such release.

It is up to the seller to prove that an obligation is an indemnity and not a guarantee, if that is what the seller wants or needs to demonstrate. A court will generally interpret an obligation to be less onerous if it can. However if the guarantor has a strong connection with the underlying transaction (for example if it is a parent company or director) then it may be more willing to find that the more onerous indemnity has been provided[6]. The heading of the document relied upon will not help, so any guarantee document a seller agrees with a third party must be carefully drafted.

The seller will want to be satisfied that the guarantor has the ability to meet any demand made under the guarantee, and should seek security for any guarantee liability.

If the guarantor is a company, the seller will want to be satisfied the guarantor has an express power to provide a guarantee in its Memorandum of Association, and that its Articles provide for the directors to exercise that power without restriction (or that any limitations on the exercise of the power are satisfied).

If there is no apparent direct benefit to the guarantor in giving the guarantee then the security may well be challenged by any insolvency office-holder who is appointed to the guarantor in due course should the guarantor go into liquidation or bankruptcy. An office-holder might assert a claim for misfeasance[7] against the directors, or that the transaction was a transaction at an undervalue[8] or a preference[9].

Directors have a duty to promote the success of the company[10], and the seller should insist on seeing board minutes for a corporate guarantor demonstrating that the board has considered this point, has taken all relevant factors into account, and has concluded that in causing the guarantor to enter into the guarantee the directors are complying with their duties and obligations, and that it benefits the company giving the guarantee. There is a general assumption that if a parent company provides a guarantee and indemnity in relation to the business of a subsidiary then there is sufficient benefit to the guarantor. It

---

[6] *Couturier v Hastie* (1852) 8 Exch 40.
[7] IA 1986, s 212.
[8] IA 1986, s 238.
[9] IA 1986, s 239.
[10] CA 2006, s 172.

will benefit from increased profitability of the subsidiary, enhanced dividend payments and a greater share value if the subsidiary trades successfully. If a subsidiary provides a guarantee and indemnity in relation to the business of its parent company, or in relation to a sister company within the same group, it may be more difficult to demonstrate a direct benefit. However it might, for example, be the case that a parent company provides services to all of its subsidiaries across a group, or is the principal debtor to a bank and the parent then manages the funding amongst the group members. Providing cross-guarantees in similar circumstances can have a direct benefit to a subsidiary.

A cash deposit

5.9 It is unlikely that the buyer will agree to tie up its funds in a deposit or escrow account but this might be negotiated.

A fixed charge can be taken by the seller over a cash deposit which will enable it to draw on the cash should the buyer fail to meet its obligation to pay deferred consideration. The seller would need to exercise absolute control over the deposit in order for the charge to take effect as a fixed rather than a floating charge.

Security created over a cash deposit may well attract the benefits provided by the Financial Collateral Arrangements (No 2) Regulations 2003 (SI 2003/3226).

A bank guarantee

5.10 The buyer may be willing to procure a bank guarantee where there is a substantial transaction with a significant value to any deferred consideration.

Set-off

5.11 The seller will need to be wary of deferred consideration being used by the buyer as a mechanism to avoid payment if the buyer later finds that it has not made the bargain it envisaged. The seller in a distressed or insolvency situation will give very limited or no warranties in the sale agreement, and the scope for the buyer to raise claims against the seller and seek to set them off against the deferred consideration it would otherwise be obliged to pay is more limited than in a typical situation where a business is sold. Nevertheless the buyer may seek to effect a set-off, and the seller must ensure set-off is excluded in the sale contract.

Security and the position of a secured creditor are considered further in Chapter 6.

Shares

5.12 Consideration can be paid by the buyer issuing shares to the seller, and in some circumstances where the seller is not in a close-down situation (whether under the control of an administrator or other office-holder or not) this might be preferable to it for capital gains tax purposes.

The issue of shares is an appropriate method of payment for assets when the seller is undergoing a solvent reconstruction under the provisions of IA 1986, s 110, but in a distressed or insolvency situation it is highly unlikely that the seller will agree to accept payment in shares as its need for cash will take priority. The seller also has to consider the difficulty in valuing and selling shares at a future date in a private company.

Loan notes

5.13   The buyer might also issue loan notes to the seller to satisfy the consideration. As with the issue of shares, this might be appropriate where the seller will continue as a going concern and the loan notes might be converted to cash over a period of time, but in an insolvency situation the seller or its administrator will need the consideration to be paid in cash.

Loan notes may be preferable to shares if the buyer is a private company, as they give the seller priority over shareholders on any insolvency of the buyer, and avoid the problem of valuing and finding a buyer for shares in a private company. They may enable the seller to spread the payments it receives over a period of years, so making use of a number of capital gains tax allowances or other reliefs.

From the seller's point of view, it needs to consider matters such as the rate of interest to be applied to the loan notes. Is this greater than it would achieve by depositing the equivalent amount of cash? What is the buyer's covenant strength? Loan notes are a risk to the seller unless they are adequately secured by a bank or over assets. The terms of any security granted to support the loan notes are vital. The buyer needs to consider whether it can avoid granting security for loan notes, and to make sure that the rate of interest applied to them is less than that at which it could borrow cash to pay the consideration on completion.

As a general rule issuing shares and loan notes will not be an option for the buyer when it is acquiring an insolvent company or business.

Raising cash

5.14   Most buyers of an insolvent business will not have a ready source of money available to them, and they will need to raise funds from one or a number of sources. They will usually need to do so quickly and effectively, as a buyer in a distressed situation will often be seeking to take advantage of an opportunity that presents itself at short notice. The seller will usually want to be paid quickly in cash, and will want to see proof of funding when an offer to buy the business is made. The terms on which the consideration is to be paid will be a vital part of the decision-making process for a seller when it comes to compare one offer against another, and it decides which of the competing bids is to be successful.

There are a number of ways in which cash can be raised to fund the purchase of an insolvent business, and the buyer may look to any one of them or a combination depending on a number of factors. These include the amount it needs to raise for the acquisition and to fund working capital and other requirements; the nature of the business and assets it is acquiring or already owns; and its own private circumstances.

Bank funding

5.15   Particularly where the acquisition is of a small business, traditional bank funding (whether by way of overdraft or term loan, or a combination of the two), may be appropriate. This is particularly so where the buyer has a good existing relationship with a bank, and may well have been discussing opportunities for expansion with a relationship manager in the event that the right opportunity presented itself. If the groundwork has been laid, the process of raising funds from the bank will be much simplified.

An overdraft is a flexible form of lending, and provides a borrower with a revolving facility that can be repaid and drawn down as required. A term loan provides a borrower with certainty in terms of the amount it can borrow and when, and its obligations on repayment.

A bank may be able to come to a quick decision on new borrowing subject to it being provided with:

- reliable historic financial information relating to the distressed or insolvent business for sale;

- good forecasts and revenue projections for the business once it has been acquired, taking account of future costs and contingencies; the bank will want to see that the lending can be serviced comfortably;

- a well-prepared business plan addressing the issues that led to the failure of the old business such that it will be a success in future; and

- valuations for the assets to be acquired; the bank will undoubtedly want to secure its lending by way of a debenture over the assets of the business and will need to know what is available to it should the business fail a second time.

If the bank does want security the buyer needs to bear in mind that a standard form of debenture will invariably include a prohibition on other security being created by the buyer, which can stifle its ability to seek other sources of funding if the bank does not co-operate. There can also be an impact on the buyer providing the seller with security for any deferred consideration.

The bank will also want to see a degree of personal investment from the directors, including actual cash injected into the business and potentially by way of personal guarantees.

The main disadvantage of bank funding, over and above the level of security it may require, can be on pricing. Bank funding can be expensive compared to other sources of money that might be available. In the current economic conditions where banks are risk-averse the lack of availability of funding may also mean that this is not a viable option for some buyers.

Further, an overdraft will usually be repayable on demand or be subject to reduction by the bank on review, which can create uncertainty. However the bank would not usually make a demand or reduce the permitted amount of borrowing unless the buyer breached its banking covenants or it otherwise became concerned as to the buyer's ability to satisfy its obligations to the bank.

For a larger transaction bank funding may be syndicated, where each of a group of lenders commits to loan funds to the buyer under common terms, with one of their number acting in a lead role in relation to collecting and distributing repayments, collecting and distributing information, and taking and enforcing security. Where there are different lenders, or different types of lenders who rely on different assets as their source of recovery on any insolvency of the buyer (see below for the types of assets that funders might lend on), their rights and remedies in the event of the failure of the buyer may well be governed by an agreement which regulates ranking and priority arrangements as between the lenders. A deed of priority will establish who has first claim to which assets on a sale, and would ordinarily be agreed at the time the funding arrangements were created.

This can impact on the time taken to obtain syndicated or multi-lender funding. The more complex the situation that exists between different lenders the more time and effort and cost it takes to put the arrangements in place, and the less likely it is that they will be relevant to an opportunistic buyer taking advantage of an insolvency scenario. However where there has been long-term planning in relation to the sale of a distressed business, and time pressure is less immediate, the whole range of options that would be available to a buyer outside of an insolvency-related purchase can be utilised.

Tax and future accounting considerations will also be relevant when structuring debt positions, particularly as they become more complex.

Government-backed schemes

5.16   Various schemes are put in place from time to time by the Government or centrally funded agencies to support small enterprises. They may be restricted, for example, to funding working capital requirements, but when used in conjunction with other types of bank or similar finance, whether the government-backed loan is raised at the time of acquisition or shortly afterwards, it can be very useful.

Typically, a scheme backed by government or a central agency will involve a guarantee of a bank loan, or a substantial part of it, such that the borrower (the buyer of the insolvent business) will not need to provide its own security to the bank. The fact that the lender has a reliable security in place may mean that it is willing to relax its usual lending criteria, and can be more flexible on repayment terms. The application process can, however, be unduly bureaucratic and this may put off some potential applicants and some banks which might otherwise participate in such schemes.

Different types of programmes to support lending to business have also been put in place.

The Business Finance Partnership ('BFP') is a scheme to increase the supply of capital to businesses through non-bank sources[11]. Under the BFP the government has made £1.2bn available to invest, alongside private sector funding, in small and mid-sized UK businesses.

The National Loan Guarantee Scheme ('NLGS') was launched on 20 March 2012 with a view to helping businesses to access cheaper bank loans by reducing the rate of interest charged by banks to the business by one percentage point. Under the NLGS the government guaranteed unsecured loans obtained by certain banks, rather than providing a guarantee to the bank for the obligations of its customers. The guarantee enabled the lenders to access funding at a cheaper rate, on the basis that the banks passed on the entire benefit to its customers. By August 2012 banks had lent a total of more than £2.5bn to over 16,000 customers under the NLGS[12].

On 1 August 2012 the government opened the Funding for Lending Scheme ('FLS') to banks and building societies, to be available for a period of 18 months[13]. Under the FLS banks are incentivised to increase lending to businesses and households. Those that increase net lending will be able to borrow additional funds from the Bank of England on a pound for pound basis at a much lower cost than banks that reduce their net lending. The amounts borrowed by banks and building societies are made public by the Bank of England on a quarterly basis, with a view to increasing competition amongst the lenders.

Venture capital funds

5.17 There are a number of venture capital funds in the UK which will invest in companies with growth potential. A distressed or insolvency situation would not necessarily be attractive to many venture capitalists, where there is limited scope for due diligence and warranties. However a number of funds

---

[11]   http://www.hm-treasury.gov.uk/bfp.htm.
[12]   Source; HM Treasury http://www.hm-treasury.gov.uk/nlgs.
[13]   http://www.bankofengland.co.uk/markets/Pages/FLS/default.aspx.

understand the insolvency market and specialise in investing in distressed companies where the acquisition cost is comparatively low, the risk is comparatively high but also the potential reward is high.

Funds specialising in distressed and insolvency scenarios are highly skilled at spotting and supporting good opportunities for their business. For a buyer who is willing to relinquish part of the equity in the acquired business to the funder, they can be the right source of money to fund the acquisition, bringing a ready and immediate source of cash and the specialist skills that the buyer may not have to turn the business around from the failed company that it is acquiring into a successful and profitable enterprise. In addition to the skills that a venture capitalist can bring to the board, the pricing of venture capital funding can be keen compared to bank funding, and the knowledge that there is a specialist working alongside the buyer to develop the business can be a big help to the buyer from a reputational and PR point of view.

The disadvantage to the buyer is of course that it will have to relinquish a share of its equity to the venture capitalist, and will lose an element of control over its business going forward. The buyer will usually be required to enter into an investment agreement with the equity provider to regulate the manner in which the business should be carried on after completion of the acquisition. In a distressed acquisition the control exercised by the funds may be tighter than usual in view of the increased risk. It may require representation on the board and will require regular detailed financial and other information, so that any potential failure of the ongoing business can be spotted and addressed at an early stage. The equity provider is likely to have far greater experience of distressed scenarios than the management.

There will also be additional matters for the buyer to take into account, such as warranties in favour of the funder within the investment agreement, to be given by directors and/or retained senior employees; an obligation to provide a personal investment; revised Articles of Association with restrictions on share transfers, pre-emption rights and drag-along provisions; and the cost of key-man insurance.

Invoice financing

5.18   Invoice financing can be achieved in one of two ways: either invoice discounting or factoring. In both scenarios the buyer will assign its debtor book to the lender in return for an advance payment of an agreed proportion of the assigned invoices. The lender also levies a charge for the service, depending on the number of invoices raised or to be raised by the buyer, and the quality of those invoices. The greater the risk of non-payment to the lender, the greater the cost to the buyer.

In invoice discounting the buyer continues to collect payment of the invoices on behalf of the lender and accounts to it afterwards, whereas in factoring the lender takes over control of the debtor ledger. Customers are notified of the funding arrangement and informed that they must pay the invoice amount directly to the lender.

The advantage of invoice financing is immediate in terms of cashflow. There is no need for the buyer to wait for customers to pay invoices, and as a method of raising working capital it is an invaluable tool. Should the buyer opt for factoring it can also take the need to monitor and control the debtor ledger out of the hands of the seller and place it with people who are skilled and experienced at managing credit control. However it can be seen as an expensive option, and when a company wants to end invoice financing arrangements, termination charges can be high.

Invoice financing is often used in conjunction with other sources of funding, particularly that provided in a more traditional manner by banks, and with a degree of co-operation between the lenders it works very well. The invoice discounter or factor may well be a separate division or subsidiary of the main bank, but even if it is not they will usually work together. The bank will need to release any security it has over a company's debts so they can be assigned to the provider of invoice finance, and the security the invoice discounter or factor takes over other assets of the company may well be postponed to any debenture or other charge in favour of the bank.

Asset financing

5.19   Specific assets may be acquired by the buyer without any existing security or funding in place, and their true value may be greater than their book value, particularly if an aggressive policy has been in place to write down the book value of assets over time.

There are lenders in the marketplace who specialise in providing finance secured on assets such as plant, machinery, or fixtures and fittings. This can be a useful source of funding where asset values are high, and they are not already charged to the bank or another lender under the terms of a debenture. As with all situations, a mix of funding sources might be appropriate providing the different lenders can work together to allocate security where it can best assist the buyer to purchase the business and fund its requirements going forward.

The nature of the finance provided can vary from one situation to another and tax savings may be achieved with funding by way of lease finance, or operating leases, or secured loans, depending on the relevant scenario.

Stock financing

5.20   This is a form of asset financing where only stock is funded. It is less commonly appropriate or available, and may be more expensive than raising funds on assets generally.

A buyer might be able to look to stock finance in a retail or wholesale business where levels of stock are relatively high, and it can be a flexible and long-term solution.

Business angels

5.21   A business angel might be appropriate where the buyer finds that its bank will not lend to it because the bank perceives the risk as too high, but the value of the business is too small for a traditional venture capitalist. An individual business angel might, however, be willing to invest in the buyer by way of loan or equity or both, in order to assist with both the acquisition of the business and its future growth. Like a venture capitalist, a business angel may well want to take an active part in the business going forward, and his or her experience can be invaluable in turning around what was a failing or failed enterprise.

The business angel may also help to raise bank funding. For example if a bank loan is dependent on the director providing an equivalent amount of funding to that to be injected by the bank, the lender may be willing to deem the funding provided by the business angel as having been provided by the director. His or her presence may also add to the credibility of the business going forward.

The main disadvantage of relying on a business angel is that he or she will want a share of the business in terms of equity, and is likely to want to take an active role at board level. As a business angel is likely to be appropriate in relation to a small enterprise, there has to be a good working and personal relationship between the buyer and the hands-on investor.

Directors' loans

5.22   Directors' loans have already been alluded to above. A director may seek to raise funding privately, perhaps by remortgaging his or her personal property, and possibly in conjunction with bank borrowing, and then lend the money raised to the buyer to fund the acquisition and/or working capital requirements of the business. The loan may then be repaid by the company in a tax-efficient manner to mitigate the director paying tax on his or her earnings.

A common problem with this form of funding is that if the business does not succeed and a second insolvency follows, repayments of a director's loan ahead of payment to other creditors may be seen as a preference or misfeasance by any subsequently appointed administrator or liquidator, leading to personal claims against the director and, potentially, disqualification from acting as a director in the future.

Equity finance

5.23   Where there is a more significant transaction taking place, the buyer may want to fund the acquisition by way of issuing shares. As noted above, that may not be attractive to the seller as it is likely to have a need for cash. If time permits, a listed buyer may still be able to secure funding by way of a share issue in any of the following ways:

- *Rights issue*. This is where a company offers new shares to its existing shareholders in proportion to their existing holdings. The offer will usually be made at a discount, and to be subscribed for in cash.

  Arrangements may be put in place to provide for shares that are not taken up on the rights issue to be sold to other investors, so a shareholder who does not respond to a rights issue may find that their allotted shares have been sold at a profit to an outsider, and they still benefit from the arrangements as they earn the profit that is made.

- *Open offer*. In an open offer shares are offered to existing shareholders on a pre-emptive basis rather than in accordance with their existing shareholding. Usually no arrangements are made to sell shares where the offer is not taken up.

- *Placing*. Shares are usually placed with institutional shareholders who will retain them as a long-term investment.

- *Vendor placing*. Although the seller wants the consideration for the transaction to be paid in cash and not in shares, the buyer issues and allots shares to the seller in exchange for the assets it is buying. The shares that are allotted are placed in the market on the seller's behalf by the buyer or its agent, and the seller receives the proceeds of sale of the shares rather than the shares themselves. This process has the advantage of overcoming statutory pre-emption rights that exist on a placing for cash.

  Vendor placings used to be popular for accounting purposes as goodwill arising on the acquisition of a business could be written off against a merger reserve, but this is no longer the case as goodwill is now written off against the profit and loss account.

Chapter 6

Secured Creditors

Security interests

6.1   Security is a right given by a debtor to a creditor over an asset or assets it owns in order to secure performance of an obligation, typically the payment of a debt. Forms of security available to a creditor are as follows.

Charge

6.2   Under a charge, the company agrees to the lender appropriating an asset for the satisfaction of a debt without the lender taking possession or control of the asset. The security does not grant the lender legal or beneficial ownership of the asset, or a right of possession. Instead the charge gives the lender a right to realise the asset to recover the debt in the circumstances described in the charge, typically an event of default.

A charge may be fixed or floating. A fixed charge gives the lender control over an asset, and indeed unless the lender has, and exercises, sufficient control over the charged asset a right described as a fixed charge may be re-characterised and take effect as a floating charge only[1]. A fixed charge will typically prevent the company from selling the asset without the lender's consent and enable the lender to claim the proceeds of sale in priority to all other creditors. A fixed charge can be created by individuals and companies, whereas a floating charge can be created by companies and limited liability partnerships only[2]. A floating charge effectively 'hovers' over a shifting pool of assets. It is a charge over a class of assets both present and future and which may change from time to time in the ordinary course of a company's business[3]. The company may dispose of floating charge assets in the ordinary course of its business without the consent of the lender.

A fixed charge is important to a lender as it gives it certainty and a far greater degree of control over its security than a floating charge. However a floating charge is also vital to provide a secured lender with a 'catch-all' form of security

---

[1]   For example *National Westminster Bank plc v Spectrum Plus Limited and others and others* [2005] UKHL 41, [2005] 2 AC 680; *Re Beam Tube Products Limited* [2006] EWHC 486 (Ch).
[2]   Save that an individual or a partnership may create an agricultural charge as a floating charge over farming stock and other agricultural assets under the Agricultural Credits Act 1928.
[3]   *Re Yorkshire Woolcombers' Association Ltd* [1903] 2 CH 284.

over a business without interfering with the company's day-to-day trade, and most importantly, providing the floating charge falls within the definition of a Qualifying Floating Charge[4], it gives the lender the ability to appoint an administrator on default[5]. Floating charge creditors are disadvantaged by the fact that on insolvency, funds which are subject to a floating charge will first be applied to pay any fixed charge over the same asset(s), preferential claims[6], the prescribed part payable to unsecured creditors[7] and costs and expenses[8] before the balance is made available to the secured creditor. Costs and expenses payable in priority to a floating charge might include liability under a Financial Support Direction issued by the Pensions Regulator[9], and potentially other forms of statutory liabilities which could be imposed on a company.

In practice lenders will often take a fixed charge over assets that they can exercise sufficient control over and a floating charge over all other assets to give them the maximum possible advantage. Fixed charge assets will typically include:

- freehold and leasehold premises;

- fixed plant and equipment;

- shares in subsidiary undertakings;

- goodwill.

A lender will often also purport to take a fixed charge over other assets, but unless it has the right to and exercises sufficient control over those assets the charge may be re-characterised and take effect as a floating charge only[10]. The description of the security interest in the charge instrument as a fixed charge has no bearing on the legal position. A fixed charge is particularly vulnerable to re-characterisation in relation to:

- **Book debts**

    If the company is permitted to collect in its book debts and use the proceeds in the ordinary course of its business without reference to the lender, any charge over them will be a floating charge only. A lender can have the benefit of a fixed charge over book debts but it must effectively and actually exercise absolute control over the debts and their proceeds to do so. A bank or other lender will usually take an assignment of book debts as security where possible, rather than seek to rely on a charge over them. The bank will then own the book debts rather than rely on security over them.

---

[4]   IA 1986, Sch B1 para 14(3).
[5]   IA 1986, Sch B1 para 14(1).
[6]   IA 1986, s 175.
[7]   IA 1986, s 176A.
[8]   IA 1986, s 176ZA.
[9]   *Bloom and others v Pensions Regulator and others* [2011] EWCA Civ 1124, [2012] 1 All ER 1455.
[10] *National Westminster Bank plc v Spectrum Plus Limited and others and others* [2005] UKHL 41, [2005] 2 AC 680; Re Beam Tube Products Limited [2006] EWHC 486 (Ch).

- **Cash deposits**

    It is simpler to create a fixed charge over a cash deposit than over a current account, where by its very nature the company will pay money in and draw it out in the ordinary course of its business. However if there is an effective fixed charge over a cash deposit it means the funds are not readily available to the company for the purpose of carrying on its business. This would be appropriate for security such as a rent deposit.

- **Plant and machinery and other chattels**

    The position is less clear in relation to plant and machinery and other chattels. If the company cannot and does not deal with its chattels, possibly by reference to an agreed and fixed schedule of items, without prior consent from the lender, then a fixed charge can be created. However if the company can buy and sell plant and machinery and other chattel assets as it sees fit, without recourse to the lender, it is likely that any charge over such assets will be floating in nature.

Typical floating charge assets will include stock, work in progress and the company's undertaking generally.

Mortgage

6.3   A mortgage involves the transfer of title of an asset to the lender on terms that it will be transferred back to the company when the debt it secures is paid. Possession of the charged asset will stay with the company, subject to the lender's right to prevent the company from dealing with the asset without its consent. A mortgage will typically be taken over land but may be taken over other physical assets.

Lien

6.4   A lien gives a right to a creditor who comes into possession of a company's asset to retain the asset and potentially sell it until and unless a debt is paid. The creditor usually takes possession of items that are subject to a lien for some purpose other than to take security, and typical examples are a warehouseman who takes possession of goods to store them for the owner, or a mechanic who takes possession of a vehicle to carry out repairs.

A lien can arise as a matter of law, under statute or under contract. If it arises under the operation of law there is no right to sell to recover the debt[11]. However a contractual lien, which might, for example, be included in a warehouseman's terms and conditions, will usually give the creditor a right to sell. A contractual lien may or may not take priority over other security depending on the facts[12].

---

[11]   *Thames Iron Works Co v Patent Derrick Co* (1860) 1 John & H 93.
[12]   *See The Trustees Corporate Trustees Limited and another v Capmark Bank Europe Plc* [2011] EWCA Civ 380, [2011] 26 EG 86 for an example of a contractual lien not ranking ahead of a debenture.

Pledge

6.5   A pledge arises where the company gives possession of an asset to a lender for the purpose of providing him or her with security. Ownership remains with the company, but the lender can sell the pledged asset in the event of default on repayment. As the company has to hand over possession of a pledged asset, this form of security only applies to tangible items and is not often used as a form of security. Delivery of possession can be given by practical means, such as the debtor handing over the keys to a warehouse where the relevant goods are stored.

Other forms of 'security'

6.6   There are other ways in which a lender or other creditor can take steps to improve its position, in terms of ensuring payment of its debt. However these are not true forms of security. Anyone seeking to acquire an insolvent company needs to be aware of this when carrying out due diligence, as quasi-security interests can have an adverse impact on a buyer if it does not gain title to all those assets it may think it is acquiring.

Retention of title

6.7   When specific goods are sold under a contract, title to the goods passes from the supplier to the customer when the parties intend it to pass[13]. The contract can specify when title passes, and many standard terms and conditions of supply include a retention of title ('ROT') clause which provides that title to goods does not pass from the supplier to the customer until either the goods supplied have been paid for, or all sums due from the supplier to the customer have been paid.

Until such time as payment is made the customer holds the goods as bailee for the supplier, and although the customer is able to use the goods in the ordinary course of its business the supplier retains ownership until such time as title passes either on payment or as a matter of law as the goods are used. Many ROT terms will also provide that the supplier should store the goods separately from other stock; mark them as the supplier's property; and provide the supplier with rights of access permitting it to attend on the customer's premises to inspect and collect its goods if payment is not made.

The object of an ROT clause is to give the supplier priority over secured and unsecured creditors if the customer fails to pay for the goods because it is insolvent, or for some other reason which may be specified in the clause. ROT provisions have limitations:

---

[13]   Sale of Goods Act 1979, s 17.

- They must be properly incorporated in the contract between the supplier and the customer in order to be enforceable as a contract term. Where the customer has its own standard terms and conditions of purchase there can be doubt as to which terms apply to a contract and the so called 'battle of the forms' can arise. The party whose terms were brought to the attention of the other immediately before the contract was formed will generally prevail, although that can be overridden where there has been a course of dealing over time.

- The supplier must be able to identify its goods. This may not be simple if there is more than one supplier of similar items and those items delivered by each supplier have not been kept apart, or goods are held at a large number of sites.

- Title must not have passed by operation of law. This can happen where goods are incorporated into other products by the customer and have lost their original identity.

- An ROT clause does not of itself give the supplier the right to enter onto the buyer's land to inspect or recover its goods.

- ROT clauses that purport to transfer rights into new products or into proceeds of sale are likely to be ineffective on insolvency as they will be found to be void as unregistered charges[14].

- They are of little or no practical benefit where goods supplied are perishable or have a low scrap value.

- ROT clauses cannot be enforced in administration without consent of the administrator or permission of the court as a result of the moratorium that arises[15].

In many cases a supplier will not actually want its goods back and would prefer payment in full or in part. ROT clauses have value as a quasi-security interest as they may enable a supplier to negotiate a payment that it would not otherwise receive on the failure of a business.

ROT clauses are becoming ever more important to potential buyers of insolvent businesses, particularly when doing due diligence before agreeing on a price. Suppliers have become ever more aware of their rights under ROT provisions, especially following the continuing retail insolvencies, where suppliers who lost out with badly drafted clauses the first time a business became insolvent have made sure that did not happen on a subsequent failure. A potential buyer should identify how many suppliers have ROT clauses; check whether or not they are incorporated; review how well-drafted they are; identify whether they are simple or all-monies clauses; and investigate whether or not the supplier can identify its goods. All of these factors will tend to point to what level of settlement a buyer may have to offer to an ROT creditor in order for the

---

[14] *Re Bond Worth Limited* [1980] Ch 228.
[15] IA 1986, Sch B1, paras 43 and 111(1).

company it is considering acquiring to be able to retain and sell goods the target has in its possession. It is worth looking at ROT in more detail.

Legal issues and ROT clauses

Sale of Goods Act 1979

The Sale of Goods Act 1979 sets out the law on when ownership of goods passes to a buyer. Under section 17(1) this is when the parties intended it to pass and regard is had under section 17(2) to the contract terms, the conduct of the parties and the circumstances of the case. Section 19 provides:

> **'19. Reservation of right of disposal**
>
> (1) Where there is a contract for the sale of specific goods or where goods are subsequently appropriated to the contract, the seller may, by the terms of the contract or appropriation, reserve the right of disposal of the goods until certain conditions are fulfilled; and in such a case, notwithstanding the delivery of the goods to the buyer, or to a carrier or other bailee or custodier for the purpose of transmission to the buyer, the property in the goods does not pass to the buyer until the conditions imposed by the seller are fulfilled.'

Goods on-sold

Where the buyer has sold the goods they may have acquired good title either because of section 25(1) of the Sale of Goods Act 1979 or where the contract terms allow a resale or do not restrict it:

> **'25. Buyer in possession after sale**
>
> (1) Where a person having bought or agreed to buy goods obtains, with the consent of the seller, possession of the goods or the documents of title to the goods, the delivery or transfer by that person, or by a mercantile agent acting for him, of the goods or documents of title, under any sale, pledge, or other disposition thereof, to any person receiving the same in good faith and without notice of any lien or other right of the original seller in respect of the goods, has the same effect as if the person making the delivery or transfer were a mercantile agent in possession of the goods or documents of title with the consent of the owner.'

If a well-drafted ROT clause is part of the supply contract this means the goods remain the supplier's property if payment has not been made. However there is a legal trap in drafting such clauses, and if the supplier tries to go too far what is meant to be an ROT clause may amount to a charge or mortgage over goods. Where that happens the clause must, like certain other charges, be registered at Companies House under the Companies Act 2006[16]. If it is not

---

[16]   CA 2006, s860.

registered then it will be void as against an administrator or liquidator[17]. This means it is invalid when it is needed most. A number of the court cases over retention of title have been over the issue of when a clause amounts to a charge. Where there is a significant, high value contract, a supplier may choose to register a charge at Companies House, although in practice this is rarely done, particularly as most contracts are numerous, or involve repeat arrangements, and few suppliers would want to be registering a charge at Companies House on a daily basis.

There are many different versions of retention of title clause wording:

(a) Simple clauses. These say ownership is retained in goods until full payment is made for those particular goods. Even these clauses can be void if the goods lose their form and are incorporated into other goods yet the supplier still seeks to recover their value.

(b) 'All-monies' or 'current account' clauses. Here the supplier retains ownership until all amounts due to the supplier are paid, not just the amount due for the particular goods in question.

Other types of clauses are sometimes collectively called multi-purpose clauses and are as follows:

(a) 'Tracing', 'prolonged' or 'proceeds of sale' clauses. The supplier seeks to retain ownership of the goods until the full purchase price for those goods has been paid. If the insolvent company sells the goods, the supplier seeks to acquire ownership of the proceeds of sale or debts owed by the sub-buyer(s), but this depends upon the existence of a fiduciary relationship or a validly registered charge.

(b) An 'aggregation' or 'enlarged' clause. Here the supplier seeks to retain ownership of the goods until the full purchase price has been paid by the insolvent company, but if the goods are manufactured into some other property, with or without the addition of other goods, the supplier claims ownership of the resulting property or a proportionate part of it equal to the contribution made to the manufacturing process by the original goods. This can occur where there is a fiduciary relationship or the contract expressly provides for the ownership of the finished goods to vest in the supplier. However in the latter case a charge is likely to have been created, which would require registration under the CA 2006 to be effective, and in the case of an individual may be void.

Tracing is a legal principle which entitles the owner of goods or money to 'trace' or follow those goods or money out of the hands of the company into the hands of a third party or a new product, and to recover them in certain limited cases. Usually tracing clauses amount to charges and are void if not registered.

---

[17] CA 2006, s874.

Sometimes clauses have elements which create valid ROT clauses and other elements which do not, and it is perfectly possible that one subclause is valid whilst another is void. Clauses should therefore have separate subparagraphs so that if any part is held void the rest might stand, and they should also include a 'severance' clause in the terms which says that if any clause or part of a clause is void the remainder will still continue in full force and effect.

Incorporation

The onus is on the supplier to prove it has a valid retention of title clause.

Under the general law of contract an offer made by one party has to be accepted by the other before there is a valid contract. Therefore an administrator or liquidator should ensure that an ROT clause was notified to the insolvent company prior to the supplier accepting the company's offer to buy. An ROT clause will be effectively incorporated into a contract if:

- it is in contractual documentation signed by the company; or

- it is in an unsigned document which, prior to entering into the contract, the company knew contained contract terms even though it was not aware of their effect; or

- it is in a separate document and the supplier had done all that was reasonably necessary to draw the contract terms to the attention of the company prior to entering into the contract; it is not necessary for the company to have actual knowledge that the document contained the contractual terms for a clause to be effective, and since ROT clauses are common, such a clause need not have been specifically drawn to the attention of the insolvent; or

- there was a sufficient course of dealing between the parties.

Ideally the terms of business should have been sent to the company prior to entering into any contract (or made clear in any conversation during which the contract was entered into) as well as appearing on all documents. However, this will very rarely be the case and the method used by the supplier to inform the company of its terms of business will vary. The terms may have been notified by the supplier before trading began or in the acknowledgement of the order, quotation, catalogue or pricelist. Usually the offer to enter into a contract will be an order by the company and the contract will be entered into on the despatch of the acknowledgement of order or despatch of the goods themselves by the supplier. In considering an ROT claim the following matters are relevant:

- Conflict of the terms of the businesses. If the supplier purported to accept the company's offer (based upon the company's terms of business) but the supplier's terms of business conflict with those of the company, then there will not have been an unconditional acceptance of the company's offer but instead the supplier will have made a counter-offer. If the company then proceeded with the transaction it should be treated as having accepted the supplier's terms of business and the ROT clause will be part of the contract.

- Where there have been regular transactions between the company and the supplier, the terms of business of previous contracts may be applied to the contract which is subject to the ROT claim.

- If the clause is contained in the terms of business on the supplier's invoice and was not previously agreed by the company and the supplier, the clause should be rejected as the contract was made prior to the invoice being sent. It is post-contractual. A clause on an invoice might be valid if there was an agreement between the parties after the contract had been entered into, but only if the company provided new consideration for the introduction of the clause as a term. It might also be valid under a course of dealing.

- Alteration of terms of business. Enquiries should be made to see whether either the company or the supplier have changed their terms of business during the period when the contracts were made for the goods.

Identifying goods

In an ideal world each supplier's goods would have a unique serial number upon them which would also appear on the contract documentation and invoice, and the supplier could identify that those goods were not paid for. If the goods have been used in a manufacturing process the supplier may still seek to recover them if they remain identifiable and are easily removable. In one case title was retained by the supplier where a product was incorporated into an engine but did not change in substance and could easily be removed[18], whereas title was lost to resin which had been melted and become part of a chipboard product[19].

Where a supplier relies on a simple ROT clause it must be able to prove that the goods it seeks to recover are those for which payment has not been made. If 100 items were supplied and 50 have been paid for, the supplier cannot recover the 50 left in the warehouse. It has to be able to prove that it is exactly those 50 for which no payment has been made.

An 'all-monies clause' clause is where the goods are not owned by the buyer until the buyer has paid all money owed to the supplier, not just for those goods. If however goods were supplied when no money was owed, then title will have passed and the supplier may still have to show which goods were supplied after the account balance was at zero.

Where there are multiple suppliers of the same goods, each supplier will have to identify its own stock save where a supplier can demonstrate that it supplied a substantial part of the goods, when that may be sufficient[20].

---

[18] *Hendy Lennox (Industrial Engines) Ltd v Graham Puttick Ltd* [1984] 1 WLR 485.
[19] *Borden (UK) Limited v Scottish Timber Products Ltd* [1979] 3 All ER 961.
[20] *Hachette UK Limited and others v Borders (UK) Limited and others* [2009] EWHC 3487 (Ch).

Manufactured goods

In considering the wording of an ROT clause it is necessary to look at how the goods are to be used.

In *Borden (UK) Limited v Scottish Timber Products Limited*[21] the court examined this area and said if the seller purports to retain ownership of a finished product then the clause will be void if not registered. Here resin supplied was used in chipboard manufacture and had lost its identity, so it could not be recovered. In *Re Peachdart Limited*[22] leather was sold and used to make handbags. Once the leather was cut as part of the manufacturing process it could not be reclaimed and the clause failed. In *Hendy Lennox (Industrial Engines) Limited v Grahame Puttick Limited*[23] the court said that an engine attached by a bolt to a generator did not lose its identity as an engine. The bolt could be undone and the engine could be recovered.

Goods fixed to land usually become part of the land, so cannot be taken back.

All-monies clauses

As mentioned above, in these clauses the supplier retains ownership until all sums owed to it are paid, and these clauses are usually valid. This was made clear in *Aluminium Industrie Vaassen BV v Romalpa Aluminium Limited*[24] and *Armour and another v Thyssen Edelstahlwerke AG*[25].

In *Clough Mill Limited v Martin*[26] it was held that all-monies clauses do not always create a registrable charge, but if the clause tries to recover the proceeds of subsales then a charge is created.

Creating a charge

Where an ROT clause purports to do the following it will create a charge in favour of the supplier which will be void as against a liquidator or administrator for lack of registration at Companies House:

- **Attempts to retain 'equitable and beneficial ownership' of goods for the supplier**. Following the decision in the case of *Re Bond Worth Limited*[27], this will be interpreted as a charge securing a debt, since the term 'equitable ownership' means the company as the legal owner holds the goods for the supplier in a trust-like fashion until payment is made for them.

---

[21] [1979] 3 All ER 961.
[22] [1983] 3 All ER 204.
[23] [1984] 2 All ER 152.
[24] [1976] 2 All ER 552.
[25] [1990] 3 All ER 481.
[26] [1985] 1 WLR 111.
[27] [1979] 3 All ER 919.

- **Seeks to retain title to goods supplied once they have lost their identity** in the manufacturing process of the company.

- **Seeks to claim the proceeds of sale of the goods or the proceeds of sale/debts owed by subpurchasers.**

- **Claims the proceeds of sale** where no fiduciary relationship exists.

Context of the ROT arrangements

In *Bulbinder Singh Sandhu v Jet Star Retail Ltd and others*[28] the High Court held that a contract containing an ROT clause must be read in its entirety when construing the effect of the clause, and should be interpreted in the context of the commercial bargain made between the parties as a whole.

In this case, the ROT clause in question was part of a contract for the sale of stock to a retailer. The stock was supplied for resale, as distinct from a sale of tools or equipment that the purchaser might intend to use in its business. The court noted that a contract for the sale of goods that are not intended for resale may often contain effective ROT clauses. However in this instance the ROT clause was not effective, as it was inconsistent with the parties' clear intention that the stock would be sold on to customers of the buyer. Although the ROT terms provided that the supplier could terminate the buyer's right to re-sell the goods, it had failed to exercise that right. Accordingly the ROT clause was ineffective to preserve the supplier's title to the stock against a sale by administrators of the retailer on considering the contract as a whole, and on looking at how the parties had operated the contract.

The High Court decision was subsequently confirmed by the Court of Appeal.

Summary

When considering whether a supplier has a valid ROT claim, an administrator or potential buyer carrying out due diligence must be satisfied on each of the following legal and practical issues (and perhaps many more, as the position will vary from one situation to another):

- That the wording of the clause includes the goods or monies being claimed.

- That the clause has been incorporated into the supply contract.

- That any goods claimed can conclusively be identified.

- Where the clause is not an 'all-monies' clause, that the goods supplied and indentified relate to an unpaid invoice.

- That physical access to the goods is possible. It is unlawful, without a court order, to force entry, but if the goods are present on site and the clause allows entry it is possible for the supplier to proceed.

---

[28] [2010] EWHC B17 (Mercantile) and [2011] EWCA Civ 459.

- Whether the company is or will be in an insolvency process. Enforcement of ROT terms is subject to the statutory moratorium that arises where the company may go into administration or is in administration[29].

- Where the goods are located. Are they at one site or distributed over a wide area? Identification and collection are not easy if goods are widely distributed.

- Whether the ROT clause allows goods to be sold in any event. Were goods supplied with the intention of resale? Is the right of resale (contractual or implied) limited to 'the ordinary course of business'?[30]

- Whether the right of resale terminates on insolvency, with or without notice from the supplier[31].

- Whether the wording of the clause extends to cover the goods and/or monies representing proceeds of sale.

- Where proceeds of sale are claimed, that the monies represent the proceeds of sale of the items which incorporated the goods from the supplier or the proceeds of sale of the goods themselves.

- Whether the goods have lost their form, or are mixed with or attached to other goods in such a way that they cannot be separated out.

Set-off

6.8   A creditor may have an agreement with the company as a term of a contract that it can set off amounts due from it to the company against amounts due from the company to the creditor. Set-off has the effective advantage of ensuring that the creditor is paid in full to the extent that mutual debits and credits exist, by extinguishing (in so far as the company has a corresponding liability to the creditor) a claim that the company may otherwise have against it.

Set-off can also arise automatically as a matter of law and in certain insolvency processes[32]. Parties cannot contract out of insolvency set-off[33]. It provides for an account to be taken of what is due from each party to the other in respect of mutual dealings and for the two sums to be set off. The balance only is then either due to the company or provable as a claim in the insolvency.

Factoring or invoice discounting

6.9   This occurs when a company that supplies goods or services on credit assigns its debts to a factoring company in return for an immediate discounted

---

[29]   IA 1988, Sch B1 Paras 43(1), 43(3), 44 and 111(1).
[30]   *Bulbinder Singh Sandhu v Jet Star Retail Ltd and others* [2010] EWHC B17 (Mercantile) and [2011] EWCA Civ 459.
[31]   *Bulbinder Singh Sandhu v Jet Star Retail Ltd and others* [2011] EWCA Civ 459.
[32]   Rules 2.85 and 4.90.
[33]   *National Westminster Bank Limited v Halesowen Pressworks & Assemblies Limited* [1972] AC 785.

payment. The debt no longer belongs to the company and so it cannot be sold by the company to a buyer.

Finance leasing and sale and leaseback

6.10   A company may finance the purchase of an asset in this manner, or refinance an asset it already owns. A lender will purchase the asset and become owner. It then leases the chattel to the company, such that the company usually pays regular monthly instalments which total the purchase price plus an amount equivalent to interest over an agreed term. The company never owns the asset during the course of the lease (although it may acquire it afterwards) so cannot grant security over it or pass title to a buyer.

Hire purchase and conditional sale

6.11   This is a form of leasing arrangement whereby the company hires the asset in question from a finance company with an option to buy for a nominal sum at the end of the term. During the hire period the lender retains ownership of the asset although possession is with the company. A conditional sale agreement is similar save that title passes automatically to the company where the condition of paying all the agreed instalments is satisfied.

Distress for rent arrears

Introduction

6.12   Distress is a common-law remedy available to a landlord. Distress arises outside of the terms of lease, and enables a landlord who is owed rent to take possession of goods on the leasehold premises, and to either hold the goods as security for payment or sell them in order to use the proceeds to satisfy the arrears. Distress can give a landlord priority over other unsecured creditors in respect of the tenant's goods. It is often criticised as an outdated remedy and the law relating to distress is due to be reformed.

If the landlord's intention is to sell goods to recover arrears of rent then the goods over which he or she distrains must be of sufficient value to defray the costs that are incurred in the processes of taking possession and sale. The landlord may not know before he or she distrains whether or not goods are subject to existing charges or other encumbrances, or are owned by third parties. However distress may be used if the landlord knows or suspects that an insolvency proceeding is about to commence, as a method of exerting pressure to pay on an office-holder who wants to make use of the company's assets or dispose of them. As with other creditors who have security, a landlord will need to release any distraint before clear title can be passed. Distraint can also give a landlord greater bargaining strength if an office-holder seeks to assign or surrender a lease.

It is only a person who was landlord at the time the arrears accrued and is landlord at the time of the distraint who has the right to distrain. A person who takes a transfer of a leasehold reversion from a landlord cannot distrain in respect of arrears that arose before the transfer.

What can a landlord distrain for?

6.13   Distress is a remedy available to a landlord in respect of rent. That has been described as 'payment made to [the landlord] in consideration of the enjoyment by a tenant of land belonging to the landlord'[34]. Other sums may fall due under a lease, such as insurance, service charges, interest and costs. Many leases will call such items rent with a view to allowing the landlord to distrain for payment of them. However the validity of such provisions is not clear as payments of insurance, service charges and other such amounts are not rent. If the lease provides as a matter of contract that sums due other than rent can be recovered in the same manner as rent or by distress that may be effective, and the court has found an attempt to recover service charge by distraint as valid[35] (although in this instance the landlord failed as the amount of service charge was not certain).

A landlord may only distrain for a certain sum. If the amount due has not been ascertained distraint is not available[36]. A tenant can set a claim against the landlord off against rent to avoid the right to distrain[37], and if the tenant seeks to set off an unliquidated claim that may affect the landlord's right to distrain in its entirety, as he or she will not know what amount he or she claims is undisputed.

The right to distrain for unpaid rent arises the day after payment fell due, which in most leases will be the day after each quarter day if rent remains unpaid.

What goods can a landlord distrain over?

6.14   A landlord can distrain over all goods found on the leasehold premises whether they belong to the tenant or a third party. A third party may avoid the distress by removing his or her goods from the premises before the distraint starts, or in some circumstances by serving an appropriate notice on the landlord afterwards.

Some goods are protected from distraint. These include:

- property belonging to the Crown[38];

---

[34]   *T & E Homes Limited v Robinson* [1979] 2 All ER 522.
[35]   *Concorde Graphics Limited v Andromeda Investments* SA (1982) 265 Estates Gazette 386.
[36]   See n 20.
[37]   *Eller v Grovecrest Investments Limited* [1995] QB 272.
[38]   *Secretary of State for War v Wynne* [1905] 2 KB 845.

- property belonging to persons with diplomatic privilege;

- tenant's fixtures;

- perishable items;

- money;

- tools, books, vehicles and equipment needed personally in the tenant's business;

- clothing and bedding;

- books of record.

Goods owned by third parties can be made subject to distraint, subject to certain remedies. The third party can tender rent to the landlord and claim an indemnity from the landlord[39]. A creditor with security over goods can require a landlord to look first to other goods to recover the arrears under the doctrine of marshalling.

The Law of Distress Amendment Act 1908 ('LDAA 1908') enables certain third parties to serve a notice on a landlord stating the goods he or she has distrained over do not belong to the tenant and so protect them from distress[40]. If the third party is a lawful[41] subtenant he or she must pay rent directly to the landlord to take advantage of the LDAA 1908, and in doing so is relieved of his or her obligation to pay rent to the tenant[42]. The LDAA 1908 also applies to a lodger, and to a person who is 'any other person whatsoever not being a tenant of the premises or of any part thereof, and not having any beneficial interest in any tenancy of the premises or of any part thereof'[43].

Some goods cannot be protected from distraint. These include goods:

- belonging to the tenant's spouse[44]; a tenant cannot avoid distress by transferring ownership to his or her spouse;

- belonging to a partner of the immediate tenant[45];

- subject to a hire-purchase agreement or conditional sale agreement[46];

- in the possession of the tenant with the consent of the true owner but where the tenant is the reputed owner[47]; accordingly the LDAA 1908 does not apply to goods that the tenant purports or appears to own;

---

[39] *Exall v Partridge* (1799) 8 Term Rep 308.
[40] LDAA 1908, s 1.
[41] LDAA 1908, s 5.
[42] LDAA 1908, s 1.
[43] LDAA 1908, s 1(c).
[44] LDAA 1908, s 4(1).
[45] LDAA 1908, s 4(2)(a).
[46] LDAA 1908, s 4A.
[47] LDAA 1908, s 4(1).

- on premises where a trade or business is carried on in which both the tenant and subtenant have an interest[48].

Notice must be served on the landlord or its bailiff in the form of a written declaration that the tenant has no property or interest in the goods that have been distrained upon and that they are not goods to which LDAA 1908 does not apply[49]. The notice must have an inventory of relevant goods to be protected from distress attached to it, and may be signed by the owner or his/her solicitor[50].

There is no time limit for service of a notice set out in the LDAA 1908 and it can be served at any time until the distress is complete. Once the notice is served the landlord cannot proceed with the distraint and the owner can apply to the court to recover his or her goods.

In view of the fact that there is no time limit for serving notice under the LDAA 1908 ownership of goods is something a seller and buyer of an insolvent business should check on if a landlord seeks to assert a distraint.

What is the effect of an insolvency proceeding on distraint?

Administration

6.15   No distress may be levied without the consent of the administrator or the permission of the court[51].

Receivership

6.16   Assets that are subject to the receivership are likely to be charged to the appointer and will be of no value to the landlord. A landlord may still distrain over assets that are subject to a floating charge[52].

Compulsory liquidation

6.17   Once a winding-up order has been made against a company no actions or proceedings against the company may be proceeded with or commenced against the company or its property without leave of the court[53], and any distress put in force against its estate is void[54]. Once a winding-up petition has been presented the company, a creditor or a contributory may apply to stay any

---

[48]   LDAA 1908, s 4(2)(b).
[49]   LDAA 1908, s 1.
[50]   *Lawrence Chemical Co Limited v Rubenstein* [1982] 1 All ER 653.
[51]   IA 1986, Sch B1, para 43.
[52]   *Re Roundwood Colliery* [1897] 1 Ch 373.
[53]   IA 1986, s 130(2).
[54]   IA 1986, s 128.

action or proceedings[55]. Distress has been held by the court to be an action or proceeding falling within the relevant provisions[56].

The court is likely to allow a landlord to complete a distress that started before the liquidation. A landlord may also be given permission to distrain in respect of arrears of rent that fall due as an expense during the course of the liquidation.

Voluntary liquidation

6.18 In voluntary liquidation there is no restriction on a landlord's right to distrain, although a liquidator may apply to the court for an order[57] applying the provisions which come into effect on compulsory liquidation.

Walking possession agreements

6.19 A landlord can exercise his or her right to distrain in person or by a certified bailiff[58]. A bailiff acts as the landlord's agent and the landlord may be liable for any wrongful acts of the bailiff.

The landlord or certified bailiff must enter onto the premises to distrain, and is not able to enter by force or will be a trespasser. It is also an offence to use or threaten force if there is someone on the premises who objects to the landlord or bailiff entering and the landlord is aware of this[59]. The landlord or his/her agent may enter through an open window or door[60], and once inside force can be used to gain access to other parts of the premises. The landlord can also use force to re-enter premises once he or she has effected a lawful distraint, although has to be wary of the risk of committing an offence[61].

Once the landlord has entered the premises he or she must seize the goods by taking some action which shows that they are being distrained upon. This might mean attaching a label to the goods or by being provided with a list of goods. After seizure the goods may be impounded on or off the premises[62] either by clearly separating them from other goods or by listing them. If goods are impounded on the premises the landlord or bailiff may leave them unattended, in which case the landlord is said to be in walking possession of the goods. It is usual for a walking possession agreement to be signed by the tenant under which he or she agrees to pay the bailiff's costs; allow re-entry at any time whilst the distress is in force; and confirms that he or she will not remove the goods from the premises. The agreement usually also includes a statement of the amount of arrears due.

---

[55] IA 1986, s 126(1).
[56] *Re Memco Engineering Limited* [1986] Ch 86.
[57] Under IA 1986, s 112.
[58] Law of Distress Amendment Act 1888, s 7.
[59] Criminal Law Act 1977, s 6.
[60] *Tutton v Darke* (1860) 5 H&N 647.
[61] Criminal Law Act 1977, s 6.
[62] Distress for Rent Act 1737, s 10.

Sale of goods

6.20   If the landlord wishes to sell the goods impounded, he or she must serve notice on the tenant stating:

- the amount of the rent arrears;

- an inventory of the goods impounded;

- the place where the goods are impounded; and

- the time when they will be sold.

The landlord must wait 5 clear days between seizure and sale[63] during which time the goods must be returned to the tenant if the arrears and costs are paid. That time can be extended by the tenant to a period of not more than 15 days subject to the tenant providing security for the landlord's additional costs[64]. The landlord has a duty to obtain the best price on any sale[65], and can sell by private treaty or by auction.

Once the goods are sold the landlord may take the arrears of rent and costs from the proceeds. Any surplus should be left with the bailiff for the benefit of the owner[66]. It is up to the owner to claim the surplus rather than for the landlord or the bailiff to seek the owner out.

Other creditors with the right to distrain

6.21   Certain other creditors may also have a right to distrain over goods, including those with a judgment debt, HM Revenue & Customs for unpaid tax, local authorities for unpaid rates and Magistrates for unpaid fines.

Validity of security

6.22   In order for it to be effective, a security interest needs to be entered into carefully. There are a range of issues which a lender or creditor needs to consider when taking security, and which a prospective buyer of an insolvent business should review when carrying out due diligence.

Terms of the security interest

6.23   An agreed security interest is created by a contract, so the usual requirements of offer, acceptance and an intention to create legal relations

---

[63]   Distress for Rent Act 1689, s 1.
[64]   Law of Distress Amendment Act 1888, s 6.
[65]   Distress for Rent Act 1689, s 1.
[66]   Distress for Rent Act 1689, s 1.

apply. The parties must have capacity to enter into the contract, and there must be consideration (unless created as a deed), certainty of subject matter, and an appropriate form of execution.

A security interest can secure present and future liabilities; actual debts and contingent claims; certain and uncertain amounts; and whether or not the time for repayment is certain. Security taken for existing debts may be subject to the avoidance provisions of the Insolvency Act 1986 as a transaction at an undervalue[67], a preference[68] or an invalid floating charge[69] on the administration or liquidation of the debtor.

The debtor might also secure not only payment of its own liabilities, but also those of a third party.

Perfection

6.24   A security interest must be perfected to be valid and effective as against third parties including other creditors, administrators and liquidators[70]. That may mean any of the following:

- an agreement to create a security interest in land must be in writing and signed on behalf of each party to the security; the agreement must contain all of the terms which the parties have agreed and it must be executed as a deed[71];

- for a lien or pledge to be effective the lender must generally have actual possession of the security asset, although constructive possession (such as by holding the keys to a warehouse where goods are stored) may be sufficient;

- security created by a company or an LLP must be registered at Companies House[72] within 21 days of creation[73];

- security over registered land must be registered at the Land Registry[74];

- there are specific rules and registers for registering security over intellectual property rights[75]; ships[76]; aircraft[77]; and personal chattels[78].

---

[67] IA 1986, s 238.
[68] IA 1986, s 239.
[69] IA 1986, s 245.
[70] CA 2006, s 874.
[71] Law of Property (Miscellaneous Provisions) Act 1989, s 2.
[72] CA 2006, s 860.
[73] CA 2006, s 870.
[74] Land Registration Act 2002.
[75] Held at the UK Patent Office.
[76] Merchant Shipping Act 1995, Sch 1.
[77] Civil Aviation Act 1982, s 86.
[78] Bills of Sale Act 1878; Bills of Sale Act (1878) Amendment Act 1882.

If a security interest is not perfected it may be subject to attack by an administrator or a liquidator, and/or may constitute a transaction at an undervalue[79], a preference[80] or an invalid floating charge[81]. However a floating charge that constitutes a financial collateral arrangement under the Financial Collateral Arrangements (No 2) Regulations 2003[82] ('FCA Regulations') is not vulnerable under IA 1986, s 245.

Priority

6.25   A lender will want to be certain of the order of payment of creditors on the insolvency of a company. Although a secured creditor will have priority over unsecured claims, if the company has created more than one security interest, priority arrangements as between the secured lenders will be relevant.

The general rules are that:

* a fixed charge takes priority over a floating charge even if it is created at a later date[83];

* fixed charges and mortgages take priority in accordance with their date of creation[84];

* floating charges take priority in accordance with their date of creation[85].

A number of specific rules then operate to vary the general position, including the following:

* where security has to be registered not only at Companies House but also in a specialist register (such as security over land, intellectual property rights, ships and aircraft) priority is determined in the order of registration in the specialist register;

* an earlier equitable interest will take priority over a later legal interest unless the legal interest is transferred to a bona fide purchaser without notice[86];

* under the FCA Regulations[87] security over relevant collateral is effectively first-ranking in priority.

Creditors may also agree to regulate priority arrangements by contract in an inter-creditor deed. A typical inter-creditor deed will include provisions which

---

[79]   See note 60.
[80]   See note 61.
[81]   See note 62.
[82]   SI 2003/3226.
[83]   *Re Robert Stephenson & Co Limited* [1913] 2 Ch 201, CA.
[84]   *James v Boythorpe Colliery Co* [1890] 2 Meg 55.
[85]   *Smith v English and Scottish Mercantile Investment Trust Limited* [1896] 40 Sol Jo 717.
[86]   *Pilcher v Rawlins* (1872) 7 Ch App 259.
[87]   SI 2003/3226.

regulate the ranking and priority of debt and security between each creditor or class of creditors; specify circumstances in which each of the creditors or class of creditors may and may not claim payment of its debt and/or enforce its security without the consent of others; and regulate the distribution of the proceeds of enforcement or sale. As funding arrangements become more complex other forms of subordination may become appropriate.

A further method by which lenders seek to retain priority for a floating charge is the use of a negative pledge in a security agreement. A negative pledge prohibits the creation of further security by the company without the lender's consent, and seeks to prevent the company from creating a subsequent fixed charge over an asset which would, if created, take precedence over the existing lender's floating charge. If a subsequent creditor takes security in breach of a negative pledge of which it has notice, the new security will rank behind the original floating charge in any event. The difficulty for the original floating charge creditor is ensuring that any other potential lender has notice of the negative pledge. In practice notice is given by including details of the negative pledge in the particulars of the original security when it is registered at Companies House, although there is no certainty that this will be effective.

Corporate benefit

6.26   Where a company creates security over its assets in return for a loan to the company or some other form of credit arrangement given to the company, the benefit of entering into the security is clear. However where security is given by a group company or an unconnected third party the corporate benefit to the company giving the security, which may not take any direct advantage from the loan or credit facility, needs to be considered carefully.

The directors of a company have a duty to act in the way they consider would be most likely to promote the success of the company for the benefit of its members as a whole[88], and must consider and document how granting security for the liabilities of another company satisfies that duty. It may be more difficult to establish the benefit to a company in charging its assets for the liabilities of a parent company than it is for a parent company to justify granting security for the liabilities of a subsidiary (profits in the subsidiary arising after the provision of underlying secured funding may lead to the declaration of dividends by the subsidiary and increased share value, both of which are of clear benefit to the parent company). It may be particularly difficult to establish the benefit to a company in charging its assets for the liabilities of a sister company. In such instances it might be appropriate for the shareholders of the charging company to approve the actions of the directors in resolving to grant the security[89]. The directors themselves must balance the risks to the company granting the

---

[88]   CA 2006, s 172.
[89]   See *Rolled Steel Products Limited v BSC* [1985] 3 All ER 52; *West Mercia Safetywear Limited v Dodd* [1988] BCLC 250.

security against the benefit to the group company or other entity with the direct obligation to pay the debt.

The rights of a secured creditor

Introduction

6.27 The position of secured creditors has to be considered carefully in any acquisition of a distressed company or business. A secured creditor generally has the right to:

- take possession of secured property (to the extent that it has not already done so);

- sell secured property; and

- depending on the nature of the security, to appoint a receiver to manage or sell the secured property or appoint an administrator.

A secured creditor who takes possession of property is accountable to the company for loss caused to the company by his or her negligence or wilful default[90]. Where the charged asset is land a lender in possession can also become liable for environmental damage and clean-up costs, and for public-liability claims. Most lenders will only take possession if they are proposing to sell.

A power of sale must be exercised by the lender in good faith for the purpose of recovering his or her debt. There is a duty to obtain the best price that could reasonably be obtained on a sale. The duties and obligations on a lender exercising a power of sale are similar to those that apply to a receiver appointed by a lender under a charge instrument[91].

As a result of the direct liabilities that may be imposed on a lender which takes possession or exercises a power of sale in relation to security property, most creditors prefer to appoint a receiver or an administrator to exercise their remedies. The advantage to the lender is that the office-holder appointed acts as the company's agent[92] and not as agent of the lender, and the secured creditor is accordingly not responsible for the actions or defaults of the receiver or administrator. The receiver's role as agent of the company will also usually appear as a term of the security instrument under which he or she is appointed.

Enforcement of security

6.28 A secured creditor who wishes to enforce his or her security will usually consider appointing a receiver under a fixed charge or an administrator under a Qualifying Floating Charge.

---

[90] *White v City of London Brewery Co* (1889) 42 Ch D 237.
[91] *Silven Properties Limited v Royal Bank of Scotland plc* [2003] EWCA Civ 1409, [2004] 4 All ER 484.
[92] LPA 1925, s 109(2); IA 1986, Sch B1, para 69.

The advantages of appointing a receiver are:

- a receiver owes his or her primary duty to their appointer, whereas an administrator owes his or her duty to the creditors of the company generally. Unsecured creditors have a much greater say in the process of administration than they do in receivership;

- a receiver does not need to be a licensed insolvency practitioner. Many receivers appointed over property are surveyors;

- the costs and expenses of a receiver are likely to be less than those of an administrator. There is no equivalent regime of expenses in receivership, and the statutory obligations imposed on a receiver to creditors generally are significantly reduced;

- receivership is available wherever the company's Centre of Main Interests ('COMI') is located, whereas administration is only available if COMI is in the UK.

The advantages of administration over receivership are:

- it provides a moratorium, which gives the office-holder the opportunity to avoid the actions of other creditors who wish to assert their individual rights;

- IA 1986 gives an administrator the ability to take control of and sell the entire business and assets of the company[93] whereas a receiver's interest will be limited to the assets over which the lender has security;

- an administrator has all the powers set out in IA 1986[94], whereas a receiver relies very much on the extended powers set out in the security instrument under which he or she is appointed;

- an administrator may require a receiver appointed over a specific asset by another secured creditor to vacate office[95];

- administration is an internationally recognised process under the EC Regulation. This is vital where the company has assets situated in other European jurisdictions.

It is also possible for the court to appoint a receiver over a company's assets or certain of them, but where a creditor has his or her own security it is unlikely they would want to follow this course of action. It might however be relevant if the lender was concerned that its security was defective in any way. A court-appointed receiver derives his or her powers from the order under which he or she is appointed.

---

[93]   IA 1986, Sch 1.
[94]   Sch 1 and Sch B1.
[95]   IA 1986, Sch B1, para 41(2).

Receivership

6.29   A receiver appointed by the holder of a fixed charge owes his or her primary duty to their appointer as a matter of contract (under the terms of the appointment) and tort. The receiver's role is to procure repayment of the secured debt. This compares favourably for the purposes of the secured creditor to the role of an administrator, who must perform his or her functions in the interests of the company's creditors as a whole[96].

The receiver also owes certain duties to other persons who have an interest in the secured property or its equity of redemption, including the company itself[97], the holder of a lower ranking security[98] and a guarantor of the secured debt[99]. However he or she does not owe a duty to individual unsecured creditors or shareholders[100].

The secondary duties imposed on a receiver are:

- to act in good faith;

- to obtain the best price reasonably obtainable at the time on a sale of the charged property. In deciding when to sell, the receiver can give priority to the interests of the secured creditor[101], but once the decision to sell is made a receiver has a duty to other interested parties to expose the property to the market and sell it fairly;

- to manage property over which he or she is appointed with due diligence:

    — a receiver has no duty to carry on a business of a company, but if he or she does so they must take reasonable steps to do so profitably[102];

    — he or she must act and exercise their powers to preserve and protect the charged property; for example failing to trigger an advantageous rent review clause was found to be a breach of this duty[103].

The powers of a receiver are those given to him or her both by law and in the security instrument under which he or she is appointed. Powers given to a receiver under the LPA 1925 are limited to collecting rent and insuring the property[104], and so the security instrument invariably widens his or her powers, often so they are equivalent to the powers of an administrator set out in IA 1986, Sch 1.

---

[96]   IA 1986, Sch B1, para 3(2).
[97]   *Gomba Holdings Limited v Homan* [1986] 3 All ER 94.
[98]   *Midland Bank Limited v Joliman Finance Limited* (1967) 203 Estates Gazette 1039.
[99]   *Burgess v Augur, Burgess v Vanstock* [1998] 2 BCLC 478.
[100]   *Medforth v Blake* [1999] BCC 771.
[101]   *Silven Properties Limited v Royal Bank of Scotland plc* [2003] EWCA Civ 1409, [2004] 4 All ER 484.
[102]   *Medforth v Blake* [1999] BCC 771.
[103]   *Knight v Lawrence* [1991] BCC 411.
[104]   LPA 1925, s 109.

A secured creditor has the right to appoint a receiver in accordance with the terms of the relevant security instrument. Usually there must be a breach on the part of the company, and under most security agreements the lender will have to first of all make demand for payment on the company and give the company a reasonable time to pay the debt. A 'reasonable time' may only be the amount of time it takes for the company to arrange a bank transfer if demand is made in banking hours[105]. If the company has stated that it cannot meet the demand then the lender does not have to give the company even that amount of time before appointing[106]. Allowing the company less than one hour between demand and appointment does not invalidate the receivership.

The decision to appoint a receiver and the timing of it is a matter for the secured creditor only, and providing the terms of the security instrument are complied with, the decision to appoint cannot be challenged[107].

The actual appointment is made by the lender sending the receiver a written notice of appointment. The notice does not have to be by way of a deed[108] unless that is a term of the security instrument. It must state the property over which the receiver is to be appointed, and the powers he or she is entitled to exercise. If there are joint receivers it should also specify whether their powers are to be exercised jointly or if specific appointees will have specific powers. The receiver must accept the appointment before the end of the business day after the day on which he or she receives the appointment document[109], and if he or she accepts orally the receiver must confirm his or her acceptance in writing within seven days[110]. Providing the receiver complies with the statutory requirements, the appointment is made when he or she receives the appointment document[111].

If the appointment of the receiver is invalid, or he/she acts outside the scope of the powers given to him/her by the appointment, the receiver may be personally liable to the company for trespass or conversion. He or she cannot however be personally liable for wrongful interference with a company's contractual relations or commit an act of conversion with regard to a company's contractual rights[112]. Most receivers will ensure that the validity of their appointment is verified by solicitors before or shortly after their appointment, and they may require the secured creditor to provide them with a contractual indemnity which applies in the event of an invalid appointment. A clearing bank would not usually give such an indemnity, but other secured creditors may do so. A receiver can also apply to court for an order that the secured creditor who

---

[105]   *Cripps (Pharmaceutical) Limited v Wickendon* [1973] 2 All ER 606.
[106]   *Sheppard & Cooper Limited v TSB Bank plc* [1996] 2 All ER 654.
[107]   *Shamji v Johnson Matthey Bankers Limited* [1991] BCLC 36.
[108]   *Phoenix Properties Limited v Wimpole Street Nominees Limited* [1992] BCLC 737.
[109]   IA 1986, s 33(1)(a).
[110]   Rule 3.1.
[111]   IA 1986, s 33(1)(b).
[112]   *OBG Limited v Allan* [2005] EWCA Civ 106, [2005] QB 762.

appointed him or her provide an indemnity for liability arising solely as a result of an invalid appointment[113].

As stated above a receiver acts as agent of the company[114] notwithstanding that he or she is appointed by the secured lender. However the receiver's status as agent of the company is lost if the company goes into liquidation. The prior appointment of a receiver does not prevent a company from entering into administration, and there is no moratorium on other enforcement action in a receivership. A receiver who has been appointed does not automatically lose office on the appointment of an administrator, but can be required by an administrator to vacate office[115]. A receiver cannot be appointed once a company is in administration as a result of the moratorium[116]. Notice of the receiver's appointment must be filed at Companies House by the lender within seven days of the appointment[117]. In practice this is usually done by the receiver himself.

The directors will remain in office on the appointment of a receiver to manage any property not subject to the appointment, as the receiver's powers extend to dealing with the security property only.

The receivership will come to an end when the debt due to the secured lender has been repaid, or when the receiver has dealt with all of the security property and has distributed the proceeds to the secured lender and to anyone taking priority over him or her. The receiver does not have a duty to distribute any moneys to unsecured creditors. If there is a surplus after his or her appointer has been paid in full, the receiver must hand it to any subsequent secured creditor who ranks next in the order of priority, or to the company itself (or its administrator/liquidator if in office). The receiver must then file his or her final accounts at Companies House[118] and give notice to the registrar that he or she is no longer in office[119].

Administration

6.30   The process of administration is considered more fully in Chapter 1 and will not be considered further in this Chapter.

Financial Collateral Arrangements (No 2) Regulations 2003[120]

6.31   The purpose of the FCA Regulations was to implement an EC Directive setting out minimum criteria for the creation, perfection and enforcement of

---

[113] IA 1986, s 34.
[114] LPA 1925, s 109(2).
[115] IA 1986, Sch B1, para 41(2).
[116] IA 1986, Sch B1, para 43(1).
[117] CA 2006, s 871.
[118] IA 1986, s 38.
[119] CA 2006, s 871.
[120] SI 2003/3226 as amended.

security in the form of financial collateral throughout the EU. They apply to arrangements entered into on or after 26 December 2003 and include matters where a lender or creditor takes a security interest over financial collateral which is in the possession or control of the lender or creditor. 'Security interest' is defined to include a fixed or floating charge, a mortgage, a lien or a pledge. 'Financial collateral' is defined as cash, financial instruments or credit claims[121] including shares and equivalent securities.

Certain provisions of IA 1986 do not apply to security interests which fall under the FCA Regulations[122]. When a company is in administration the secured creditor can enforce its security without the consent of the administrator or permission of the court; the administrator cannot deal with the property; nor can he or she require a receiver appointed over the collateral to vacate office. Further, under FCA, reg 10 the prescribed part does not apply to any property that falls under the FCA Regulations, and any floating charge cannot be avoided under IA 1986, s 245.

Certain requirements relating to the perfection of security are also disapplied by the FCA Regulations. An agreement only has to be in writing and does not have to be signed. Also, a security interest will not be invalidated by failure to register it under CA 2006, s 860. In practice most lenders will perfect their security in the usual manner, but these exceptions to the usual position may provide a useful back-up if there has been any defect in standard procedure.

Assignment of security interests

6.32   A secured creditor will usually have the right under its security instrument to assign its interests to a third party without the company's consent. That provides an interested person with an opportunity to assert the control of a secured lender over the company, potentially with a view to acquiring an actual interest in the business itself.

A secured creditor may often be persuaded to assign its interest at a discount. If the lender faces a significant shortfall on the value of its security as against the level of its debt, it may prefer to receive a certain payment immediately rather than wait for an uncertain payment at an unknown point in the future. Accordingly it is not uncommon for lenders to assign their rights in loan or other funding agreements, and in the security instruments taken out to support the debt, to a third party at a significant discount. The new owner of the debt and security may then exercise all of the rights of the original lender, often with a view to taking either immediate steps to crystallise its new position in anticipation of making a quick profit, or with a more long-term view than the original creditor was willing to take.

---

[121]   Introduced by Financial Markets and Insolvency (Settlement Finality and Financial Collateral Arrangements) (Amendment) Regulations 2010 (SI 2010/2993).

[122]   Financial Collateral Arrangements (No 2) Regulations 2003 (SI 2003/3226), reg 8.

In either scenario there will be a period of uncertainty for the company and the prospect of a distressed sale of the business.

The position of a factor/invoice discounter

6.33   Factoring and invoice discounting are receivables financing procedures which involve a form of quasi-security. A company sells its book debts and other receivables at a discount to a finance company for immediate cash. In factoring the lender assumes responsibility for administering the company's sales ledger and collecting the debts, whereas in invoice discounting the company continues to administer its sales ledger and collect the debts. It then accounts to the finance company for the proceeds.

Under the terms of the financing agreement the company assigns its existing and future debts to the lender. There will be a number of other terms to deal with matters such as draw-down and repayment; acceptance or disapproval of debts; recourse; charges and interest; giving notice to customers (if factoring); provision of information to the lender; set-off; representations and warranties; term; termination provisions. Factoring and discounting is beneficial to the company as it enables it to raise funds quickly, and in a small organisation the company can outsource credit control. It is often available when more traditional sources of funds are not. However the charges can be high, and when collection of debts is out of the company's control it may find its customers complaining about methods of recovery employed. This will not apply to invoice discounting save in the event of default. In factoring, as notice of the assignment of debts is given to debtors the factor can immediately sue to recover moneys in its own name. Under an invoice discounting agreement notice is not given to debtors and the ability to sue remains with the company. The discounter can give notice of the assignment to a debtor and sue for the money owing in its own name, but before doing so it would usually give the company an option to repurchase the debt.

Most factors and invoice discounters will have the benefit of a debenture over the assets of a company, including the usual array of fixed and floating charges. However it is often the case that they will hold a second-ranking debenture behind the main funder, possibly a clearing bank. There will usually be a waiver and priority agreement in place with the first-ranking debenture holder. The waiver will provide that the first-ranking lender's prior charge over book and other debts which are assigned or to be assigned to the factor under the factoring or discounting agreement is waived so that the factor acquires the debt free of charge. The deed of priority will then typically provide that the factor has a first-ranking charge over book and other debts which fail to vest in it, and a second-ranking charge over all other assets. There may also be provisions regulating enforcement of the security, such as an obligation on each lender to give notice and/or to consult with the other before any enforcement steps are taken (save where assets are in jeopardy).

On any insolvency or distressed sale of a company or business, the position of a factor or invoice discounter has to be considered not only as secured creditor but also as one who has a particular relationship with the company's customers. A factor will already have a role in which it is engaged with the company's customers as it manages the sales ledger. That is not the case in a discounting arrangement, but as stated above the finance company may give notice to creditors and collect the company's debts itself, particularly in the event of default. The lender will not have a customer/supplier relationship to protect and may adopt an aggressive collection procedure with the company's customers. If the buyer of an insolvent business is looking to take over and build on the company's customer base this can be a damaging turn of events. It may be necessary for a buyer to ensure that any debt due to a factor or discounter is paid as part of the acquisition process to ensure that customer relationships are maintained. The insolvency of a company leading to the end of a factoring or invoice discounting arrangement may involve the company incurring significant termination charges which also have to be dealt with.

The position of a secured creditor

Introduction

6.34   Why is the position of a secured creditor so important in buying and selling insolvent companies? The key point is that a secured creditor has control over assets. Save for in certain circumstances in administration (see 6.37 below), a secured creditor must provide a release of its security over assets on a sale of a company or its property, or the buyer will acquire the assets subject to that security. No buyer would wish to acquire assets already charged to a third party, and no funder to the buyer would advance monies in circumstances where it could not obtain its own (usually) first ranking security interest in the assets after completion. A secured creditor will only generally provide a release on payment in full, or on being satisfied that there is no prospect of any greater recovery than that on offer. In some circumstances (a lien or pledge) the secured creditor will have possession of the company's assets and will not release them without payment. The same may apply to creditors with quasi-security such as retention of title creditors.

When structuring a transaction, the parties will have to consider the outcome for secured creditors. If the sale is proposed outside of a formal insolvency proceeding, the creditor will invariably want to measure the proposed outcome against that in insolvency to ensure that it results in an enhanced recovery for it. If a secured creditor is offered anything less than full repayment it will want to ensure that it is getting the best possible recovery.

Classes of assets

6.35   Reference has been made in this chapter to differing security interests and classes of assets that may be subject to security interests. When considering whether or not, and if so when, a secured creditor might be paid it is necessary

173

to consider the nature of both the security interest held by a creditor and the assets they attach to. It is also important to bear in mind those assets which appear to belong to the company but in fact do not, as a result of quasi-security interest. Any payment for assets subject to retention of title, factoring or invoice discounting, finance leasing, sale and leaseback, hire purchase or conditional sale agreements will be paid to the asset-owner and will not be available for the company's secured creditors at all.

A secured creditor with a fixed charge will be entitled to recover the entire proceeds of realisation of the asset, subject to the costs of realisation. A creditor with a floating charge will find his or her potential recoveries subject to the claims of preferential creditors, the prescribed part for unsecured creditors and costs and expenses of any insolvency proceeding. Where a creditor has a debenture including fixed and floating charges it is therefore vital to ascertain which assets are subject to a fixed charge and which are not. Then the value of each asset has to be determined and apportioned out of the total consideration. There may be competing interests if the company wants to put a low value on assets where a sale will result in a charge to capital gains tax, whereas the secured lender wants a high value as that asset is subject to a fixed charge. Each individual asset or class of assets will often have to be valued separately.

Order of priority of payment

6.36   On insolvency, subject to any agreement made between the creditors as to the ranking of their security, the usual order of priority of payment to creditors is as follows:

(1)   To holders of a fixed charge or those with a proprietary interest.

   The costs of realisation will usually be paid out of the proceeds of sale of a fixed charge asset, or one sold on behalf of the owner[123], but otherwise the secured creditor or owner will recover the entire sale proceeds to the extent that they are required to be paid to him or her to satisfy his or her debt.

(2)   Payment of the expenses of the insolvent estate.

   Costs and expenses are paid before the office-holder pays any other claims[124]. The expenses of an administration or liquidation are paid in a prescribed order of priority[125].

(3)   Payment of preferential claims.

   All preferential debts rank equally in priority[126].

(4)   Payment of the claims of the holders of floating charges.

---

[123]   *Re Berkeley Applegate (Investment Consultants) Limited* (No 2) (1988) 4 BCC 279.
[124]   IA 1986, s 155; IA 1986, Sch B1, paras 65 and 99.
[125]   Rule 2.67(1); rule 4.218(3).
[126]   IA 1986, s 175(2)(a); IA 1986, Sch B1, para 65(3).

Floating charge holders are paid in accordance with the relevant order of priority, determined either by the date of creation or as agreed between the secured creditors. Payment to floating charge creditors is subject to any prescribed part that is to be made available for the benefit of the company's unsecured creditors[127].

(5)   Payment of unsecured creditors.

Unsecured claims also rank equally for payment out of any remaining assets of the company. A secured creditor who has a shortfall under his or her security may make a claim as an unsecured creditor, but cannot participate in any distribution made out of the prescribed part[128] (save where it has released its security[129]).

(6)   Finally any remaining funds are returned to shareholders.

This is unusual where the company has been in an insolvency proceeding.

It is often the case that an estimated outcome statement, showing what the likely return to secured creditors would be in an insolvency scenario, has to be prepared and provided to a secured creditor to demonstrate to it that it will not be disadvantaged by a proposed sale of a business, either in or outside of an insolvency proceeding.

Administrators and secured creditors

6.37   Whilst it is usually necessary to obtain the consent of a secured creditor to a sale of assets, failing which the creditor may refuse to release his or her security, the provisions of IA 1986, Sch B1 provide a mechanism for an administrator to overcome any such difficulties.

An administrator may dispose of or take action in relation to property which is subject to a floating charge as if it were not subject to the charge[130]. This applies to a charge that was a floating charge on its creation[131], so it does not matter that the floating charge will have crystallised and taken on the characteristics of a fixed charge. Accordingly an administrator can sell floating charge assets without the secured creditor's consent. The floating charge creditor is protected by having the same priority in the proceeds of sale as he or she had in the property the administrator has sold[132].

127   IA 1986, s 176A.
128   *Re Permacell Finesse Ltd (in liquidation)* [2008] BCC 208; *Thorniley v HMRC* [2008] EWHC 124 (Ch), [2008] 1 WLR 1516.
129   *Robert Hunter Kelly and Jonathan Peter Sumpton (Liquidators of PAL SC Realisations 2007 Limited) v Inflexion Fund 2 Limited Partnership, Autocruise Co-Investment Limited Partnership* [2010] EWHC 2850 (Ch), [2011] BCC 93.
130   IA 1986, Sch B1, para 70(1).
131   IA 1986, Sch B1, para 111(1).
132   IA 1986, Sch B1, para 70(2).

6.37 *Secured Creditors*

An administrator may make an application to court for an order enabling him or her to dispose of property subject to security other than a floating charge as if it were not subject to the security[133]. The court must be satisfied that the sale would be likely to promote the purpose of administration[134]. The secured creditor is protected in this instance as it is a condition of any such order that the net proceeds of sale of the security property are paid to the secured creditor, together with any further amount required to bring the net proceeds of sale up to market value[135].

Similar provisions apply in relation to any property that is subject to a chattel-leasing agreement, retention of title agreement, hire-purchase agreement or conditional sale agreement[136].

These useful provisions enable an administrator to dispose of charged property, subject to the agreement of the court, in the absence of agreement from the secured creditor or owner. The creditor can oppose the application and/or produce evidence as to the true market value, but the court will assist the administrator if doing so would achieve the purpose of administration. The provisions of IA 1986, Sch B1, paras 70–72 should be borne in mind when structuring a transaction if secured creditors may be unwilling to co-operate.

Nevertheless it is always appropriate to seek the consent and approval of secured creditors to a transaction, usually at an early stage.

---

[133] IA 1986, Sch B1, para 71(1).
[134] IA 1986, Sch B1, para 71(2).
[135] IA 1986, Sch B1, paras 71(3), 111(1).
[136] IA 1986, Sch B1, paras 72, 111(1).

Chapter 7

Goodwill, Intellectual Property Rights and Data Protection Act Issues

This chapter examines the purchase of goodwill, intellectual property rights and also data protection issues on buying a business. An Appendix to the chapter sets out important Insolvency Service rules about re-use of a company name after a business goes under[1]. This book also includes as a precedent an example of an IPR assignment to which reference should be made (see Appendix, 'B. Assignment of intellectual property and rights').

Goodwill

7.1   A company which is failing may have much 'badwill'. Suppliers are cross they have not been paid. They are incensed about the powers of the administrator. Customers have not received the goods they have expected and may even be in danger of losing deposits paid up-front for goods or services. However, if the business acts soon enough much goodwill is preserved and often comprises a substantial part of the business sale.

Most sales of assets agreements set out in detail the assets to be transferred including the 'goodwill' and seek to define that term. Chapters 11 and 12 look at issues with customers and suppliers respectively.

A typical definition of 'goodwill' in a sale agreement might be:

> '**"Goodwill"** means the goodwill of the Business and the exclusive rights of the Buyer to represent itself as carrying on the Business in succession to the Seller, including, without limitation, the right to use the Name, all telephone numbers, fax numbers and e-mail addresses insofar as such rights are vested in and are capable of being transferred by the Seller.'

Goodwill would then be listed in the sale of assets clause as an item of the 'Assets' being sold. The Name in the definition above may be a registered trade mark, either a UK trade mark or even an EU-wide Community Trade Mark and/or foreign registered trade mark rights or could simply be goodwill built up in an unregistered trade mark which under English law could be a right to sue for passing off where someone misuses that unregistered trading name (which may also be an internet domain name).

---

[1]   March 2010 URN 10/831.

In each case an initial check can be made at www.ipo.gov.uk under Trade marks to search names and owners free of charge and also at companieshouse. gov.uk of course to check the corporate registrations of the limited company name/names and also check domain name ownership at www.whois.com[2].

Goodwill, VAT and transfer as a going concern

7.2   Probably the most important tax point relating to the business transfer agreement is to get the VAT treatment right. A person registered for VAT must, in principle, charge VAT on anything which is sold unless it is an exempt or zero-rated supply. VAT is not solely chargeable on the sale of stock; it is also chargeable on the sale of capital assets, be it the sale of a surplus typewriter or the goodwill of a business. However, relief is available where a business is sold as a going concern, which will often be the case, but it is important to distinguish this from cases where the seller is merely selling a collection of assets, and it is also important to be sure that the business is being sold as a going concern.

Administrators can be very difficult over confirming that the business they are selling has continued as a going concern, and this is a crucial issue to sort out early on in any purchase from them.

HMRC guidance states the following:

> **'The business, or part business, must be a "going concern" at the time of the transfer**. It can still be a "going concern" even though it is unprofitable, or is trading under the control of a liquidator or administrative receiver, or a trustee in bankruptcy, or an administrator appointed under the Insolvency Act 1986.'[3]

Article 5 of the VAT (Special Provisions) Order 1995 (SI 1995/1268) treats the supply of a business, or part of a business, as neither a supply of goods nor a supply of services provided that the necessary conditions are satisfied. The overriding condition is that the supply must consist of a transfer of a business (or part) as a going concern, but there are also special conditions in relation to land.

Article 5 is mandatory, so if an error is made in its application either the seller or purchaser can be at a severe financial disadvantage. For example, if a seller sells its business to a purchaser and charges VAT where it should not have been charged, HMRC may refuse to allow the purchaser to reclaim the VAT – ie they

---

[2]   www.whois.com will show owners of dot com domain names although the registration may be in the name of the website designer in some cases.

[3]   See HMRC 32-page guidance Transfer of business as a going concern (HMRC Reference: Notice 700/9 (April 2008)) at: http://customs.hmrc.gov.uk/channelsPortalWebApp/channels PortalWebApp.portal?_nfpb=true&_pageLabel=pageLibrary_ShowContent&id=HMCE_CL _000093&propertyType=document#downloadopt.

would disallow any input tax credit to the purchaser. Alternatively, if the seller sells business assets in a transaction which does not attract the relief and fails to charge VAT to the purchaser, HMRC will demand output tax from the seller which it may, depending on how the contract was worded, be in no position to recover from the purchaser, the presumption being that if the contract is silent on the point, the purchase price is VAT-inclusive.

The conditions contained in Article 5 involve determining questions of fact which may not be all that clear. In deciding whether a transaction amounts to a taxable supply, regard must be had to its substance rather than its form, and consideration must be given to all of the circumstances, weighing the factors which point in one direction against those which point in another. The points listed should be adopted as standard tests:

(a) the effect of the transfer must be to put the purchaser in possession of a business which can be operated as such – a sale of capital assets alone is not in itself enough;

(b) the assets transferred must be intended for use by the new owner in carrying on the same kind of business;

(c) there must be no significant break in the normal trading pattern before or immediately after the transfer;

(d) if only a part is being transferred, that part must be capable of operating alone; and

(e) the purchaser must be registered for VAT or, at the time of the transfer, become liable to be registered.

The overriding consideration is, of course, that the business must be a going concern at the time of the transfer and not a mere collection of assets. There is a restriction on the operation of Article 5 where land is concerned. The first point is to work out whether VAT will be charged on the sale of the land without Article 5. This would be the case either if the seller had made an election to charge VAT over the land (Value Added Tax Act 1994, Sch 10, para 2) or because it is the sale of the freehold of a new commercial building or civil engineering works (Value Added Tax Act 1994, Sch 9, Group 1, item 1). In these cases, the sale of the land will only be within Article 5 if the purchaser, normally before the date of the contract, both makes an election to charge VAT in respect of the land and has given written notification to HMRC. There are also anti-avoidance provisions in relation to elections over land and these need to be borne in mind as well.

The factors listed below are worth considering in order to determine whether the transaction is a transfer as a going concern. No one factor is conclusive – for example, the absence of the assignment of premises and outstanding contracts is not conclusive. Nevertheless, some factors will carry particular weight. Particular emphasis should be placed on the transfer of goodwill, the right to use the business name and the preservation of some continuity in the activities of the business.

What is stated in the written sale agreement?

- Is goodwill, intellectual property or know-how expressly or de facto transferred?

- Is the right to use the business name or the product names transferred and used?

- Is the equipment, outstanding contracts, specialists tools or trading stock taken over?

- Are customer lists transferred, and does the purchaser have the right to approach customers of the seller?

- Are existing staff employed by the purchaser? (This is more relevant in the case of expert staff but not so relevant in the case of unskilled or semi-skilled staff.)

- Is the business to be conducted by the purchaser in the same way as by the seller?

- Can the activities be carried on without interruption? (A short closure by the purchaser may not be enough to preclude a going concern.)

- What was stated in any advertising, and what is said or implied in any announcements to actual or potential customers?

These factors are listed in no order of priority. It is not necessary for them all to exist for Article 5 to apply, but they should allow the seller to build up the necessary overall picture. In cases of doubt a ruling should be obtained from HMRC prior to exchange of contracts.

All contracts for the transfer of a business should be carefully worded. Where acting for the seller, it is important that it is expressly stated that the price is VAT-exclusive (see Appendix, precedent 'A. Business transfer agreement', clause 5.1). The seller should reserve the right subsequently to charge VAT, and if possible this should cover both the charge to VAT and any penalty and interest which may be raised by HMRC (see Appendix, precedent 'A. Business transfer agreement', clause 6).

Where a business is transferred as a going concern the seller must notify HMRC in writing within 30 days that it has ceased to make or have any intention of making taxable supplies. This procedure should also be followed where part of a business is transferred as a going concern. Additionally, where a transfer of the whole business occurs, it is possible for the purchaser to take over the seller's old VAT registration number provided an appropriate application is made on behalf of both parties. The purchaser then assumes responsibility for submitting any tax returns due at the date of the transfer and accounting for any continuing tax liability. Both parties should give careful thought to these conditions and their inherent dangers. In practice, transferring registration in this way would be most relevant to transfers between related or friendly parties (eg in the context of family businesses or a group reorganisation). A purchaser would be ill-advised to agree to it in a transaction at arm's length, because it would also be taking over the seller's VAT liabilities.

As regards business records, these must be kept for six years unless HMRC have agreed a shorter period. The seller must transfer any VAT records it was obliged to keep to the purchaser unless, exceptionally, it applies to the local VAT office for permission to retain them. Permission may be forthcoming where only part of the business is sold and it would be impracticable to split the records. Either way, the seller would normally wish to reserve a right to access over any records that are taken over by the purchaser.

Intellectual property rights

7.3   Intellectual property rights exist in every business, as every business at the very least has a name. However, depending upon the nature of the business, intellectual property rights may or may not be a key asset. There are four main categories of intellectual property rights:

- copyright;

- designs (registered and unregistered – unregistered designs being called 'design right');

- patents; and

- trade marks.

Of these, registered designs, patents and trade marks are registered rights and title to them is determined conclusively by the state of the register kept by the appropriate body. A search of the appropriate registers at the Intellectual Property Office (www.ipo.gov.uk) will reveal UK rights. Some companies possess valuable know-how too, although this is not strictly in law a property right.

Assuming assets rather than shares are being purchased, an assignment of intellectual property ('IP') rights will be needed. Sometimes, if the rights are still owned by subcontractors an assignment from them is needed instead/as well. This book includes a sample IPR assignment precedent to which reference should be made (see Appendix, 'B. Assignment of intellectual property and rights').

Although there are no registers of copyright, unregistered design right and know-how, enquiry can be made of the management of the target to establish what unregistered IP rights exist and whether they have been challenged or enforced in the past.

Always ask who wrote the unregistered works, if they have the original drawings or designs and if they are dated. Also check if the person who wrote the unregistered works were an employee at the time of creation of the works. If not, for copyright, the ownership may remain with the consultant or other author and an assignment where possible may be necessary at the time of the acquisition. Ask what licences have been granted to third parties of the rights and check the terms of such licences. If revenue is paid under those licences, check if they may be terminated by the licensee in the event of a change of control or sale of the IP right, where an asset sale and if the licence is assignable.

If a business has IP as a principal asset, as is very much the case with a software company, for example, then even in insolvency situations the IP ownership position must be examined. At the very least ask:

(a)   Who wrote the software (which individual person – ie not their company or employer)?

(b)   Were they an employee or self-employed? And if self-employed, what written contract is there with the company for whom they did the work? (If there was none then the copyright probably remains with them and an assignment should be procured now, in writing, before the business is bought).

(c)   What existing licences of the IP have been granted, and are any exclusive?

(d)   Is the company sure it owns all rights in the IP, and are there any disputes with directors or shareholders over ownership of the IP?

(e)   What registered IP is there, and what are the registration numbers? (Then check the registrations.)

A common question is whether the insolvent business can continue with the same name when purchased by the ex-directors or shareholders. At the end of this chapter is the Insolvency Service guidance on this point[1]. The law restricts the re-use of a name previously used by a company that has gone into liquidation (Insolvency Act 1986, s 216). Chapter 3 dealt with section 216 in more detail. This restriction applies personally to a director of the company in liquidation. The name which cannot be used is known as the 'prohibited name'. This can be a danger area in the field of buying an insolvency business as an ex-director, so it is best to take legal advice in cases of doubt.

The business is likely to have a name which the buyer may wish to continue to use after the purchase. Below is a typical clause an administrator might use in this regard in the sale agreement:

1.   'NAME

1.1   So far as the Seller can legally grant it, the Buyer shall be entitled to use the Name in connection with the operation of the Business by the Buyer.

1.2   The Buyer acknowledges that:

(a)   it is aware that the Name is not a registered trade mark;

(b)   the Name has never been registered as a trading name; and

(c)   no warranties, guarantees, representations or statements of any kind whatsoever have been given or made to it by or on behalf of the Seller (or by anyone else) as to their having any proprietary or other rights to or in respect of the Name.'

Compared with a non-insolvency situation, very little is warranted above. Of course if the name is a registered trade mark then this would alter the words above. Buyers can check free online if a mark is a UK-registered trade mark or not at www.ipo.gov.uk.

Data Protection Act 1998

7.4   On buying a business the buyer will have access to personal data about living individuals from the seller, and this must be handled carefully under the Data Protection Act 1998. In addition, an asset of the business might be data protected by the Act, and indeed in many purchases in the dot com boom/bust the only asset the buyers could purchase from an administrator was a customer list of individuals' data which, technically in law, there was no right to pass on without a breach of the Act, although many such sales did, however, proceed.

If any of the information is 'personal data' under the Data Protection Act 1998 then it should not be used other than in accordance with that Act. Information such as employee home addresses, wages and sickness records should be disclosed only under conditions of confidence, and even then the Act may be breached if the individuals have not given consent, such as a general data-protection consent to future processing, when they joined the company. Wherever possible, anonymised and sample employment contracts and details should be supplied with the aim of ensuring that the data is not identifiable as relating to particular individuals. A new draft EU data protection regulation has been proposed (in 2012) but it is still not law. However do check the up to date rules in force from time to time.

Information Commissioner's Office *The Employment Practices Code* addresses these issues in relation to mergers, etc. Paragraphs 2.12 provide as follows:

'2.12 Merger, acquisition, and business re-organisation

Business mergers and acquisitions will generally involve the disclosure of information about workers. This may take place during evaluation of assets and liabilities prior to the final merger or acquisition decision. Once a decision has been made disclosure is also likely to take place either in the run-up to or at the time of the actual merger or acquisition. A similar situation arises in business re-organisations that involve the transfer of workers' employment from one legal entity to another. This sub-section of the Code will be relevant to such situations.

2.12.1 Ensure, wherever practicable, that information handed over to another organisation in connection with a prospective acquisition, merger or business re-organisation is anonymised.

Key points and possible actions

- Ensure that in any merger or acquisition situation, those responsible for negotiation are aware of the Code, including its provisions on sensitive data.

- Assess any request for personal information from the other organisation. If at all possible, limit the information given to anonymised details.

2.12.2 Only hand over personal information prior to a final merger or acquisition decision after securing assurances that it will be used solely for the evaluation of assets and liabilities, it will be treated in confidence and will not be disclosed to other parties, and it will be destroyed or returned after use.

Key points and possible actions

- Remind those negotiating that they must receive strict assurances about how personal information will be used and what will happen to it should discussions end.

- Consider setting up a "data room" with accompanying rules of access.

2.12.3 Unless it is impractical to do so, tell workers if their employment records are to be disclosed to another organisation before an acquisition, merger or re-organisation takes place. If the acquisition, merger or re-organisation proceeds make sure workers are aware of the extent to which their records are to be transferred to the new employer.

Key points and possible actions

- In some circumstances "insider trading" or similar restrictions will apply. An example is where providing an explanation to workers would alert them to the possibility of a takeover of which they would otherwise be unaware and could thereby affect the price of a company's shares. The obligation to provide an explanation to workers is lifted in such circumstances.

2.12.4 Where a merger, acquisition or re-organisation involves a transfer of information about a worker to a country outside the European Economic Area (EEA) ensure that there is a proper basis for making the transfer.

Key points and possible actions

- Review the Information Commissioner's guidance at *www.ico. gov.uk: Data Protection: Your Legal Obligations: International Transfers* if you intend to pass workers' information outside the EEA.

- Check that there is a legal basis for the transfer that you intend to make.

2.12.5 New employers should ensure that the records they hold as a result of a merger, acquisition or re-organisation do not include excessive information, and are accurate and relevant.

Key points and possible actions

- Remember that a new employer's use of workers' information acquired as the result of a merger, acquisition or re-organisation is constrained by the expectations the workers will have from their former employer's use of information.

- When taking over an organisation assess what personal information you now hold as outlined in 0.3 and 0.4 (see pages 10 and 11 [*of the Code*]).'

The *Supplementary Guidance* provides:

'2.12 Merger, acquisition and re-organisation

2.12.1 Wherever practicable, information from which individual workers cannot be identified should be used, so details such as names and individual job titles should be omitted. This might be possible where, for example, a company merely wants to know how many workers of a particular type are employed and their average rates of pay. In other cases a company might require detailed information about particular workers in order to appraise a company's human resources assets properly. This might be the case where the expertise or reputation of individual workers has a significant bearing on the value of the company. Similarly where a company has a significant liability, perhaps as the result of a worker's outstanding legal claim, it may have to disclose information identifying the worker with details of the company's liability.

In some cases even the removal of names from the information will not prevent identification, for example where without a name it is still obvious that the information relates to a particular senior manager. Removal of names may nevertheless help protect privacy, even if identification is still possible.

Remember that handing over sickness records will entail the processing of sensitive personal data (see page 72 [*of the Supplementary Guidance*]).

2.12.2 It is important to gain formal assurances about how the information will be used. Information should be returned or destroyed by the shredding of paper or the expunging of electronic files, should the merger or acquisition not go ahead. The provision of information is sometimes achieved by the use of a "data room" in which information about the business is made available to prospective purchasers. Strict conditions must be accepted by those granted access to the "data room".

2.12.3 Businesses may not always expect to be involved in mergers, acquisitions or reorganisations and may not therefore have told their workers, at the time they were recruited, what would happen to their personal information in such an event. Reasons of commercial confidentiality and legal duties relating to matters such as "insider trading" may make it difficult to be explicit at the time the merger or acquisition is being considered. In some circumstances the corporate finance exemption in the Act may be relevant and may relieve companies of the obligation to inform workers of the disclosure of their information. This could occur, for example, where providing an explanation to workers could affect the price of a company's shares or other financial instruments.

One business may also be under a legal obligation to disclose to another. Where there is a legal obligation to disclose, there is an exemption from some of the provisions of the Act. The employer is relieved of the obligation to inform workers of the disclosure if this would be inconsistent with the disclosure, perhaps because it would breach commercial confidentiality. The processing of sensitive personal information involved in a disclosure related to an acquisition or merger must satisfy a sensitive data condition. This will not be an obstacle where there is an employment related legal obligation on one business to disclose to another, but may well prevent the disclosure of sensitive personal information in the run up to a merger or acquisition where there is no such obligation and the worker has not been asked for and given explicit consent.

See page 72 [of the *Supplementary Guidance*] for conditions to be satisfied.

2.12.4 The Act imposes restrictions on the transfer of personal information to countries outside the EEA. Countries in the EEA are the member states of the European Union together with Iceland, Norway and Liechtenstein. The Information Commissioner provides separate detailed guidance on international transfers The European Commission provides both a model contract that can be used to legitimise a transfer outside the EEA and a list of countries outside the EEA that are deemed to provide adequate protection by virtue of their data protection law. The European Commission has also entered into a special arrangement with the USA known as "the safe harbor".

See the Information Commissioner's website: *www.ico.gov.uk: Data Protection: Your Legal Obligations: International Transfers.* The European Commission website is at www.europa.eu.int/comm/internal_market/privacy/index_en.htm

2.12.5 It is the new employer who now has a responsibility for the type and extent of personal information retained and who will have liability for it under the Act. The new employer must not assume that the personal information it receives from the original employer is accurate or relevant and not excessive in relation to its purposes. Within a few months of the merger or takeover it should review the records it has acquired, for example by checking the accuracy of a sample of records with the workers concerned and should make any necessary amendments.

This ICO guidance helps ensure those purchasing insolvent businesses comply with data protection legislation. In many cases there will not be much time or opportunity, however, to engage in large amounts of due diligence, particularly in flat-pack administration purchases. In those cases, at the very least seek to ensure that:

(a)   if a large part of what is being bought is mailing lists that those on the lists consented to their data being passed to the buyer of assets of that business; and

(b)   caution is exercised in undertaking due diligence to restrict what personal data is examined and in particular disclosed before a sale, and ensure a confidentiality agreement is signed. Few sellers would omit to require a buyer to sign a confidentiality agreement in any event.

Data protection clause example

7.5   Below is an example of a data protection clause from an agreement for sale of a business from administrators:

'DATA PROTECTION

1.1   The Buyer agrees to comply with the provisions of the Data Protection Act 1998 when dealing with any Personal Data.

1.2   The Buyer agrees that it shall, within two months of the Transfer Date, write to all those natural persons whose details are recorded on the Databases to notify them (at least in general terms) of their rights under part II of the Data Protection Act 1998.

1.3   The Buyer shall not transfer any Personal Data (including, without prejudice to the generality of the foregoing, the Databases) outside the European Economic Area without first obtaining the specific written consent of the subjects of that Personal Data.

1.4   The Buyer shall indemnify and keep indemnified the Administrators and each of them against any Liabilities arising from or in relation to a failure by the Buyer to comply with the terms of this Clause.'

Summary

7.6   This chapter has examined goodwill, intellectual property rights and data protection issues in relation to business purchases. The buyer from an administrator may not have large amounts of time to undertake due diligence in these areas. However some checks, as has been seen, are easy to undertake and this should be done.

Appendix

7.7

Insolvency Service Guidance on 'Re-use of a company name after liquidation' (March 2012 URN 12/640)

The law restricts the re-use of a name previously used by a company that has gone into liquidation (section 216 of The Insolvency Act 1986). This restriction applies personally to a director of the company in liquidation. The name which can't be used is known as the "prohibited name".

This leaflet explains what re-use of a prohibited name means. It does not give a complete list of everything you must and must not do, nor does it give you legal advice.

To understand exactly how the restrictions affect you, you should always take your own independent professional advice.

What is a prohibited name?

A prohibited name is a name by which the liquidated company was known at any time in the 12 months immediately before the liquidation: whether this is its registered name at Companies House, or its trading name, or any name so similar to its registered or trading name as to suggest an association with the liquidated company.

Who is restricted?

The restriction applies to a person who was registered as a director or acted as a director of the company in liquidation at any time during the 12 months immediately before the liquidation.

What is the restriction?

For 5 years from the date of liquidation, you are not permitted to be a director of or take part in the promotion, formation or management of a limited company that is using a prohibited name. In addition you may not be concerned in or take any part in carrying on a business that is using a prohibited name if the business is not a limited company (for example, if it is a partnership or sole trader).

What is an example of a prohibited name?

Say the company in liquidation was registered at Companies House as ABC Limited and it used the trading name XYZ, then the following would apply:

- The registered name ABC Limited or XYZ Limited would be prohibited.

- The trading name ABC or XYZ would be prohibited.

- The trading name ABC or XYZ used by an unincorporated business (such as a sole trader or partnership) would be prohibited.

- If a company or business had a registered name or trading name so similar as to suggest an association with ABC or XYZ, the name would be prohibited.

Exceptions

There are three exceptions to the restrictions on the re-use of a prohibited name.

First exception: Sale of business

You may use the name if you are or intend to be a director of a company or are or intend to be proprietor of a business and the company or business buys the whole, or substantially the whole, of the business of the company in liquidation from the liquidator. If this happens or is intended to happen under arrangements made by an administrator, administrative receiver or supervisor of a voluntary arrangement of the insolvent company, you must use a prescribed form (form 4.73) to publish a Notice in the Gazette and also send it to all creditors known to you or whose names and addresses could be obtained by you by making reasonable enquiries. The prescribed form 4.73 can be downloaded through the following internet link: http://www.opsi.gov.uk/si/si2007/uksi_20071974_en_1 The Notice may be published and given before the completion of the sale arrangements but must be published and given no later than 28 days after completion.

Second exception: Immediate application to court for permission

You can get permission from the court to use the prohibited name. You should apply to the court within 7 business days of the liquidation. If you apply within that time, you may carry on using the prohibited name for 6 weeks from the date of the liquidation or until the court decides whether to grant you permission, whichever is the earlier. It is important that your application is heard within the 6 weeks; otherwise the restriction will again apply to you.

The court can grant permission at any time during the 5 years that a name is prohibited, but it cannot retrospectively authorise use of a prohibited name for any time during the period before it gave permission.

If a company has gone into compulsory liquidation (i.e. your company in liquidation was wound up in the court and was dealt with by the official receiver), you should apply for permission to the same court that made the winding-up order. If a company has gone into voluntary liquidation, you should apply for permission to any county court in the area where the company traded, as long as that county court has the jurisdiction to wind up companies.

If you apply to the court for permission to use a prohibited name, you should send a copy of your application to Hotline and S216(3) Applications Team, 3rd Floor, Cannon House, 18 Priory Queensway Birmingham B4 6FD. Email: intelligence.live@insolvency.gsi.gov.uk. This is because the court may call on the liquidator, or any former liquidator, to report the circumstances in which the liquidated company became insolvent, and the extent (if any) of your responsibility for the insolvency.

Third exception: Previous use of name by another company or business

The restriction on the re-use of a prohibited name does not apply to you if you are a director of another company that has used a prohibited name continuously for 12 months up to the date of the liquidation of the liquidated company. In these specific circumstances your use of a name would not be prohibited, even though the name was also used by the liquidated company. However, your company must have been actively trading during the whole of the 12 months up to the date of the liquidation of the liquidated company, and must have used the name during the whole of that period. If your company was dormant (not actively trading) during any part of the 12 months or used the name during only part of the period, then the restriction will apply and you will not be allowed to re-use the prohibited name, without the permission of the court.

Penalties

If you contravene section 216 of the Act, you are committing a criminal offence. You may be prosecuted by the Department for Business Innovation and Skills and could go to prison if you are convicted. In addition, under section 217 of the Act you could be made personally liable for the debts incurred during the time that you were involved in managing a business using a prohibited name, even if it was a limited company. This could happen whether you are prosecuted under section 216 or not.

Employee who helps someone else contravene section 216

Even if you are not contravening section 216 of the Act, you will be personally liable for the debts of a company if you are involved in managing a business and you act on instructions from someone you know is contravening section 216. This is because you are helping someone to commit a criminal offence by contravening section 216.

Where can I find out more?

Our publications give more details of insolvency procedures. You can obtain further copies of this publication from The Insolvency Service website: http://www.insolvency.gov.uk/. All our publications are also available on this website.For general enquiries you can contact The Insolvency Service Insolvency Enquiry Line on 0845 602 9848 or email Insolvency.EnquiryLine@ insolvency.gsi.gov.uk.Please note that the Enquiry Line can only give general information about insolvency. If your query relates to a specific case then you should either contact the officer dealing with that case or obtain independent professional advice as appropriate.Her Majesty's Courts and Tribunals Service publishes a series of information publications and contact details on their website at: http://www.justice.gov.uk/global/contacts/hmcts/index.htm.This leaflet provides general information only. Every effort has been made to ensure that the information is accurate, but it is not a full and authoritative statement of the law and you should not rely on it as such. The Insolvency Service cannot accept any responsibility for any errors or omissions as a result of negligence or otherwise.

(March 2012 version)

Chapter 8

Excluded Assets

Introduction

8.1   The sale and purchase of an insolvent business usually takes place very quickly. Timing is often critical to the seller, who will often be in the position of having little or no funding to carry on the business. There might be pressure to pay certain crucial liabilities on time, including employees and key suppliers, either of which could walk away if left unpaid so destroying much of the value of the business. Other pressing creditors such as landlords and retention of title suppliers can be kept at bay for a time by way of the moratorium that arises on administration[1], or the interim moratorium that arises on filing a Notice of intention to appoint an administrator or making an administration application[2] pending the appointment of an administrator taking place. There can be a very short period of time for the parties to agree which assets are to be included in the sale and which are to be excluded from it, and the speed of the transaction may mean that is a significant amount of work to do post-completion to perfect the transfer of the included assets, such as the assignment of property leases, obtaining consent to use licences and/ or intellectual property, or the novation of contracts. There is unlikely to be a delay between exchange and completion during which such matters might otherwise be dealt with.

Agreement on included and excluded assets can be a vital part of the sale transaction, particularly if the sale is of a division or part of the seller's business only. All assets which the seller needs to carry on the remaining part of its business must be excluded from the sale. If both parties wish or need to use the same asset (for example the business name, or intellectual property rights) then licensing arrangements will have to be agreed.

Even if the buyer is acquiring the whole of the seller's business certain assets will necessarily be excluded from the sale, particularly by an office-holder. The buyer will want to ensure that it does not acquire liabilities it was not expecting and did not bargain for when it agreed the price.

The seller, if in an insolvency process, will only sell whatever right, title and interest it has in the assets that are sold, and the risk of assets being excluded

---

[1]   IA 1986, Sch B1, para 43.
[2]   IA 1986, Sch B1, para 44.

as the seller did not have title to them will usually fall on the buyer. The sale agreement will be drafted in favour of the seller, often providing that such interest in the assets that the seller purports to transfer will be sold subject to all claims that third parties may have to them. The buyer will agree that if the seller does not have title, or such title as it has is subject to any third-party interest, the buyer cannot rescind the contract and will not be entitled to a reduction in the purchase price. The seller will not provide any warranties as to title, and the time for the buyer to carry out due diligence and the information provided to it will invariably be limited.

The buyer will also be aware that an administrator acts as agent of a seller in administration, and that the office holder will exclude all liability that may arise against him or her personally in the terms of the sale agreement. Accordingly even if the seller does breach the agreed sale terms and a claim arises against it, that claim will almost undoubtedly be against the insolvent seller only, rather than against the administrator, his or her firm, or his or her insurers.

Book debts

8.2   Book debts are often a key and valuable asset of the seller, and one of the main benefits of a sale of an insolvent business as a going concern will be to enhance the recovery of book debts and retentions. It is well known as a matter of practice that where a company gets into financial difficulties or enters into an insolvency procedure, and there is any threat of a breakdown in continuity of supply of goods or services whether in the immediate or long-term future, debtors will use that as a reason to avoid payment. Customers will often assert counterclaims and set-offs against debts, whether those counterclaims are genuine current claims that can be demonstrated as having arisen before the financial difficulties arose, or are anticipated claims that might arise in the future in relation to defects or losses that have not yet occurred. As a result the collection of book debts due to an insolvent business can often be difficult.

It is a matter of negotiation between a seller and buyer as to whether or not book debts are sold. First of all the seller may not have title to book debts if they are subject to a factoring or invoice discounting agreement, and those debts which the seller does own may be those debts transferred back to it for the very reason that they are old and/or subject to disputes and difficult to recover.

If the seller is willing to transfer its book debts it will want to transfer them for full value. An office-holder appointed to the company has a duty to realise the assets of the company at the best possible price for the benefit of the company's creditors. The buyer will of course want to acquire them at a discount to reflect the risk of disputes, non-payment and set-offs. The result is that book debts are often not transferred to the buyer, although the buyer may be authorised to collect them on behalf of the seller for a fee or a commission.

As part of the sale agreement the buyer will usually take possession of the seller's non-statutory books and records, and having acquired the goodwill of the business it will be in contact with customers and promoting itself as carrying on the business. Employees with knowledge of customer relationships and the sales ledger may have transferred to the buyer under TUPE. The buyer is often therefore in a better position to collect the debts than the seller. However the seller will want to retain control over how the buyer deals with debtors. The seller no longer has an ongoing relationship with customers to protect, and would usually wish to take an aggressive attitude to debt collection after a sale of its business. The buyer is trying to establish relationships and would usually prefer to take a much more conciliatory line. Therefore the sale agreement may provide that the seller retains ownership of the debts but the buyer is authorised to collect them. Financially this may not be ideal for the buyer notwithstanding the potential longer term gain from the commission, as it may incur up-front collection costs in the short term. However the ability to control the collection of debts and ensure that an aggressive approach is not automatically taken in every instance against its new customers may mean it is worth incurring the cost at a time when customer relationships may be vulnerable.

Money collected will be held on trust for the seller pending payment of the proceeds across to it, and the buyer will usually be obliged to provide statements showing recoveries, and to pass moneys received to the seller on a regular basis. If an ongoing customer pays any debt to the buyer, the sale agreement may well provide for payment to be allocated to moneys due to the seller first of all, and the buyer will not be permitted to compromise or discount debts over a certain level without the seller's consent.

The seller will also usually be able to take back control of collection of the debts if it is not satisfied that the buyer is taking appropriate or sufficient steps to collect them. In that event, or if the seller retained the benefit of the book debts from the outset, the buyer may seek to impose some restrictions on the seller, for example:

- an agreed process of debt collection;
- an undertaking not to commence court proceedings against a debtor for an agreed period of time;
- an agreement that the seller will:
  - give notice to the buyer before it commences any court proceedings against a debtor; and/or
  - it will offer a debt for sale to the buyer before it commences any court proceedings against the debtor.

Books and records

The company's books and records

8.3   Where the buyer is acquiring the business and certain assets of the company rather than the company itself it will not acquire ownership or possession of the seller's statutory books.

The buyer will want to have access to other books and records of the company, including items such as sales ledgers, supplier and customer lists, and employee records. Unfortunately the seller, and in particular any office-holder appointed to it, will also want access to the same company books and records in order that he or she can deal with claims made against the company and carry out his or her investigations into events before his or her appointment and into the reasons for the company failure. There are clear competing interests, and the question of how an administrative receiver should deal with a company's books and records after a sale of its business[3] forms part of the subject matter of one of the Statements of Insolvency Practice which office-holders are required to adhere to as best practice.

The usual compromise is for the seller to retain ownership of the company's non-statutory books and records but to hand possession of them over to the buyer, perhaps for a limited period of time. This is subject to a further term that the buyer will allow the seller and any office-holder appointed to it to have access to the books and records to inspect and copy them as they may reasonably require. The buyer will usually be obliged to provide adequate facilities to the seller to enable inspection and copying to proceed efficiently.

If the company's books and records are computerised and held electronically this problem may be overcome by the seller taking and retaining an image of its records,[4] which means that both parties will have identical copies.

Where a business is sold as a going concern and the buyer takes over the seller's VAT registration, the obligation to maintain and preserve such records as is required by the Value Added Tax Act 1994 will fall on the buyer[5]. VAT records will be excluded from the sale but possession will necessarily be handed over to the buyer subject to a term that the buyer will allow the seller and any office-holder appointed to it to have access to the books and records to inspect and copy as they may reasonably require. If the buyer does not take over the seller's VAT registration (which would be the usual scenario in an insolvency sale), both ownership and possession of the VAT records will be retained by the seller.

The office-holder's books and records

8.4   If an office-holder is appointed to the seller, different classes of records will be in his or her possession. SIP 17 identifies the following in relation to an administrative receivership. It is likely that the same classes of records will apply in administration:

- Company records maintained prior to the office-holder's appointment. These will comprise the statutory books of the seller and the accounting and all other non-statutory records, such as the sales ledgers, supplier and customer lists and employee records.

---

3   SIP 17, paras 13–19.
4   Subject to the provisions of the Data Protection Act 1998.
5   Value Added Tax Act 1994, s 49 and Sch 11, para 6.

- The statutory books and records must be kept at the company's registered office[6], and as noted above will be excluded from the sale. Ownership of all other accounting and non-statutory records may be retained by the seller but possession subject to appropriate terms may be given to the buyer. A liquidator appointed in due course is entitled to such records.

- Company records generated from the time of the office-holder's appointment. These are records which are generated for accounting purposes or as a result of the company carrying on its business. A liquidator is also entitled to such records, and they should also be excluded from the sale, but possession subject to appropriate terms may be given to the buyer.

- The office-holder's personal records. These are the records the office-holder generates in the course of carrying out his or her duties, and relate to the office-holder's appointment and the duties and obligations arising out of it. These records are his or her personal property and should be excluded from the sale and not provided to the buyer.

Business name

8.5   The name of an established and reputable company or business is often a significant part of its goodwill, and a valuable asset available to be sold, particularly where it is one which brings with it notions such as customer confidence, reliability and prestige. The failure of the business may not affect such notions and the seller and buyer will want to make the most of their value. However where the seller is part of a group which carries on its entire business under the same name, it may wish to exclude the name from the sale to maintain control of the name and associated branding within the group. Or the seller may wish to retain ownership of the name but license the buyer to use it on terms. The buyer may well want to exclude the business name from the sale if it believes that the seller's failure has tarnished the name irreparably and it has no wish to make use of it in the future.

If the buyer acquires the name of the seller the directors of an insolvent seller will need to take note of the provisions of IA 1986[7] in relation to the re-use of company names if they are, or intend to act as, directors of the buyer, or to be in any way, whether directly or indirectly, concerned or take part in the promotion, formation or management of the buyer.

Cash

8.6   Cash at the bank or elsewhere will almost always be an excluded asset. In some situations cash may be transferred to the buyer on a pound for

---

[6]   CA 2006, s 1136.
[7]   IA 1986, s 216 and s 217.

pound basis, for example where it is a till float, or petty cash that is needed for use immediately post completion.

Claims

8.7 All claims against third parties, policies of insurance, and the proceeds of claims will usually be excluded, save for claims relating specifically to the assets that are transferred (such as warranty claims against manufacturers).

The right to pursue claims in the name of the company is often a useful asset to an office-holder. They may be set off against claims made against the company in administration[8] and liquidation[9] to reduce the level of creditor claims and enhance distributions to other creditors.

Claims vested in the seller may also be the subject of a separate sale to a buyer by way of an assignment of a chose in action. The buyer may be willing to pursue a claim at its own cost and risk when the insolvent company itself cannot do so because of a lack of funding. An office-holder can either assign the balance remaining due to the seller once insolvency set-off has been applied[10], or if there is no set-off he or she can assign the entire claim. Or the office-holder can assign the proceeds of a claim[11]. The terms of any sale can vary such that the buyer either pays a fixed price on completion of the assignment of a claim (or on making a recovery), or a percentage of net recoveries.

The office-holder cannot assign the right to bring and prosecute a claim that vests in him or her personally under the provisions of IA 1986[12].

Customer contracts

8.8 Whilst many sale agreements provide for all customer contracts to be assigned to the buyer on completion, that need not be the case. If the seller is carrying on a part of its business it may want to exclude certain contracts from the sale where there is a significant realisation to be made with little or no further cost to incur. The buyer may want to exclude certain contracts where there are significant actual or potential liabilities attaching to them and little or no reward to be earned. Whether the parties can agree a schedule of transferring contracts to attach to the sale agreement as a definitive statement of which contracts form part of the sale and which do not may well depend on the amount of time available to them, and the amount and quality of

---

[8] Rule 2.85.
[9] Rule 4.90.
[10] *Stein v Blake* [1995] 2 All ER 961.
[11] *Glegg v Bromley* [1912] 3 KB 474, CA.
[12] *Ruttle Plant Hire Ltd v Secretary of State for Environment, Food and Rural Affairs* [2008] EWHC 238 (TCC), [2009] 1 All ER 448.

information provided by the seller to the buyer for the purpose of carrying out due diligence.

In order to effectively transfer the benefit and burden of a contract, the parties will need to enter into a novation agreement.

Intellectual property rights

8.9   It would be usual for a sale agreement and assignment to transfer intellectual property rights ('IPR') to the buyer. However where the seller is transferring a part of its business only it needs to consider whether it needs to retain IPR or part of it, and if necessary enter into a license arrangement with the buyer to enable it to exploit the IPR.

The buyer also needs to consider and investigate whether the seller is the owner of the IPR and can transfer it in any event. It can carry out searches of the relevant registers. IPR may be excluded from the sale simply because it is not owned by the seller but instead has vested in an individual (perhaps one of the directors of the seller) or in a different company, such as a holding company which might then licence use of the IPR amongst the members of the group.

Similar considerations may apply to domain names and links and websites.

Plant and machinery

8.10   Plant and machinery in the ownership of the seller will usually transfer to the buyer as part of the sale agreement. However assets of this nature are often subject to lease, hire purchase or other similar financial arrangements and title may be held by a lender to the company.

If there is substantial equity in the plant and machinery the seller may consider repaying any outstanding finance on it such that title passes to the seller, and it can then be transferred to the buyer. Otherwise the seller must exclude all financed assets and other third-party assets from the sale. The sale agreement will provide that the buyer acquires no interest in third-party assets and that it holds them as bailee. The buyer will have no right to take possession of or make use of financed or third-party assets and will not be permitted to sell, charge or otherwise create any encumbrance over them. Typically the buyer will be required to provide access to third-party assets to the seller, any office-holder and the owner and to deliver them up to, or make them available for collection by, the owner. The buyer will usually also be required to provide the seller and any office-holder with an indemnity in relation to any claims that arise in relation to third-party assets after completion.

If the buyer wishes to make use of plant and machinery that is subject to finance, or any other third-party assets, it will need to negotiate a novation of any finance agreements with the owner, or enter into a new agreement with it.

In the absence of suitable arrangements being made with the lender, the owner is likely to make arrangements to collect and sell its assets and make a claim against the seller in respect of any shortfall.

It may be necessary for the parties to agree schedules of that plant and machinery and any other third-party assets to be transferred to the buyer as part of the sale, and that which is not.

Premises

8.11   One of the most significant assets on the sale of an insolvent company or business may be its premises.

The value of the company's land, whether freehold or leasehold, will depend very much on current property market conditions at the time of the sale. It will however often be less susceptible to the stresses caused by the failure of the company. The buyer may offer a low price with a view to persuading the seller that it should accept it to achieve a quick sale, and a 'forced sale' transfer of premises by an office holder will usually result in a lower value than a sale as part of a going concern on the open market by a willing seller. Other than that, premises will be valued very much in accordance with market conditions.

Subject to agreement on price there is usually no bar to the sale of freehold premises by a company or office-holder in an insolvency situation. It may take some time for the usual searches to be obtained, but other than that there is no reason why a freehold sale cannot proceed quickly.

That may not be the case with leasehold premises. The buyer often wishes to retain the company's leasehold premises, certainly in the short term, either with a view to persuading customers that there will be a seamless transfer of the business into new ownership or simply because it does not have the time to find new premises and agree terms with the new landlord. Most leases can be assigned but only with the landlord's consent, and this can take time to obtain and may be subject to conditions. The mechanics of dealing with the assignment of a lease and the problems that can arise will be considered further in Chapter 13, but for the time being it should be noted that leasehold premises in particular are often excluded from the sale of a business, certainly on the day on which the transaction generally is completed.

Retention of title assets

8.12   When specific goods are sold under a contract title to the goods passes from the supplier to the customer when the parties intend it to pass[13]. Many standard terms and conditions of supply include a retention of title ('ROT')

---

[13]   Sale of Goods Act 1979, s 17.

clause which provides that title to goods does not pass from the supplier to the customer until either the goods supplied have been paid for, or all sums due from the supplier to the customer have been paid.

Until such time as payment is made the customer holds the goods as bailee for the supplier, and although the customer is able to use the goods in the ordinary course of its business the supplier retains ownership until such time as title passes either on payment or as a matter of law as the goods are used. Many ROT terms will also provide that the supplier should store the goods separately from other stock; mark them as the supplier's property; and provide the supplier with rights of access permitting it to attend on the customer's premises to inspect and collect its goods if payment is not made.

The object of an ROT clause is to give the supplier priority over secured and unsecured creditors if the customer fails to pay for the goods because it is insolvent, or for some other reason which may be specified in the clause. ROT provisions have limitations. They must be properly incorporated in the contract between the supplier and the customer in order to be enforceable as a contract term; they are of little or no practical benefit where goods supplied are perishable or have a low scrap value; and they cannot be enforced in administration as a result of the moratorium that arises[14]. In many cases a supplier will not actually want its goods back. Nevertheless ROT clauses have value as they enable a supplier to negotiate a payment that it would not otherwise receive on the failure of a business.

As title to goods supplied under ROT terms does not pass to the customer, the seller will have no right to sell such goods. If the seller or the buyer appropriates such goods either of them may be liable to a claim in conversion asserted by the owner. On a practical level it is often difficult to ascertain whether or not goods are held subject to ROT terms, as most companies do not keep ROT goods separate from others or mark them as the owner's property notwithstanding that they are obliged to do so. Usually ROT goods will be an excluded asset in the sale agreement, but the buyer will take possession of them on terms that it holds the goods as bailee and does not hold itself out as the owner. The sale agreement will specify that the buyer does not obtain title to ROT assets and that they may not be charged or otherwise made subject to any encumbrance over them. The seller or the buyer may be required to deal with ROT claims asserted by suppliers, and if they are proved to be valid the buyer will be required to permit the supplier to uplift the goods, or it will be obliged to pay the supplier for them, usually with no right to rescind the contract or to an abatement of the purchase price. If an ROT claim is settled or disproven, title to the former ROT assets will pass to the buyer.

There will also usually be an indemnity in favour of the seller and any office-holder if the supplier successfully brings a claim for conversion against either of them.

---

[14] IA 1986, Sch B1, para 43.

Shares

8.13   Shares owned by the seller are also usually excluded. They are not part of the assets of the seller which are needed to carry on its business as a going concern, and shares may be the subject of a separate sale, often to a special purchaser such as the ultimate shareholder of a group, where they are shares in a private limited company.

Third-party assets

8.14   See section 8.10 'Plant and machinery'.

Chapter 9

Employees

Introduction

9.1   The Transfer of Undertakings (Protection of Employment) Regulations 2006[1] ('TUPE') came into force on 6 April 2006 to replace the 1981 version of the Regulations[2] ('TUPE 1981').

Prior to the introduction of TUPE 1981, when a business or assets were sold the parties could select which employees (if any) transferred to the buyer, and the buyer could employ those employees who transferred on whatever terms it chose, without taking on liability for any rights or obligations under their contract of employment with the seller. The remaining employees would be made redundant without any obligation on the parties to the transaction to consult with the affected persons or their representatives.

TUPE 1981 was adopted in the UK to implement the Acquired Rights Directive[3] ('Acquired Rights Directive'), as subsequently revised[4]. On considering those provisions of TUPE that give effect to the Acquired Rights Directive (but not on considering other provisions[5]), courts and employment tribunals are required to give TUPE a purposive construction such that it gives effect to the underlying purpose of the Acquired Rights Directive to protect employees' rights on the transfer of a business. TUPE 1981 introduced three key concepts into UK law:

- employees transfer to a buyer on the sale of a business, and the buyer takes on all rights, liabilities and obligations in relation to the employees;

- employees are protected from dismissal in relation to a TUPE transfer;

- employers are required to consult with representatives of affected employees or, if none, with the affected employees directly.

---

[1]   SI 2006/246.
[2]   SI 1981/1794.
[3]   Council Directive 77/187/EEC ([1977] OJ L61/26) on the approximation of the laws of the Member States relating to the safeguarding of employees' rights in the event of transfers of undertakings, businesses or parts of businesses.
[4]   Council Directive 2001/23/EC ([2001] OJ L82/16) on the approximation of the laws of the Member States relating to the safeguarding of employees' rights in the event of transfers of undertakings, businesses or parts of undertakings or businesses.
[5]   *McCarrick v Hunter* [2012] EWCA Civ 1399, [2013] IRLR 26 (CA).

In 2006 a number of changes were introduced to the TUPE regime:

- the scope of TUPE was widened to provide clarification regarding the application of TUPE to service-providers;

- the seller was put under an obligation to provide certain information about the transferring employees to the buyer;

- provisions were introduced in relation to the transfer of insolvent businesses;

- employers and employees were able to agree changes to terms of employment where there is an economic, technical or organisational ('ETO') reason entailing changes in the workforce;

- clarification was made as to when it was unfair for employees to be dismissed for reasons connected to a transfer;

- the seller and buyer were made jointly and severally liable for any failure to inform and consult with employees in some circumstances;

- the right to resign and claim constructive dismissal where a transfer involves a substantial change in working conditions to the employee's material detriment.

General provisions of TUPE

9.2   TUPE applies to a relevant transfer, which is a transfer of a business or undertaking where a transfer or an economic activity that retains its identity takes place. There are three basic elements to a TUPE transfer:

- an economic entity;

- a transfer of that entity;

- the entity retaining its identity after the transfer.

TUPE does not apply where there is simply a sale of the shares of a company as there is then no transfer of a business or undertaking.

TUPE applies where the business is situated in the UK immediately prior to the transfer even if the transfer is subject to the laws of a foreign jurisdiction, or the employee's rights are governed by the laws of a foreign jurisdiction, or the employees ordinarily work outside of the UK.

Where there is a relevant transfer:

- the contracts of the employees who are assigned to a group of resources or employees that form the subject of the transfer automatically transfer to the buyer on existing terms[6]; this applies to all employees employed in

---

[6]   TUPE, reg 4.

the grouping immediately prior to the transfer, or who would have been so employed had they not been dismissed because of the transfer or a reason connected with it which is not an ETO reason entailing changes in the workforce;

- the buyer takes over the position of the seller in relation to the transferring employees. All of the seller's rights, duties and obligations under the transferring employee's contracts pass to the buyer (other than occupational pension scheme rights for private-sector employees), and any acts or omissions of the seller prior to the transfer are treated as if they had been done by the buyer;

- the contracts of employees who object to the transfer are terminated by operation of law on the date of the transfer;

- where employees resign as the transfer involves substantial changes to their material detriment they are treated as if they had been dismissed.

Any changes to terms of employment of the transferring employees will be void if the sole or principal reason for the change is either:

- the transfer; or

- a reason connected with the transfer which is not an ETO reason entailing changes in the workforce.

Changes to terms of employment of the transferring employees before of after the transfer can be made where the sole or principal reason for the change is:

- a reason unconnected with the transfer;

- a reason connected with the transfer which is an ETO reason entailing changes in the workforce.

Any dismissal of an employee with at least one year's service, or two year's service if employment commenced on or after 6 April 2012[7], will be automatically unfair[8] if the sole or principal reason for the change is either:

- the transfer; or

- a reason connected with the transfer which is not an ETO reason entailing changes in the workforce.

If an employee resigns as a result of a repudiatory breach of contract or as a result of substantial changes in working conditions to his material detriment then he may claim that his employment has been terminated unfairly by way of constructive dismissal.

---

[7]   Unfair Dismissal and Statement of Reasons for Dismissal (Variation of Qualifying Period) Order 2012 (SI 2012/989).
[8]   TUPE, reg 7.

9.3 *Employees*

The seller and buyer have an obligation to inform and consult with their employees (via trade unions or representatives as appropriate) who might be affected by a transfer or any measures taken in connection with it, and to provide certain information to them. A failure to comply with this requirement may result in a cost of up to 13 weeks' gross pay uncapped for each affected employee, for which the seller and buyer may be jointly and severally liable. The seller is also required to provide the buyer with certain information about the transferring employees not less than 14 days before the transfer takes place.

TUPE has been seen as a barrier to the rescue of insolvent businesses by the insolvency profession, principally because of the prospect of a buyer becoming responsible for significant and often unknown liabilities. In the absence of warranties in the sale contract to protect a buyer, it may be reluctant to proceed with a transaction. Directive 2001/23 gave EU member states the option to relax the provisions of the Acquired Rights Directive in certain aspects in relation to insolvent companies, and in the UK that option was taken up in 2006 with a view to promoting the rescue of a failing business but still providing employees with appropriate safeguards and protections.

Specific TUPE provisions where the seller is insolvent

Introduction

9.3   TUPE 1981 did not distinguish between the transfer of a solvent and an insolvent business, save that it included specific rules relating to the hive-down of a business by a liquidator or receiver which purported to enable a buyer of an insolvent business to acquire it without effecting a TUPE transfer. However these provisions were contrary to the Acquired Rights Directive and were not of any practical use once interpreted by the court[9]. They were therefore not retained in 2006 when TUPE was revised. Instead specific insolvency-related provisions of TUPE were introduced to modify the general rules where there is a transfer of an insolvent business. TUPE now makes separate provision for the transfer of a business that is subject to 'relevant insolvency proceedings'[10] and one that is subject to 'bankruptcy proceedings or any analogous insolvency proceedings'[11].

Unfortunately the relevant provisions of TUPE itself are not sufficiently certain. There is no clear definition of those insolvency procedures that are 'relevant insolvency proceedings' or 'bankruptcy proceedings or any analogous insolvency proceedings', and no certainty as to those liabilities that pass to the buyer and those that do not. It is only as a result of interpretation of regulation 8 by the Court of Appeal that certainty now exists[12].

---

[9]   *Litster v Forth Dry Dock & Engineering Co Limited* [1989] ICR 341.
[10]   TUPE, reg 8(6).
[11]   TUPE, reg 8(7).
[12]   See section 9.8.

'Relevant insolvency proceedings'

9.4   Where the seller is subject to 'relevant insolvency proceedings' TUPE is modified such that:

*   certain of the seller's debts to employees will not transfer to the buyer[13], but instead will be paid out of the National Insurance Fund ('NIF') by the Redundancy Payments Office ('RPO'). Liabilities include statutory redundancy pay, arrears of pay, payment in lieu of notice and holiday pay up to the current statutory limits (as of 1 February 2013) as follows:

    —   statutory redundancy pay: £13,500;

    —   payment in lieu of notice: up to 12 weeks' pay, capped at £5,400;

    —   arrears of pay: up to 8 weeks' pay capped at £3,600;

    —   holiday pay: up to 6 weeks' pay capped at £2,700.

    The maximum weekly sums paid are capped at £450 per week, with that figure reviewed by the Department for Business, Innovation and Skills ('BIS') on 1 February each year.

    Liability to pay any amounts owed above the statutory limits will pass to the buyer.

*   The seller and the buyer may agree certain changes to the employees' contracts of employment[14] with a view to safeguarding employment by ensuring the survival of the business.

'Relevant insolvency proceedings' means[15]:

> 'insolvency proceedings which have been opened in relation to the [seller] not with a view to the liquidation of the assets of the [seller] and which are under the supervision of an insolvency practitioner'.

However those insolvency proceedings which fall within the definition are not specified and there has been uncertainty as to which proceedings they are. *A guide to the 2006 TUPE Regulations for employees, employers and representatives*[16] ('the Guide') issued by BIS in June 2009 states that in the view of BIS the definition means[17]:

> 'any collective insolvency proceedings in which the whole or part of the business or undertaking is transferred to another entity as a going concern. That is to say, it covers an insolvency proceeding in which all creditors of the debtor may participate, and in relation to which the insolvency office-holder owes a duty to all creditors. The Department considers that "relevant insolvency proceedings" does not cover winding-up by either creditors or members where there is no such transfer'.

---

[13]   TUPE, reg 8(5).
[14]   TUPE, reg 9(1).
[15]   TUPE, reg 8(6).
[16]   http://www.bis.gov.uk/files/file20761.pdf.
[17]   The Guide, Part 6.

Further guidance has also been issued by BIS in a note on *Redundancy and insolvency payments*[18] ('the Note'). The Note is intended to set out the Secretary of State's approach in determining whether or not the RPO will make payments to employees out of the NIF. The Note states that the correct approach as to whether an insolvency proceeding is a 'relevant insolvency proceeding' is to look at:

> 'the main or sole purpose of the procedure rather than its outcome in a specific instance'.

The approach adopted by the Secretary of State as set out in the Note is that 'relevant insolvency proceedings' are:

- administration;
- voluntary arrangements; and
- administrative receiverships.

Proceedings that are not 'relevant insolvency proceedings' are:

- compulsory liquidation;
- creditors' voluntary liquidation;
- members' voluntary liquidation; and
- receivership.

BIS does not consider members' voluntary liquidation and receivership to be insolvency proceedings.

However it should be noted that the Guide and the Note only reflect the view and approach of the Secretary of State. The Court of Appeal has resolved previously conflicting authority to reach a position of certainty[19].

No transfer of debts

9.5   Under TUPE, where the seller is subject to 'relevant insolvency proceedings' liability to pay sums owed to a 'relevant employee' under 'relevant statutory schemes' will not transfer to the buyer[20]. Accordingly it is only sums owed that fall outside of the statutory scheme that the buyer will become liable for.

'Relevant employee' means[21] an employee of the seller whose contract of employment transfers to the buyer by virtue of TUPE, or whose employment with the seller is terminated before the relevant transfer where the sole or

---

[18]   http://www.bis.gov.uk/files/file30031.pdf.
[19]   *Key2Law (Surrey) LLP v De'Antiquis* [2011] EWCA Civ 1567, [2012] ICR 881.
[20]   TUPE, reg 8(5).
[21]   TUPE, reg 8(2).

principal reason for the dismissal is the transfer itself or a reason connected with the transfer that is not an ETO reason entailing changes in the workforce.

'Relevant statutory schemes' are those schemes that provide for the RPO to pay the amounts stated in section 9.4 above out of the NIF.

The date of the transfer of the business is treated as the date on which the employee's employment was terminated[22] for the purpose of TUPE, reg 8, so that it is not necessary for the employee's employment to actually have been terminated in order for him or her to claim payment from the NIF.

The RPO adopts the following position. It will pay out of the NIF up to the statutory limits for:

- Arrears of wages and pay for holiday taken to employees who transfer to the buyer. It will not pay statutory redundancy payments, pay in lieu of accrued holiday not taken or pay in lieu of notice, as the employees have not been dismissed.

- Arrears of wages and holiday pay to employees who have been unfairly dismissed by reason of the transfer. It will not pay statutory redundancy payments or pay in lieu of notice as the affected employees were not made redundant. If employees bring a successful claim for unfair dismissal or breach of contract it is for the employment tribunal to decide on liability as between the seller and buyer.

- Arrears of wages, holiday pay, redundancy payments and pay in lieu of notice to employees who are dismissed for an ETO reason. They will be considered to be redundant.

- Arrears of wages and pay for holiday taken to employees who refuse to transfer to the buyer. It will not pay statutory redundancy payments, pay in lieu of accrued holiday not taken or pay in lieu of notice, as the employees have not been made redundant but left of their own accord.

No payments will be made for arrears of wages or holiday pay where the transfer takes place before insolvency and employees transfer to the buyer or are unfairly dismissed. That situation will be treated as a solvent TUPE transfer and regulation 8 will not apply.

The Employment Appeal Tribunal ('EAT') has clarified that the NIF will only be liable to pay debts due as at the date of the transfer, or at any earlier date on which an employee was unfairly dismissed for a reason related to the transfer. Where an employee transfers to the buyer no liabilities relating to dismissal will have arisen as at the transfer date and if the employee is then dismissed by the buyer the new employer, rather than the NIF, will be liable for any redundancy pay or unpaid holiday[23].

---

[22] TUPE, reg 8(3).
[23] *OTG Ltd v Barke and others* UKEAT 0320/09, [2011] ICR 781; *Pressure Coolers Ltd v Molloy and others* [2011] IRLR 630.

Permitted variations to contracts

9.6   TUPE provides for the parties to a sale and purchase to make 'permitted variations' to contracts of employment where the seller is subject to 'relevant insolvency proceedings'[24].

The seller or buyer or insolvency practitioner must agree the variations with 'appropriate representatives' of the affected employees. 'Appropriate representatives' are[25] union representatives where there is a recognised trade union, or in any other case appointed or elected representatives providing they have authority to agree permitted variations. Where there are no trade-union representatives the text of any variations to be agreed must be provided to all affected employees with such guidance as they may need to understand it before agreement is made, and the agreement must be recorded in writing and signed by each of the representatives[26].

The variations must not breach any other statutory requirements and the sole or principal reason for the variation must be[27] the transfer itself or a reason connected with the transfer that is not an ETO reason entailing changes in the workforce, and it must be designed to safeguard employment opportunities by ensuring the survival of the undertaking, business or part of it.

Any permitted variation agreed will take effect as a term of the employees' contract of employment in place of the term it varies[28].

It can be seen that an individual employee does not have to agree to the changes providing his or her trade union or authorised representatives give their consent, and regulation 9 is on the face of it a significant inroad into the usual effects of TUPE. However it is not a change that has had a significant impact in practice.

Dismissal of employees

9.7   The appointment of an insolvency practitioner to a company does not result in the automatic dismissal of employees (save for compulsory winding up[29]). However it is not unusual for an insolvency practitioner to make redundancies, or indeed for a company going through financial difficulties to do so. This may be part of a cost-cutting and restructuring exercise, or dismissals may be made with a view to creating a more attractive business for a potential buyer. In the absence of a formal insolvency the usual TUPE rules will apply to an employee who is dismissed shortly before a transfer.

---

[24]   TUPE, reg 9(1).
[25]   TUPE, reg 9(2).
[26]   TUPE, reg 9(5).
[27]   TUPE, reg 9(7).
[28]   TUPE, reg 9(6).
[29]   *Re General Rolling Stock Co (Chapman's case)* (1866) 1 Eq 346.

The position where an office-holder makes an employee redundant shortly before a transfer has been before employment tribunals on many occasions. It can be difficult to ascertain whether or not dismissals are connected to the transfer and are for an ETO reason entailing changes in the workforce, particularly when they occur when there is no definite sale planned or agreed and no transfer takes place for some time. The general provisions of TUPE giving employees protection from dismissal apply as modified where the seller is subject to 'relevant insolvency proceedings'. However they are disapplied where the seller is subject to 'bankruptcy proceedings or any analogous insolvency proceedings'[30].

If an employee who has been continuously employed for one year or more (two years or more if employment commenced on or after 6 April 2012[31]) is dismissed, that will automatically be an unfair dismissal if the sole or principal reason is either the transfer itself or a reason connected with the transfer that is not an ETO reason entailing changes in the workforce[32]. Liability for any such unfair dismissal will automatically transfer to the buyer[33].

However if the sole or principal reason for the dismissal was not the transfer itself, or it was a reason connected with the transfer that was an ETO reason entailing changes in the workforce of either the seller or the buyer then that may not be for a potentially fair reason and liability for the dismissal may remain with the seller.

Instances where employees have been dismissed when an office-holder was marketing the business of an insolvent company with a view to finding a buyer, but had not yet identified the other potential party to the transfer, have still been found to be connected to the subsequent TUPE transfer[34]. Other instances have been decided differently[35]. The Court of Appeal has found[36] that a pre-transfer dismissal of an employee by administrators was connected with the transfer within the meaning of regulation 7(1) even where the identity of the buyer was not known, identified or contemplated at the date of dismissal. There was no ETO reason as the administrators had dismissed the employee to make the business more attractive to potential buyers. There was no intention to change the workforce and to carry on the business. Most recently in *Kavanagh and others v Crystal Palace FC (2000) Ltd and others*[37] the EAT found that where an administrator had made redundancies with a view to mothballing the company's business so that a buyer could be found in due course, rather than with a view to carrying on the business, that was not an ETO reason for the dismissals. The Eat

---

30   TUPE, reg 8(7).
31   Unfair Dismissal and Statement of Reasons for Dismissal (Variation of Qualifying Period) Order 2012 (SI 2012/989).
32   TUPE, reg 7(1).
33   TUPE, reg 4(3).
34   *Harrison Bowden v Bowden* [1994] ICR 186; *CAB Automotive Limited v Blake and others* 0298/07, EAT.
35   *Ibex Trading Co Limited v Walton* [1995] IRLR 564.
36   *Spaceright Europe Ltd v Baillavoine and another* [2011] EWCA Civ 1565, [2012] ICR 520.
37   UKEAT/0354/12/SM (15/03/2013).

said the only conclusion it could draw was that the dismissal of the employees was for the purpose of selling the business, albeit it was not at that stage certain that there would be a sale, or who the eventual buyer (if any) would be. Accordingly the dismissals were automatically unfair and the liabilities which arose as a result would transfer to the buyer under TUPE.

Where an employee was dismissed because the buyer would not acquire the business unless the office-holder made a number of redundancies, that was not an ETO reason entailing changes in the workforce[38]. However where an administrator made redundancies before a sale because he or she had no funds available to pay the employees, that was an ETO reason entailing changes in the workforce[39]. The difference seems to be that a lack of funds to pay employees was a business reason to make dismissals rather than a reason connected with the eventual sale and transfer of the business. The thought process of the office-holder making the redundancies should be examined in determining the likelihood of whether TUPE will apply or not[40].

Sellers are advised to exercise caution and assume that TUPE will apply, particularly (but not only) where the time between an employee's dismissal and the transfer is short[41]

Under section 188(1) of the Trade Union and Labour Relations (Consolidation) Act 1992 ('TULRCA'), employers are obliged to collectively consult where they propose to dismiss as redundant 20 or more employees at one establishment within a period of 90 days or less. The question of what constitutes an 'establishment' for the purpose of consulting with affected employees on a proposed collective redundancy is currently the subject of an appeal to the EAT. In *USDAW and others v WW Realisation 1 Limited (in liquidation)*[42] the ET considered claims for breach of the duty to inform and consult under TULRCA section 188 in connection with the mass redundancies of Woolworths' employees resulting from the closure of its stores. A key issue before the tribunal was whether the duty to inform and consult was triggered in stores which had less than 20 employees. The duty would be engaged (and employees in those stores would benefit from any protective award) if all of Woolworths' stores were a single establishment. However, the duty would not be triggered in respect of these employees working in a store with less than 20 employees, and they would not benefit from any protective award, if each individual Woolworths store was defined as a single establishment. The ET upheld the claim for breach of TULCRA section 188 and made protective awards for 60 days' gross pay, but expressly excluded awards for

---

[38] *Wheeler v Patel & Golding Group of Companies* [1987] IRLR 211.
[39] *Honeycombe 78 Limited v Cummins and others* 100/99, EAT; *Dynamex Friction Limited and another v Amicus and others* [2008] EWCA Civ 381, [2008] IRLR 515.
[40] *Dynamex Friction Limited and another v Amicus and others* [2008] EWCA Civ 381.
[41] *Morris v John Grose Group* [1998] IRLR 499; *CAB Automotive Limited v Blake and others* 0298/07, EAT; *Spaceright Europe Ltd v Baillovoine and another* [2011] EWCA Civ 1565, [2012] ICR 520.
[42] ET 3201156/2010.

those employed at stores with less than 20 employees. The ET rejected the argument put forward by the union and employee representatives that the whole of Woolworths' retail operations nationwide should be aggregated to constitute a single establishment, and found that each employee was assigned to the particular store in which they worked and each Woolworths store was a distinct establishment from any other store. This fact based decision is helpful to administrators, but has created uncertainty, and the outcome of the appeal is awaited with interest.

On 18 December 2012 the Department for Business, Innovation and Skills announced that it had asked Acas (the Advisory, Conciliation and Arbitration Service) to publish non-statutory guidance which will expand on the meaning of 'establishment' with reference to: geographical location, management structure, management of financial autonomy, cohesion of the workforce, nature of the work undertaken or type of service provided, contractual relationship between employer and employee, and the level within the company at which the decision to dismiss is taken[43]. The guidelines are intended to give flexibility to employers and they too are awaited with interest.

Further, the minimum period of consultation in relation to collective redundancies of 100 or more employees will reduce from 90 to 45 days[44], although any failure to comply may still lead to a protective award of up to 90 days pay per employee. Both the Acas guidance and the revised consultation period are intended to have effect from 6 April 2013.

'Bankruptcy proceedings or any analogous insolvency proceedings'

9.8   Where 'bankruptcy proceedings or any analogous insolvency proceedings' have been instituted with a view to the liquidation of the assets of the seller under the supervision of an insolvency practitioner, employees will not automatically transfer to the buyer on a transfer of the business and any dismissals will not be automatically unfair[45].

Acting as an insolvency practitioner in relation to a company is defined as acting as a liquidator, provisional liquidator, administrator or administrative receiver[46]. The Guide and the Note provide further guidance from BIS and the RPO as to the insolvency proceedings which fall within the definition of 'bankruptcy proceedings or any analogous insolvency proceedings'. These are:

- compulsory liquidation; and

- creditors' voluntary liquidation;

---

[43]   https://www.gov.uk/government/consultations/collective-redundancies-consultation-on-changes-to-the-rules.
[44]   See note 43.
[45]   TUPE, reg 8(7).
[46]   IA 1986, s 388(1).

Proceedings that are not 'bankruptcy proceedings or any analogous insolvency proceedings' are:

- administration;

- voluntary arrangements;

- administrative receiverships;

- members' voluntary liquidation; and

- receivership.

The question of whether or not administration, and particularly a pre-pack administration where an immediate sale of the business and assets takes place, can fall within the ambit of 'bankruptcy proceedings or any analogous insolvency proceedings', and so enable the buyer to avoid the liabilities relating to the dismissal of employees that would otherwise follow a transfer under TUPE, has come before the EAT and the court on a number of occasions. The position has now been clarified by the Court of Appeal in the case of *Key2Law (Surrey) LLP v De'Antiquis*[47]. The Court of Appeal found that administration can never be insolvency proceedings which would fall within the ambit of TUPE, reg 8. It rejected the uncertainty of a fact based approach, which had been asserted in *Key2Law* and a number of previous cases. The court noted that when an administrator is appointed the primary objective under paragraph 3(1) of Schedule B1 IA 1986 is to rescue the company as a going concern. As a result it could not be said that as at the moment of appointment of an administrator the object of the process was to liquidate the assets. Whilst that might be the outcome, the administrator must always consider the primary objective to rescue the company. The position is now clear, and TUPE does apply on a pre-pack administration and all other administrations.

In a Consultation on Proposed Changes to TUPE issued by BIS on 17 January 2013[48] the government stated that it believed that the decision of the Court of Appeal in *Key2Law* had given sufficient clarity and that no change to TUPE was required to give certainty as to which insolvency proceedings fell TUPE, reg 8 and which did not.

No transfer of employees or automatic unfair dismissal

9.9   Under TUPE, regulation 8(7) employees do not automatically transfer to the buyer on a sale where the seller is subject to 'bankruptcy proceedings or any analogous insolvency proceedings'. All liabilities remain with the insolvent seller, and the buyer can choose whether or not to employ all or any of the employees, and on what terms it employs them. This remains the case

---

[47]   [2011] EWCA Civ 1567, [2012] ICR 881.
[48]   https://www.gov.uk/government/consultations/transfer-of-undertakings-protection-of-employment-regulations-tupe-2006-consultation-on-proposed-changes.

where liquidation may have been chosen over administration as the preferred insolvency process in order to take advantage of regulation 8(7)[49].

As a result of regulation 8(7) the business is much more attractive to a potential buyer, as often transferring employee liabilities are one of the most significant costs the buyer of an insolvent business takes on. The buyer can cherry-pick those employees it wishes to have working for it, and as their contracts do not transfer to the buyer it can employ such individuals on whatever terms it agrees with them.

Employees who are employed by the buyer in such circumstances will retain their continuity of employment[50], and that will need to be taken into account for the purpose of calculating their future redundancy entitlement should they be made redundant in due course, and in relation to rights to claim unfair dismissal.

Although employees who are dismissed prior to the transfer will not be able to rely on TUPE, reg 7 to assert that their dismissal was automatically unfair for a reason related to the transfer, they will still be able to rely on the usual grounds of a potentially unfair dismissal.

Information and consultation

Introduction

9.10   The obligations in TUPE to inform and consult with 'appropriate representatives'[51] apply to all transfers of a business, including where the seller is insolvent. The nature of the insolvency proceedings is irrelevant. The obligation to inform and consult (and to provide Employee Liability Information – see section 9.17 below) also forms part of the BIS Consultation issued on 17 January 2013[52] referred to in section 9.8 above.

The obligation to inform

9.11   The employer must provide the appropriate representatives of the affected employees with certain information long enough before the relevant transfer to enable the affected employees to consult with the representatives[53].

---

[49]   *Bowater & Ors v NIS Signs Ltd (in liquidation) & Ors* (Leicester Employment Tribunal, 29–31 March 2010, Judge Lancaster).
[50]   *Oakland v Wellswood (Yorkshire) Ltd* [2009] IRLR 250, 0395/08, EAT; Employment Rights Act 1996, s 218(2).
[51]   TUPE, reg 13.
[52]   https://www.gov.uk/government/consultations/transfer-of-undertakings-protection-of-employment-regulations-tupe-2006-consultation-on-proposed-changes.
[53]   TUPE, reg 13(2).

There is no minimum prescribed time limit, and the time frame is likely to vary in accordance with the nature and effect of the proposed transfer.

The information to be given

9.12   The seller must give the following information to the recognised trade union or employee representatives[54]:

- the fact of the transfer, the (approximate) date when it is to take place and the reasons for it;

- the legal, economic and social implications of the transfer for the affected employees; what is meant by 'legal, economic and social implications' will be a question of fact in each case;

- the measures which the employer envisages it will take in connection with the transfer in relation to 'any affected employees' or, if no measures are to be taken, that fact; 'measures' includes any 'action, step or arrangement' taken in connection with the transfer[55];

- any measures that the buyer envisages it will take in relation to the transferring employees in connection with the transfer or, if the buyer envisages taking no measures, that fact;

- suitable information relating to the use of agency workers (if any) by the employer[56]. 'Suitable information' includes:

  - the number of agency workers working temporarily for and under the supervision and direction of the employer;

  - the parts of the employers' undertaking in which those agency workers are working; and

  - the type of work those agency workers are carrying out.

Information about agency workers must be given in respect of the employer's entire business, not just that part that is to be transferred, and is not limited to those agency workers who are employees.

The information must be given to each of the employee representatives in writing[57], and must be accurate and disseminated carefully[58]. It does not need to include information on the right to object to becoming employed by the transferee[59].

---

[54] See n 45 above.
[55] *IPCS v Secretary of State for Defence* [1987] IRLR 373.
[56] Agency Workers Regulations 2010 (SI 2010/93).
[57] *NALGO v British Waterways Board* 11548/88/LN/A, ET.
[58] *Hagen v ICI Chemicals & Polymers Ltd* [2002] IRLR 31.
[59] *Marcroft v Heartland (Midlands) Ltd* [2011] EWCA Civ 438, [2011] IRLR 599.

The obligation to consult

9.13   Where the buyer 'envisages that he will take measures in relation to an affected employee, in connection with the relevant transfer, the seller shall consult with the appropriate representatives of that employee with a view to seeking agreement to the intended measures'[60]. This is a separate obligation from that to provide information to the relevant trade union or elected employee representatives. However, in practice, the mere fact of providing that information to the union will often trigger a dialogue which satisfies the obligation to consult.

The word 'envisages' suggests that the seller must have a definite plan or proposal which the employer intends to carry out in connection with the TUPE transfer. 'Measures' is given a wide interpretation and includes a positive act or omission by the employer.

Consultation must be with a view to seeking the agreement of the trade union or employee representatives to the relevant measures that are envisaged, and the seller must negotiate in good faith over all areas of the proposed redundancies and the measures it intends to take over the TUPE transfer.

It is not uncommon for the buyer to seek to agree with the seller that the buyer shall participate with the seller in the consultation process with the seller's employees to ensure that the employees are properly consulted with, and reduce the potential liability for any failure by the seller to consult to fall to the buyer under TUPE, since liability for such failure is joint and several.

'Special circumstances' defence for failure to inform or consult

9.14   The seller has a defence for failure to inform or consult if it can show that there were special circumstances making it not reasonably practicable for information to be given or consultation to take place, and that it had done the best it could to comply in the circumstances[61]. In practice, this defence is likely to be construed very narrowly and it is unlikely that insolvency of itself will amount to 'special circumstances'[62].

Liability for claims

9.15   Where an employer has failed to comply with a requirement to inform or consult, a claim may be brought by affected employees, employee representatives

---

[60]   TUPE, reg 13(6).
[61]   TUPE, reg 13(9).
[62]   See *USDAW and others v WW Realisation 1 Limited (in liquidation) and another* ET 3201156/10, 19 January 2012 for a recent example.

or the trade union depending on the circumstances[63]. The employment tribunal may award compensation payable of up to 13 weeks' gross pay for each affected employee. There is no limit on the amount of a week's pay.

It may order the seller or the buyer to pay the compensation, depending on the facts. Where the seller has breached its obligations to inform and consult, the tribunal can[64] make the buyer and seller jointly and severally liable to pay any compensation awarded against the seller. It may also make both jointly and severally liable to pay where either the seller or the buyer fails to pay a compensation award made against it.

Where the seller is insolvent

9.16   Insolvency practitioners often work to a very tight timetable, and there may be insufficient time for an office-holder to comply with the seller's obligation to inform and consult with employees or their representatives. If there is a breach of regulation 15, the principle of joint and several liability means that payment of compensation is likely to fall on the buyer, as it is unlikely that the insolvent seller will be able to pay.

The 'special circumstances' defence may give some comfort to the buyer in an insolvency situation. However the defence is likely to be construed very narrowly by the employment tribunal, and the onus is on the seller to show that it took all such reasonably practicable steps that it could take to comply with the obligation to inform and consult[65]. Even a minimal amount of information and consultation from the office-holder will provide some mitigation.

Employee liability information

9.17   The seller is under an obligation to provide 'employee liability information' to the buyer at least 14 days before a transfer or, if special circumstances make this not reasonably practicable, as soon as reasonably practicable thereafter[66].

'Employee liability information' ('ELI') means[67]:

- the identity and age of each employee;

- particulars of his or her employment;

- information as to any disciplinary procedure taken against an employee and any grievance procedure taken by an employee within the last two years;

---

[63]   TUPE, reg 15(1).
[64]   TUPE, reg 15(9).
[65]   TUPE, reg 15(2).
[66]   TUPE, reg 11(6).
[67]   TUPE, reg 11(2).

- information of any court or tribunal case, claim or action brought by an employee within the last two years or which the seller has reasonable grounds to believe an employee may bring;

- information of any collective agreement which will have effect after the transfer.

It may simply not be possible for an office-holder who transfers a business very shortly after he or she is appointed to comply with this obligation. The office-holder will not have a detailed knowledge of the business and information may not be available to him or her if the seller did not keep accurate and current records. The Guide notes[68] that it would not be reasonably practicable to provide information on time where the identity of the buyer was not known until late in the sale process, or where a transfer takes place at short notice.

If the seller fails to comply with the obligation to supply ELI, the buyer may complain to the ET and the buyer may be compensated for the losses it suffers as a result of the seller's failure to comply. However, the more practical solution is that the seller provides warranties and indemnities to the buyer which should provide the buyer with an avenue for compensation if the buyer has not been given an accurate portrait of the relevant ELI in advance of completion of the sale. It is rare though for insolvency practitioners to agree to provide warranties and indemnities and a claim against an insolvent seller is unlikely to be of real value, so the buyer may prefer to use any failure to provide ELI as a negotiating lever to secure a reduction on the purchase price. Provisions in relation to any failure to supply ELI, or failure to supply it in full, should be included in a sale agreement entered into by administrators.

The Consultation on Proposed Changes to TUPE issued by BIS on 17 January 2013[69] includes a proposal to remove the requirement on a seller to supply ELI, which if implemented will go some way to reduce the burden on administrators when they are selling a business over which they have been appointed. However any prudent buyer of a business out of administration is still likely to want detailed information on employees in order to calculate the potential employee liability that will follow a TUPE transfer, and so in real terms the impact of removing the requirement to supply ELI under TUPE may not lead to a significant change in practice.

Practical considerations

9.18   It is very important for both the seller and the buyer to consider the specific implications of TUPE on the sale of an insolvent business, as compared to a sale in a situation where the seller is solvent. The implications may have a big impact on the terms of the transaction, particularly price. Whilst the

---

[68] At p 21.
[69] https://www.gov.uk/government/consultations/transfer-of-undertakings-protection-of-employment-regulations-tupe-2006-consultation-on-proposed-changes.

exclusions from certain of the TUPE provisions that are considered in this chapter only arise when the seller is in a formal insolvency process, the parties to a proposed transaction should bear in mind that other provisions will also have an impact on a distressed sale outside of formal insolvency, such as the obligation to inform and consult, and the principle of joint and several liability.

The following matters need to be kept in mind at all times:

- What is the nature of the seller's insolvency? Employees' contracts do not generally come to an automatic end on the appointment of an office-holder to a company. However employment contracts are automatically terminated when a compulsory winding-up order is made[70].

- The TUPE insolvency provisions will not apply at all if the seller is not in a formal insolvency proceeding.

- If the seller is in a formal insolvency proceeding, the parties must ascertain if it is a 'relevant insolvency proceeding' or a 'bankruptcy or any analogous insolvency proceeding' as there are different implications for the buyer in each situation.

- Following the Court of Appeal Decision in *Key2Law*[71] it is clear that a pre-pack administration is a 'relevant insolvency proceeding' and TUPE will apply.

- Information made available to the buyer when it carries out its due diligence exercise is likely to be limited. The insolvency practitioner will have no personal knowledge of the seller and records many be incomplete. Further, there is unlikely to be sufficient time for the buyer to ask all of the questions it would like answered. The buyer should as a minimum seek to ascertain:

  — the numbers of employees likely to transfer, and their roles;

  — key terms of employment, including salary, benefits, notice period, change of control provisions, rights on termination;

  — any debts owed to employees by the seller;

  — information as to any recent dismissals and proposed dismissals;

  — information as to any ongoing or threatened litigation by employees.

- What is the potential level of employee liabilities? This may depend on the nature of the insolvency proceeding and the impact of the insolvency provisions of TUPE.

- Where the seller is subject to a 'relevant insolvency proceeding' the buyer may become liable to pay:

  — relevant costs relating to all of the seller's employees;

---

[70] *Re General Rolling Stock Co (Chapman's case)* (1866) 1 Eq 346.
[71] *Key2Law (Surrey) LLP v De'Antiquis* [2011] EWCA Civ 1567, [2012] ICR 881.

— debts owed to the employees over and above the amounts paid by the RPO on behalf of the NIF;

— any amount awarded in relation to any transfer-related dismissals, unless there was an ETO reason entailing changes in the workforce; failure to comply with the obligation to inform and consult in relation to collective redundancies[72]; failure to comply with the obligation to inform and consult in connection with the transfer[73], which may be joint and several with the seller.

• Where the seller is subject to a 'bankruptcy or any analogous insolvency proceeding' the buyer may become liable to pay:

— relevant costs relating to the seller's employees who transfer; they retain continuity of service[74];

— any amount awarded in relation to failure to comply with the obligation to inform and consult in connection with the transfer, which may be joint and several with the seller.

• The potential scope for changing the terms of employment by way of a 'permitted variation' where the seller is subject to a 'relevant insolvency proceeding'.

• The seller's obligation to provide ELI[75], which in practice is likely to remain if and when the proposed changes to TUPE are enacted.

• The seller's obligation to inform and consult[76]. Even a small amount of information and consultation given in a short time frame can mitigate future claims and the buyer should consider carrying out a joint information and consultation process with the seller where possible.

• The likelihood of redundancies. Is a redundancy consultation required? What constitutes an 'establishment' for the purpose of a redundancy consultation[77]? This may be fact specific and vary from case to case.

• The quantum of employee liabilities generally and the risk of employee claims against the buyer. These are often key drivers as to whether or not a proposed sale takes place, and if so are highly relevant in determining the price the buyer is willing to pay.

• Warranties and indemnities in relation to employees will not be provided by the seller where it is subject to insolvency proceedings.

• It would be usual for the seller to require the buyer to provide an indemnity in relation to employee claims brought against the seller after

---

[72] Trade Union and Labour Relations (Consolidation) Act 1992, ss 188–194.
[73] TUPE, reg 13.
[74] *Oakland v Wellswood (Yorkshire) Ltd* [2009] IRLR 250, 0395/08, EAT; Employment Rights Act 1996, s 218(2).
[75] TUPE, reg 11.
[76] TUPE, reg 13.
[77] *USDAW and others v WW Realisation 1 Limited (in liquidation)* ET 3201156/2010.

the transfer, particularly if the seller has made employees redundant at the buyer's request.

• The lack of warranties in favour of the buyer and the request for indemnities in favour of the seller will also often form a significant part of the negotiations on price, or the manner in which the consideration is paid. The buyer may seek to defer payment of part of the purchase price pending any employee claims being made.

• Can and should the buyer obtain insurance against employee liabilities to mitigate the risk?

Future reforms

9.19   Employment law is a fast changing area, and the government published a progress report on its reforms to Employment Law on 14 March 2013.[78] Further changes to procedures which will impact on the transfer of insolvent companies and businesses are likely.

---

[78]   https://www.gov.uk/government/uploads/system/uploads/attachment data/file/141918/1/3-P136-employment-law-2013-progress-on-reform 1 pdf.

Chapter 10

Pension Schemes

This chapter contains an overview of pension issues that may arise on the sale or purchase of an insolvent business. This is a complex and specialist area of law, much of which is outside the scope of this book, and appropriate legal advice must always be taken in relation to pension matters.

Introduction

10.1   There are a number of scenarios which a buyer might find in relation to pension arrangements provided to employees of the seller.

Workplace pensions

10.2   With effect from October 2012 employers with at least one worker in the UK became or will become subject to an obligation to provide employees with a workplace pension. The start date by which an employer must provide a workplace pension varies between 1 October 2012 and 1 February 2018[1], and depends on the number of people in the employer's PAYE scheme. The provisions require employers to:

- enrol certain employees into a pension scheme;

- make contributions to the scheme on behalf of the employees; and

- register with The Pensions Regulator.

10.3   A company may provide a defined benefits (final salary) scheme, or a money purchase benefits (a defined contribution) scheme, or a mixture of both. In a defined benefit scheme the amount payable to the employee on retirement is known, but not the cost of providing it. In a defined contribution scheme the amount of contributions to be made is known, but not the benefit to the employee on retirement.

The insolvent seller may be the sole or principal employer under an occupational scheme or it may be a participating employer in a scheme where the principal employer is not in financial distress or subject to an insolvency proceeding.

---

[1]   http://www.thepensionsregulator.gov.uk/employers/staging-date-timeline.aspx.

10.4   Alternatively an employer may offer a contract-based scheme, also known as a group personal pension scheme, in which employees and the employer make contributions on a money-purchase basis to a third-party pension provider who is engaged to run the scheme.

TUPE

10.5   Article 3 of the Acquired Rights Directive[2] provides that:

- the seller's rights and obligations arising from a contract of employment or from an employment relationship existing on the date of a transfer of a business should, by reason of such transfer, be transferred to the buyer;

- the buyer should continue to observe the terms and conditions agreed in any collective agreement on the same terms applicable to the seller under that agreement.

Paragraph 3 of Article 3 provides that the above does not apply to employees' rights to old age, invalidity or survivors' benefits under supplementary company or inter-company pension schemes outside of the statutory schemes in member states. This is known as the 'pensions exception'.

The Transfer of Undertakings (Protection of Employment) Regulations 2006 (SI 2006/246) ('TUPE') implements the Acquired Rights Directive, and on a relevant transfer of a business all the seller's rights, powers, duties and liabilities under or in connection with a contract of employment are transferred to the buyer[3]. Where, at the time of a relevant transfer, there is a collective agreement made by or on behalf of the seller with a trade union recognised by the seller in respect of any employee whose contract is preserved by TUPE, reg 4, then that agreement will have effect as if it was made by or on behalf of the buyer with that trade union[4].

The 'pensions exception' to TUPE is set out in regulation 10(1). It provides that regulations 4 and 5 shall not apply:

- to so much of a contract of employment or collective agreement as relates to an occupational pension scheme; or

- to any rights, powers, duties or liabilities under or in connection with any such contract or subsisting by virtue of any such agreement and relating to such a scheme or otherwise arising in connection with that person's employment and relating to such a scheme.

---

[2]   Council Directive 77/187/EEC ([1977] OJ L61/26) on the approximation of the laws of the Member States relating to the safeguarding of employees' rights in the event of transfers of undertakings, businesses or parts of businesses.
[3]   TUPE, reg 4(2).
[4]   TUPE, reg 5.

The usual view is that the pensions exception does not apply to personal pension schemes, including contract based workplace schemes such as group personal pensions.

Regulation 10(2) of TUPE states that:

'for the purposes of Regulation 10(1) ... any provisions of an occupational pension scheme which do not relate to benefits for old age, invalidity or survivors shall be treated as not being part of the scheme'.

This takes such provisions of an occupational pension scheme out of the TUPE exception, and uncertainty as to what is meant by '... which do not relate to benefits for old age, invalidity or survivors' has led to references to the European Court of Justice[5].

Prior to the 2006 amendments to TUPE, an employee who rejected employment with the buyer because of inadequate pension provision could claim constructive dismissal on the ground of a repudiatory breach of contract. A claim could include wrongful dismissal[6] and unfair dismissal. Regulation 10(3) of TUPE now provides that employees who transfer to the buyer under TUPE cannot bring a claim for breach of contract or constructive unfair dismissal arising in a loss or reduction of rights under an occupational pension scheme in consequence of the transfer.

It is likely that changes to pension arrangements are matters in respect of which the seller must consult with representatives of affected employees[7], notwithstanding that rights relating to occupational schemes will not transfer to the buyer because of the 'pensions exception'. Even if the seller itself is not proposing to make any changes to pension arrangements it will still have an obligation to inform affected employee representatives.

Pension issues on the transfer of the business

10.6   Whatever scenario exists, the buyer will want to ensure that it does not acquire any liabilities in relation to any form of pension provision.

Defined benefit schemes

10.7   Benefits will generally be provided by way of a registered scheme administered by trustees. Active members of the scheme will leave pensionable service on a sale, and the buyer will not acquire any liability in relation to the

---

[5]   See *Beckmann v Dynamco Whicheloe Macfarlane Limited* (Case C-164/00); [2002] ECR I-4893 and *Martin and others v South Bank University* [2003] 85 PBLR below.
[6]   *University of Oxford v Humphreys and the Associated Examining Board* [2000] IRLR 183.
[7]   TUPE, reg 13.

seller's scheme. Occupational pension rights are excluded from TUPE[8] and do not transfer to the buyer[9]. If the seller's defined benefit scheme is underfunded there may be a significant debt due from the seller to the trustees, and the question will arise as to whether the scheme is eligible for transfer to the Pension Protection Fund ('PPF').

Defined contribution schemes

10.8   If the seller provides employees with personal pensions contributions paid before the sale, the pension arrangements remain with the third-party provider. Under TUPE any obligation to pay employee contributions for a period of service after the sale will transfer to the buyer.

If the seller provides an occupational scheme, past contributions will be held by the scheme trustees and the buyer will not take over any obligation in respect of arrears. Occupational schemes do not transfer under TUPE but the buyer will be obliged to make provision for a workplace pension from the relevant date applicable to it[10].

Future arrangements

10.9   The buyer has a range of options for making pension provision for transferring employees when it acquires a business.

Where there is a relevant transfer under TUPE, existing contractual obligations to provide and contribute to a personal pension arrangement will transfer to the buyer. If there are no contractual obligations to fulfil the buyer may have to provide access to a workplace pension in the usual manner. If the seller was obliged to make contributions to a personal pension scheme they must continue.

The minimum provision to be made by the buyer following a TUPE transfer (but only where the seller had an occupational pension scheme, whether defined benefit or defined contribution, to which it was obliged to pay or has in fact paid contributions) is as follows:

- contributions to a stakeholder pension scheme that match the employee's contributions up to an amount equal to six per cent of his or her remuneration;

- a defined benefit scheme that satisfies the minimum contracting-out reference scheme test;

---

[8]   TUPE, reg 10(1).
[9]   But note *Beckmann v Dynamco Whicheloe Macfarlane Limited* (Case C-164/00); [2002] ECR I-4893 and *Martin and others v South Bank University* [2003] 85 PBLR.
[10]   See section 10.1 and http://www.thepensionsregulator.gov.uk/employers/staging-date-timeline/aspx.

- a defined benefit scheme that provides benefits of an overall equivalent value to the contributions made to the seller's scheme where the employer's element of contributions is at least six per cent of pensionable pay and the employee is not required to contribute more than 6% of pensionable pay;

- a defined contribution occupational scheme where the employer matches employee contributions up to six per cent of pensionable pay.

Exceptions to the general rule

10.10   There are case law exceptions to the general rule that obligations under occupational pension schemes do not transfer to a buyer under TUPE.

Early retirement provisions on redundancy may transfer to the buyer by operation of law under TUPE following the decision of the European Court of Justice ('ECJ') in *Beckmann v Dynamco Whicheloe Macfarlane Limited*[11]. The scope of *Beckmann* is not clear and it can be argued that it does not apply to occupational schemes set up under a trust. However it cannot be certain that early-retirement rights will remain with an insolvent seller.

Mrs Beckmann worked for the NHS and contributed to the NHS Superannuation Scheme ('NHS Scheme'). On 1 June 1995 the body for which she worked was subject to a TUPE transfer to Dynamco Whicheloe Macfarlane Limited ('DWM'). On 6 May 1997 she was made redundant. DWM paid Mrs Beckmann the lump-sum redundancy payment she was entitled to save for an amount in respect of her early retirement benefits under the NHS Scheme. Mrs Beckmann brought legal proceedings seeking a declaration that she was entitled to those benefits. There were a number of differences between the NHS Scheme and a private-sector occupational pension scheme:

- retirement benefits were paid by the UK government, although amounts due in respect of early-retirement benefits paid on redundancy were paid by the NHS employing authority;

- administration of the NHS Scheme was outside the control of the employer or trustees;

- the NHS Scheme was regulated by statutory instrument rather than by a trust deed and rules.

The High Court referred two questions to the ECJ: did early-retirement benefits fall within Article 3(3) of the Acquired Rights Directive ('Article 3(3)')? And if not, was there an obligation falling on a transferee employer arising from the contract of employment, the employment relationship or a collective agreement which transferred to the transferee which made it liable to pay the benefits to an employee on a dismissal?

---

[11]   Case C-164/00; [2002] ECR I-4893.

On the first question the ECJ found that early-retirement benefits paid in the event of the dismissal of an employee who had reached a certain age were not benefits that were excluded from TUPE transfers. It was only benefits that are paid when the employee reaches the end of his or her normal working life as laid down by the general structure of the pension scheme in question that fall within the definition, not those that are payable in other circumstances including on dismissal for redundancy.

In relation to the second question, Mrs Beckmann submitted that the early-retirement benefits derived from her contract of employment or from her employment relationship with the NHS, and her contract expressly provided that she would benefit from the rights set out in the statutory instrument. DWM submitted that as the rights were provided for by statutory instrument and payment to NHS employees was made by the Secretary of State, TUPE was not applicable. The ECJ looked at the Acquired Rights Directive and found that there was no provision for any exceptions save for those set out in Article 3(3). Accordingly the fact that the benefits in this instance derived from a statutory instrument rather than a contract made no difference and they transferred to DWM.

The judgment created uncertainty as to what was meant by 'benefits that are paid when the employee reaches the end of his normal working life'. Did that mean all pensions paid before normal retirement age were excluded from TUPE?

The 'pensions exception' was again considered by the ECJ in *Martin and others v South Bank University*[12]. It is beyond the scope of this chapter to review the *Martin* judgment in detail. However the following propositions can be derived from it:

- The effect of the decision in *Beckmann* has apparently been extended beyond rights arising on redundancy.

- The following rights will transfer under TUPE as they are not old-age, invalidity or survivors' benefits within the meaning of Article 3(3):

  — early-retirement benefits;

  — benefits intended to enhance the conditions of early retirement, paid in the event of early retirement and arising by agreement made between the employer and the employee.

- The following rights were not part of the *Martin* decision:

  — rights to apply for an early-retirement pension as a deferred pensioner no longer employed by the employer;

  — rights to take a transfer value from the scheme;

  — rights to be consulted in relation to the selection of member-nominated trustees.

---

[12]   [2003] 85 PBLR.

- Rights that are within the 'pensions exception' are:

  — pensions payable on or after normal retirement age;

  — ill-health early-retirement benefits;

  — benefits payable to members' dependants on the death of a member before or after normal retirement age.

  Rights falling within the 'pensions exception' are likely to include death-in-service lump-sum payments and incapacity early-retirement pensions.

There has been just one High Court decision which has considered *Beckmann, The Procter & Gamble Company v Svenska Cellulosa Aktiebolaget SCA and another*[13]. Procter & Gamble transferred a business to Svenska Cellulosa Aktiebolaget ('SCA') in 2007 and the sale and purchase agreement provided that SCA would be liable for any accrued liabilities that transferred under TUPE. The Procter & Gamble Pension Fund scheme provided for early retirement, with the employer's consent, on or after 55 with a discount applied for early receipt of a pension before normal retirement age. The level of discount varied according to whether or not the employee had 15 or more years continuous service on retirement. The court had to consider whether the early retirement benefits transferred under TUPE, and it found that the right to have an application for early retirement considered did transfer, as did the liability to provide enhancements to early retirement benefits.

A number of matters remain in question after *Beckmann*, *Martin* and *Procter*:

- *Procter* has extended the *Beckmann* decision beyond the scope of redundancy to include the right to be considered for an early retirement pension, and to receive a bridging pension pending normal retirement date.

- It was unclear after *Beckmann* and *Martin* whether obligations that transfer relate to just those benefits payable up to the normal retirement date or to all obligations under the pension scheme. *Procter* confirmed that only the liability to fund the enhanced early retirement benefits transferred, and not the full early retirement benefit (in other words, only the obligation to fund the additional benefits to members that would otherwise be lost transferred).

- It remains unclear if the exception applies to the statutory right to take a transfer of benefits from one scheme to another. The right has to be exercised before normal retirement age, but it relates to benefits payable from the normal retirement age.

- It remains unclear what the position is if the provision of early-retirement benefits is subject to the consent of the employer or the trustees of the scheme. Where the decision is that of the employer and the obligation

---

[13]   [2012] EWHC 1257 (Ch), [2012] IRLR 733.

to provide early-retirement benefits has passed to the buyer, then the decision to give consent will also transfer to the buyer. However where the decision rests with the trustees it is not clear that the obligation to provide early-retirement benefits will transfer to the buyer.

- It may still be possible to amend benefits under TUPE, regulation 4(5) where the sole or principal reason for the change is a reason unconnected with the transfer or a reason connected with the transfer which is an ETO reason.

Most buyers would wish to carry out due diligence on pension schemes to determine what early-retirement benefits they might acquire on the transfer of a business, but in the context of a distressed or insolvency sale this may not be possible in view of the short amount of time available to the buyer and the limited information that is likely to be available.

Existing pension scheme

10.11   Where the seller is the sole or principal employer and its pension scheme meets the requirements of the Pensions Act 2004 ('PA 2004') the buyer can take over the scheme by becoming the sole or principal employer. Most buyers would not wish to do this, in particular for a defined benefit scheme where it would become liable for any deficit. Most buyers will leave the seller's pension scheme behind to ensure that it does not assume any liability under it:

- A buyer may adopt all pension obligations in contracts between the seller and employees.
- The buyer would become subject to all existing terms of the scheme, including funding requirements and obligations in favour of the trustees.
- The buyer would become liable for any debt on the employer in a winding up of the scheme. That would bring responsibility for any past investment decisions, erroneous valuations, incorrect actuarial data, etc.
- The buyer would be subject to the regime of the Pensions Regulator and the moral hazard provisions of PA 2004.

Bulk transfer payments

10.12

- Historically a buyer might agree to provide equivalent defined benefit pension provisions to those provided by a seller. This would involve arranging a bulk transfer payment from the seller's pension scheme to satisfy the accrued liabilities.
- In an insolvency situation such a transfer is not an appropriate option as the buyer will not obtain any warranties from an office-holder or the scheme trustees to the effect that the amount of any transfer payment will be sufficient to meet the scheme liabilities.

The Pensions Regulator

Introduction

10.13   The Pensions Regulator ('TPR') is the UK regulator of work-based pension schemes. It is empowered by the Government to regulate work-based pensions, and it has been given certain specific objectives:

- to protect the benefits of members of work-based pension schemes;

- to promote and improve understanding of the good administration of work-based pension schemes;

- to reduce the risk of situations arising which may lead to compensation being payable from the PPF; and

- to maximise employer compliance with employer duties and with certain employment safeguards.

The PPF is a fund whose main function is to provide compensation to members of eligible defined benefit pension schemes in situations where the employer has become insolvent and there are insufficient assets in the pension scheme to satisfy certain amounts due to members.

Powers

10.14   TPR has a number of powers available to it under the moral-hazard provisions contained within PA 2004 to enable it to meet its objectives, including the ability to issue Financial Support Directions[14] ('FSD') and Contribution Notices[15] ('CN') to relevant parties to require them to make payments to underfunded pension schemes. The purpose of these powers is to prevent stakeholders abusing and relying on the PPF to satisfy amounts payable to scheme members.

Employers and scheme trustees have an obligation to notify TPR of any 'notifiable event' in relation to a pension scheme or an employer[16] so that TPR can minimise the risk of circumstances which might give rise to compensation being payable by the PPF. Notifiable events in relation to an employer are[17]:

- any decision by the employer to take action which will, or is intended to, result in a debt which is or may become due to the scheme not being paid in full;

- a decision by the employer to cease to carry on business in the UK, or in fact ceasing to carry on business if no decision to do so was taken;

---

[14]   PA 2004, s 43.
[15]   PA 2004, s 38.
[16]   PA 2004, s 69.
[17]   The Pensions Regulator (Notifiable Events) Regulations 2005 (SI 2005/90).

- where applicable, receipt by the employer of advice that it is trading wrongfully within the meaning of IA 1986, s 214 (wrongful trading), or circumstances being reached in which a director or former director of the company knows that there is no reasonable prospect that the company will avoid going into insolvent liquidation within the meaning of that section;

- the conviction of an individual, in any jurisdiction, for an offence involving dishonesty, if the offence was committed while the individual was a director or partner of the employer,

and in certain circumstances:

- any breach by the employer of a covenant in an agreement between the employer and a bank or other institution providing banking services, other than where the bank or other institution agrees with the employer not to enforce the covenant; and

- where the employer is a company, a decision by a controlling company to relinquish control of the employer company.

A number of these events may be found and give rise to a duty to notify TPR in a distressed sale situation. The employer must give notice in writing as soon as reasonably practicable (in practice as a matter of urgency). Whilst a failure to notify may give rise to a civil penalty of up to £50,000, it will not of itself lead to the unravelling of any transaction that takes place. It can be a ground which TPR considers when deciding whether to issue a CN.

TPR has exercised its power to issue FSDs and CNs, and has demonstrated a willingness to intervene in an insolvency situation by other means to protect the PPF.

Financial Support Directions and Contribution Notices

10.15   An FSD is a notice given to an employer under an occupational pension scheme which is not a money purchase scheme, or a person connected or associated with an employer[18] which requires that person or persons to secure that:

- financial support for the scheme is put in place within the period specified in the direction[19]; and

- thereafter that financial support or other financial support remains in place while the scheme is in existence[20].

An FSD may be issued when TPR considers it is reasonable to do so, and the employer is a service company or is insufficiently resourced. A company is

18   As defined in IA 1986, s 435.
19   PA 2004, s 43(3)(a).
20   PA 2004, s 43(3)(b).

'insufficiently resourced' if the value of its resources is less than 50% of the estimated section 75 debt[21], and either:

- the value of the resources of a person who is connected to or associated with the employer when added to the resources of the employer is at least 50 per cent of the estimated section 75 debt; or

- at any time falling on or after 14 April 2008, the aggregate value of the resources of two or more persons who are connected to or associated with the employer and with each other when added to the resources of the employer are at least equal to 50% of the estimated section 75 debt.

The status of FSDs in an administration has been the subject of a Court of Appeal judgment and will be considered in section 10.21.

A CN is a notice given to an employer under an occupational pension scheme which is not a money purchase scheme, or to a person connected to or associated with an employer[22] which requires that person or persons to pay the sum specified in the notices to the scheme trustees.

A CN may be issued when TPR considers it is reasonable to do so, and is of the opinion that the person who it serves the notice on was a party to an act or a deliberate failure to act and the material detriment test is met or that the main purpose or one of the main purposes of the act or failure was[23]:

- to prevent the recovery of the whole or any part of a section 75 debt; or

- to prevent such a debt becoming due, to compromise or otherwise settle such a debt, or to reduce the amount of such a debt which would otherwise become due.

The act or acts may have taken place at any time within the period of six years ending with the issue by TPR of a warning notice in relation to the CN.

The 'material detriment' test will be met if TPR is of the opinion that the act or failure has detrimentally affected in a material way the likelihood of accrued scheme benefits being received[24]. Regard must be had to such matters as TPR considers relevant, including:

- the value of the assets and liabilities of the scheme;

- the effect of the act or failure on the value of those assets or liabilities;

- the scheme obligations of any person;

- the effect of the act or failure on any of those obligations;

- the extent to which any person is likely to be able to discharge any scheme obligation in any circumstances (including insolvency).

---

[21] See Pensions Act 1995, section 75.
[22] As defined in IA 1986, s 435.
[23] PA 2004, s 38(3), (5)(a).
[24] PA 2004, s 38A.

There is a defence to a CN issued by reference to the 'material detriment' test. The person on whom a warning notice of the CN is served must show that:

- he or she gave due consideration to the extent to which the act or failure might detrimentally affect in a material way the likelihood of accrued scheme benefits being received; and

- he or she took all reasonable steps to eliminate or minimise the potential detrimental affects; and

- it was reasonable for him or her to conclude that the act or failure would not detrimentally affect in a material way the likelihood of accrued scheme benefits being received.

A CN may also be issued where there have been a series of acts or failures to act and either the 'material detriment' test or the 'main purpose' test is met in relation to the series.

TPR must have regard to the extent to which, in all the circumstances of the case, it was reasonable for the person to act or fail to act in the way he did. TPR must also have regard to any other matters it considers relevant when deciding whether or not it would be reasonable to issue an FSD[25] or a CN[26] on grounds other than the 'material detriment' test. In both cases such 'other matters' would include:

- the relationship which the person has or has had with the employer and whether the person has or has had control of the employer;

- the value of any benefits received directly or indirectly by that person from the employer;

- any connection or involvement which the person has or has had with the scheme;

- the financial circumstances of the person.

In the case of a CN it must also consider:

- if the act or failure to act was a notifiable event for the purposes of PA 2004, s 69 (duty to notify the Regulator of certain events), any failure by the person to give notice of the event;

- all the purposes of the act or failure to act (including whether a purpose of the act or failure was to prevent or limit loss of employment);

- the degree of involvement of the person in the act or failure to act; and

- the likelihood of relevant creditors being paid.

---

[25]   PA 2004, s 43(7).
[26]   PA 2004, s 38(7).

Clearance statements

10.16   There is a procedure under PA 2004, ss 46 and 42 in relation to FSDs and CNs, by which the parties to a proposed transaction can apply to TPR for a clearance statement to the effect that the arrangements they propose will not give rise to TPR issuing an FSD or a CN. This can eliminate any uncertainty that might otherwise arise on the sale of any business, but particularly one where the seller is insolvent and pension scheme deficits may well be a live issue. TPR encourages parties to apply for clearance statements whenever there is a risk that a transaction will or may be detrimental to a pension scheme, and will work quickly with a view to fitting in with the very short timeframe within which a transaction may have to be completed.

Usually the parties to the transaction will agree a joint approach to TPR for clearance. The applicants should have agreed steps to mitigate any detriment to the pension scheme, and they must provide full disclosure of all relevant matters. A clearance statement binds TPR in relation to the exercise of the power to issue an FSD or a CN in relation to the scheme unless[27]:

- the circumstances in relation to which the exercise of the power under that section arises are not the same as the circumstances described in the application; and

- the difference in those circumstances is material to the exercise of the power.

Accordingly, failure to provide full disclosure can effectively result in a clearance statement being set aside at a later date. TPR can seek further information from the parties in relation to any application[28].

TPR has issued guidance as to when it expects an application for clearance to be made[29]. It expects a clearance statement to be sought only in relation to 'type A' events. All 'type A' events are events that are materially detrimental to the ability of the scheme to meet its pension liabilities. Employer-related events will only be 'type A' events if the scheme has a relevant deficit. Events which fall into this category include those which:

- prevent the recovery of the whole or any part of the employer's section 75 debt;

- prevent the employer's section 75 debt becoming due or compromise the section 75 debt;

- reduce the amount of the employer's section 75 debt which would otherwise become due; or

- weaken the employer covenant because:

---

[27]   PA 2004, ss 46(5), 42(5).
[28]   PA 2004, ss 46(3), 42(3).
[29]   http://www.thepensionsregulator.gov.uk/guidance/guidance-clearance.aspx#s1386.

— they have an impact on the ability of the employer to meet its ongoing funding commitments to the scheme, or an impact on those commitments; or

— they reduce the dividend that would be available to the scheme in the event of employer insolvency.

Relevant events might include:

• granting further security;

• paying dividends;

• a change in group structure, or change of control, or change of group financial support;

• a 'phoenix' of a business.

In any restructuring, consideration must be given as to seeking a clearance statement from TPR if relevant and time permits.

If there is a wish to compromise a section 75 debt as part of a restructuring it is likely that the PPF will be involved in any negotiations, in addition to the scheme trustees and the employer, in order that the PPF can ensure its position is not worsened and the risk of FSDs and CNs can be reduced or eliminated. If one result of a restructuring is that the seller's pension scheme transfers to the PPF, TPR will not issue a clearance statement unless the PPF is satisfied with the arrangements.

The scheme apportionment arrangements[30] introduced on 6 April 2008 and the employer debt 'easement' procedure [31] introduced on 6 April 2010 (which will help employers of underfunded schemes to manage a restructuring process without triggering a section 75 debt) are examples of how the Department for Work and Pensions is working with stakeholders to introduce a more flexible and workable regime.

Other powers

10.17   Under Pensions Act 1995 ('PA 1995'), s 7 as modified by Pensions Act 2008, s 131(1) TPR has the power to appoint a trustee of a trust scheme where it is satisfied that it is reasonable to do so in order:

(a)   to secure that the trustees as a whole have, or exercise, the necessary knowledge and skill for the proper administration of the scheme;

(b)   to secure that the number of trustees is sufficient for the proper administration of the scheme;

---

[30]   Occupational Pension Schemes (Employer Debt – Apportionment Arrangements) (Amendment) Regulations 2008 (SI 2008/1068).

[31]   Occupational Pension Schemes (Employer Debt and Miscellaneous Amendments) Regulations 2010 (SI 2010/725).

(c)   to secure the proper use or application of the assets of the scheme; or

(d)   otherwise to protect the interests of the generality of the members of the scheme.

On 23 February 2009 the Determination Panel of TPR appointed a trustee under PA 1995, s 7(3) to the Graphex Limited ('Graphex') Pension and Life Assurance Scheme ('Graphex Scheme'). Graphex was the principal employer and the Graphex Scheme was underfunded. An actuarial estimate showed that as at 19 September 2008 there was a buyout deficit of £1.4 million based on assets of £2.5 million. Graphex was insolvent but was continuing to trade on the basis of a parent company guarantee. TPR learned that certain directors of Graphex and its parent company, which was also a participating employer, were planning to place Graphex into administration and buy the business back by way of a pre-pack, leaving the pension deficit behind. Indeed it appeared that avoiding the pension liability was the main purpose of the administration in so far as certain of the directors of Graphex and the parent company were concerned. The same directors were also trustees of the Graphex Scheme.

The Determinations Panel of TPR found that the relevant trustees were faced with conflicts of interest as trustees of the Graphex Scheme and directors of the participating employers which they had failed to manage properly. It appeared that the proposed pre-pack was imminent and in the circumstances it was necessary to appoint an independent trustee to the Graphex Scheme using the Special Procedure (without notice) on the basis that if any other course of action was taken there would have been an immediate risk to the scheme members and assets. Further, on review of the decision the Determinations Panel added that an additional ground for the appointment of an independent trustee was that a pre-pack would have posed a risk to the PPF.

In all pre-packs unsecured creditors do not have the opportunity to comment on the proposed sale of the business before it takes place, and a pension scheme creditor is in no different a position. It will receive SIP 16 information after the sale, but nothing beforehand. In relation to the Graphex Scheme it was the trustees themselves who had created the risk to the scheme as they were also the directors of Graphex who were considering the pre-pack. TPR's decision to appoint an independent trustee to the scheme in such circumstances shows that it will intervene in such a situation where the trustees/directors fail to manage what is an obvious conflict of interest, and of course where it knows of the risk to the scheme in advance.

Pensions issues on insolvency

Winding up the scheme

10.18   If the principal employer under a defined benefit pension scheme enters into a specified insolvency proceeding, this may well crystallise the winding up of the pension scheme, and a debt due from the company to the pension scheme of an amount by which the value of the assets of the scheme is insufficient to fund its liabilities[32]. Other events, such as the transfer of a business outside of insolvency, can trigger crystallisation of the debt arising under PA 1995, s 75. The section 75 debt is calculated on a full buyout basis, being the cost of securing the liabilities of the scheme by purchasing matching annuities with an insurance company. This can be a significant, in some circumstances the largest, debt a company has. Unless the company has specifically secured the debt to the pension scheme it will be an unsecured claim. However as the pension scheme may well be the largest unsecured creditor it does enable the trustees to wield a certain amount of power.

Notice obligations

10.19   An insolvency event also brings with it an obligation on the part of the office-holder to notify the PPF, TPR and the scheme trustees of the insolvency[33] within 14 days of the later of the insolvency event and the office-holder becoming aware of the insolvency. Relevant insolvency events[34] which trigger the obligation to give notice in relation to a company are:

- where a nominee in relation to a proposal for a voluntary arrangement submits his or her report to the court and states that in his or her opinion meetings of the company and its creditors should be summoned to consider the proposal;

- the directors of the company file with the court documents and statements to obtain a small-company moratorium where they propose a voluntary arrangement;

- an administrative receiver is appointed in relation to the company;

- the company enters administration;

- a resolution is passed for the creditors' voluntary winding up of the company;

- a meeting of creditors is held in relation to the company under IA 1986, s 95 (a creditors' meeting which has the effect of converting a members' voluntary winding up into a creditors' voluntary winding up);

- an order for the winding up of the company is made by the court.

The obligation to give notice does not apply when:

- a resolution is passed for the members' voluntary winding up of the company;

- a provisional liquidator is appointed;

---

[32]   PA 1995, s 75.
[33]   PA 2004, s 120.
[34]   PA 2004, s 121.

- a receiver other than an administrative receiver is appointed;

- a company enters into an overseas insolvency process.

Scheme transfer to the PPF

10.20   Giving notice will cause the start of an assessment period to determine whether or not the scheme will be transferred to the PPF. During an assessment period the PPF will ascertain whether:

- the scheme can be rescued; or

- it can afford to secure benefits at least equal to those that the PPF would provide if it assumed responsibility for it.

If the answer to both questions is no, the PPF will assume responsibility for the pension scheme from the end of the assessment period.

The PPF broadly offers two levels of compensation to scheme members:

- for those who have reached the scheme retirement age or were already receiving a survivors' pension or an early-retirement pension payable on the grounds of ill health, 100 per cent of the pension already being paid;

- for those who have not reached the scheme retirement age, 90 per cent of the benefits payable subject to a cap depending on the age of the scheme member when the compensation falls due to be paid.

The principal issues for any party to a transaction involving an insolvent seller are similar to those that have been set out in section 10.4 above in relation to the powers of TPR and avoiding the exercise and effect of any of those powers. Additionally, they have to bear in mind that where there is a large number of employees and an underfunded defined benefit scheme, the scheme trustees or the PPF may well be the largest unsecured creditor in the insolvency proceeding.

Nortel and Lehman Brothers

10.21   In July and September 2010 respectively TPR published a determination to issue FSDs against a number of companies within the Nortel and Lehman Brothers groups, in each case after the relevant companies had gone into administration. The administrators appointed to both Nortel and Lehman Brothers issued applications in the High Court to determine the status of liability under the FSDs, and how they should be treated in the administrations. The High Court found that liability under FSDs issued after a company had gone into administration constituted an expense of the administration. The administrators appealed that decision.

In October 2011 the Court of Appeal unanimously dismissed the appeal and upheld the decision of the High Court on giving judgment[35]. The court found that liability under the FSDs and any subsequent CN was an expense of the administrations, which fell to be paid as a necessary disbursement under Rule 2.67(1)(f) of the Insolvency Rules 1986 so ranking ahead of the administrators' remuneration in terms of priority. The administrators obtained permission to appeal to the Supreme Court, and the further appeal is due to be heard on 14 May 2013.

The Court of Appeal decision has created a real concern for insolvency practitioners, who will be aware of the risk of liability under FSDs when considering their strategy for an administration. It significantly strengthens the position of TPR, and may well stifle some business rescues. As a result of concerns raised by insolvency practitioners TPR issued a statement on 26 July 2012 to help the pensions and insolvency industries understand its approach to FSDs in insolvency situations[36].

This issue will only affect a very small number of administrations, but nevertheless it is an important point and the outcome of the appeal to the Supreme Court is awaited with interest.

---

[35]   *Bloom and others v Pensions Regulator and others* [2011] EWCA Civ 1124, [2012] 1 All ER 1455.
[36]   http://www.thepensionsregulator.gov.uk/docs/financial-support-directions-and-insolvency-july-2012.pdf.

Chapter 11

How to Deal with Existing Customers and Work in Progress

Customers of an insolvent or almost insolvent business are never happy. If they have also been forced by the administrator to accept part payment only of monies due it can be very hard to maintain their goodwill. There may be the possibility of offering them more repayments over time if they will remain loyal customers of the business under its new ownership, but clearly buyers have an uphill struggle to maintain credibility and keep the business. Yet the customer base and goodwill are often a principal asset acquired. This is one major area where the insolvent and solvent sales differ. Goodwill may not be much in existence if a customer has not received goods for which they have paid. This chapter examines how to deal with existing customers of the business being purchased. Chapter 7 examined some issues of goodwill, data protection and intellectual property which will also have an impact on the future relationship between the parties. Chapter 4, which addressed due diligence, gave guidance on areas to watch. If due diligence has been undertaken even on a preliminary level it is hoped that it will, at the very least, have looked at which are the key customers and the likelihood of them staying with the business after a purchase. Reference should also be made to precedent 'C. Novation of contract' in the Appendix.

Advance protection

11.1   Protecting a business during difficult economic times requires both obvious and more subtle legal measures. The almost insolvent business may have taken the following steps or may choose to do so when difficulties arise:

1. **Require payment in advance**

    Any change to a contract requires agreement between both parties. However most sales are on one-off purchase-order terms rather than longstanding distribution or supply contracts so new terms can be presented for each purchase. Where there is a long-term agreement with payment terms already in place then changes to the agreement can be made if both parties agree. Always look at the terms in place already as they may well set out how variations or changes are negotiated. A typical clause might fix prices or payment terms for a 12-month period and provide for regular reviews.

    Some buyers have simply said that suppliers will not be allowed to supply them unless they accept new terms, such as longer payment periods, in the current economic climate and suppliers desperate for the business have had to accede to such requests. Legally this is simply a matter of commercial negotiation once any fixed-payment period/fixed-terms period is up. The obvious risk however is that the supplier not agreeing to an immediate contract change can lead to termination by the buyer, and the supplier may not be able to afford to lose that business. If the aim is to keep a buyer afloat so that suppliers have a customer to supply then changing terms even to the detriment of the supplier may be commercially wise. There are no difficult legal issues in this. Simply agree the document changes. Ensure they are signed, and that where there is a pre-existing contract its variation or change control provisions are followed so far as possible and ensure the variation to the agreement is kept safely with the original contract.

Force majeure

Some companies argue that the current recession/depression could amount to circumstances of force majeure which might entitle them to suspend the operation of the contract. This depends on the clause concerned, where there is one. Force majeure is usually defined to mean circumstances which make it impossible for one party to perform the contract, such as act of God, fire, earthquakes, civil unrest on a worldwide scale caused by the economic instability and sometimes strikes, although wise buyers always delete strikes and industrial action when negotiating force majeure clauses in contracts. It is conceivable that a failure by a bank could mean a supplier cannot pay, such as happened for a period with those with savings in the Icelandic banks. Force majeure clauses would need to be scrutinised carefully to see if that would mean a buyer did not have to pay under the terms of the contract. However, often failure to pay is not excused by force majeure. Some contracts expressly state that force majeure reasons may not be used to excuse a failure to pay. Even where the force majeure clause does not refer to failures to pay most customers have other sources of finance they can use so they would not be prevented from paying due to circumstances beyond their control unless there were a ban on payments between that country and the other, sanctions and the like. Recent examples have included swine flu, where some clauses cover pandemics, and the April 2010 Icelandic volcano fallout which caused flight transport from the UK to be stopped, although the availability of 'by sea' alternatives may mean that would not be force majeure under many clauses.

Anti-competitive agreements with competitors about price

Questions from clients on this issue have included whether they can agree with other suppliers to a customer in known difficulties to require this or limit credit periods to a certain level. Under the Competition Act 1998 such collusion could amount to an anti-competitive practice when done by agreement or understanding with other suppliers. When simply taken as unilateral action it is lawful. Similarly, collectively agreeing to boycott a customer with competitors is illegal. Information on this area can be obtained from the Office of Fair Trading – www.oft.gov.uk. The

EU in 2011 revised its competition law-guidelines on horizontal agreements – see www.europa.eu under 'Competition'. These for the first time include a new section on information exchange under competition law. Some industries with competition law investigations in their past require competition solicitors to attend credit group discussions to ensure discussion does not stray into areas which would breach Article 101 TFEU or the Competition Act 1998. Detailed guidance is also provided in writing by such lawyers to clients involved in such competitor discussions about credit issues.

Currency fluctuation risks

2. Hedge against currency risks or specify fees in sterling. A large number of questions from clients to solicitors of late have been about, for example, currency fluctuations, pricing changes, and rights to vary a price given the unprecedented slump in the pound. Ensure that all contracts with businesses abroad adequately reflect currency risks. The pound at the date of writing is at the lowest it has ever been against the euro. In some ways this should help exports, but as few people are buying abroad whatever the price it has not, to date, proved the boon it might otherwise have been.

3. Reduce credit periods if they have to be offered at all. At a time when some big customers with economic power have demanded longer credit periods this suggestion can be difficult, but for suppliers who cannot obtain new bank finance reduction in credit periods can be essential to survival. Some companies have had to factor their debts and this is obviously one solution, although not favoured by many and does not always give the right impression to customers about the viability of the supplier. Also, sometimes there is a customer-relations problem if the factoring company then vigorously enforces debts which result in adverse publicity for the original supplier.

4. Look at what contracts are in place whether formal or informal, and which are the more important commercial arrangements which the business has undertaken. Some companies have no written contracts at all with key suppliers and customers. Of course it is very hard to change the status quo and 'if it ain't broke, don't fix it' is sometimes commercially wise, but it may well be possible to tell a supplier or customer that a written agreement is needed to formalise the business arrangement. This might then make it clear that rights given are 'exclusive' where that was simply the custom and practice before. It may also specify that a lengthy notice period of three months or even a year or more must be given to terminate the arrangement. Without that in place contracts can be terminated on 'reasonable notice' at common law under English law. That is too vague a principle under which to operate for many businesses, and it may well be that the directors or company secretary get blamed if the business is in difficulties because a big supplier or customer terminates a longstanding unwritten arrangement with very little notice, when had there been a written contract with a fixed notice period, the business might have had time to find alternative customers or suppliers to plug the gap. It can be wise to undertake a general review within the business

now, before it has financial problems, to find out which contracts are important and which are in writing.

5. Retention of title: increasing numbers of companies are looking at their terms of business, or drafting them if they have none, in particular to check they have binding retention of title clauses.

6. Do a very thorough investigation into the credit-worthiness of all suppliers or customers. Request payment up front in cash/by bank transfer/ letter of credit in cases where that is appropriate and also obtain director or parent-company guarantees of obligations and ensure they are drawn up by lawyers so they are legally binding.

7. Include payment on the basis of results, where possible.

Redundancies

8. In some cases it may be necessary to terminate the employment contracts of staff if the overhead cost cannot be afforded. Ensure if people are made redundant that this is done within the law, following all procedures; www.bis.gov.uk has useful guidance from the Department for Business, Innovation and Skills on the procedures to be followed on redundancy and dismissal of employees. If someone is truly redundant then they will be entitled to a redundancy payment, although these are fairly low, set statutory rates. However some employers choose to offer a more generous package, particularly where they are seeking to persuade employees to leave. The business will need to engage in consultation in advance in many cases. The steps that had to be gone through before terminating an employment contract until 5 April 2009 were set out in the Employment Act 2002 (Dispute Resolution) Regulations 2004. These were abolished by the Employment Act 2008 on 6 April 2009 – see http://www.berr. gov.uk/whatwedo/employment/Resolving_disputes/index.html. The Act abolished the mandatory 'three-step' processes for disciplinary and dismissal procedures undertaken by an employer and for grievances raised by an employee. In its place businesses must act fairly and are advised to follow a revised statutory ACAS Code of Practice which sets out the principles of what an employer and employee should do to achieve a reasonable standard of behaviour in termination of employment. It is generally best to take legal advice before making staff redundant.

Debt Recovery

9. Recover debt. Often he who proceeds first recovers money. Consider issuing statutory demands (there has been a huge increase in these of late), starting legal action and pursuing other parties for breach of contract. When money is tight every penny counts. Do not let big debts build up with those who may not be able to pay. Take action. Require payment up front, security or even an equity stake in a business. Refuse to provide goods or services if no payment is forthcoming. Consider paying your supplier's own supplier instead of your supplier as a compromise to ensure projects can continue.

10. Look at getting out of onerous contracts which cannot be afforded. Check with lawyers if legally binding obligations have been formed or

not. Consider the cost of terminating contracts, which may be cheaper than continuing.

11. Every seller ought to have written conditions of sale which reserve ownership of the goods (or intellectual property where copyright such as computer software or designs is being written for a customer) until full payment is made.

12. Assess if contracts can be transferred. Some suppliers have been assigning contracts to new subsidiaries with very poor credit records. Sometimes the contract forbids this.

Rights to vary contracts

11.2   In practice most commercial contracts, other than one-off sales of goods and services on standard terms/purchase orders, expressly include a clause which states that the terms may not be varied without agreement signed by both parties. For longer term service agreements there will often be even more detailed change-control provisions. Many such contracts have annexed to them a special form to be used by the parties in agreeing changes to the contract which must be signed and agreed before the work proceeds. However in law it is permissible in a long-term contract to give one party the right to vary the terms at will on notice to the other party if that is preferred and if the other party will accept those terms. That is not the case however for contracts with consumers. Most will not accept such an onerous position but it is not unlawful to impose it on a business if the other party agrees at the outset.

Assuming there is no such right to vary without consent, a business worried about insolvency of a supplier or customer which is therefore seeking to improve contract terms will need to consider how it can agree new contract terms with the other party. For example prices may be fixed for a year or a right to increase prices if costs go up agreed. In such a case the obvious route is to offer some terms which improve the legal position of the other party whilst also seeking changes to the benefit of the first party. In this way it may be possible to persuade them to accept terms which might on the other hand be onerous to them. Similarly, if one party is in a very strong negotiating position because they know the other party has to have their goods and there are few alternative products available, then they may be able to agree amended terms more easily than would otherwise be the case.

Other contract terms

11.3   Consider revising contract terms to check that there are rights to terminate agreements, not only where the customer goes into liquidation, but also when it cannot pay its debts as they fall due or other earlier insolvency 'hint' rather than event. In that case the supplier can bail out early without being in breach of contract. Even if the contract requires the supplier to continue with the agreement, in appropriate cases it may be best to stop work. Most insolvent companies will not sue suppliers who breach a contract simply because they do not have the funds to do so, but obviously take legal advice before engaging in such a bullish stance, and ideally ensure the contract allows work to cease in such a case.

Other credit issues

11.4   Good credit control is crucial. Employ good credit controllers and take up references for new customers. The Madoff/Stanford and other alleged frauds/Ponzi schemes which came to light in the recession in 2009/2010 seem to have continued unchecked because people followed the herd, did not undertake their own due diligence and relied on others to take the lead. In difficult economic times it is crucial for buyers to undertake regular checks on the credit-worthiness of customers before offering credit. Cash up front is demanded in appropriate cases.

After a customer goes out of business

11.5   The measures above provide some legal protection in advance of a customer getting into financial difficulties. Once notification is received of liquidation or administration (or for sole traders, bankruptcy or other arrangements with creditors), act quickly.

Arrange to retrieve goods subject to retention of title clauses. No court order is needed, and most liquidators, once the clause is proven to apply, will allow suppliers to enter premises and take goods back. If the goods are locked up then a court order is needed to break down a door, but if they are lying on shelves or in a corridor or in a factory a supplier is entitled simply to arrive and retrieve them if the contract says so. Possession remains nine-tenths of the law in practice and most liquidators start by looking at how much money is in the bank to decide which disputes are worth fighting. Also consider negotiating with a liquidator who may need stock and may instead choose to pay sums owed simply to help carry on trading if he or she hopes to sell the business as a going concern.

Example

Pedestrian Thickos Ltd never had any terms of sale. When their best customer went bust they assumed they could recover goods they had sold but for which they had received no payment. They found the goods were owned by the buyer from the date of delivery. They got nothing on the liquidation. In one part of their business they had terms of sale, but had contracts on the buyer's conditions of purchase on its purchase order, so their terms did not apply. They similarly lost out.

Bright CoSec Ltd had good terms of sale which contained an RoT Clause. They always rejected terms and conditions on purchase orders and imposed their terms of sale. On a liquidation of a customer they were able to enter the premises of the buyer and recover £50,000 worth of stock by enforcing their RoT clause.

Determine if as a supplier the business will be crucial to a liquidator who may choose to pay cash up front if a prospective sale is likely.

Consider making an offer to buy the customer as a means of securing debt. Suppliers often find they are a natural buyer for a customer in financial difficulties. Sometimes a consortium with other suppliers together can effect a sale or put in some funding, perhaps in conjunction with a management buyout.

Check if the debt is secured in any way. It may be that a floating or fixed charge was granted over assets which will put the supplier higher up the list of payees on a liquidation or entitle the supplier to sell the asset over which any charge was granted.

If a company has not yet gone into liquidation, be careful about accepting payments where there is a connection in case the rules on preferences are breached or the directors are wrongfully or fraudulently trading. If there is even a hint of an attempt to defraud creditors, take legal advice. Not everyone will be the recipient of $1m of jewellery allegedly posted by Bernard Madoff, but the corporate equivalent of such an action when the company is on the verge of going out of business is not uncommon and buyers need to be wary of deals that appear too good to be true.

Finally, remember that most liquidators and administrators will negotiate and want the affairs of the company settled in a cost-effective fashion so do not always accept the first proposal put forward. Once the company is out of business there may be possibilities to buy back stock, buy assets, parts of the business and even intellectual property.

Bona vacantia

11.6   Companies which are instead wound down and struck off without debts may inadvertently find they still own some assets. These go to the Crown under a principle called Bona Vacantia. Details of this are at http://www.bona-vacantia.gov.uk/. Solicitors have experience of buying assets, even computer source code, from that office, eg in 2013 £1000 was a typical fee charged by the Treasury Solicitor's office for purchase of a trade mark by a company which had been struck off the register. However in most commercial liquidations described in this chapter the company goes into insolvency liquidation and the liquidation would normally dispose of all the assets. Above all think ahead. Do not wait until a problem occurs to wish there were terms of sale with an ROT clause in them or a commercial contract with a long notice period. Seek to negotiate them now before problems arise.

Purchase agreement and assignment of contracts

11.7   One of the assets to be purchased will be goodwill (see Chapter 7), and part of that will be assignment of existing contracts, where they are assignable. Part of due diligence (see Chapter 4) is ascertaining if contracts can be assigned. Even with the limited due diligence involved in fire-sales of this kind it is essential to check the issue of assignment for major contracts with customers. If the customer may terminate the agreement and it may not be assigned and they are not minded to novate (sign a new contract) with the buyer then there may be in effect no business to purchase.

The legal position is that the benefit of contracts under English law can be assigned unless the contract says otherwise – hence the importance of checking existing contracts for such a restriction. Then once the assignment has taken place the buyer will notify the other contracting party that from henceforth they are dealing with the buyer. Obviously where shares not assets are acquired it is a very different matter as the same legal entity continues as do its contracts, seamlessly, but even then the contract may contain a right to terminate on a 'change of control', so due diligence on that issue in cases of acquisitions of shares, not assets, should be carried out.

A novation agreement conversely is a new agreement which the customer may or may not accept – in other words it may not be foisted on a contracting party in the way an assignment can be.

In some cases the prospective buyer may be able to visit an important customer with the seller in advance of the sale to seek at least verbal non-binding assurances about continuing business after a sale.

Below is an example of a clause in a contract from an administrator:

1. **THE CONTRACTS**

1.1   The Buyer acknowledges that the Seller may not be entitled to assign or novate the Contracts and to that extent neither it nor the Administrators on its behalf purport to do so.

1.2   The Seller shall, for a period of six months from the Transfer Date, use reasonable efforts to co-operate with the Buyer in trying to persuade the other parties to any Contract to have that contract assigned or novated to the Buyer, although it is agreed and understood that the Seller and the Administrators may have little or no influence with such other parties and shall be under no obligation to make any payments directly or indirectly to such other parties to persuade them to effect an assignment or novation.

1.3   The Buyer accepts the risk that some or all of the Contracts may prior to the Transfer Date have been breached or terminated and that the contracting party may refuse to continue with the performance of its contractual obligations on the same terms and conditions or at all unless the Buyer is willing to remedy such breach and that further a contracting party may exercise or purport to exercise rights of set-off or counterclaim against the Buyer.

1.4   Without limitation to the above, the Buyer shall indemnify and keep indemnified the Seller and the Administrators on a full indemnity basis from and against all and any Liabilities arising in respect of all and any Contracts after the Transfer Date in so far as the Buyer chooses to take a novation to such Contracts to itself.

As can be seen very little is promised by administrators compared with a different type of business sale where insolvency is not an issue. The seller does here agree to co-operate after the sale but it is clearly placed as a liability on the buyer that the contract may not be successfully transferred. The indemnity from buyer to seller in the last part of the clause will also be of concern to some buyers.

Work in progress

11.8   Finally, the agreement will address work in progress. Here is an example definition of this:

> '**"Work in Progress"** means all partly completed contracts or partly performed services in respect of the Business as at [   ] 2013 together with the benefit of all leads or other pre-contract opportunities of the Business as at [   ] 2013.'

Work in progress is one of the assets which is purchased in many purchases, and clearly it needs to be made certain what happens about contracts which are mid-stream when the sale occurs.

Practical steps to take if a customer is in difficulties

11.9   Where a customer has gone into liquidation or administration, contact the liquidator or administrator as soon as possible. Assess the total financial exposure to that customer. Look at whether there was credit insurance – this has been a major issue in the recession with many companies withdrawing credit insurance cover for well-known high-street businesses such that suppliers have no longer been prepared to supply those companies unless cash is paid up front.

Checklist of practical immediate steps

- Call your purchasing department at once and put an immediate halt on any payments to that customer, as there may be rights of set-off of money they owe to the business against money the business owes that customer.

- If the liquidator or administrator needs the supplies of goods, insist on cash up front and instalment payments for other sums which are due for earlier supplies, on credit where possible.

- Immediately begin an examination of the paperwork to ascertain what retention of title clauses there were, whose terms apply and whether that can be proved.

- Contact the liquidator about recovery of goods – complete their form for recovery of goods and keep copies of all papers sent to them.

- Arrange a date to attend at the premises to take back goods.

- If there is any doubt about whether the RoT clause is a registrable charge and the supplies were made less than 21 days before, consider registering the charge now at Companies House.

- Go to the premises, assuming there is an RoT clause, and recover the goods – take members of staff who will be able to recover the goods physically and be calm but assertive – take the relevant paperwork and if necessary legal advice from the company's solicitor about the right to recover the goods.

- Check whether goods which are on third-party premises could be taken back too if title was not yet passed – certainly in practice often the buyer will have left the goods at a customer's premises which may sometimes not even be on private property so the supplier may be able to recover the goods.

- If there are no goods of this kind or no RoT clause, look at other goods of the buyer at the premises of the supplier such as goods sent for repair or remanufacture, and look at whether they could be held on to if that is legal – take legal advice on the contract clauses concerned.

- Cease making goods for that customer if there is no prospect of payment, unless there is a ready market for them elsewhere.

- Check contracts with suppliers for that project, and subcontractors, and have them cease work – see if there is a legal obligation to pay them or not.

Acquiring the customer's business and contracts – Insolvency Service Guidance

11.10   A customer with a business which is going under may have valuable customer contracts. The supplier may be able to acquire cheaply equity/shares in that customer or take an assignment of the customer's contracts direct so that the customer is removed from the contractual matrix and in their place there is a direct contract between the supplier and the ultimate customer.

These options are not always possible, but they can represent a compromise where the customer is otherwise unable to pay anything for the goods and parts of the business could continue profitably. The various parties will have to check if contracts can be freely assigned (often they cannot be due to contractual restrictions) and also, very importantly, look at whether any such deals will breach any insolvency legislation such as amounting to a fraudulent preference.

In terms of what happens next, when the customer is in liquidation the following Insolvency Service guidance sets out the position for creditors:

'Your role as a creditor

When will I be notified?

The OR will normally notify all known creditors within 12 weeks of the date of the court order. The OR will say whether a meeting of creditors will be held. The OR will decide to hold a meeting to appoint an IP if there are significant assets, otherwise the OR will be the trustee or liquidator.

You will also be sent a report giving estimates of the insolvent's assets and liabilities and what the causes of the failure are considered to be. If you think that a bankrupt or company is withholding information about the assets, you should write to the OR dealing with the case.

How do I make a claim?

If you have been contacted by the OR/IP they already have a note of your claim. If you contacted the OR/IP your details will have been added to the list of creditors.

If the OR/IP intends to hold a meeting of creditors or to make a payment to creditors you will be sent a 'proof of debt' form. The official receiver does not automatically send out proof of debt forms. If you receive a proof of debt form you should complete and sign it and return it to the OR/IP. The rights of a creditor who holds a fixed charge, or security, on assets (such as a mortgage) to sell the asset to recover their debt are not affected by insolvency. The chargeholder (secured creditor) is the first to get paid when the asset is sold. Any surplus will be handed over to the trustee/liquidator.

When all the assets available to unsecured creditors have been realised, the trustee/liquidator will distribute the proceeds in a strict order of priority as follows:

1. The fees and charges of the liquidation/bankruptcy.

2. Debts due to preferential creditors. These debts are set out in the Insolvency Act 1986 and include wages owed in the four months before the date of the insolvency order and contributions to occupational pension schemes.

3. In company cases, any creditor holding a floating charge over an asset, such as a debenture.

4. All unsecured creditors.

5. Any interest payable on debts.

6. In company cases, the shareholders.

Therefore, unsecured creditors will usually only be paid when the fees and charges of the insolvency procedures and the claims of secured and preferential creditors have been paid. Where a company which is being wound up has assets subject to a floating charge, part of the net proceeds from their sale will, in appropriate cases, be set aside for distribution to the unsecured creditors.

If full repayment of claims is not possible, payments are made to creditors by way of a dividend in proportion to the value of each claim.

If a dividend is to be paid, all creditors whose addresses are known will be notified. If you have not already submitted a proof of debt, this may be your last chance to do so. If you submit your proof of debt after the dividend has been declared, you may lose your right to share in the money available at that time.

How much you are paid will depend on the amount of money that can be realised and the number of claims. If there are few assets, you may not receive anything.

You can ask for a full list of creditors from the OR/IP. The OR/IP is allowed to charge a fee for this service. The list will show how much each creditor is owed. You also have a right to inspect the court file unless the court directs otherwise. If a statement of affairs has been submitted, the OR/IP will not send you a list of creditors, instead you will be directed to the court file for details of creditors and their claims.

When paying a dividend, the OR/IP can reject the whole or part of a creditor's claim. The OR/IP must provide reasons for doing so in writing. If you are dissatisfied with the decision on your claim, you may apply to the court for the decision to be reversed or varied.

Meeting of creditors

A first meeting of creditors is held so that the creditors can appoint an IP as trustee or liquidator in place of the OR. This is likely to be the only meeting of creditors before the final meeting is called. If the OR does not believe the assets available are enough to attract an IP, the OR will send notice to all creditors that no first meeting is to be held and as a result the OR will be trustee/liquidator. The OR must hold a first meeting if it is requested by one quarter in value of the creditors. If the creditors request a meeting, they will have to lodge a deposit for any costs of the meeting with the OR. If the creditors do not choose an IP at the meeting, the OR can apply to the Secretary of State to make an appointment or remain as trustee/liquidator. The OR can also apply to the Secretary of State when an appointment of an IP is needed in an emergency, for example to deal with urgent transactions involving assets. When this happens the IP must notify the creditors of his or her appointment. This may be done by advertisement in a newspaper if the court allows, for example where there is a large number of creditors.

Further meetings of creditors (called general meetings) are sometimes held if the trustee/liquidator wants to find out the creditors' wishes in any matter relating to the insolvency proceedings, or if requested by 10 per cent in value of the creditors.

Where an IP is trustee/liquidator, a final meeting of creditors will be called (see details under 'Completion of the case' below).

Conduct and voting at a meeting of creditors

You can normally only vote at a meeting if you have returned your proof of debt to the OR/IP within the time stated in the notice. You can vote at the meeting without attending personally but you must also have submitted a proxy form allowing someone else to vote on your behalf. The proxy form is supplied by the OR/IP at the same time as the notice calling the creditors' meeting and you must return it by the time specified. The proof of debt and proxy form must be signed by the same person. Voting at a meeting of creditors is by value, and is calculated by the amount of the creditor's claim that is admitted (accepted) by the chair of the meeting for voting purposes. The chair will check all the proofs of debt and proxy forms, and confirm the amount admitted for voting purposes.

Briefly, at a first meeting of creditors, the chair will check that everyone present is allowed to be at the meeting; s/he will explain the purpose of the meeting, and provide details about the insolvent's assets. The meeting then votes on the appointment of an IP as trustee or liquidator. A first meeting of creditors is not an opportunity for you to question the bankrupt/director (it is unlikely they will be at the meeting) or to discuss matters relating to the insolvency.

For an IP to be appointed by the meeting of creditors, there must be a majority in value of those present or represented (by proxy) voting for the IP.

Creditors'/liquidation committee

A creditors'/liquidation committee can also be appointed at a meeting of creditors unless the official receiver remains as trustee/liquidator. The committee supervises and assists the trustee/liquidator on behalf of the creditors. In bankruptcies it is called a creditors' committee; in liquidations it is a liquidation committee. The committee consists of at least 3 and not more than 5 elected creditors.

An individual creditor who has been elected can act personally or appoint a representative.

You have a right to nominate yourself or any other creditor as a member of a committee. You can also vote for yourself.

If certain actions are proposed by the trustee/liquidators, a creditors'/liquidation committee must first give approval for them. Each committee has different powers but they include agreeing to carry on the bankrupt's or company's business and bringing or defending legal actions. A liquidation committee must first approve payments to any class of creditors (for example, preferential creditors) in full and any arrangements made with creditors or in relation to assets.

The trustee's/liquidator's remuneration

The OR's remuneration (payment) as trustee/liquidator is specified under insolvency law. An IP's remuneration as trustee/liquidator is fixed by the creditors'/liquidation committee. If there is no committee, it may be fixed at a meeting of creditors. The remuneration can be fixed as a percentage of the value of the assets realised and distributed or on a time basis. Any creditor, with the support of 25% in value of unsecured creditors, can apply to the court for the remuneration to be reviewed if they consider it too high. If the creditors do not agree a remuneration, the IP will receive the same as would have been paid to an OR, but s/he can apply to the court to agree a higher amount.

Completion of the case

If an OR is dealing with the case and you have sent in a proof of debt, the OR will inform you when he or she has completed the insolvency and intends to apply to the Secretary of State for release.

This means that the OR's role as trustee/liquidator comes to an end. The creditors have a right to object to the OR's release. Please note that the release of the OR as trustee is not relevant to, and does not affect, a bankrupt's discharge. Generally the OR's release can only be withheld if the OR has failed to realise assets that were available to be realised or has misapplied the proceeds of any assets realised. You will also be sent a summary of the OR's receipts and payments as trustee/liquidator.

If an IP is dealing with the case, you will be sent a notice of the final meeting of creditors. At this meeting the IP will report on his or her conduct of the case and will give a summary of the receipts and payments. The creditors give the IP his/her release at this meeting. Creditors have a right to refuse to the IP's release.

Buying a business – taking over a project

11.11 Where the customer is a middleman or prime contractor and the works will be provided to an ultimate customer where the prime contractor goes out of business it is common that the ultimate customer may want the supplier to continue with the services so the project can be completed or to secure the raw materials or products which that customer needs. In some cases where the customer is very dependent on that supplier the supplier may be able to negotiate that some of the sums owed to it by the original customer are paid by the ultimate customer/buyer.

Summary

11.12   This chapter has examined issues of preparation for insolvency and contractual and business issues that can be anticipated and addressed for companies in difficulties before insolvency arises. It then looked at clauses in agreements relating to assignment of contracts and finally work in progress issues.

Chapter 12

How to Deal with Suppliers

When dealing with suppliers consider if contracts can be assigned. See Chapter 11 for assignment and rules relating to it.

Assigning and novating supplier contracts

12.1   The contracts with suppliers may be terminable even if shares in the insolvent company are acquired (under a change of control clause); and on a sale of assets, which is more usual for insolvency situations, the existing contracts with suppliers to the business will often provide that agreements may not be assigned without consent, perhaps not to be unreasonably withheld or delayed. If there is no such restriction then the benefit of supplier contracts can be assigned at common law (assuming English law applies to the particular agreements) and after the assignment the buyer will send written notice to the supplier as required by law.

(See Appendix, 'C. Novation of contract' for a sample novation agreement precedent.)

Tactics

12.2   However even when an assignment as described above is possible, it may be more sensible to approach key suppliers before a purchase occurs if that can be arranged. A last-minute pre-pack administration situation, however, may not allow sufficient time for supplier contact before a purchase. In such cases quick contact with suppliers after it, to reassure them, is essential.

Suppliers will want to know:

- With whom they are now dealing, trading reputation, ability to pay, stability of buyer.

- Will the prices paid be the same?

- What is to happen about existing payments due from the insolvent company to the supplier – sometimes administrators will have kept the business going as a going concern and ensured key suppliers are paid, however.

- Could they impose worse terms on a buyer? Not if contracts are assigned as they are and there is no restriction on assignment; but otherwise the answer is that they may, as usually they are not obliged to supply at all.

Negotiation with suppliers

12.3   After the sale has occurred, very swiftly approach the most important suppliers to ensure continued supplies. In some cases they may, before the purchase, have been prepared to give non-binding letters of intent setting out their intention to continue the business after the sale has occurred.

In these ways the position with suppliers can be secured.

Chapter 13

Leasehold Premises

Introduction

13.1   Landlords have an important role to play in the sale of any insolvent business involving leasehold premises in respect of which the seller is the tenant. Landlords have some very specific rights and remedies not available to other interested parties, and they have a wide range of options and potential courses of action available to them. The rights a landlord enjoys vary from one insolvency proceeding to another, and so the position of a landlord may form a key part of the planning process when deciding whether or not an insolvent seller enters into a formal insolvency proceeding as part of a sale process, and if so which proceeding and when it should commence.

The particular issues that should be considered are the landlord's rights to:

* recover arrears of rent;

* recover ongoing rent; and

* forfeit the lease.

Administration

13.2   A landlord will be an unsecured creditor in respect of any arrears of rent as at the time a company enters into administration. The landlord cannot take any steps to recover the unpaid rent by way of court proceedings or distraint without the consent of the administrator or permission of the court as a result of the moratorium that arises[1] on administration. Consent or permission is unlikely to be given, and the landlord will form a part of the general body of unsecured creditors, subject to its ability to recover arrears as a condition of consenting to an assignment of the lease. A landlord who submits a proof of debt to the administrator will participate in any eventual distribution to unsecured creditors, whether under the prescribed part or otherwise.

Rent accruing during the period of an administration may in certain circumstances be paid as an expense or a necessary disbursement of the administration, in accordance with the statutory order of payment of expenses[2].

---

[1]   IA 1986, Sch B1, para 43.
[2]   Rule 2.67(1).

13.2 *Leasehold Premises*

If the administrator enters into a lease, rent will be paid as an expense of the administration in any event[3]. If a company in administration makes use of the premises for the purpose of the administration rent will be paid as an expense in accordance with the terms of the lease[4]. Otherwise rent accruing due after the date of commencement of the administration under an existing lease will not be paid as an expense unless the administrator agrees to do so.

In *Goldacre (Offices) Limited v Nortel Networks UK Limited (in administration)*[5], a decision handed down by the court in January 2010, the landlord made an application to the court for an order that rent accruing under two leases be paid as an expense of the administration of the tenant. The leases predated the commencement of the administration, so there was no question of them being contracts entered into by the administrator. Part of the premises had been used by the company in administration and rent that fell due in relation to that part of the premises was paid to the landlord. However the landlord sought an order that as the administrators continued to make use of the premises for the purpose of the administration, the entire rent falling due under the leases ought to be paid as an expense of the administration in accordance with the terms of the leases. The court found that rent was payable under the Insolvency Rules 1986 (SI 1986/1925, as amended) ('the Rules') as either an expense[6] or a necessary disbursement[7] of the administration. Rent falling due on the next quarter day was a payment in advance that was not subject to apportionment, and the entire rent falling due on the next quarter day under the terms of the leases was payable as an expense. There was no discretion available to enable the court to consider how much it would be fair for the administrators to pay, taking into account the proportion of the entire leasehold space the company used, or to apportion the rent so that it was only paid up to the date on which the company vacated the premises. If the administrator used any part of the space then the entire quarter's rent was to be paid as an expense on the quarter day. Liability would cease only if the company had vacated the premises by the next quarter day.

The *Goldacre* case was a blow to administrators and a very welcome outcome for landlords. Prior to the decision administrators had denied that rent was payable as an expense of administration, or had relied on the *Atlantic Computers*[8] principles to pay only for the time the company in administration was in occupation of the premises and for that part of the premises which it used.

It is not however all bad news for administrators and good news for landlords. In *Leisure Norwich (II) Limited and others v Luminar Lava Ignite Ltd*[9], a

---

3   IA 1986, Sch B1, para 99(4).
4   *Goldacre (Offices) Limited v Nortel Networks UK Limited (in administration)* [2009] EWHC 3389 (Ch), [2010] 1 Ch 455.
5   See n 4.
6   Rule 2.67(1)(a).
7   Rule 2.67(1)(f).
8   *Re Atlantic Computer Systems plc* [1992] Ch 505, CA.
9   [2012] EWHC 951 (Ch), [2012] BCC 497.

decision handed down by the High Court in March 2012, the court confirmed that rent accrued prior to the appointment of administrators does not rank as an expense even where the company continues to use the premises during the administration. Any unpaid rent due when administrators were appointed was a provable debt in the insolvency and could only be treated as such. It has been reported[10] that this outcome has been challenged by a group of landlords affected by the administration of the retailer Game, which went into administration on 26 March 2012, one day after the quarter day.

The fact that a tenant has gone into administration will usually be a ground on which the landlord can forfeit a lease. Any arrears of rent will also be a further ground. However the landlord cannot take steps to forfeit with the consent of the administrator of permission of the court as a result of the administration moratorium. When it comes to forfeiture, rather than proceedings to collect arrears of rent, a landlord may well succeed on an application brought under IA 1986[11] for permission to commence proceedings. On making an application for permission the court will consider the guidance given in *Atlantic Computers* to decide whether or not permission should be granted. The court will weigh up and balance the rights of the landlord against the rights of the unsecured creditors. It will consider:

- whether granting permission to the landlord to bring forfeiture proceedings would be likely to impede achieving the purpose of the administration:

    — if not then permission would usually be given;

    — otherwise the court will carry out a balancing exercise weighing the legitimate interests of the landlord against those of the other creditors;

    — great importance will be given to the landlord's proprietary rights; an administration for the benefit of unsecured creditors should not be conducted at the expense of those with proprietary rights;

    — permission will be given if significant loss would be caused to the landlord by refusing it; however if substantially greater loss would be caused to the unsecured creditors that would outweigh the loss to the landlord;

- the financial position of the company and its ability to pay ongoing rent;

- the administrator's proposals for achieving the purpose of the administration and the prospects of success;

- the length of time the landlord might be kept out of possession of the premises; and

- whether or not to impose conditions.

---

[10] http://www.propertyweek.com/5049940.article.
[11] IA 1986, Sch B1, para 43.

The usual outcome of the balancing exercise is that if the administrator is using the premises in order to achieve the purpose of the administration, it is likely that permission to commence forfeiture proceedings will be refused on condition that the administrator pays accruing rent and other sums due under the terms of the lease as an expense of the administration for the period during which the company makes use of the premises. Usually the landlord and administrator would negotiate such terms in order to avoid the costs of an application to court.

Accordingly prior to *Goldacre* an administrator might agree with the landlord to pay rent as an expense for the period during which the company used the premises for the purpose of the administration only. As soon as the company ceased to occupy the premises payment of rent would stop, as the administrator had no further interest in the premises and would be willing to allow the landlord to forfeit the lease. The administrator would seek to pay only for that proportion of the entire space that the company actually used, and might seek to renegotiate the terms of payment such that rent was paid weekly or monthly in arrears rather than quarterly in advance. However since *Goldacre*, once rent becomes payable under the terms of the lease (as may have been varied by agreement between the landlord and tenant prior to administration, say if the landlord has agreed that the tenant may pay rent monthly rather than quarterly for a period of time to assist the tenant's cashflow), if the company makes use of any part of the premises rent and other sums reserved by the lease for the entire next period falls due for payment in accordance with the usual terms of the lease (as may have been varied) as an expense of the administration.

Rent is not payable as an expense under *Goldacre* as soon as the tenant goes into administration. The obligation to pay as an expense only arises when rent and any other amounts fall due for payment under the terms of the lease, and if at that time the company is making use of the premises for the purpose of the administration. Further, administration expenses are not necessarily paid when they fall due, and if there is doubt that the assets of the tenant will be sufficient to pay all of the expenses of the administration, the administrator can properly wait and see to what extent the assets are (or are not) sufficient.There is no obligation under *Goldacre* to pay rent as an expense for any period between the commencement of the administration and the next quarter day (or such other date as rent falls due for payment), as confirmed by the Court in *Luminar*[12]. Any such unpaid rent is a provable debt only and is not payable as an expense.

An administrator must be aware of any variation in the terms of the lease with regard to when payment falls due. In certain sectors that have faced particularly difficult trading conditions, such as retail, it is not unusual for landlords to have agreed with tenants that rent will fall due monthly rather than quarterly.

Nor is there any obligation to pay rent as an expense if the company is not making use of the premises for the purpose of the administration. There is

---

[12]   *Leisure Norwich (II) Limited and others v Luminar Lava Ignite Ltd* [2012] EWHC 951 (Ch).

little guidance in *Goldacre* as to what constitutes making use of the premises. Cases in relation to liquidation state that where the company makes use of the entire premises that will constitute use[13]. *Goldacre* itself confirms that where the company only occupies part of the premises for the purpose of the administration that will also constitute use. Where the company completely vacates the premises that will not constitute use[14]. Storing assets on the premises in order to achieve a better sale price for them is likely to constitute use[15], whereas simply allowing assets to remain on site without making any use of the premises to achieve a sale may not[16]. Failing to offer a surrender of the lease will not constitute use[17]. Although there is no guidance on this it is likely that granting a licence to occupy to a buyer of the company's business will constitute use.

The administrator is not personally liable to the landlord for payment of the rent as he or she acts as agent of the company[18]. The landlord may still find therefore that rent is not paid if the company has insufficient funds to discharge it as an expense of the administration. However in view of the priority that rent enjoys under *Goldacre* that is likely to be an unusual scenario. As noted above, rent may also not be paid until the end of the administration when the administrator pays all of his or her expenses.

Although this was not considered in the *Goldacre* judgment, it may be the case that other amounts falling due under the terms of a lease may also fall to be paid as an expense of the administration if the obligation to pay arises at a time when the company is making use of the premises for the purpose of the administration. This could include insurance, service charges and, potentially, claims for dilapidations.

Goldacre and *Luminar* may well have an impact on the timing of the commencement of an administration. From the company's point of view it is often an inability to pay a significant sum that is shortly due to be paid, such as rent, which results in a decision to enter into administration. From the administrators' point of view it would make sense for administration to commence shortly after rent has fallen due, and for the administrator to ensure that by the time the next rent payment is due the company has ceased to make any use of its leasehold premises. Also an administrator would want to ensure that any licence to occupy granted to a buyer of the business has been terminated either because the buyer has agreed an assignment of the lease or because the buyer itself has vacated the premises. Alternatively the buyer must be required to fund passing rent for the entire next rent payment period.

Other categories of creditors could also seek to make use of the *Goldacre* decision, such as the owners of assets subject to lease or hire-purchase agreements.

---

[13] *Re Oak Pitts Colliery Co* (1882) 21 Ch D 322.
[14] *Re ABC Coupler and Engineering Co Limited (No 3)* [1970] 1 WLR 702.
[15] *Re Linda Marie Limited (in liquidation)* [1988] 4 BCC 463.
[16] See n 12.
[17] *Re Toshuku Finance UK plc* [2002] UKHL 6, [2002] 1 WLR 671.
[18] IA 1986, Sch B1, para 69.

Receivership

13.3   Receivership has little impact on a tenant's liability to pay rent. The tenant remains liable to pay under and in accordance with the terms of the lease, and there is no moratorium to prevent enforcement of the terms of the lease. Accordingly the landlord can sue or distrain for payment of existing arrears and take steps to forfeit the lease.

A receiver acts as agent of the tenant[19] and as such does not incur personal liability for the rent even if he or she causes the company to continue to make use of the premises whilst not paying amounts that fall due under the lease. The court will not order a receiver to pay rent[20] and the landlord must rely on its usual remedies where there is a tenant in default.

Liquidation

13.4   A landlord will be an unsecured creditor in respect of any arrears of rent as at the time a company enters into liquidation, and can submit a proof of debt in the usual manner and participate in any distribution to unsecured creditors.

A lease does not automatically come to an end on a company going into liquidation. Similarly to administration, if the tenant makes use of the premises for the benefit of the liquidation then rent may fall to be paid as an expense of the liquidation in accordance with the statutory order of payment of expenses[21]. A liquidator may however disclaim a lease[22] which will bring the obligation to pay rent to an end.

A tenant in liquidation is unlikely to be trading (other than possibly for a very short period), and is unlikely to make use of the premises for the purpose of carrying on its business. However if the liquidator takes steps to sell or assign the lease for a premium he or she may well have to pay rent as an expense. Similarly if he or she agrees to pay rent to preserve a lease it will be payable as an expense[23]. However mere inactivity on the part of the liquidator is not likely to trigger an obligation to pay rent as an expense, and if the lease is preserved for the benefit of the landlord rather than the benefit of the liquidation the landlord will not be able to claim rent as an expense[24].

Where the liquidator disclaims a lease, rent accruing for the period of the liquidation up to the disclaimer may be payable as an expense or necessary disbursement if the liquidator has used the premises for the benefit of the liquidation.

---

[19]   LPA 1925, s 109.
[20]   *Hand v Blow* [1901] 2 Ch 721.
[21]   Rule 4.218.
[22]   IA 1986, ss 178, 179.
[23]   *Re Linda Marie Limited (in liquidation)* [1989] BCLC 46.
[24]   *Re Bridgewater Engineering Co* (1879) 12 Ch D 181.

Disclaimer

13.5   If a lease has a value a liquidator will usually seek to assign or surrender it for a premium. However if a lease has no realisable value and the premises are not needed for the benefit of the liquidation the liquidator may wish to disclaim the lease so that the landlord cannot seek to claim rent as an expense. Disclaimer has the effect of bringing all of the tenant's obligations under the lease to an end, and as it has no further right to occupy the premises all other liabilities accruing in respect of it cease, such as any obligation to pay rates, insurance and utilities.

A liquidator may disclaim any onerous property of the company notwithstanding that he or she has taken possession of it, endeavoured to sell it or otherwise exercised rights of ownership in relation to it[25]. 'Onerous property' may include a lease, and where it does further provisions apply which the liquidator must satisfy in order that the disclaimer of a lease takes effect[26]. The disclaimer notice must be served on all persons claiming to be an underlessee or mortgagee of the tenant, and there must be no application made within 14 days for the lease to be vested in the applicant or, if an application is made, the court must have ordered that the disclaimer shall take effect.

The liquidator can decide to disclaim a lease at any time, unless he or she has been served with a notice to elect. A landlord may choose to do this to avoid uncertainty. A person interested in the relevant property may apply in writing to the liquidator requiring them to decide whether they will disclaim or not, and the liquidator then has 28 days in which to make a decision. If they fail to serve a disclaimer notice within that period the liquidator and any person who replaces them as office-holder may not disclaim in the future[27]. The court can extend the 28-day time limit but would not usually do so once it has expired. If the liquidator fails to disclaim having received a notice to elect, he or she may face a claim for payment of rent as an expense of the liquidation.

The effect of a disclaimer is to terminate the relationship of landlord and tenant, and any future rights and liabilities under the lease. The landlord is entitled to possession of the premises [28] and the tenant has no right to remain in the property[29]. The landlord can prove in the liquidation to the extent of the loss or damage caused as a result of the disclaimer[30]. The landlord is not entitled to claim all future rent due under the terms of the lease. Instead it has a statutory right to compensation, the amount of which is to be calculated on the same basis as if the landlord was claiming damages for breach of contract[31]. That means that the landlord must mitigate its loss by seeking to re-let the

---

[25]   IA 1986, s 178(2).
[26]   IA 1986, s 179(1).
[27]   IA 1986, s 178(5).
[28]   *Re Hyams, ex p Lindsay v Hyams* (1923) 93 LJ Ch 184.
[29]   *Smalley v Quarrier* [1975] 2 All ER 688.
[30]   IA 1986, s 178(6).
[31]   *Re Park Air Services plc* [2000] 2 AC 172.

premises, and may see its claim reduced by reason of the fact that payment to it is accelerated. If the landlord can only re-let at a reduced rent, it can include in its claim an amount equal to the difference between the contractual rent under the disclaimed lease and the actual rent it can now recover from a new tenant for the remainder of the original term[32], or at least until such time as the tenant could have broken the lease[33].

Company voluntary arrangement ('CVA')

13.6   The role of landlords in connection with CVAs has been in the spotlight for some time, with a number of high-profile retail restructurings and insolvencies involving large leasehold property portfolios occurring since 2009.

A landlord will be an unsecured creditor in respect of any arrears of rent as at the time a company proposes a CVA, and can submit a claim in the usual manner and participate in the voting and in the distribution to unsecured creditors.

Every creditor who has notice of the creditors' meeting called to consider a proposal for a CVA is entitled to vote at the meeting and any adjournment of it[34]. Votes are calculated according to the amount owed to the creditor as at the date of the meeting[35]. A creditor may vote in respect of a debt that is unliquidated or whose value is not ascertained, and any unliquidated or unascertained claim will be valued at £1 for voting purposes unless the chairman of the meeting agrees to put a higher value on it[36].

Future rent and other amounts due under a lease are more difficult to deal with than arrears, and claims made by landlords for voting purposes have come before the court from time to time[37]. Landlords may submit a claim to the chairman and seek to vote for all future rent due under the terms of a lease. However it is likely that any such claim will be rejected, and the landlord may find its claim for future sums due under the lease reduced to £1 under rule 1.17(3) if the chairman does not agree to put any higher value on the claim. The same applies to claims for dilapidations[38]. The law on creditor's claims for voting purposes in a CVA is outside of the scope of this book.

On a practical level this may not be of great concern to a landlord. Whilst it can be bound by a CVA in respect of future rent and other amounts falling

---

[32] *Re Hide, ex p Llynvi Coal and Iron Co* (1871) 7 Ch App 28.
[33] *Re McEwan, ex p Blake* (1879) 11 Ch D 572.
[34] Rule 1.17(1).
[35] Rule 1.17(2).
[36] Rule 1.17(3).
[37] Eg *Re Cranley Mansions Limited* [1994] 1 WLR 1610; *Doorbar v Alltime Securities Limited* [1996] 1 WLR 456; *Re Newlands (Seaford) Educational Trust* [2007] BCC 195.
[38] *Re Newlands* (see n 34).

due under the terms of a lease, if there are grounds for forfeiture other than non-payment of rent (and usually insolvency of the tenant would be such a ground) the landlord can require future rent to be paid in full as a condition of not forfeiting. Accordingly notwithstanding that the landlord is an unsecured creditor alongside others it has a special position in that if the company needs to retain use of the premises, the landlord can use that position as a bargaining tool to ensure that it is paid in full without the company and the supervisor of the arrangement facing the risk of a challenge to the CVA by other creditors as being an arrangement that is unfairly prejudicial to them[39].

The issue that has arisen in recent cases is how the CVA procedure can and should be used as an alternative to administration to rescue an insolvent business where landlords have control of the voting process. It will be recalled that in order for a resolution approving a CVA to be passed a majority of three-quarters or more in value of the creditors present and voting must vote in favour of it[40].

In the restructuring of a retail (or other) business with a large property portfolio it is not uncommon for the company to wish to retain its better performing sites, but to close down those outlets that perform poorly or are in unsuitable locations, and for the company to divest itself of ongoing obligations under the leases of the closed units. That could be achieved by a sale of part of the business, in or out of administration, with the insolvent company then moving into liquidation so that any remaining leases that cannot be surrendered may be disclaimed. The business then continues in a restructured form, making use of only the cherry-picked sites. However that is a costly process, and one which would require the landlords of the outlets which the business wishes to retain agreeing to assign leases to the buyer. A restructuring by way of a CVA where the company remains as tenant of the retained leases avoids that problem. However there is no way to divest the company of the leases it does not wish to retain absent agreement with relevant landlords.

Early attempts to restructure by way of a CVA failed[41], but in the case of JJB Sports ('JJB') a CVA was approved by creditors on 27 April 2009 as an alternative to administration. JJB was the tenant of some 250 open and trading stores and some 140 closed stores. Under the terms of the CVA it proposed a 12-month variation in the terms of the leases of the open stores such that rent was to be paid on a monthly basis rather than quarterly. In respect of the closed stores JJB set aside a fund of £10 million against which landlords could make a claim, each receiving a dividend which was equivalent to some 6 months' rent. JJB would also continue to be liable to pay rates due for the empty stores. It was very important to the commercial landlords affected by the proposal that JJB did not seek to limit their rights in relation to the trading stores, save for the variation to pay rent monthly rather than quarterly. They recognised that the

---

[39]   IA 1986, s 6.
[40]   Rules 1.19(2), 1.19(4).
[41]   Eg *Prudential Assurance Co Limited v PRG Powerhouse Limited* [2007] EWHC 1002 (Ch), [2008] 1 BCLC 289.

fund of £10 million created to pay claims in relation to the closed stores would give them a better return than liquidation, which was the ultimate outcome for JJB if the CVA had been rejected. The success of the JJB CVA has since been followed by many other companies.

It is not clear whether similar CVAs will continue to be approved on the same terms in future, although at present they show no sign of abating[42]. Voting rights for future liabilities in a retail CVA remain a contentious subject, although none have been subject to challenge in the courts. The concern is that landlords of premises that are to remain open may be given the same voting rights as landlords of premises that are to close. Therefore those landlords who will be relatively unaffected by the process, as they will retain a tenant who will pay rent following the restructuring, can vote through a CVA and bind all landlords, including those who will be significantly affected as their premises will close down and be left empty. Certain landlords have also pointed out that on a successful restructuring, the share price of publicly quoted tenants may increase significantly, giving a substantial benefit to shareholders. It is possible that landlords will require that they participate in that benefit as a term of agreeing to future proposals.

Restructuring

13.7 If a tenant is entering into an informal restructuring process as a result of its insolvency, the position of a landlord is usually unaffected save to the extent that the landlord agrees to participate in the process.

The tenant may seek permission to charge a lease as a way of raising new funds, and it may also seek permission to assign or surrender a lease as part of the sale of its business or part of it. Any such request would be dealt with by the landlord in the usual manner.

A landlord may be asked to participate more directly in the process by way of the tenant seeking to renegotiate and vary the terms of the lease. It is not uncommon for a tenant in financial difficulty to seek to vary the terms of payment of rent, perhaps for a finite period of time, such that it is payable monthly in arrears rather than quarterly in advance. The tenant may seek to defer payments of rent or seek a reduction in rent in accordance with current market conditions. Whether or not a landlord will agree to such requests may depend on the bargaining strength of the parties. The landlord will not want to set a precedent by agreeing to a variation of the terms too easily. However in a market where there is a lot of empty leasehold property which is difficult to let, it will be anxious to keep the tenant in occupation. A landlord may prefer a tenant paying a reduced rent, or paying other than in accordance with the terms of the lease, than no tenant at all. In the latter situation the landlord not only loses its income stream, but also incurs liabilities in respect of the premises

---

[42] For example Fitness First, CVA approved June 2012; La Tasca, CVA approved August 2012.

such as the obligation to pay rates, insurance and maintenance costs. The landlord may also benefit from the improved covenant strength of the tenant after restructuring.

This can be a difficult situation for a landlord, whose own business is based on an established level of income, and with cash-flow forecasts showing income on certain specified dates. However landlords, particularly those with large portfolios of property, are often of necessity flexible, and when the property market is weak it is not unusual for some temporary variations in lease terms to be agreed.

Distress

13.8   The landlord's remedy of distress for arrears of rent is considered in Chapter 6.

Forfeiture

Introduction

13.9   A landlord may wish to forfeit a lease when a tenant becomes insolvent, depending on market conditions at the time. The landlord may be able to secure vacant possession of the premises by forfeiting the lease and then either sell the reversion at an enhanced value or relet the premises at a premium or an increased rental yield. The ability to forfeit a lease can put a landlord in a very strong position to the detriment of the other unsecured creditors of the company, and a number of restrictions are placed on a landlord's ability to forfeit.

Most leases will provide for forfeiture on insolvency, although the terms of the lease should always be carefully checked. The right to re-enter will also be provided for where there are arrears of rent or other breaches of covenant on the part of the tenant, including parting with possession of the premises or creating a sub-lease or licence without consent. A lease will always be voidable at the instance of the landlord on breach, rather than void, to prevent the tenant from avoiding the terms of the lease by effecting a deliberate breach of covenant.

Forfeiture on insolvency

13.10   Insolvency of itself will not be an event giving the landlord a right to forfeit in the absence of an express term to that effect. The court has found that it is not unusual for a lease to be subject to forfeiture on insolvency[43] but no

---

[43]   *Hyde v Warren* (1877) 3 Ex D 72.

such term has been implied into a lease. The case law is, however, very old and the court may now imply a term providing for forfeiture on insolvency into a lease of commercial premises as it is effectively a standard term.

The right to forfeit will usually be subject to a strict construction by the court. When a right to forfeit arises the landlord can elect to bring the lease to an end or permit it to continue. The landlord cannot take the benefit of the lease and at the same time reserve the right to forfeit. Accordingly if it takes any step that recognises the existence of the lease, such as making a demand for rent under the terms of the lease, its right to forfeit will be lost. Waiver of the right to forfeit only applies to past breaches and not future events, and where there is a continuing breach of the lease the right to forfeit will arise on a daily basis. The appointment of an administrator, receiver, liquidator or supervisor to a tenant will usually be a one-off breach in respect of which a right to forfeit can be waived. However continued insolvency may be a continuing breach in respect of which the right to forfeit arises on a daily basis.

When a tenant is in administration the right to forfeit is subject to the statutory moratorium that arises[44]. A landlord cannot take any steps to forfeit by peaceable re-entry or by way of court proceedings without consent of the administrator or permission of the court. When a landlord makes an application to the court for permission to forfeit the court will carry out a balancing exercise under the guidance set out in the *Atlantic Computers*[45] case, weighing up the proprietary interests of the landlord against the rights of the unsecured creditors (see section 13.2). If the landlord is to be denied the right to forfeit the lease the administrator will usually be required to pay accruing rent as an expense of the administration.

If the tenant is in receivership there is nothing to prevent the landlord from taking steps to forfeit the lease. The tenant can apply to the court for relief from forfeiture, subject to any conditions the court may impose which as a minimum are likely to include the payment of all arrears of rent and costs. The lack of any moratorium against forfeiture in receivership, and in restructuring outside of a formal insolvency proceeding, is a key factor when deciding how best to proceed with the sale of an insolvent business. If a lease needs to be protected then administration may be the only viable way forward.

Where the tenant is in compulsory liquidation different considerations apply. The landlord does not require leave of the court to forfeit between presentation of a winding-up petition and a winding-up order, but the company, a creditor or a contributory may apply to the court to stay the proceedings[46]. Once a winding-up order is made the landlord requires leave of the court[47]. The court is likely to give leave if there are no grounds on which the company or the liquidator can defend the proceedings[48].

---

[44] IA 1986, Sch B1, para 43.
[45] [1992] Ch 505, CA.
[46] IA 1986, s 126(1).
[47] IA 1986, s 130(2).
[48] *General Share and Trust Co v Wetley Brick and Pottery Co* (1882) 20 Ch D 260.

Where the tenant is in voluntary liquidation the landlord is not prohibited from taking steps to forfeit the lease, although the liquidator can apply to the court to ask it to apply the relevant provisions that arise in compulsory liquidation[49]. The court is unlikely to do so if the company or the liquidator is unable to defend the proceedings.

Method of forfeiture

13.11 If the landlord has a right of forfeiture it may be able to exercise that right by peaceable re-entry, without a court order. This is particularly so in the case of commercial premises. The landlord must obtain a court order where premises are wholly or partly residential[50].

Peaceable re-entry is prohibited when a moratorium arises in administration[51] or when a CVA is proposed and the procedure to obtain a moratorium in respect of a small company is invoked[52].

Alternatively a landlord may forfeit by way of court proceedings, in which case service of the claim results in forfeiture.

Relief from forfeiture in cases of insolvency

13.12 If the breach of the lease relied on is the liquidation of the tenant, the liquidator can only apply for relief within the first year of the winding up. Providing the application is made during the first year it does not matter when the relief is granted[53].

It may be difficult for a liquidator to persuade the court to grant relief from forfeiture, although if he or she has a proposed assignee in place who is willing to take an assignment of the lease from the tenant and to pay all of the arrears of rent and other amounts due under the lease relief may be granted[54]. However if the proposed assignee does not have a good covenant relief may be refused as the court will not impose an unsatisfactory assignee on the landlord[55].

If the landlord is bound by a voluntary arrangement under which it is obliged to accept a reduced figure for arrears of rent, the tenant may be granted relief from forfeiture on paying the reduced amount[56].

---

[49] IA 1986, s 112.
[50] Protection from Eviction Act 1977, s 2.
[51] IA 1986, Sch B1, para 43(4).
[52] IA 1986, Sch A1, para 12(1)(f).
[53] *Gee v Harwood* [1933] Ch 712.
[54] *Pakwood Transport Limited v 15 Beauchamp Place Limited* (1977) 36 P & CR 112.
[55] *Geland Manufacturing Co v Levy Estates Co* (1962) 181 Estate Gazette 209.
[56] *Re Naeem (a bankrupt)* [1990] 1 WLR 48.

Assignment

Introduction

13.13   Where there is a sale of an insolvent business the buyer will often want to take over the seller's occupation of leasehold premises. The office-holder benefits by realising the capital value (if any) in the lease. The buyer is able to continue the business seamlessly without the upheaval of relocating the business, which may be impossible in the very short timescales often involved on an insolvency sale. Maintaining the same location for the business helps to maximise the benefit to be realised out of the seller's goodwill and helps retain and build confidence in the business on the part of suppliers, customers and employees. For the landlord the prospect of replacing an insolvent tenant with a solvent one may be attractive, and an assignment offers the opportunity for the landlord to recover arrears of rent which might not exist on taking a surrender of the lease. It also avoids a void period during which the landlord not only loses its rental income but also incurs the costs associated with the space.

Assignment by the company

13.14   The company may wish to assign a lease before any formal insolvency proceeding commences as part of a restructuring of its business. The directors of the company retain all of their powers to deal with the company's property at this time. However the landlord and the buyer must bear in mind that if the company does enter into administration or liquidation in due course, prior transactions which occurred at a relevant time[57] will be investigated by the office-holder and they may be declared void by the court as a transaction at an undervalue[58] or a preference[59].

Any disposition of the company's property that occurs between the presentation of a petition for the winding up of the seller and the winding-up order is void unless the court otherwise orders[60]. 'Disposition' includes the assignment of a lease[61]. The court may validate transactions that occur during the period between presentation of a petition and a winding-up order. The purpose of IA 1986, s 127 is to ensure that where a company is insolvent all creditors of the same class are treated equally, and:

(a)   if the transaction does not have the effect of reducing the company's assets available to creditors[62]; or

---

[57]   IA 1986, s 240.
[58]   IA 1986, s 238.
[59]   IA 1986, s 239.
[60]   IA 1986, s 127.
[61]   *Re Al Levy (Holdings) Limited* [1964] Ch 19.
[62]   *Re Tramway Building and Construction Co Limited* [1988] Ch 293.

(b)   is not at an undervalue[63]; or

(c)   will not result in one creditor being preferred over another[64]; or

(d)   will benefit creditors by realising a profit pending the hearing of the petition,

the court is likely to exercise its discretion to make a validation order.

If the company, buyer and landlord enter in an agreement to assign a lease before a winding-up petition is presented but the assignment is not completed until after presentation, the transaction should not fall foul of IA 1986, s 127 as the disposition of the lease takes place when the contract is made[65].

Although any assignment that takes place between the presentation of a winding-up petition and the making of a winding-up order is void, the buyer nevertheless acquires legal title to the premises[66]. It holds the beneficial interest on trust for the seller. It is arguable that the buyer is liable to pay the rent accruing until the winding-up order is made notwithstanding that the assignment is void[67].

A buyer and a landlord should always carry out a winding-up search at the Central Index at the Companies Court before entering into an assignment of a lease, to check whether a winding-up petition has been presented against the tenant company.

Assignment by an administrator

13.15   An administrator has power to take possession of, collect and get in the company's property[68] and to sell or otherwise dispose of the property by public or private auction or by private contract[69]. 'Property' will include any lease. He or she also has power to grant or accept a surrender of a lease or tenancy of any of the property of the company[70].

If a lease is subject to a floating charge the administrator can deal with it as if the lease were free from the charge[71]. If it is subject to a fixed charge the administrator can apply to court for an order to enable him or her to assign the lease free of the charge[72] if the creditor has not agreed to provide a release. The

---

[63]   *Re Rescuepine Limited* [2003] EWHC 216 (Ch), [2003] 1 BCLC 661.
[64]   *Re Gray's Inn Construction Co Limited* [1980] 1 All ER 814.
[65]   *Re French's (Wine Bar) Limited* [1987] BCLC 499.
[66]   See n 61.
[67]   *Stein v Pope* [1902] 1 KB 595.
[68]   IA 1986, Sch B1, para 60; Sch 1, para 1.
[69]   IA 1986, Sch 1, para 2.
[70]   IA 1986, Sch 1, para 17.
[71]   IA 1986, Sch B1, para 70(1).
[72]   IA 1986, Sch B1, para 71(1).

court may make an order if it is satisfied that the proposed assignment would be likely to promote the purpose of the administration[73]. Any order will be subject to a condition that the net proceeds of the assignment are paid to the chargeholder towards satisfaction of the secured debt, together with any further amount required to bring the net proceeds up to the net market value of the lease[74].

Assignment by a liquidator

13.16   A liquidator has power to sell any of the company's property by public auction or by private contract, with power to transfer the whole of it to any person[75]. 'Property' will include any lease. He or she also has power to do all such other things as may be necessary for winding up the company's affairs[76]. He or she also has the power to do all acts and execute in the name of the company all deeds, receipts and other documents[77].

Assignment by a receiver

13.17   A receiver appointed under LPA 1925 does not have power to assign a lease[78]. However most charges over property will extend a receiver's powers to include a power to sell.

A mortgagee may also assign a lease in the exercise of its statutory power of sale[79] or in exercise of a power of sale arising under the mortgage or charge document. A benefit of taking an assignment from a mortgagee is that he or she can overreach any subsequent mortgage or charge that has been created over the lease[80], although they cannot sell free of any prior encumbrance[81].

The assignment

13.18   Most commercial leases will include a provision that the landlord's consent is required to any assignment, and that such consent is not to be unreasonably withheld. Any such term of a lease remains binding on an insolvent tenant, including a tenant subject to an insolvency proceeding.

The terms of any restriction on assignment in a lease should be reviewed carefully as there may be ways in which the parties to a proposed transaction

---

[73]   IA 1986, Sch B1, para 70(2)(b).
[74]   IA 1986, Sch B1, para 70(3).
[75]   IA 1986, ss 165, 167 and Sch 4, para 6.
[76]   IA 1986, Sch 4, para 13.
[77]   IA 1986, Sch 4, para 7.
[78]   LPA 1925, s 109.
[79]   LPA 1925, s 101(1).
[80]   LPA 1925, ss 88, 2(1)(iii).
[81]   LPA 1925, s 104(1).

can overcome a refusal to give consent. A restriction on assignment will not prevent a company from subletting premises[82] or granting a third party a licence to occupy[83]. A restriction on subletting will not prevent an assignment[84]. A restriction on parting with possession will prevent an assignment, subletting[85] and granting a third party a licence to occupy where the tenant relinquishes control of the premises[86]. However there may not be a breach of the lease if the tenant retains control.

If the lease contains an unqualified prohibition on assignment then it is a matter for the landlord as to whether or not it waives the term. It does not have to act reasonably in making its decision and can impose such terms as it may require to be met. The only qualification is that the landlord cannot discriminate on grounds of race or sex when making its decision.

It is usual for a prohibition on assignment to be qualified such that it is subject to the landlord's consent, usually not to be unreasonably withheld. If any qualified prohibition on assignment is not expressly subject to that proviso it will be implied[87]. Where the prohibition on assignment is qualified the landlord cannot claim a payment that would amount to a fine in return for giving its consent[88], although it can charge its reasonable legal expenses.

A request for licence to assign should be made in writing, and the landlord must give its consent or refuse on reasonable grounds within a reasonable time[89]. What is a reasonable time depends on the facts of the case[90], and in an insolvency situation where time is of the essence the time afforded to the landlord may be reduced from that which it would usually enjoy. A landlord is required to give consent save where it is reasonable not to, and it must give the tenant written notice of its decision with reasons for refusing consent if that is the case, and any conditions that consent is subject to[91].

The question of whether or not a landlord is acting reasonably has been the subject of a number of decisions of the court[92], and the following guidelines may be applied:

- the purpose of the covenant is to protect the landlord from having its premises used or occupied in an undesirable way or by an undesirable tenant or assignee;

---

[82]   *Sweet & Maxwell Limited v Universal News Services Limited* [1964] 2 QB 699.
[83]   *Edwardes v Barrington* (1901) 50 WR 358.
[84]   *Marks v Warren* [1979] 1 All ER 29.
[85]   See n 80.
[86]   *Lam Kee Ying Sdn Bhd v Lam Shes Tong* [1975] AC 247.
[87]   Landlord and Tenant Act 1927, s 19.
[88]   LPA 1925, s 144.
[89]   Landlord and Tenant Act 1988, s 1(3).
[90]   *Go West Limited v Spigarolo* [2003] EWCA Civ 17, [2003] QB 1140.
[91]   See n 85.
[92]   The leading case is *International Drilling Fields Limited v Louisville Investments (Uxbridge) Limited* [1986] Ch 513.

- a landlord may not refuse consent on grounds that have nothing to do with the relationship of landlord and tenant in regard to the subject matter of the lease;

- the onus of proving that consent has been unreasonably withheld is on the tenant;

- the landlord does not have to prove that its reasons for withholding consent were justified as long as they are reasons that might be formed by a reasonable person in the circumstances;

- it may be reasonable to refuse consent on the grounds of the proposed use of the premises by the assignee even though the proposed use is not forbidden by the lease;

- while a landlord need only usually consider its own relevant interests, there may be cases where there is such a disproportion between the advantage to the landlord and detriment to the tenant that it is unreasonable to refuse consent;

- subject to these principles it is a question of fact whether consent has been unreasonably withheld.

Circumstances in which it has been found to be reasonable for a landlord to refuse consent include where:

- references have not been supplied;

- the proposed assignee's financial standing is unsatisfactory;

- the assignment will reduce the value of the landlord's reversionary interest;

- the landlord requires a serious breach of covenant to be remedied;

- the proposed assignee is likely to breach the terms of the lease.

A landlord will often make it a condition of granting consent that any arrears of rent are discharged, and as the tenant is insolvent any such obligation will fall on the buyer. The buyer may then seek to negotiate with the seller that any payment of arrears of rent that has to be made is set off against the purchase price for the premises or the business. It is also likely that the buyer will be required to pay the landlord's costs of the assignment, and to deal with any requirements to register the assignment.

It is not reasonable for a landlord to refuse consent on the ground that the insolvency of the tenant has given rise to a right of forfeiture. If a landlord attempts to forfeit without giving due consideration to a proposed assignment the court may grant the tenant relief from forfeiture[93].

---

[93] *Pakwood Transport Limited v 15 Beauchamp Place Limited* (1977) 36 P & CR 112.

In view of the fact that the tenant is insolvent it would not be usual for the company to enter into an authorised guarantee agreement with the landlord on assignment.

Other practical points to consider include that the office-holder may not have access to the company's original copy of the lease, which the company would usually hand over to the buyer on completion of an assignment. He or she may have to carry out a search of the company's books and records or make enquiries of the directors as to its whereabouts. If the original lease cannot be located the directors may be required provide a statutory declaration setting out the circumstances in which it came to be missing. If the lease is missing the office-holder should take steps to deal with the situation sooner rather than later as the longer he or she waits the less likely it may be that the directors are willing to co-operate with him or her.

If the consent of any superior landlord is required this should be sought as soon as possible to avoid delay to completion of the assignment.

The landlord and the buyer may wish to agree variations to the lease on the assignment, or to agree a licence to make alterations or for a change of use. Whilst this is a matter for them to negotiate, the seller may find it delays completion.

Delay for any reason can have ramifications for an administrator of the seller under *Goldacre (Offices) Limited v Nortel Networks Limited (in administration)*[94] if it means that a quarter day (or other date for payment of rent under the terms of the lease) passes, and the seller remains in occupation of the premises and makes use of them for the purpose of the administration (see 13.2 and 13.19).

Consideration should also be given as to how any rent deposit is dealt with.

To the extent that it was not done on completion of any earlier sale of the business, the seller must also make provision for removing any items that are not transferring to the buyer from the premises, as unless otherwise agreed it will have no rights of access following assignment.

Licence to occupy

13.19   In many sales of an insolvent business there is insufficient time for the seller to request the landlord's licence to assign, for the landlord to consider the request and for the parties to agree terms and prepare the necessary documentation. This is particularly so in the case of a pre-pack administration where the sale takes place immediately on, or very shortly after, the appointment of the administrator.

---

[94]   [2009] EWHC 3389 (Ch), [2010] 1 Ch 455.

In such circumstances it is usual for the seller to permit the buyer to occupy the premises under the terms of a licence to occupy, notwithstanding that this may constitute a breach of the terms of the lease. The buyer will then be allowed by the seller to take possession of the leasehold premises whilst negotiations take place with the landlord to obtain consent to an assignment of the lease, or to provide the buyer with time to carry out an orderly relocation of the business.

A licence to occupy would typically include the following terms:

- The buyer is permitted to occupy the premises as a bare licencee only and not as subtenant of the seller.

- The rights granted are personal to the buyer and not capable of assignment.

- The licence may be terminated at any time by the seller.

- The buyer will pay the seller a licence fee equivalent to the passing rent and all other sums falling due under the terms of the lease for the period of occupation. The licence fee will usually be payable weekly or monthly in advance and will apportioned on a daily basis.

- The buyer will pay all other sums falling due in relation to the premises for its period of occupation, including utilities, rates, insurance and all other outgoings and expenses associated with the premises.

- The buyer will comply with all of the tenant's covenants under the lease other than the covenant to pay rent. Specific obligations which might give rise to third-party claims against the seller may be included, such as covenants not to cause damage to the premises or any equipment on them, and to make good any damage caused; to leave the premises in a clean and tidy condition; not to display signs or advertising; not to cause a nuisance.

- Unless it is terminated forthwith, the term of the licence will expire when the landlord refuses to give consent to an assignment, or the lease is assigned or such other long-stop date as may be agreed between the parties.

- The buyer will indemnify the administrator and the company in respect of any claims or losses which arise in respect of the premises, the lease or the licence.

The administrator will usually pass the licence fee on to the landlord, which will not accept payment directly from the occupier as it will not want to create a landlord and tenant relationship prior to any formal assignment of the lease.

The practice of an administrator entering into a licence to occupy with a buyer in breach of the terms of a lease was considered by the Court of Appeal in *Innovate Logistics Limited (in administration) v Sunberry Properties Limited*[95]. The company was tenant under a lease of premises used to store frozen and chilled goods pending distribution to its customers. When the company went into administration some £20 million worth of frozen food

---

[95]   [2009] BCC 164.

was stored at the premises. The lease contained the usual prohibitions against assignment and parting with possession, and also provided for the landlord to re-enter the premises for breach of covenant, failure to pay rent and insolvency. The company was in arrears of rent when it went into administration. The administrators agreed a sale of the company's business to a third party, with a view as far as the administrators were concerned of ensuring continuity of the business to assist with the orderly collection of the company's debts. The buyer did not want an assignment of the lease as it had existing cold-storage facilities. It was granted a licence to occupy the premises for up to six months in order to enable it to distribute the frozen and chilled goods at the premises. The licence fee was to be paid monthly, each payment to be of a sum equal to one month's passing rent. The administrators agreed to pay the licence fee on to the landlord. There was no question that on the administrators entering into the licence to occupy the company was in further breach of the terms of the lease.

The landlord asked the administrators to terminate the licence to occupy. They refused, and the landlord applied to the court for permission to commence proceedings under IA 1986, Sch B1, para 43(6) for an injunction to enforce the terms of the lease.

The tenant opposed the application and submitted that:

- In order to achieve the purpose of administration it was essential that the buyer took over the seller's contracts, and that it stored and delivered the £20 million of goods at the premises to the company's customers. Some £8.9 million of book debts may not otherwise be recovered.

- The court should carry out the balancing exercise in the *Atlantic Computers* case in the context of the administrator's attempts to maximise recovery of the book debts. The immediate termination of the licence to occupy would put collection of £8.9 million at risk. The administrator had no choice but to grant the licence to occupy.

- Although breach of the lease was a factor for the court to take into account when carrying out the balancing exercise, it did not displace the discretion of the court when considering whether permission should be given to commence proceedings.

- Any temporary loss that the landlord would suffer had to be balanced against the loss to other creditors if proceedings were commenced and successful.

- The financial position of the company was such that it could not pay rent falling due under the lease. The arrangements the administrators had agreed meant that the landlord would receive payments for the next six months that it would not otherwise receive. The only potential loss to the landlord would be the interest it might have earned on the rent had it been paid quarterly in advance rather than monthly.

- The landlord in this case did not want to forfeit the lease. Rather it was seeking to exert pressure on the buyer to take an assignment.

The landlord submitted that:

- A party with proprietary rights should ordinarily be given permission to commence proceedings against a company in administration.

- The moratorium was being used to deprive it of its proprietary rights and to weaken its bargaining position with the buyer.

- The application would leave the lease in place. The landlord merely sought to enforce the covenant, not to part with possession.

- The landlord's rights under the lease had been deliberately breached by permitting a complete stranger to occupy the premises under a pre-pack arrangement that had been presented to creditors, including the landlord, as a fait-accompli. There was no longer any business of the company to protect.

- Accordingly this case was outside of the balancing exercise described in *Atlantic Computers*. In this case the landlord was not seeking to enforce its proprietary rights as against the company, but rather its legitimate aim was to strengthen its bargaining possession with the third-party buyer.

On consideration of the arguments, the Court of Appeal dismissed the application for permission to commence proceedings. It found that in order to achieve the purpose of the administration it was essential for the buyer to occupy the premises and take over the contracts to store and distribute goods to customers, many of whom were debtors to the company. The order the landlord sought would, if granted, terminate the buyer's ability to carry out the contracts. The court should carry on the balancing exercise in accordance with the *Atlantic Computers* guidance. In order to protect the landlord the court also found that the administrators should pay the monthly licence fee to the landlord together with any interest earned on that money. The administrators were not ordered to pay contractual rent and interest as an expense of the administration.

The *Innovate* case demonstrates that the court will carry out a balancing exercise in respect of the rights of a landlord and the rights of creditors in a range of situations, not just where the landlord complains of a failure to pay rent. The court may find that on balance the landlord should be denied its proprietary rights when that would tend to achieve the purpose of administration, notwithstanding a breach of the terms of the lease, on terms that the landlord is not prejudiced financially in the meantime. In *Innovate* the court did not find that the loss of bargaining position was a sufficient ground to persuade it to exercise its discretion in favour of the landlord and give permission to commence proceedings.

The decision gives support to the practice of administrators granting a licence to occupy to buyers in such circumstances.

The decision in *Innovate* must be considered in the light of the subsequent decisions of the court in *Goldacre (Offices) Limited v Nortel Networks Limited (in administration)*[96] and *Leisure Norwich (II) Limited and others v Luminar*

---

[96]   [2009] EWHC 3389 (Ch), [2010] 1 Ch 455.

Lava Ignite Ltd[97] *(see section 13.2).* In *Goldacre* and *Luminar* the court was considering a different point to that which arose in *Innovate*. Rather than the exercise of its discretion when considering an application for permission to commence proceedings against a company brought under IA 1986, Sch B1, para 43, the court in *Goldacre* was concerned with the question of whether rent fell to be paid under the expenses regime in administration[98]. The guidance in *Atlantic Computers* is not relevant to that question. However the *Goldacre* decision is important in the context of granting a buyer a licence to occupy premises, as it confirms that a company in administration is liable to pay rent as an expense of the administration if rent and any other amounts fall due for payment under the terms of the lease, and at that time the company is making use of the premises for the purpose of the administration.

There is little guidance in *Goldacre* or *Luminar* as to what constitutes the company making use of the premises for the purpose of the administration. However in *Innovate* the company argued that it needed to grant a licence to occupy the premises to the buyer in order to facilitate the collection of book debts for the purpose of the administration, and the Court of Appeal expressly relied on that argument in coming to its decision. It therefore appears highly likely that an administrator who grants a licence to occupy to a buyer will find that the landlord can successfully argue that the company is making use of the premises such that a landlord relying on *Goldacre* will claim rent as an expense. An administrator therefore needs to consider that although he or she may be collecting the licence fee from the buyer on a monthly basis, and for an uncertain term, if rent falls due under the terms of the lease during the period of the licence to occupy (usually on a quarter day) the administrator will have to pay rent as an expense of the administration for the entire demised premises and for the entire next quarter, whatever the amount he or she recovers from the buyer under the terms of the licence.

Surrender

Introduction

13.20   As an alternative to an assignment of a lease a landlord and tenant may agree a surrender. Depending on market conditions at the time a landlord may be willing to pay a premium to agree a surrender if it can relet the premises at a greater rent. For the tenant it brings obligations under the lease to an end on terms that may be agreed in relation to any existing claims.

A surrender operates to end the lease and bring all future obligations arising under it to an end. A landlord has been prevented from bringing a claim against a tenant in relation to goods left on the premises after a surrender of the lease

---

[97]   [2012] EWHC 951 (Ch), [2012] BCC 497.
[98]   Rule 2.67(1).

had taken place[99]. It does not operate as an automatic waiver of existing claims at the time of the surrender, but the parties can agree to such a waiver as a term of the surrender. Otherwise any breaches of covenant prior to the surrender will have given rise to a right of action that has accrued[100] and must be released.

The tenant will also be required to satisfy any obligation in relation to a period prior to the surrender which has not been satisfied at the time. Therefore if rent is payable in arrears, it will still have to pay for the period up to the time of the surrender[101]. If rent is paid in advance in the usual manner, the tenant is not entitled to be reimbursed rent applicable to the period after the surrender unless there is an express agreement to that effect[102]. If a rent review date has passed before the surrender but the new rent is not determined until afterwards the tenant is also at risk. It will have to pay any increased amount of rent for the period from the review date to the surrender[103].

Form of surrender

13.21 A lease may be surrendered formally by deed or informally by a dealing between the landlord and the tenant which shows that the lease has come to an end. Whilst an informal surrender is attractive in an insolvency situation, as it keeps costs to a minimum, it may not be the best option as there is then no opportunity to agree a waiver of any existing claims which have arisen prior to the date of the surrender. A formal surrender will be required if the lease is registered at the Land Registry.

A formal surrender of a lease not exceeding three years must usually be by way of deed[104]. There is no prescribed form of words to be used but it must be clear that the lease has come to an end, and there must be a surrender by the tenant and an acceptance of the surrender by the landlord. The deed should also deal with any waivers of existing breaches or claims.

An informal surrender can take place by any course of dealing between the landlord and tenant that demonstrates that the lease is at an end. The most usual form of dealing is for the tenant to hand the keys back to the landlord, and for the landlord to accept them[105]. However there must be an intention that this will effect a surrender, and if the landlord makes it clear that it does not accept a surrender when keys are handed back to it then the lease will continue. There will be no surrender if the landlord does not return the keys but does nothing to demonstrate that it has accepted a surrender[106]; or if it simply markets the

99   *Re ABC Coupler and Engineering Co Limited (No 3)* [1970] 1 WLR 702.
100 *Dalton v Pickard* [1926] 2 KB 545.
101 Apportionment Act 1870, s 3.
102 *William Hill (Football) Limited v Willen Key and Hardware Limited* (1964) 108 Sol Jo 482.
103 *Torminster Properties Limited v Green* [1983] 2 All ER 457.
104 LPA 1925, s 52.
105 *Dodd v Acklom* (1843) 6 Man & G 672.
106 *Cannan v Hartley* (1850) 9 CB 634.

premises for rent to a new tenant where there are arrears[107] (in which case the lease will not come to an end until a new tenancy is granted); or if it accepts the keys for the purpose of carrying out repairs[108] or redecoration; or if it changes the locks to secure abandoned premises[109]. However if the landlord markets premises for its own benefit a surrender will be presumed[110]; also where the landlord has relet to a new tenant[111].

In view of the uncertainty surrounding an informal surrender some form of documentation is always advised.

Other options available to the tenant

13.22 The tenant should consider whether or not it can exercise a break clause in the lease.

It may be possible to limit future liability under the lease by exercising a break, and the expense of doing so may be favourable as compared to the expense arising on a disclaimer. Most break clauses require the tenant to have complied with its obligations under the terms of the lease so any break clause will have to be reviewed carefully to ensure that insolvency does not mean it cannot be complied with.

Other remedies available to the landlord

13.23 A landlord may have a number of other remedies available to it on the insolvency of a tenant, any of which might impact on a sale of the company's business.

The landlord may have the benefit of a rent deposit, and if so the insolvency of the tenant will usually give the landlord the right to draw down on it. A rent deposit is often secured by way of a fixed charge over a deposit of cash at bank, and it will need to be registered at Companies House in the usual manner[112], although registration may not be necessary under the FCA Regulations (see Chapter 6, section 6.31).

Drawing down on a rent deposit would constitute enforcement of a security, and if the tenant is in administration that would require the consent of the administrator or permission of the court[113]. However a rent deposit created after 26 December 2003 is likely to fall under the FCA Regulations, in which case

---

[107] *Oastler v Henderson* (1877) 2 QBD 575.
[108] *Boynton-Wood v Trueman* (1961) 177 Estates Gazette 191.
[109] *Relvok Properties v Dixon* (1972) 25 P & CR 1.
[110] *Phene v Popplewell* (1862) 12 CBNS 334.
[111] *Wallis v Hands* [1893] 2 Ch 75.
[112] CA 2006, s 860.
[113] IA 1986, Sch B1, para 43.

the moratorium does not apply. An administrator is likely to give consent to a landlord to draw down on a rent deposit if he or she is satisfied that the arrears claimed are properly due and the rent deposit has been properly registered. An administrator is unlikely to be able to argue on an application for permission to enforce brought by the landlord that he or she needs to retain the rent deposit for the purpose of the administration, notwithstanding that if it is preserved there may be further cash available for the benefit of the company's creditors.

In addition to being a potential source of money available for the benefit of the creditors of the company, if a rent deposit is preserved it may be transferred on terms as part of any assignment of the lease.

There is nothing to prevent a landlord from drawing down on a rent deposit if the tenant is in receivership or liquidation.

If the tenant is subject to a CVA the landlord may be unable to draw down on a rent deposit if it has agreed to such a term as part of the CVA. Creditors cannot approve a proposal or modification which affects the rights of a secured creditor to enforce its security without its consent[114].

A landlord may also bring a claim against any guarantors on the insolvency of the tenant, although a CVA might prevent the landlord from doing so if its terms are not unfairly prejudicial to the landlord[115].

A landlord may also serve notice on any subtenant enabling it to collect rent due to the tenant directly[116]. Service of such a notice is not the equivalent to levying distress[117] so is not prevented by the moratorium arising on administration.

---

[114]   IA 1986, s 4(3).
[115]   *Prudential Assurance Co Limited v PRG Powerhouse Limited* [2007] EWHC 1002 (Ch), [2007] BCC 50.
[116]   LDAA 1908, s 6.
[117]   *Wallrock v Equity and Law* [1942] 2 KB 82.

Precedents

Warning:

Use of all precedents carries dangers. There are major risks in using these precedents without competent legal advice. It is unlikely that any precedent will be able to be used in any transaction without considerable modification.

A.   Business transfer agreement

The form of business transfer agreement set out below is typical of those used in the sale of a business as a going concern by an administrator.

The business transfer agreement is an indicative draft only and must be modified as appropriate for the transaction in which it is being used. As business transfers vary greatly, this precedent should be treated as being little more than a collection of useful clauses. It has been drafted from the point of view of an administrator as typically an administrator will provide the first draft of a business transfer agreement and will not be willing to negotiate many amendments.

Any sale of the property would be subject to further terms which are not included here.

Any deferred consideration should always be supported by security granted by the Buyer and/or by a third party guarantor.

THIS AGREEMENT is made the [ ] day of [ ] 20 [ ].

BETWEEN:

(1) [ ] **Limited** (in administration) registered in England and Wales with company number: [ ] whose registered office is at [ ] (**'Seller'**) acting by the Administrators; and

(2) [ ] **Limited** registered in England and Wales with company number: [ ] whose registered office is at [ ] (**'Buyer'**); and

(3) [ ] and [ ] as joint administrators of the Seller both of [ ] (**'Administrators'**).

BACKGROUND:

(A) The Seller carries on the Business.

(B) The Administrators were appointed as joint administrators of the Seller on [ ] by the directors of the Seller under paragraph 22 of Schedule B1 of the Insolvency Act 1986.

[Or]

The Administrators were appointed as joint administrators of the Seller on [ ] by [*Charge Holder*] under paragraph 14 of Schedule B1 of the Insolvency Act 1986.

[Or]

The Administrators were appointed as joint administrators of the Seller on [ ] by an order of the [ ] court made in proceedings under matter number [ ].

(C) The Seller has agreed to sell, and the Buyer has agreed to buy such right title and interest (if any) as the Seller has in the Business, the Assets and the Property with a view to carrying on the Business as a going concern on the terms of this Agreement.

(D) The Administrators are a party to this Agreement solely for the purpose of obtaining the benefit of the provisions in their favour and they shall incur no personal liability of any kind under or in connection with this Agreement.

IT IS AGREED as follows:

1. Definitions and interpretation

1.1 In this Agreement, unless the context otherwise requires, the following words have the following meanings:

'Administrators' Records' all records produced by or at the direction of the Administrators, their staff, agents or representatives in connection with the administration of the Seller and any other records which the Administrators are required by law to retain;

'this Agreement' this Agreement, including any Schedule or Annexure to it and any document referred to in it or in agreed form;

'Assets' the assets to be sold pursuant to sub-clause 2.1;

'Bank' [   ];

'Book Debts' all trade and other debts and amounts owing to the Seller at the Transfer Date in respect of the Business (whether or not due and payable) including interest payable on those sums and the benefit of any security or guarantee for their payment;

'Business' the business of [   ] carried on at the Property by the Seller;

'Business Day' a day (other than a Saturday or a Sunday) on which clearing banks are open for business in the City of London;

'Business Information' all information, know-how and techniques (whether or not confidential and in whatever form held) which in any way relate to:

    (a) all or any part of the Business and the Assets;

    (b) any products manufactured and/or sold or services rendered by the Business;

    (c) any formulas, designs, specifications, drawings, data, manuals or instructions;

    (d) the operation, management and administration or financial affairs of the Business including any business plans or forecasts, information relating to future business development or planning, information relating to litigation or legal advice; and

    (e) the sale or marketing of any of the products manufactured and/or sold or services rendered by the Business, including, but not limited to, all customer names and lists, sales and marketing information (including but not limited to targets, sales and market-share statistics, market surveys and reports on research);

'Business Name' [   ] or any representation or application of it, whether in terms of packaging, get-up or otherwise, as used in the Business on or before the Transfer Date, and any other name which is similar to it or capable of being confused with it;

'Buyer's Solicitors' [   ] of [   ] (Ref:[   ]);

'Cash'	cash in hand of the Seller or in the Seller's bank accounts on the Transfer Date and all cheques and securities representing it;
'Charge Holder'	[ ];
'Charge Holder's Security'	[ ];
'Claims'	all rights and claims, demands, actions or proceedings of any kind of the Seller against third parties relating to any of the Assets or otherwise arising (whether before or after Completion) out of or in connection with the Business under any warranties, conditions, guarantees, indemnities or insurance policies or otherwise;
'Completion'	the performance by the parties of the obligations set out in clause 5 (Completion);
'Completion Date'	the date of this Agreement;
'Consideration'	the purchase price for the Business and the Assets referred to in sub-clause 3.1;
'Contracts'	(a) the Customer Contracts; (b) Leasing Agreements; (c) the Intellectual Property Licences; and (d) save for the Excluded Contracts and contracts of employment, all undischarged contracts, pending contracts, commitments and orders entered into by or on behalf of the Seller relating to the Business, and where such contract has a value greater than £[ ] in aggregate, that contract has been listed in Annexure 1;
'Customer Contracts'	all contracts, engagements or other commitments in connection with the Business entered into by or on behalf of the Seller with Customers which remain to be performed in whole or in part by the Seller as at the Transfer Date;
'Customer Data'	the personal data (as defined in the DPA 1998) of Customers which form part of the Customer Database;
'Customer Database'	any database owned by the Seller for the purpose of providing products and/or services to Customers;
'Customers'	the customers and former customers of the Business;
'Data Controller'	as defined in section 1 of the DPA 1998;
'Data Employees'	the Employees and all persons formerly employed by the Seller in the Business at any time before the Transfer Date;
'DPA 1998'	the Data Protection Act 1998;
'Employee Data'	the personal data (as defined in the DPA 1998) of the Data Employees who form part of the Employee Database;
'Employee Database'	any database owned by the Seller in connection with the Data Employees;

'Employee Liability Information'	in respect of each of the Employees:

(a) the identity and age of the Employee;

(b) the Employee's written statement of employment particulars (as required under section 1 of the Employment Rights Act 1996);

(c) information about any disciplinary action taken against the Employee and any grievances raised by the Employee, where a Code of Practice issued under Part IV of the Trade Union and Labour Relations (Consolidation) Act 1992 relating exclusively or primarily to the resolution of disputes or any other applicable code or statutory procedure applied, within the previous 2 years;

(d) information about any claim either brought by the Employee against the Seller within the previous 2 years or where the Seller has reasonable grounds to believe that a claim may be brought against the Buyer arising out of the Employee's employment with the Seller; and

(e) information about any collective agreement which will have effect after the Transfer Date in relation to the Employee pursuant to regulation 5(a) of TUPE;

'Employees' — all the employees of the Seller engaged in the Business at the date of this Agreement whose names are set out in Annexure 2, and **'Employee'** means any of them;

'Encumbrance' — any mortgage, charge (fixed or floating), pledge, lien, hypothecation, guarantee, trust, right of set-off or other third party right or interest including any assignment by way of security, reservation of title or other security interest of any kind or other arrangement or agreement having similar effect;

'Excluded Assets'

(a) the Administrators' Records;

(b) the Book Debts;

(c) Cash;

(d) Claims;

(e) the Excluded Contracts;

(f) the ROT Assets;

(g) the Third Party Assets;

(h) the VAT Records;

(i) all policies of insurance relating to the Business together with the benefit of any claims under them;

(j) any freehold or leasehold property owned, leased or used by the Seller other than the Property;

(k) any shares or other securities owned by the Seller;

(l) any other property, rights or assets of the Seller which are not listed in the list of Assets;

'Excluded Contracts'	those contracts relating to the Business listed in Annexure 3;
'Fixed Assets'	all fixtures and fittings, plant, machinery, equipment and other tangible assets physically attached to the Property and owned or used by the Seller in relation to the Business at the Transfer Date including those listed in Annexure 4;
'the Freehold Property'	the freehold property details of which are set out in Part 1(a) of Schedule 1;
'Goodwill'	the goodwill, custom and connection of the Business and the exclusive right for the Buyer to represent itself as carrying on the Business in succession to the Seller and to use all the Business Name and any trade-names associated with the Business;
'HMRC'	Her Majesty's Revenue & Customs;
'Intellectual Property Licences'	the licences and other agreements granted by third parties to the Seller for the use of the Intellectual Property Rights including those listed in Annexure 5;
'Intellectual Property Rights'	patents, trademarks or names and service marks (whether or not registered or capable of registration), registered designs, design rights, copyrights and related rights, database rights, the right to apply for and applications for any of the preceding items, together with the rights in inventions, processes, software, know-how, trade or business secrets, confidential information, internet domain names, and any process or other similar right or asset capable of protection enjoyed, owned, used or licensed in relation to the Business;
'Landlord'	the person or persons from time to time entitled to the reversion (whether immediate or not) expectant upon the termination of the Lease;
'Landlord's Consent'	the consent of the Landlord authorising a transfer or an assignment of the residue of the Lease to the Buyer in accordance with the terms of the Lease, such consent being given in a written formal licence to assign, dated and signed or executed by or on behalf of each of the parties to it;
'Lease'	the lease under which the Leasehold Property is held as set out in Part 1(b) of Schedule 1, including every deed varying or supplemental to the Lease, every licence granted under the Lease and every collateral agreement as defined in the Landlord and Tenant (Covenants) Act 1995;
'the Leasehold Property'	the leasehold property details of which are set out in Part 1(b) of Schedule 1;
'Leasing Agreements'	any leasing, conditional sale, credit sale, hire-purchase and like agreements to which the Seller is a party, under which title to assets used by the Seller in or in relation to the Business does not pass or has not passed to the Seller, including those listed in Annexure 6;

'Liabilities'	all claims, liabilities, obligations and debts of the Seller on the Transfer Date relating to the Business whether matured or not, fixed or contingent including, but not limited to, any and all liabilities in respect of bank loans, overdrafts and other loans owing by the Seller;
'Motor Vehicles'	the motor vehicles owned or used by the Seller in relation to the Business as listed in Annexure 7;
'Moveable Assets'	all plant, machinery, equipment, tools, furniture and other tangible assets not physically attached to the Property and owned or used by the Seller in relation to the Business at the Transfer Date, including those listed in Annexure 8;
'Notice'	includes any notice, demand, consent or other communication;
'the Property'	the Freehold Property and the Leasehold Property;
'ROT Assets'	all assets in the possession of the Seller at the Transfer Date that are or become subject to an ROT Claim;
'ROT Claim'	a claim made by a supplier of goods (or a person deriving title from such a supplier) delivered to the Buyer for the return of such goods, or for the payment of damages for wrongful interference with them on the basis that title had not passed to the Seller before delivery;
'Security'	the Charge Holder's Security and other charges and Encumbrances over the Assets;
'Seller's Records'	the books, accounts, lists of clients, Customers and suppliers, credit reports, sales literature, price lists, advertising and publicity material, stock records, lists of outstanding and unfulfilled orders and contracts, and other files, books, correspondence and all the other documents, papers and records however stored of the Seller relating to the Business, Employees or any of the Assets, but excluding the Administrators' Records and the VAT Records;
'Seller's Solicitors'	[ ] of [ ] (Ref: [ ]);
'Stock'	all stock-in-trade, raw materials, components, spare parts, finished and unfinished goods, bought-in goods, consumables, stores, packaging materials, packages and work in progress relating to the Business as at the Transfer Date;
'Tax Authority'	any taxing or other authority, body or official competent to administer, impose or collect any Taxation;
'Taxation'	all forms of taxation and statutory governmental, supra-governmental, state, provincial, local governmental or municipal impositions, duties, contributions, and levies (including withholdings and deductions) whether of the United Kingdom or elsewhere in the world, whenever imposed and however arising, and all penalties, fines, charges, costs and interest, together with the cost of removing any charge or other encumbrance relating thereto, and **'Tax'** shall be construed accordingly;

'Third Party Assets'	all assets in the possession of the Seller in relation to the Business which are on loan, subject to lease, hire purchase, conditional sale, rental, contract hire or other agreements which do not pass title to the Seller, or of which it is for any reason bailee;
'Third Party Consent'	a consent, licence, approval, authorisation or waiver required from a third party for the conveyance, transfer, assignment or novation in favour of the Buyer of any of the Assets;
'Transfer Date'	[ ];
'TUPE'	the Transfer of Undertakings (Protection of Employment) Regulations 2006;
'VAT'	Value Added Tax charged under VATA 1994 and any replacement or similar or additional Tax;
'VATA 1994'	the Value Added Tax Act 1994 and all other statutes, statutory instruments, regulations and notices containing provisions relating to VAT;
'VAT Records'	all records of the Seller relating to the Business referred to in section 49 of VATA 1994.

1.2   In this Agreement, unless the context otherwise requires:

(a)   words in the singular include the plural and vice versa, and words in one gender include any other gender;

(b)   a reference to a statute or statutory provision includes:

   (i)   any subordinate legislation (as defined in section 21(1) of the Interpretation Act 1978) made under it;

   (ii)   any repealed statute or statutory provision which it re-enacts (with or without modification); and

   (iii)   any statute or statutory provision which modifies, consolidates, re-enacts or supersedes it;

(c)   a reference to:

   (i)   any party includes its successors in title and permitted assigns;

   (ii)   a **'person'** includes any individual, firm, body corporate, association or partnership, government or state (whether or not having a separate legal personality);

   (iii)   clauses and schedules are to clauses and schedules of this Agreement, and references to sub-clauses and paragraphs are references to sub-clauses and paragraphs of the clause or paragraph in which they appear;

   (iv)   any provision of this Agreement is to that provision as amended in accordance with the terms of this Agreement;

(v) any document being **'in the agreed form'** means in a form which has been agreed by the parties on or before the date of this Agreement and for identification purposes signed by them or on their behalf by their solicitors;

(vi) **'indemnify'** and **'indemnifying'** any person against any circumstance includes indemnifying and keeping him harmless from all actions, claims and proceedings from time to time made against him and all loss or damage and all payments, costs or expenses made or incurred by that person as a consequence of or which would not have arisen but for that circumstance;

(vii) a **'loss'** includes any loss, damage, cost, charge, penalty, fee or expense;

(viii) **'records'** includes information held in any form, including paper, electronically stored data, magnetic media and microfilm; and

(ix) **'representatives'** includes partners, agents, employees and any other person acting on behalf of and with the authority of any relevant person;

(d) except as set out in sub-clause 1.1, terms defined in the Companies Act 2006 have the meanings attributed to them by that Act;

(e) **'sterling'** and the sign **'£'** mean pounds sterling in the currency of the United Kingdom save that if, following the introduction of the Euro, pounds sterling ceases to exist as the currency of the United Kingdom, then all references in this Agreement to **'pounds sterling'** and **'£'** shall be construed as references to the Euro at the conversion rate applicable at the close of the business day before that on which the pound sterling ceased to exist;

(f) the table of contents and headings are for convenience only and shall not affect the interpretation of this Agreement;

(g) general words shall not be given a restrictive meaning:

(i) if they are introduced by the word 'other' by reason of the fact that they are preceded by words indicating a particular class of act, matter or thing; or

(ii) by reason of the fact that they are followed by particular examples intended to be embraced by those general words;

(h) where the words **'include(s)'**, **'including'** or **'in particular'** are used in this Agreement, they are deemed to have the words 'without limitation' following them;

(i) **'writing'** or **'written'** includes faxes but not email;

(j)   a reference to the Administrators and the Seller includes each of them jointly or either of them individually; and

(k)   where any liability or obligation is undertaken by two or more persons, the liability of each of them shall be joint and several.

2.   Sale of the Business and the Assets

2.1   Subject to the terms of this Agreement the Seller shall sell to the Buyer and the Buyer shall purchase such right title and interest (if any) as the Seller has and can transfer at the Transfer Date in the following assets:

(a)   the Business Information;

(b)   the benefit (subject to the burden) of the Contracts;

(c)   the Fixed Assets;

(d)   the Goodwill;

(e)   the Intellectual Property Rights;

(f)   the Moveable Assets;

(g)   the Motor Vehicles;

(h)   the Seller's Records; and

(i)   the Stock.

2.2   The Property is sold in accordance with the terms set out in Part 2 of Schedule 1.

2.3   For the avoidance of doubt and without limitation the Excluded Assets are not included in the sale under this Agreement.

2.4   The Business and Assets are sold free from the Charge Holder's Security.

2.5   Risk of loss or damage to the Assets shall pass to the Buyer from the Transfer Date.

3.   Consideration

3.1   The Consideration is the payment by the Buyer to the Seller of the sum of £[ ] (exclusive of VAT), which is payable in cash at Completion in accordance with clause 5 (Completion).

3.2   The Consideration shall be apportioned between the Assets as set out in Schedule 2.

3.3   In addition, the Buyer shall assume the burden of the Contracts and any liabilities associated with them in accordance with this Agreement.

3.4   The Seller confirms that the Administrators or the Seller's Solicitors may give a good receipt for the Consideration and any and all other amounts due or payable under this Agreement.

4.   Value Added Tax

4.1   All amounts payable by the Buyer pursuant to this Agreement are expressed to be exclusive of any VAT that may be chargeable thereon.

4.2   The Seller and the Buyer agree that the sale of the Assets is for VAT purposes the transfer of the business of the Seller as a going concern for the purposes of both section 49(1) of VATA 1994 and article 5 of the Value Added Tax (Special Provisions) Order 1995 (**'article 5'**). The Seller and the Buyer shall use their reasonable endeavours to secure that, pursuant to such provisions, the sale of the Assets is treated as neither a supply of goods nor a supply of services for the purposes of VAT.

4.3   The Buyer warrants to the Seller and the Administrators that:

(a)   it is, or shall be at Completion, a taxable person and duly registered for the purposes of VAT;

(b)   it is purchasing the Assets and the Property as beneficial owner in order that it may carry on the Business as a going concern in succession to the Seller, and it has no present intention of transferring any of them to any third party;

(c)   following Completion, it will use the Assets and the Property or any of them to carry on the same kind of business as that previously carried on by the Seller;

(d)   by not later than the 'relevant date' within the meaning of article 5, it (or a relevant associate for the purposes of paragraph 2 of Schedule 10 to the VATA 1994 or a relevant group member for the purposes of paragraph 21 of Schedule 10 to the VATA 1994) will:

(i)   make an option to tax in respect of the Property, to take effect not later than the relevant date; and

(ii)   notify HMRC of the option to tax; and

(iii)   supply the Seller with a copy of the option to tax and evidence of the receipt by HMRC of the option to tax;

(e)   it will not revoke the option to tax in relation to the Property (either before or after Completion) or do, cause to be done or omit to do anything which could lead to the option to tax being revoked by HMRC.

5.   Completion

5.1   Completion shall take place at the offices of the Seller's Solicitors or at such other place as the Administrators may direct on [   ] 20[   ] at [   ] [am] [pm].

5.2 On Completion:

   (a)   the Buyer shall:

      (i)   pay the Consideration (plus any VAT due for payment on it) to the Seller by telegraphic transfer to the client account of the Seller's Solicitors at [   ] Bank plc, account number [   ], sort code [   ];

      (ii)   execute and deliver to the Administrators this Agreement and any and all other documents which require execution by the Buyer;

      (iii)   deliver to the Administrators a certified copy of a resolution passed by the board of directors of the Buyer authorising the execution and delivery of this Agreement and any and all other documents delivered; and

   (b)   subject to the Buyer having complied with sub-clause 5.2 (a), the Seller shall permit the Buyer to enter into and take possession of the Business and shall deliver or cause to be delivered to the Buyer:

      (i)   physical possession of the Property;

      (ii)   if required by the Buyer, duly executed agreements in agreed form for the assignment or novation of the benefit of the Contracts to the Buyer, or as the Buyer shall direct, and all the requisite consents and licences for such assignments;

      (iii)   a duly executed assignment in agreed form to vest the Goodwill in the Buyer;

      (iv)   if required by the Buyer, duly executed assignments and licences in agreed form of the Intellectual Property Rights (including, without limitation, any required assignments of trademarks);

      (v)   a letter to the relevant domain name registrar consenting to the transfer of the Seller's registrations to the Buyer;

      (vi)   at the Property, the Assets which are capable of transfer by delivery;

      (vii)   physical possession of the ROT Assets and the Third Party Assets;

      (viii)   any instruments of transfer which the Buyer may reasonably require to vest title in the Assets (including, without limitation, any transfer or conveyance, and any Landlord's Consent and assignment) together with all deeds and documents of title relating to the Assets;

      (ix)   those of the Seller's Records which are not stored at the Property;

      (x)   releases from the Security to the extent that such releases are available at Completion; and

(xi) a special resolution passed by the shareholders of the Seller, changing its name to a name which is in no way similar to the Business Name.

5.3 Upon receipt by the Seller of any VAT due for payment in respect of the Consideration the Seller will provide the Buyer with an appropriate VAT invoice.

5.4 Without limitation of any other provision of this Agreement, from Completion, the Buyer shall do all things necessary to ensure compliance with all legal requirements as to possession, ownership or use of any of the Assets or the Property, including obtaining all necessary licences, consents, certificates, permits and other authorisations.

5.5 The Buyer shall fully indemnify the Seller and the Administrators from and against all claims and losses which may be brought against or incurred by the Seller or the Administrators in respect of the Buyer's failure to comply with clause 5.4.

6. Apportionments

6.1 All charges and outgoings relating to and payable in respect of the Business and any of the Assets and the Property which relate to a period commencing before or on and ending after the Transfer Date shall be apportioned on a time basis (save where such charges and outgoings are specifically referable to the extent of such use) so that such part of each charges and outgoings as is attributable to the period ending on the day immediately prior to the Transfer Date shall be borne by the Seller and each part of such charges and outgoings as is attributable to the period commencing on the Transfer Date shall be borne by the Buyer.

6.2 For the purposes of sub-clause 6.1, charges and outgoings shall exclude the amounts due to creditors under the Liabilities, but shall include, without limitation, rents, rates, water and other periodic outgoings, gas, electricity and telephone charges, licences, royalties, road tax licences and insurance premiums and obligations, and liabilities in respect of salaries, wages, bonuses, accrued holiday pay and other remuneration, national insurance, pension and other statutory contributions, income tax deductible under PAYE for which the Seller is accountable, contributions to retirement benefit schemes and all other payments to or in respect of the Employees.

6.3 Such part of all royalties, discounts, rebates and other sums receivable in respect of the Business or any of the Assets or the Property which relates to a period commencing before and ending on the day immediately prior to the Transfer Date shall be for the benefit of the Seller, and such part of the royalties, discounts, rebates and other sums receivable in respect of the Business or any of the Assets which relates to a period commencing on the Transfer Date shall be for the benefit of the Buyer save that this sub-clause shall not apply to the Book Debts.

6.4 The Buyer shall pay for all goods or services ordered by the Seller or the Administrators relating to the Business or the Assets or the Property, on terms either of personal liability or payment as an administration expense, which have not been delivered or performed prior to the Transfer Date (**'Seller's Orders'**). Payment shall be made within five Business Days of the date of delivery to the Buyer of an invoice in respect of those goods or services, by the Seller or the supplier. The Buyer shall fully indemnify the Seller and the Administrators from and against any claims and losses which may be brought against or incurred by the Seller or the Administrators in respect of the Seller's Orders.

6.5 For the avoidance of doubt, and except as expressly provided otherwise in this Agreement, notwithstanding that the Seller may continue to be responsible for all debts payable by it, and all claims and liabilities (including contingent claims and liabilities) outstanding against it or any of its assets it shall have no obligation to pay such amounts.

6.6 For the avoidance of doubt the Buyer shall pay, satisfy and discharge all debts and liabilities of the Business incurred on and after the Transfer Date, and shall fully indemnify the Seller and the Administrators from and against all claims and liabilities which may be brought against or incurred by the Seller or the Administrators in respect of such debts and liabilities.

7. Contracts

7.1 With effect from Completion, the Buyer shall assume and perform all of the obligations of the Seller under the Contracts, whether arising before or after the Transfer Date.

7.2 The Seller shall with effect from Completion, assign to the Buyer or procure the assignment of all of the Contracts which are capable of assignment without the consent of other contractual parties.

7.3 If any Contract cannot be assigned by the Seller to the Buyer except by an agreement or novation or with a consent to assignment or without assignment constituting an event of default or termination, no assignment shall take place by virtue of this Agreement until legally able to do so, but:

(a) the Buyer shall take all reasonable steps to procure that the Contract be novated or to obtain the consent or waiver to the event of default or to the termination, and promptly provide copies of any such novations, consents or waivers to the Seller;

(b) unless or until the Contract has been novated or assigned or the provision waived, the Seller shall hold it on trust for the Buyer;

(c) the Buyer shall, at its own cost and for its own benefit, perform the Seller's obligations under the Contract arising after the Transfer Date and shall carry out and complete it (or shall procure that it is carried out and completed), to the extent that it has not previously been carried out or completed, in the ordinary course in a proper and workmanlike manner and in accordance with its respective terms; and

(d) unless the Buyer is prevented by the other party to the Contract from performing it, the Buyer shall indemnify the Seller against the defective or negligent performance or non-performance of the Contract.

7.4 If, prior to the Transfer Date, the Seller has sub-contracted the performance of any Contract to any person, the Buyer shall, on behalf of the relevant customer, seek or accept delivery from such person of the goods or other products or services in respect of which that Contract was made and shall make it available to, or for collection by, such customer.

7.5 Any prepayment or deposit received by the Seller before the Transfer Date (other than sums held on trust) shall remain the property of the Seller, and the Buyer shall not be entitled to any refund or other allowance in respect of them.

7.6 The Buyer shall fully indemnify the Seller and the Administrators from and against all claims and losses which may be brought against or incurred by the Seller or the Administrators in respect of the Contracts insofar as such matters relate to the period, or any event occurring, after the Transfer Date.

8. Intellectual Property

8.1 The Buyer shall obtain any necessary third party licences, consents and permissions (**'Permissions'**) to use or exploit the Intellectual Property Rights and the Business Name. For the avoidance of doubt, the Seller does not authorise or purport to authorise the Buyer to use or exploit any of the Intellectual Property Rights or the Business Name before the Buyer obtains any such Permissions.

8.2 The Buyer shall be responsible for all registration, maintenance, renewal fees and other expenses in connection with the assignment, licensing or maintenance of the Intellectual Property Rights and the Business Name.

8.3 The Buyer shall fully indemnify the Seller and the Administrators from and against all claims and losses which may be brought against or incurred by the Seller or the Administrators in respect of the use of any or all of the Intellectual Property Rights or the Business Name insofar as such matters relate to the period, or any event occurring, after the Transfer Date.

9. Third Party Assets

9.1 The Seller shall leave the Third Party Assets on the Property after Completion.

9.2 The Buyer shall:

(a) hold the Third Party Assets as bailee;

(b) have no title to or further right to possess or use any of the Third Party Assets;

(c) not hold itself out as owner of any of the Third Party Assets;

    (d)   at its own expense, maintain the Third Party Assets in as good condition as they were in at the time of Completion (subject to normal wear and tear);

    (e)   not sell, charge or otherwise encumber or dispose of any of the Third Party Assets; and

    (f)   allow the Administrators, the Seller, the owners of the Third Party Assets and their respective representatives, to have access to the Third Party Assets at any reasonable time, to enable them to inspect, remove or otherwise deal with them.

9.3   The Buyer shall use all reasonable endeavours to obtain the consent of the owners of the Third Party Assets to the Buyer's continued possession, use or purchase of them. Neither the Administrators nor the Seller shall object to or hinder any arrangements which the Buyer may wish to make in this respect nor will they make any claim in relation to the Third Party Assets. The Seller shall execute such documents as the Buyer may reasonably require subject to the requirements of clause 20.8.

9.4   If the owner of any Third Party Asset refuses to sell it or otherwise make it available to the Buyer, the Buyer shall forthwith deliver up such item for collection and removal by the owner and notify the Seller of such delivery up.

9.5   The Buyer shall fully indemnify the Seller and the Administrators from and against all claims and losses which may be brought against or incurred by the Seller or the Administrators in respect of any or all of the Third Party Assets insofar as such matters relate to the period, or any event occurring, after the Transfer Date.

10.   ROT Assets

10.1   The Seller shall leave the ROT Assets on the Property after Completion, and allow the Buyer into possession of the ROT Assets as against it.

10.2   The Buyer shall:

    (a)   hold the ROT Assets as bailee;

    (b)   have no title to or further right to possess any of the ROT Assets;

    (c)   not hold itself out as owner of any of the ROT Assets;

    (d)   not charge or otherwise encumber any of the ROT Assets;

    (e)   store, maintain and insure the ROT Assets at its own expense;

    (f)   allow the Administrators, the Seller, the owners of the ROT Assets and their respective representatives, to have access to the ROT Assets at any reasonable time, to enable them to inspect, remove or otherwise deal with them.

10.3   From Completion, the Buyer shall promptly inform the Administrators and the Seller of any information received by it in respect of any ROT Claims.

10.4 The Buyer shall fully indemnify the Seller and the Administrators from and against all claims and losses which may be brought against or incurred by the Seller or the Administrators in respect of any or all of the ROT Assets.

10.5 Where it is established by agreement between the Administrators and the relevant claimant or by court order that an ROT Claim is not valid and enforceable, such right, title and interest (if any) as the Seller has in the ROT Asset, the subject of that ROT Claim, will pass to the Buyer on the date of that agreement or court order.

11. Book Debts

11.1 Collection of the Book Debts shall remain the responsibility of the Seller and the Buyer shall not seek to collect or recover the Book Debts or do anything to hinder their collection by the Seller. In particular the Buyer shall not purport to agree any discounts or compromise or otherwise settle any of the Book Debts.

11.2 If the Buyer receives any payment in respect of any Book Debt or any other sum due to the Seller, it shall hold the payment on trust for the benefit of the Seller and remit it to the Seller forthwith on receipt.

11.3 If the Buyer receives a payment from a person who is a debtor of both the Seller and the Buyer, the amount shall be first applied in respect of the debts due to the Seller, and the Buyer shall pay to the Seller an amount equal to the payment so received immediately on receipt.

11.4 The Seller and the Administrators may take such action as they think fit in relation to the collection of the Book Debts, provided that:

    (a) the Seller agrees not to threaten the commencement of proceedings or to take any other steps (other than sending accounts rendered) with regard to any Book Debt owed to it by a person it knows to be a customer of the Buyer without first offering in writing to assign the relevant Book Debt to the Buyer at its face value. An offer made by the Seller under this clause 11.4(a) shall state the name of the debtor, and the age, amount and nature of the debt to be collected;

    (b) the Buyer may, within five Business Days of receipt of an offer made under clause 11.4(a) accept it by paying the full amount of the Book Debt specified in the offer (including any specified interest or costs that the Seller is entitled to recover from the debtor) to the Seller; and

    (c) if the Buyer accepts the offer in accordance with clause 11.4(a) the Seller shall enter into an assignment of the relevant Book Debt to the Buyer.

12. Employees

12.1 The parties agree that the sale and purchase pursuant to this Agreement will constitute a 'relevant transfer' for the purposes of TUPE and that the contracts of employment of the Employees and the Seller's rights, powers, duties and liabilities under or in connection with such contracts of employment shall be transferred to the Buyer under TUPE at the Transfer Date.

12.2 Neither the Seller nor the Administrators shall have any liability to the Buyer for any claims or losses which may be brought against or incurred by the Buyer whether relating to the period before or after the Transfer Date in respect of any persons whose employment is transferred to the Buyer, whether under TUPE or otherwise.

12.3 The Buyer acknowledges that the Seller acting by the Administrators has, so far as practicable, provided it with the Employee Liability Information, and that, given the Administrators' limited knowledge of the Business and the insolvency of the Seller, such information may be incomplete or inaccurate.

12.4 The Buyer shall fully indemnify the Seller and the Administrators from and against all claims and losses which may be brought against or incurred by the Seller or the Administrators in respect of any of the Employees, whether in relation to periods before or after the Transfer Date, including any claim brought by:

(a) any of the Employees;

(b) the Buyer under Regulation 12 of TUPE; or

(c) any person under Regulation 15 of TUPE.

12.5 If the contract of employment of any Employee is found not to have transferred to the Buyer under TUPE with effect from the Transfer Date, the Buyer agrees that:

(a) it will within five Business Days of being informed of such fact make the relevant Employee an offer of employment in writing; and

(b) any such offer of employment made by the Buyer will be on terms which are not materially different from that Employee's terms immediately before the Transfer Date (save as to the identity of the employer).

On making that offer (or at any time after the offer should have been made if no offer is made), the Seller shall terminate the employment of the relevant Employee and the Buyer shall fully indemnify the Seller and the Administrators against all claims and losses which may be brought against or incurred by the Seller or the Administrators in respect of the employment of that Employee from the Transfer Date until such termination and from the termination of such employment.

13. Seller's Records

13.1 From Completion, the Buyer shall make the Seller's Records available for inspection by the Seller, the Administrators and their representatives and provide to them reasonable facilities during normal business hours to inspect and copy (at the Buyer's expense) the Seller's Records.

13.2 The Buyer shall:

    (a)   keep the Seller's Records in good order and in good and safe condition, and insured for their full value; and

    (b)   give the Administrators not less than one month's prior notice of any intended disposal or destruction of all or any of them.

13.3 For the avoidance of doubt, the Administrators' Records shall not be available to the Buyer for inspection or otherwise, and if any of them come into the possession of the Buyer, at Completion or otherwise, it shall immediately notify the Administrators and deliver them to the Administrators on demand.

14.   Buyer's Records

14.1 During normal business hours and on reasonable notice, the Buyer shall give the Seller, the Administrators and their representatives access to the premises, records and staff of the Buyer to enable the Seller and the Administrators to deal with:

    (a)   collection of the Book Debts;

    (b)   ascertainment of any sums payable under this Agreement; and

    (c)   any other matters arising in connection with this Agreement or the administration of the Seller.

14.2 For the period of six months from Completion, the Buyer shall make available to the Administrators, without charge, reasonable office, telephone, and secretarial facilities at the Property for their use during normal business hours, to enable the Administrators to deal with the matters referred to in clause 14.1.

15.   VAT Records

15.1 The Seller and Buyer intend that section 49 of VATA 1994 shall apply to the sale of the Assets and the Property under this Agreement but they do not intend to make a joint application to Customs for the Buyer to be registered for VAT under the VAT registration number of the Seller pursuant to regulation 6(1)(d) of the VAT Regulations 1995.

15.2 The Seller shall preserve and permit the Buyer reasonable access to the VAT Records for such period as may be required by law.

15.3 If any of the VAT Records come into the possession of the Buyer, at Completion or otherwise, it shall immediately notify the Administrators and deliver them to the Administrators on demand.

16.   Data Protection

16.1 Notwithstanding any other provision of this Agreement, the Buyer undertakes that, on receipt of the Customer Database and Employee Database on the Completion Date, it shall:

(a) duly observe all of its obligations as a Data Controller under the DPA 1998 which arise in connection with processing Customer Data and Employee Data;

(b) comply with the eight Data Protection Principles set out in the DPA 1998 and, in particular, it shall process Customer Data and Employee Data fairly and lawfully for the purpose of the continued provision of details of the product(s) and services to the Customers and in connection with the employment of the Data Employees and in accordance with the terms and conditions set out in this Agreement;

(c) send a fair processing notice to each Customer and Data Employee identified in the Customer Database and Employee Database within five Business Days of the Completion Date;

(d) respond to any request made by a Customer or Data Employee in relation to the provision of details of the product(s) and services in accordance with the rights of data subjects (as defined in the DPA 1998); and

(e) obtain, and at all times maintain, a notification under the DPA 1998 appropriate to the performance of its obligations under this Agreement.

16.2 The Buyer shall fully indemnify the Seller and the Administrators from and against all claims and losses incurred by the Seller or the Administrators which may be brought against or incurred by the Seller or the Administrators in respect of the processing of the Customer Data or Employee Data by the Buyer or any breach of contract, negligence, fraud, wilful misconduct, breach of statutory duty or non-compliance with the data protection obligations set out in this clause 16 or any part of DPA 1998 by the Buyer or its representatives.

17. Correspondence

After Completion, the Buyer shall promptly deliver to the Administrators all correspondence received by it addressed to the Seller or the Administrators.

18. Administrators' liability

18.1 The Administrators act as agents of the Seller and neither they nor their representatives shall incur any personal liability whatever by virtue of this Agreement, nor in relation to any related matter or claim nor in respect of any transfer, assignment or other documents made pursuant to this Agreement.

18.2 The Administrators have entered into this Agreement in their personal capacities solely for the purpose of obtaining the benefit of the provisions in their favour.

19. Exclusions

19.1 Subject to clause 19.5, all representations, warranties, conditions, guarantees and stipulations, express or implied, statutory, customary or otherwise in respect of the Assets, the Business or the Property or any of the rights, title and interests transferred or agreed to be transferred pursuant to this Agreement are expressly excluded (including warranties and conditions as to title, quiet possession, merchantable quality, fitness for purpose and description). Except as expressly set out in this Agreement, any lists contained in any schedule or annexe are for guidance only and are not exhaustive or complete lists of the items in question and shall not constitute any warranty in respect of the Seller's ownership of the listed items or otherwise.

19.2　The Assets and the Property or any of them are sold in their condition and locations at the Transfer Date and subject to all faults, liens, executions, distraints, encumbrances and claims of third parties, the expense of discharging which shall be met by the Buyer. Unless otherwise required by law (and then only to that extent), the Seller and the Administrators and each of them shall not be liable for any loss arising out of, or due to, or caused by any defect or deficiencies in any or all of the Assets and the Property.

19.3　The Buyer agrees that the terms and conditions of this Agreement and the exclusions and limitations contained in it are fair and reasonable having regard to the following:

(a)　that this is a sale by an insolvent company in circumstances where the Administrators' knowledge of the Business, Assets and Property is limited and it is usual that no representations and warranties are given by or on behalf of the Seller or the Administrators;

(b)　that the Buyer has relied solely on the opinions of itself and its professional advisors concerning the Assets and the Property or any of them, their quality, condition, description, fitness and suitability for any purpose, the possibility that some or all of them may have defects not apparent on inspection and examination, and the use it intends or proposes to put them to;

(c)　that the Buyer has agreed to purchase the Assets and the Property or any of them 'as seen' in their present state and condition for a consideration which takes into account the risk to the Buyer represented by the parties' belief that the said exclusions and limitations are or would be recognised by the court;

(d)　that the Buyer, its representatives and advisers have been given every opportunity it or they may wish to have to examine and inspect all or any of the Assets and the Property or any of them and all relevant documents relating to them.

19.4　The Buyer acknowledges that it has not entered into this Agreement in reliance upon any representations, agreements, statements or replies to specific enquiries (whether oral or written) made or alleged to have been made by the Seller, the Administrators or its or their representatives at any time.

19.5 Nothing in this Agreement operates to limit or exclude any liability for fraud or fraudulent misrepresentation.

19.6 The Buyer acknowledges that if the Seller does not have title or unencumbered title to any or all of the Assets or any of the Properties, or if the Buyer cannot exercise any right conferred or purported to be conferred on it by this Agreement, this shall not be a ground or grounds for rescinding, avoiding or varying any or all of the provisions of this Agreement, or for any reduction or repayment of any part of the consideration.

20. General

20.1 Entire agreement

This Agreement sets out the entire agreement and understanding between the parties and supersedes all prior agreements, understandings or arrangements (oral or written) in respect of the subject matter of this Agreement.

20.2 Contracts (Rights of Third Parties) Act 1999

Unless expressly provided in this Agreement, no term of this Agreement is enforceable pursuant to the Contracts (Rights of Third Parties) Act 1999 by any person who is not a party to it.

20.3 Assignment

(a) This Agreement shall be binding upon and enure for the benefit of the successors of the parties but shall not be assignable by the Buyer.

(b) The Buyer may not grant any Encumbrance over this Agreement or any document referred to in it.

20.4 Variation

No purported variation of this Agreement shall be effective unless it is in writing and signed by or on behalf of each of the parties.

20.5 Effect of Completion

Except to the extent already performed, all the provisions of this Agreement shall, so far as they are capable of being performed or observed, continue in full force and effect notwithstanding Completion.

20.6 Invalidity

If any provision of this Agreement is found by any court or competent authority to be invalid, unlawful or unenforceable in any jurisdiction, that provision shall be deemed not to be a part of this Agreement, but it shall not affect the enforceability of the remainder of this Agreement, nor shall it affect the validity, lawfulness or enforceability of that provision in any other jurisdiction.

20.7 **Releases and waivers**

(a) Any waiver by or on behalf of the Seller or the Administrators of any right under this Agreement is only effective if it is in writing and signed by the Administrators on behalf of the Seller or the Administrators on their own behalf. It applies only in the circumstances for which it is given and shall not prevent the Seller or the Administrators from subsequently relying on the provision so waived.

(b) No failure by the Seller or the Administrators to exercise or delay in exercising any right or remedy provided under this Agreement or by law constitutes a waiver of such right or remedy or shall prevent any future exercise in whole or in part.

(c) No single or partial exercise by the Seller or the Administrators of any right or remedy under this Agreement shall preclude or restrict the further exercise of any such right or remedy.

(d) Unless specifically provided otherwise, the rights of the Seller and the Administrators arising under this Agreement are cumulative and do not exclude rights provided by law.

20.8 **Further assurance**

(a) For six months following Completion, the Seller and the Administrators (provided they are, at the relevant time, the Administrators of the Seller) shall (at the Buyer's expense) execute and deliver all such documents, and do whatever the Buyer may from time to time reasonably require for the purpose of giving effect to the provisions of this Agreement, provided that the terms of any such documents:

   (i) shall exclude the personal liability of the Administrators;

   (ii) shall be no more onerous to the Seller and the Administrators than the terms of this Agreement;

   (iii) shall be subject to the Administrators' prior approval, which shall not be unreasonably withheld or delayed.

(b) Pending the execution of any documents and things in accordance with clause 20.8(a), the Seller shall hold any legal interest in the Assets and the Property or any of them on trust for the Buyer but without any legal responsibility for the Assets and the Property or any of them and, in particular, neither the Seller nor the Administrators shall be obliged to maintain any registrations or otherwise protect the Assets and the Property or any of them.

20.9 **Counterparts**

(a) This Agreement may be executed in any number of counterparts and by the parties on separate counterparts, but shall not be effective until each party has executed at least one counterpart.

(b) Each counterpart, when executed, shall be an original of this Agreement and all counterparts shall together constitute one instrument.

20.10 **Time of the essence**

Except as otherwise expressly provided, time is of the essence as regards every obligation of any party under this Agreement.

20.11 **Confidentiality**

(a) The Seller and the Administrators shall keep confidential all the information that they have acquired about the Buyer and use such information only for the purposes contemplated by this Agreement.

(b) The Buyer undertakes to the Seller and the Administrators to keep confidential the terms of this Agreement and all information that it has acquired about the Seller and to use the information only for the purposes contemplated by this Agreement.

(c) Either party may disclose any information that it is otherwise required to keep confidential under this clause 20.11:

    (i) to such professional advisers, consultants and employees or officers of its group and, in the case of the Seller and the Administrators, the Administrators' firm, employees and agents, as are reasonably necessary to advise on this Agreement, or to facilitate the underlying transaction, provided that the disclosing party procures that the people to whom the information is disclosed keep it confidential as if they were that party;

    (ii) with the written consent of the Administrators and the Buyer; or

    (iii) to the extent that the disclosure is required:

        (A) for the purposes of the administration or any subsequent liquidation of the Seller;

        (B) by law; or

        (C) by a regulatory body, tax authority or securities exchange,

but shall use reasonable endeavours to consult the Administrators (in the case of a disclosure on the part of the Buyer) or the Buyer (in the case of a disclosure on the part of the Seller or the Administrators) and to take into account any reasonable requests the party consulted may have in relation to the disclosure before making it.

(d) No announcement, circular or other publicity in connection with the subject matter of this agreement (other than as permitted by this agreement) shall be made by or on behalf of the Seller, the Administrators or the Buyer without the approval of the Administrators and the Buyer (such approval not to be unreasonably withheld or delayed).

20.12 **Default interest**

If the Buyer defaults in the payment when due of any sum payable under this Agreement (whether payable by agreement or by an order of a court or otherwise), the liability of the Buyer shall be increased to include interest on that sum from the date when such payment was due until the date of actual payment at a rate per annum of 5 per cent above the base rate from time to time of the Bank. Such interest shall accrue from day to day and shall be compounded quarterly.

20.13 **Set-off**

The Buyer shall not be entitled to set off any amount due to it against any sum due from it to the Seller or the Administrators.

21. Announcements

21.1 Subject to sub-clause 21.2, no announcement concerning the terms of this Agreement shall be made by or on behalf of any of the parties without the prior written consent of the others, such consent not to be unreasonably withheld or delayed.

21.2 Any announcement or circular required to be made or issued by any party by law or under the regulations of the London Stock Exchange plc or the City Code on Takeovers and Mergers issued by the Panel on Takeovers and Mergers may be made or issued by that party without consent if it has first sought consent and given the other parties a reasonable opportunity to comment on the subject matter and form of the announcement or circular (given the timescale within which it is required to be released or despatched).

22. Costs and expenses

22.1 Except as referred to in sub-clause 22.2 each party shall bear its own costs and expenses incurred in the preparation, execution and implementation of this Agreement.

22.2 The Buyer shall pay all stamp and other transfer duties and registration fees applicable to any document to which it is a party and which arise as a result of or in consequence of this Agreement.

23. Notices

23.1 Any notice to a party under this Agreement shall be in writing signed by or on behalf of the party giving it and shall, unless delivered to a party personally, be left at, or sent by prepaid first-class post, prepaid recorded delivery or facsimile, to the address of the party as set out on the first page of this Agreement, or as otherwise notified in writing from time to time.

23.2 Except as referred to in sub-clause 23.3, a notice shall be deemed to have been served:

(a) at the time of delivery if delivered personally;

(b) 48 hours after posting in the case of an address in the United Kingdom and 96 hours after posting for any other address; or

(c) two hours after transmission if served by facsimile on a Business Day prior to 3pm or, in any other case, at 10am on the Business Day after the date of despatch.

If the deemed time of service is not during normal business hours in the country of receipt, the notice shall be deemed served at or, in the case of faxes, two hours after, the opening of business on the next Business Day of that country.

23.3 The deemed service provisions set out in sub-clause 23.2 do not apply to:

(a) a notice served by post, if there is a national or local suspension, curtailment or disruption of postal services which affects the collection of the notice or is such that the notice cannot reasonably be expected to be delivered within 48 hours or 96 hours (as appropriate) after posting; and

(b) a notice served by facsimile, if, before the time at which the notice would otherwise be deemed to have been served, the receiving party informs the sending party that the notice has been received in a form which is unclear in any material respect, and, if it informs the sending party by telephone, it also despatches a confirmatory facsimile within two hours.

23.4 In proving service it will be sufficient to prove:

(a) in the case of personal service, that it was handed to the party or delivered to or left in an appropriate place for receipt of letters at its address;

(b) in the case of a letter sent by post, that the letter was properly addressed, stamped and posted;

(c) in the case of facsimile, that it was properly addressed and despatched to the number of the party.

23.5 A party shall not attempt to prevent or delay the service on it of a notice connected with this Agreement.

23.6 A notice under this Agreement shall not be valid if sent by email.

24. Governing law and jurisdiction

24.1 This Agreement shall be governed by and construed in accordance with English Law.

24.2 Each of the parties irrevocably submits for all purposes in connection with this Agreement to the exclusive jurisdiction of the courts of England.

This Agreement is made on the date appearing at the head of the first page.

Annexures

1. **Contracts**
2. **Employees**
3. **Excluded Contracts**
4. **Fixed Assets**
5. **Intellectual Property Licenses**
6. **Leasing Agreements**
7. **Motor Vehicles**
8. **Moveable Assets**

Schedule 1

Part 1(a)

(Description of the freehold property)

Part 1(b)

(Description of the leasehold property including details of the Lease)

Part 2

(Provisions relating to the Property.)

Schedule 2

Apportionment of Consideration

£

the Property
the Business Information
the Contracts
the Fixed Assets
the Goodwill
the Intellectual Property Rights
the Moveable Assets
the Motor Vehicles
the Stock

Signed by .... **Limited**   )   ....
(in administration)   )   Administrator
acting by its administrator without   )
personal liability pursuant to powers   )
conferred under the Insolvency Act 1986   )
in the presence of:)

Signature of witness:

Name:

Address:

Occupation:

Signed by ....   )   ....
for and on behalf of   )   Director
....…................. **Limited**   )
in the presence of:)

Signature of witness:

Name:

Address:

Occupation:

Signed by ....   )   ....
for and on behalf of the Administrators   )   Administrator
in the presence of:)

Signature of witness:

Name:

Address:

Occupation:

B. Assignment of intellectual property and rights[1]

DATED .... 20[   ]

(1)   XXXXXXXX LIMITED (in administration)
(2)   YYYYYYYY LIMITED
(3)   [A1 and A2 – ADMINISTRATORS]

ASSIGNMENT OF INTELLECTUAL PROPERTY RIGHTS

DRAFT 1 .... 20[   ]

DATE OF ASSIGNMENT: .... 20[   ]

PARTIES:

(1)   [   ] **Limited** (in administration) registered in England and Wales with company number: [   ] whose registered office is at [   ] (**'Assignor'**) acting by the Administrators; and

(2)   [   ] **Limited** registered in England and Wales with company number: [   ] whose registered office is at [   ] (**'Assignee'**); and

(3)   [   ] and [   ] as joint administrators of the Assignor both of [   ] (**'Administrators'**).

BACKGROUND

(A)   The Assignor is the legal and beneficial owner of certain intellectual property rights.

(B)   On [DATE] the Administrators were appointed as joint administrators of the Assignor.

(C)   By the Main Agreement (as defined below) the Assignor has agreed to sell to the Assignee certain intellectual property rights of the Assignor.

---

[1]   Adapted from PLC's Assignment of Intellectual Property and Rights precedent. For further information please visit http://uk.practicallaw.com/.

IT IS NOW AGREED as follows:

1.   Definitions and interpretation

1.1   In this Assignment the following words and expressions shall have the following meanings:

'Assigned Rights'	the Patents, Trade Marks and Registered Designs and all the Intellectual Property Rights [relating to the Materials] **or** [set out in Schedule 5];
'Business Day'	a day other than a Saturday or Sunday or public holiday in England when banks in London are open for business;
'Intellectual Property Rights'	patents, rights to inventions, copyright and related rights, trade marks and services marks, trade names and domain names, rights in get-up, goodwill and the right to sue for passing off and unfair competition, rights in designs, rights in computer software, database rights, rights to preserve the confidentiality of information (including know-how and trade secrets) and any other intellectual property rights, including all applications for (and rights to apply for and be granted), renewals or extensions of, and rights to claim priority from, such rights and all similar or equivalent rights or forms of protection which subsist or will subsist, now or in the future, in any part of the world;
'Main Agreement'	a business sale agreement made on the date of this assignment between (1) the Assignor (2) the Assignee and (3) the Administrators under which the Assignee agreed to buy certain of the assets and the business of the Assignor on the terms set out in the Main Agreement;
['Materials'	the materials described in Schedule 4;]
'Patents'	the patents and the applications short particulars of which are set out in Schedule 1;
'Registered Designs'	the registered designs and the applications short particulars of which are set out in Schedule 2;
'Trade Marks'	the registered trade marks and the applications and the unregistered trade marks short particulars of which are set out in Schedule 3;
'VAT'	value added tax imposed in any member state of the European Union pursuant to Council Directive (EC) 2006/112 on the common system of value added tax and national legislation implementing that Directive or any predecessor to it, or supplemental to that Directive, or any similar tax which may be substituted for or levied in addition to it or any value added, sales, turnover or similar tax imposed in any country that is not a member of the European Union.

1.2   Clause and schedule headings shall not affect the interpretation of this assignment.

1.3   The schedules form part of this assignment and shall have effect as if set out in full in the body of this assignment. Any reference to this assignment includes the Schedules.

1.4   References to clauses and schedules are to the clauses and schedules of this assignment.

1.5   Unless the context otherwise requires, words in the singular include the plural and in the plural include the singular.

1.6   Unless the context otherwise requires, a reference to one gender shall include a reference to the other genders.

1.7   A reference to a statute or statutory provision is a reference to it as amended, extended or re-enacted from time to time provided that, as between the parties, no such amendment, extension or re-enactment shall apply for the purposes of this assignment to the extent that it would impose any new or extended obligation, liability or restriction on, or otherwise adversely affect the rights of, any party. This clause does not, however, apply in relation to taxation.

1.8   A reference to a statute or statutory provision shall include any subordinate legislation made from time to time under that statute or statutory provision.

1.9   **Writing** or **written** includes faxes but not e-mail.

1.10 Any words following the terms **including, include, in particular** or any similar expression shall be construed as illustrative and shall not limit the sense of the words, description, definition, phrase or term preceding those terms.

1.11 A **person** includes a natural person, corporate or unincorporated body (whether or not having separate legal personality) and that person's legal and personal representatives, successors and permitted assigns.

2   Assignment

For the consideration set out in the Main Agreement the Assignor hereby assigns to the Assignee absolutely all its right, title and interest in and to the Assigned Rights, including:

(a)   the absolute entitlement to any registrations granted pursuant to any of the applications comprised in the Patents, Registered Designs and Trade Marks;

(b)   all goodwill attaching to the Trade Marks and in respect of the business relating to the goods or services in respect of which the Trade Marks are registered or used; and

(c)   the right to bring, make, oppose, defend, appeal proceedings, claims or actions and obtain relief (and to retain any damages recovered) in respect of any infringement, or any other cause of action arising from ownership, of any of the Assigned Rights whether occurring before, on, or after the date of this assignment.

3. VAT

3.1 All payments made by the Assignee under this assignment are exclusive of VAT. If any such payment constitutes the whole or any part of the consideration for a taxable or deemed taxable supply by the Assignor, the Assignee shall increase that payment by an amount equal to the VAT which is chargeable in respect of the taxable or deemed taxable supply provided that the Assignor shall have delivered a valid VAT invoice in respect of such VAT to the Assignee.

3.2 If the VAT invoice is delivered after the relevant payment has been made, the Assignee shall pay the VAT due within five Business Days of the Assignor delivering a valid VAT invoice.

3.3 If the Assignee fails to comply with its obligation under this clause 3 it shall additionally pay all interest and penalties which thereby arise to the Assignor.

4. Further assurance

The Assignor and the Administrators shall use all reasonable endeavours to procure that any necessary third party shall, at the Assignee's cost, execute such documents and perform such acts as may reasonably be required for the purpose of giving full effect to this assignment.

5. Waiver

No failure or delay by a party to exercise any right or remedy provided under this assignment or by law shall constitute a waiver of that or any other right or remedy, nor shall it preclude or restrict the further exercise of that or any other right or remedy. No single or partial exercise of such right or remedy shall preclude or restrict the further exercise of that or any other right or remedy.

6. Entire agreement

6.1 The Main Agreement and this assignment constitute the whole agreement between the parties and supersede all previous agreements between the parties relating to the subject matter of this assignment.

6.2 Should there be any variance between the terms of the Main Agreement and this assignment in relation to the subject matter of this assignment, this assignment shall prevail.

6.3 Each party acknowledges that, in entering into this assignment, it has not relied on, and shall have no right or remedy in respect of, any statement, representation, assurance or warranty (whether made negligently or innocently) other than as expressly set out in this assignment.

6.4 Nothing in this clause shall limit or exclude any liability for fraud.

7. Variation

No variation of this assignment shall be effective unless it is in writing and signed by the parties (or their authorised representatives).

8. Severance

8.1 If any court or competent authority finds that any provision of this assignment (or part of any provision) is invalid, illegal or unenforceable, that provision or part-provision shall, to the extent required, be deemed to be deleted, and the validity and enforceability of the other provisions of this assignment shall not be affected.

8.2 If any invalid, unenforceable or illegal provision of this assignment would be valid, enforceable and legal if some part of it were deleted, the provision shall apply with the minimum modification necessary to make it legal, valid and enforceable.

9. Counterparts

This assignment may be executed in any number of counterparts, each of which when executed and delivered shall constitute an original of this assignment, but all the counterparts shall together constitute the same agreement. No counterpart shall be effective until each party has executed at least one counterpart.

10. Third party rights

Save for those third parties referred to in clause 11.1 below, no person other than a party to this assignment shall have any rights to enforce any term of this assignment.

11. Administrators

11.1 The Administrators act as agents for the Assignor and neither they, their firm or agents will incur any personal liability under or by virtue of this deed, nor in relation to any related documents, matters or claims whatsoever.

11.2 The Administrators have entered into this Assignment solely for the purpose of obtaining the benefit of the provisions of the contract that are in the Administrators' favour.

12. Notices

12.1 Any notice or other communication required to be given under this assignment shall be in writing and shall be delivered personally, or sent by pre-paid first-class post or recorded delivery or by commercial courier, to each party required to receive the notice or communication as set out below:

   (a) Assignor and the Administrators: [NAME OF CONTACT] [ADDRESS];

   (b) Assignee: [NAME OF CONTACT] [ADDRESS];

or as otherwise specified by the relevant party by notice in writing to each other party.

12.2 Any notice or other communication shall be deemed to have been duly received:

    (a)   if delivered personally, when left at the address and for the contact referred to in this clause;

    (b)   if sent by pre-paid first-class post or recorded delivery, at 9.00 am on the second Business Day after posting; or

    (c)   if delivered by commercial courier, on the date and at the time that the courier's delivery receipt is signed.

12.3 A notice or other communication required to be given under this assignment shall not be validly given if sent by e-mail.

12.4 The provisions of this clause shall not apply to the service of any proceedings or other documents in any legal action.

13. Governing law and jurisdiction

13.1 This assignment and any dispute or claim arising out of or in connection with it or its subject matter or formation (including non-contractual disputes or claims) shall be governed by and construed in accordance with the law of England and Wales.

13.2 The parties irrevocably agree that the courts of England and Wales shall have exclusive jurisdiction to settle any dispute or claim that arises out of or in connection with this assignment or its subject matter or formation (including non-contractual disputes or claims).

This assignment has been entered into on the date stated at the beginning of it.

SCHEDULE 1

PATENTS

Country or territory	Application or publication number	Date of filing or registration	Description

SCHEDULE 2

REGISTERED DESIGNS

Country or territory	Application number	Publication number	Date filed	Date granted	Description

SCHEDULE 3

TRADE MARKS

PART 1

Registered trade marks and applications

Country or territory	Mark	Application or registration number	Date of filing or registration	Class(es)	Specification of goods or services

PART 2

Unregistered trade marks

Country or territory	Mark	Date of first use	Goods or services for which mark has been used

[SCHEDULE 4

MATERIALS

]

[SCHEDULE 5

UNREGISTERED ASSIGNED RIGHTS

]

Signed as a deed by .... **Limited**)   ....
(in administration))   Administrator
acting by its administrator without)
personal liability pursuant to powers)
conferred under the Insolvency Act 1986)
in the presence of:)

Signature of witness:

Name:

Address:

Occupation:

Signed as a deed by .... **Limited**)   ....
acting by a director)   Director
in the presence of:)

Signature of witness:

Name:

Address:

Occupation:

Signed as a deed by ....)   ....
for and on behalf of the Administrators)   Administrator
in the presence of:)

Signature of witness:

Name:

Address:

Occupation:

C. Novation of contract[2]

DATED .... 20[ ]

(1) XXXXXXXX LIMITED (in administration)
(2) YYYYYYYY LIMITED
(3) [A1 and A2 – ADMINISTRATORS]

NOVATION OF CONTRACT

DRAFT 1 .... 20[ ]

DATE OF NOVATION: .... 20[ ]

PARTIES:

(1) [ ] **Limited** (in administration) registered in England and Wales
     with company number: [ ] whose registered office is at [ ] (**'First
     Contractor'**) acting by the Administrators; and

(2) [ ] **Limited** registered in England and Wales with company number:
     [ ] whose registered office is at [ ] (**'Employer'**);

(3) [ ] **Limited** registered in England and Wales with company number:
     [ ] whose registered office is at [ ] (**'Second Contractor'**); and

(4) [ ] and [ ] as joint administrators of the First Contractor both of [ ]
     (**'Administrators'**).

BACKGROUND

(A) By an agreement in writing dated [DATE] (**Contract**) made between
     the First Contractor and the Employer the First Contractor agreed to
     [DESCRIBE THE WORKS] (**Works**).

(B) On [DATE] the Administrators were appointed as joint administrators of
     the First Contractor.

(C) The works to be carried out under the Contract have not been completed.

---

[2] Adapted from PLC's Novation of Contract precedent. For further information please visit
     http://uk.practicallaw.com/.

(D)   The parties have agreed to novate the Contract from the First Contractor and the Employer to the Second Contractor and the Employer on the terms set out below.

IT IS NOW AGREED as follows:

1.   Interpretation

1.1   The definitions and rules of interpretation in this clause and in the background of this deed apply in this deed.

['**Employees**'	those employees whose contracts of employment transfer from the First Contractor to the Second Contractor by virtue of TUPE with effect from the Transfer Date, being those employees who are listed at Schedule 2;]
'**Materials**'	any unfixed materials that are at the site of the Works at the date of this deed;
['**Transfer Date**'	the date of this deed;]
['**TUPE**'	Transfer of Undertakings (Protection of Employment) Regulations 2006.]

1.2   The headings are included for convenience only and shall not affect the interpretation or construction of this deed.

1.3   References to **Clauses** [or the **Schedule**] are to clauses of [or the schedule to] this deed.

1.4   References to any of the **masculine, feminine and neuter genders** shall include the other genders and references to the singular number shall include the plural and vice versa.

1.5   References to a **document** are to that document as varied, supplemented or replaced from time to time.

1.6   References to the First Contractor and the Administrators are a reference to any successor in title to any of them, including (but not limited to) any liquidator subsequently appointed to the First Contractor.

1.7   References to **writing** shall include any modes of reproducing words in a legible and non-transitory form but not email.

1.8   A reference to a statute or statutory provision is a reference to it as it is in force from time to time, taking account of any amendment, extension, or re-enactment and includes any statute, statutory provision or subordinate legislation which it amends or re-enacts.

1.9   A reference to a statute or statutory provision shall include any subordinate legislation made from time to time under that statute or statutory provision.

2.   Novation of contract

2.1   This deed novates the Contract from the First Contractor and the Employer to the Second Contractor and the Employer.

2.2.   The First Contractor shall no longer owe any duty or obligation to the Employer in respect of the Contract.

2.3   The Employer shall no longer owe any duty or obligation to the First Contractor in respect of the Contract.

2.4   The Second Contractor binds itself to the Employer under the Contract as if it were, and always had been, named in the Contract in place of the First Contractor. The Second Contractor undertakes with the Employer to carry out its duties and obligations under the Contract (insofar as they remain to be carried out).

2.5   The Employer binds itself to the Second Contractor under the Contract as if the Second Contractor were, and always had been, named in the Contract in place of the First Contractor.

2.6   All rights of action and remedies vested in the First Contractor against the Employer in respect of the Contract shall vest in the Second Contractor from the date of this deed.

2.7   All rights of action and remedies against the First Contractor in respect of the Contract that are vested in the Employer shall lie against the Second Contractor from the date of this deed.

2.8   The Second Contractor shall indemnify (on a full indemnity basis) the First Contractor and the Administrators against all losses, costs, expenses, charges, damages and liabilities whatsoever which the First Contractor and the Administrators may sustain as a result of having novated the Contract from the Employer and the First Contractor to the Employer and the Second Contractor by this deed.

[3.   Amendment of Contract

The Employer and the Second Contractor agree that the terms of the Contract are varied as set out in Schedule 1.]

4.   Affirmation of Contract

Subject to the terms of this deed, the Contract shall remain in full force and effect even though the First Contractor is insolvent, in administration and the Administrators have been appointed. The Employer, the First Contractor and the Second Contractor agree that the appointment of the Administrators has not terminated, and shall not be treated as grounds for terminating, the First Contractor's employment under the Contract.

5.   Assistance to Second Contractor

5.1   The Employer and, at the Second Contractor's expense, the First Contractor shall each provide the Second Contractor with all the help and information they reasonably can to enable the value of work-in-progress under the Contract to be agreed or ascertained as soon as reasonably practicable.

5.2   The First Contractor shall immediately deliver any documents it possesses that relate exclusively to the Contract to the Second Contractor.

6.   Unfixed goods

6.1   The First Contractor (without giving any warranty as to title or condition) grants such right title and interest (if any) as the First Contractor has and can transfer in the Materials to the Second Contractor.

6.2   The Second Contractor acknowledges that whilst it may take possession of the Materials on the date of this deed, they may be subject to claims by third parties with title to, or an interest in, the same. The Second Contractor acknowledges that it bears the sole risk of the Materials being subject to any such encumbrance and agrees to indemnify the First Contractor and the Administrators (on a full indemnity basis) against all actions, proceedings, claims, losses, expenses, costs, charges and liabilities whatsoever that the First Contractor or the Administrators may become subject to as a result of having given possession of the Materials to the Second Contractor.

[7.   Employees

7.1   The First Contractor and the Second Contractor believe that, pursuant to TUPE, the Second Contractor will become the employer of the Employees with effect from the Effective Time. The Second Contractor agrees that from the Effective Time it will:

7.1.1 comply with its obligations arising out of or in connection with the employment of any of the Employees; and

7.1.2 perform and observe its obligations under Regulation 13 of TUPE.

7.2   The Second Contractor acknowledges that the First Contractor has disclosed to it under Regulation 11 of TUPE such information about the Employees as is reasonable and practicable in the circumstances.

7.3   The Second Contractor agrees to indemnify the First Contractor and the Administrators (on a full indemnity basis) against all actions, proceedings, claims, demands, losses, costs, charges, damages, expenses or liabilities whatsoever that the First Contractor or the Administrators may sustain in relation to:

7.3.1 any claim brought or alleged by the Second Contractor under Regulation 12 of TUPE;

7.3.2 any claim arising from the failure of the Second Contractor to comply with its obligations under clause 7.1, or from the employment of the Employees or the termination of their employment after the Transfer Date.]

8.   Payment under the Contract

The Second Contractor and the Employer acknowledge that the sum of £[AMOUNT] has been paid to the First Contractor under the Contract and that the Second Contractor has no claim whatsoever to the same.

9. Administrators

9.1 The Administrators act as agents for the First Contractor and neither they, their firm or agents will incur any personal liability under or by virtue of this deed, nor in relation to any related documents, matters or claims whatsoever.

9.2 The Administrators have entered into this deed solely for the purpose of obtaining the benefit of the provisions of the contract that are in the Administrators' favour.

10. Third party rights

Save for those third parties referred to in clause 9.1 above, a person who is not a party to this deed shall not have any rights under or in connection with it.

11. Governing law and jurisdiction

11.1 This deed and any dispute or claim arising out of or in connection with it or its subject matter or formation (including non-contractual disputes or claims) shall be governed by and construed in accordance with the law of England and Wales.

11.2 The parties irrevocably agree that the courts of England and Wales shall have exclusive jurisdiction to settle any dispute or claim that arises out of or in connection with this deed or its subject matter or formation (including non-contractual disputes or claims).

EXECUTION:

This document has been executed as a deed and is delivered and takes effect on the date stated at the beginning of it.

SCHEDULE 1

VARIATIONS TO THE CONTRACT

SCHEDULE 2

EMPLOYEES

Signed as deed by .... **Limited**)   ....
(in administration))   Administrator
acting by its administrator without)
personal liability pursuant to powers)
conferred under the Insolvency Act 1986)
in the presence of:)

Signature of witness:

Name:

Address:

Occupation:

Signed as a deed by .... **Limited**)   ....
acting by a director)   Director
in the presence of:)

Signature of witness:

Name:

Address:

Occupation:

Signed as a deed by .... **Limited**)   ....
acting by a director)   Director
in the presence of:)

Signature of witness:

Name:

Address:

Occupation:

Signed as a deed by ....)   ....
for and on behalf of the Administrators)   Administrator
in the presence of:)

Signature of witness:

Name:

Address:

Occupation:

D. Sample retention of title clauses

1. Simple ROT clause

1. PASSING OF PROPERTY

1.1 Title to and property in the Goods shall remain vested in the Company (notwithstanding their delivery and the passing of the risk therein to the Buyer) until the price of the Goods has been paid, discharged or satisfied in full.

1.2 Until title to and property in the Goods passes to the Buyer:

(a) the Company may at any time without prior notice to the Buyer repossess and resell such of the Goods as are capable of being repossessed if any of the following events occurs:

(i) a receiver, liquidator, administrator or administrative receiver is appointed to or over the Buyer or any of its assets, or Notice of intention to appoint an administrator is given or filed at court or an administration application is made in respect of the Buyer, or

(ii) the Buyer is the subject of bankruptcy or winding up or other insolvency proceedings (including (but not limited to) presentation of a winding-up petition), ceases to trade or threatens to cease to trade, passes a resolution for winding up (except for the purpose of a solvent amalgamation or reconstruction), or

(iii) the Buyer makes any composition or arrangement with its creditors, or

(iv) the Buyer is unable to pay its debts as and when they fall due within the meaning of the Insolvency Act 1986, or

(v) if any sum due from the Buyer to the Company whether under the Contract or otherwise is not paid on the due date of payment.

For the purpose of exercising its rights under this sub-paragraph the Company, its employees or agents together with any vehicles and plant considered by the Company to be necessary shall be entitled at any time without prior notice to the Buyer to safe and unrestricted access to the Buyer's premises and/or any other locations where any of the Goods are situated;

(b) the Buyer shall store such of the Goods as are capable of being stored in a proper manner and conditions which adequately protect and preserve them without charge to the Company and ensure that they are clearly identified as belonging to the Company. Without prejudice to sub-paragraph 1.2(a) above the Company shall be entitled to examine the Goods in storage at any time during normal business hours and upon giving the Buyer reasonable notice of its intention to do so and to enter upon any premises owned or occupied by or access to which is controlled by the Buyer for that purpose;

(c)   the Buyer shall not resell the Goods save in the ordinary course of its business;

(d)   upon the occurrence of any of the events referred to in sub paragraph 1.2(a) above the Buyer shall no longer be entitled to resell the Goods and any consent or licence or authority to resell the Goods that exists or arises under sub paragraph 1.2(c) above or otherwise shall automatically and immediately terminate, and/or be withdrawn and/or be rescinded without notice to the Buyer.

1.3   The rights and remedies conferred on the Company by this Condition 1 are in addition to and shall not in any way prejudice limit or restrict any other rights or remedies of the Company under the Contract.

2.   All monies ROT clause

Example of a newly negotiated retention of title provision where the parties have other terms and conditions/a contract in place

....

....

[address]

....

[Date]

Dear [   ]

ABC Limited ('**ABC**'/'**We**'/'**Us**'/'**Our**') currently buys certain .... goods ('**Goods**') from **DEF Limited** registered in England and Wales under company number ...., registered office address ....   ('**You**'/'**Your**') under a previously agreed trading agreement ('**Agreement**').

We have agreed with You that a retention of title clause shall apply to Goods ordered from You with effect from the date of this letter and this is set out below. The Agreement shall be varied as follows:

2.1   Risk in the Goods will pass to ABC upon delivery, namely as soon as the Goods have been unloaded on Our premises (including third party premises operated by a distribution service provider or other contractor on Our behalf) and are no longer under the control of Your delivery driver.

2.2 You will retain all right, title and interest in the Goods until the earlier of the date:

2.2.1 We pay You in full:

2.2.1.1 for the Goods in accordance with the Agreement, and

2.2.1.2 any and all other sums due to You under the Agreement or otherwise; or

2.2.2 We sell the Goods to Our customers in the ordinary course of business whereupon title shall pass to Us.

2.3 You hereby agree that We may sell the Goods in the ordinary course of business (but not otherwise) notwithstanding that We may not have paid You in full for such Goods and that We shall be entitled to pass full right, title and interest in the Goods to Our customer(s) at the point of sale as envisaged by clause 2.2.2 above.

2.4 Until such time as title in the Goods passes to Us in accordance with clause 2.2 above, We agree to:

2.4.1 keep the Goods stored securely in Our facilities;

2.4.2 take all reasonable steps to protect the Goods from loss, damage, theft or destruction;

2.4.3 not remove any branding or labelling applied by You which would enable the Goods to be clearly identified as having been supplied by You.

2.5 Where You have grounds to terminate the Agreement on the basis that a receiver, liquidator, administrator or administrative receiver has been appointed over Our assets, or if a Notice of Intention to appoint an Administrator is given or filed at court in relation to Us or an administration application is made in respect of Us or We are the subject of bankruptcy proceedings, or We cease to trade or threaten to cease to trade, or We pass a resolution for winding up (except for the purpose of a solvent amalgamation or reconstruction) or a winding-up petition is presented against us or We are subject to the grant of a winding-up order, or if We make any composition or arrangement with Our creditors, or are unable to pay Our debts as and when they fall due within the meaning of the Insolvency Act 1986, both during and after termination of the Agreement, We permit You and/or Your authorised employees, agents or contractors to enter Our premises where the Goods are stored, and immediately upon written notice, to recover any Goods to which title has been retained by You pursuant to clause 2.2 above.

2.6 Where You exercise Your rights under clause 2.5 above You agree to bring all supporting documentation with You to demonstrate to Our authorised representative that You have a valid right to recover the Goods and You will not be allowed to remove any of the Goods from Our premises until an authorised representative of ABC has confirmed in writing that the value of the Goods to be collected does not exceed the value of the outstanding payment due to You under the Agreement.

2.7 Notwithstanding that We may sell the Goods under clause 2.3 above, this does not waive any right or remedy You may have against Us to recover sums due to You under the Agreement.

2.8 Upon the occurrence of any of the events referred to in sub clause 2.5 above We shall no longer be entitled to resell the Goods and any consent or licence or authority to resell the Goods that exists or arises under clause 2.3 above or otherwise shall immediately and automatically terminate, and/or be withdrawn and/or be rescinded by You without any notice to Us whatsoever whether or not You are aware of the relevant circumstances.

2.9 The passing of title and risk under this clause 2 will not negate or reduce any right of rejection or any right to return the Goods available to Us under the Agreement or in law.

2.10 This letter of amendment shall be subject to English law and the exclusive jurisdiction of the English courts.

2.11 All other terms and conditions of the Agreement remain in full force and effect and shall not be varied by this letter of amendment. This letter of amendment prevails over the Agreement if there is any inconsistency between the two.

2.12 Clause references in this letter of amendment refer to the clauses in this letter of amendment rather than those in the Agreement.

2.13 Any notices to be served upon ABC under this letter of amendment or the Agreement must be served to:

Name: Company Secretary and General Counsel

Address: ABC ....

Fax No: ....

2.14 Any such notice given under clause 2.13 may be delivered personally, by recorded signed for delivery, or facsimile transmission and will be deemed to have been received:

2.14.1 by hand delivery – at the time of delivery;

2.14.2 by recorded signed for delivery – two Business Days after the date of mailing;

2.14.3 by facsimile transmission – immediately upon transmission provided a confirmatory copy is sent by recorded signed for delivery or by hand within three Business Days.

A '**Business Day**' means any day other than Saturdays, Sundays and public holidays in the United Kingdom.

2.15 Any variations to this letter of amendment or to the Agreement must be in writing and signed by an authorised representative of the parties which in the case of ABC means a director of the company.

2.16 If any court or competent authority finds that any provision of this letter of amendment (or part of any provision) is invalid, illegal or unenforceable, that provision or part-provision shall, to the extent required, be deemed to be deleted, and the validity and enforceability of the other provisions of this letter shall not be affected. If any invalid, unenforceable or illegal provision of this letter of amendment would be valid, enforceable and legal if some part of it were deleted. the provision shall apply with the minimum modification necessary to make it legal, valid and enforceable.

Please would You indicate Your acceptance of these terms and conditions by signing and returning the enclosed copy of this letter of amendment.

Yours sincerely

....

[name]

Group Buying Director

For and on behalf of ABC Limited

We hereby agree to the above terms and conditions:-

.... (signed)

.... (print name and title)

.... (date)

For and on behalf of DEF Limited

E. Debenture[3]

DATED .... 20[   ]

(1) XXXXXXXX LIMITED
(2) YYYYYYYY LIMITED (in administration)
(3) [A1 and A2 – SELLER's ADMINISTRATORS]

DEBENTURE

DRAFT 1 .... 20[   ]

DATE OF DEBENTURE: .... 20[   ]

PARTIES

(1) [   ] **Limited** registered in England and Wales with company number: [   ] whose registered office is at [   ] (**'Buyer'**);

(2) [   ] **Limited** (in administration) registered in England and Wales with company number: [   ] whose registered office is at [   ] (**'Seller'**) acting by the Seller's Administrators; and

(3) [   ] and [   ] as joint administrators of the Seller both of [   ] (**'Seller's Administrators'**).

BACKGROUND

(A) On the date of this debenture the Seller and the Buyer and the Seller's Administrators entered into the Agreement.

(B) The Seller has agreed to enter into this debenture for the purpose of providing security for the payment of all sums that are or may fall due for payment by the Buyer to the Seller and/or the Seller's Administrators under the terms of the Agreement.

1. Definitions and interpretation

1.1 Definitions

In this debenture the following words and expressions shall have the following meanings:

---

[3] Adapted from PLC's Debenture precedent. For further information please visit http://uk.practicallaw.com/.

'Administrator'	an administrator appointed to manage the affairs, business and property of the Buyer pursuant to clause 13.7;
'Agreement'	a business sale agreement made on the date of this debenture between (1) the Seller (2) the Buyer and (3) the Seller's Administrators under which the Buyer agreed to buy certain of the assets and the business of the Seller on the terms set out in the Agreement;
'Bank'	[ ];
'Book Debts'	all present and future book debts and other debts and monetary claims due or owing to the Buyer, and the benefit of all security, guarantees and other rights of any nature enjoyed or held by the Buyer in relation to any of them;
'Business Day'	a day (other than a Saturday or Sunday) on which banks are open for general business in London;
'Charged Property'	all the assets, property and undertaking for the time being subject to the Security Interests created by this debenture (and references to the Charged Property include references to any part of it);
'Costs'	all costs, charges, expenses, taxes and liabilities of any kind including, without limitation, costs and damages in connection with litigation, professional fees, disbursements and any value added tax charged on Costs;
'Designated Account'	any account of the Buyer nominated by the Seller or by the Seller's Administrators as a designated account for the purposes of this debenture;
'Environment'	the natural and man-made environment including all or any of the air, water and land including the air within buildings and other natural or man-made structures above or below ground, ground and surface water and surface and sub-surface soil and any living organisms supported by the said media;
'Environmental Law'	all applicable laws, statutes, treaties, regulations, directives or similar measures, judgments or decisions of any court or tribunal, codes of practice or guidance notes relating to the pollution or protection of the Environment that affects the Charged Property;
'Equipment'	all present and future equipment, plant, machinery, tools, vehicles, furniture, fittings, installations and apparatus and other tangible moveable property for the time being owned by the Buyer, including any part of it and all spare parts, replacements, modifications and additions;
'Financial Collateral'	shall have the meaning given to that expression in the Financial Collateral Regulations;
'Financial Collateral Regulations'	the Financial Collateral Arrangements (No 2) Regulations 2003 (SI 2003/3226);

338

'Insurance Policy'	each contract and policy of insurance effected or maintained by the Buyer from time to time in respect of its assets or business (including without limitation any insurances relating to the Charged Property);
'Intellectual Property'	the Buyer's present and future patents, trade marks, service marks, trade names, designs, copyrights, inventions, topographical or similar rights, confidential information and know-how and any interest in any of such rights, whether or not registered, including all applications and rights to apply for registration and all fees, royalties and other rights derived from, or incidental to, these rights;
'Investments'	all present and future stocks, shares, loan capital, securities, bonds and investments (whether or not marketable) for the time being owned (at law or in equity) by the Buyer including:

    (a)   dividend, interest or other distribution paid or payable in relation to any of the Investments; and

    (b)   right, money, shares or property accruing, offered or issued at any time in relation to any of the Investments by way of redemption, substitution, exchange, conversion, bonus, preference or otherwise, under option rights or otherwise;

'LPA'	Law of Property Act 1925;
'Material Adverse Effect'	any event or circumstance which, in the opinion of the Seller or the Seller's Administrators:

    (a)   is likely to materially and adversely affect the Buyer's ability to perform or otherwise comply with all or any of its obligations under this debenture or the Agreement or any other agreement between the Buyer, the Seller and the Seller's Administrators;

    (b)   is likely to materially and adversely affect the business, operations, property, condition (financial or otherwise) or prospects of the Buyer; or

    (c)   is likely to result in this debenture or the Agreement or any other agreement between the Buyer, the Seller and the Seller's Administrators not being legal, valid and binding on, and enforceable in accordance with its terms against, the Buyer and, in the case of this debenture, not providing to the Seller and the Seller's Administrators security over the assets expressed to be subject to a Security Interest under this debenture;

'Properties'	all freehold and leasehold properties (whether registered or unregistered) and all commonhold properties, now or in the future (and from time to time) owned by the Buyer or in which the Buyer holds an interest (including (but not limited to) the properties which are briefly described in Schedule 1) and **Property** means any of them;
'Receiver'	a receiver and/or manager of any or all of the Charged Property appointed under clause 16.1;
'Relevant Agreement'	each agreement specified in Schedule 2;
'Secured Liabilities'	all present and future monies, obligations and liabilities owed by the Buyer to the Seller and/or to the Seller's Administrators, whether actual or contingent and whether owed jointly or severally, as principal or surety and/or in any other capacity whatsoever, under or in connection with the Agreement or this debenture (including, without limitation, those arising under clause12.3) together with all interest (including, without limitation, default interest) accruing in respect of such monies or liabilities;
'Security Financial Collateral Arrangement'	shall have the meaning given to that expression in the Financial Collateral Regulations;
'Security Interest'	any mortgage, charge (whether fixed or floating, legal or equitable), pledge, lien, assignment by way of security or other security interest securing any obligation of any person, or other agreement or arrangement having a similar effect;
'Security Period'	the period starting on the date of this debenture and ending on the date on which all the Secured Liabilities have been unconditionally and irrevocably paid and discharged in full and no further Secured Liabilities are capable of being outstanding.

1.2 Interpretation

Unless the context otherwise requires, in this debenture:

(a) any reference to any statute or statutory provision includes a reference to any subordinate legislation made under that statute or statutory provision, to any modification, re-enactment or extension of that statute or statutory provision and to any former statute or statutory provision which it consolidated or re-enacted before the date of this debenture;

(b) a reference to one gender includes a reference to the other gender;

(c) words in the singular include the plural and in the plural include the singular;

(d) a reference to a clause or Schedule is to a clause or Schedule of or to this debenture;

(e)   references to **the Seller** and **the Seller's Administrators** is a reference to any successor in title to any of them, including (but not limited to) any liquidators subsequently appointed to the Seller;

(f)   a reference to **this debenture** (or any specified provision of it) or any other document shall be construed as a reference to this debenture, that provision or that document as in force for the time being and as amended or novated from time to time;

(g)   a reference to a **person** shall be construed as including a reference to an individual, firm, corporation, unincorporated body of persons or any state or any agency of a person;

(h)   a reference to an **amendment** includes a supplement, variation, novation or re-enactment (and **amended** shall be construed accordingly);

(i)   a reference to **assets** includes present and future properties, undertakings, revenues, rights and benefits of every description;

(j)   a reference to an **authorisation** includes an authorisation, consent, licence, approval, resolution, exemption, filing, registration and notarisation;

(k)   a reference to a **regulation** includes any regulation, rule, official directive, request or guideline (whether or not having the force of law) of any governmental, inter-governmental or supranational body, agency, department or regulatory, self-regulatory or other authority or organisation; and

(l)   the headings do not form part of this debenture or any part of it and do not affect its interpretation.

1.3   Clawback

If the Seller or the Seller's Administrators consider that an amount is capable of being avoided or otherwise set aside on liquidation or administration of the Buyer or otherwise, then that amount shall not be considered to have been irrevocably paid for the purposes of this debenture.

1.4   Nature of security over real property

A reference in this debenture to a charge or mortgage of any freehold, leasehold or commonhold property includes:

(a)   all buildings and fixtures (including trade and tenant's fixtures) which are at any time situated on that property;

(b)   the proceeds of sale of any part of that property;

(c)   the benefit of any covenants for title given or entered into by any predecessor in title of the Buyer in respect of that property or any monies paid or payable in respect of those covenants; and

(d)   all rights under any licence, agreement for sale or agreement for lease in respect of that property.

1.5 Law of Property (Miscellaneous Provisions) Act 1989

For the purposes of section 2 of the Law of Property (Miscellaneous Provisions) Act 1989 the terms of the Agreement and of any side letters between any parties in relation to the Agreement are incorporated in this debenture.

1.6 Third Party Rights

Save for those third parties referred to in clause 26.1 of this debenture, a third party has no right under the Contracts (Rights of Third Parties) Act 1999 to enforce, or to enjoy the benefit of, any terms of his debenture.

1.7 Schedules

The Schedules form part of this debenture and shall have effect as if set out in full in the body of this debenture. Any reference to this debenture includes the Schedules.

1.8 Insolvency Act 1986

Paragraph 14 of Schedule B1 to the Insolvency Act 1986 applies to the floating charge created by this debenture.

2. Covenant to pay

2.1 Covenant to pay

The Buyer shall on demand made by the Seller or by the Seller's Administrators pay to the Seller and discharge the Secured Liabilities when they become due.

3. Grant of security

3.1 Charging clause

As a continuing security for the payment and discharge of the Secured Liabilities, the Buyer with full title guarantee:

(a) charges to the Seller, by way of first legal mortgage, each Property listed in Schedule 1;

(b) charges to the Seller, by way of first fixed charge:

    (i) all Properties acquired by the Buyer in the future;

    (ii) all present and future interests of the Buyer not effectively mortgaged or charged under the preceding provisions of this clause 3 in or over freehold or leasehold property;

    (iii) all present and future rights, licences, guarantees, rents, deposits, contracts, covenants and warranties relating to each Property;

    (iv) all licences, consents and authorisations, statutory or otherwise held or required in connection with the Buyer's business or the use of any Charged Property and all rights in connection with them;

(v)   all present and future goodwill and uncalled capital for the time being of the Buyer;

(vi)   all the Book Debts;

(vii)   all Equipment;

(viii) all the Intellectual Property;

(ix)   all the Investments; and

(x)   all monies from time to time standing to the credit of its accounts with any bank, financial institution or other person; and

(c)   charges to the Seller, by way of first floating charge, all the undertaking, property, assets and rights of the Buyer at any time not effectively mortgaged, charged or assigned pursuant to clause 3.1(a) and clause 3.1(b).

3.2   Automatic conversion of floating charge

The floating charge created by clause 3.1(c) shall automatically and immediately (without notice) be converted into a fixed charge over the relevant Charged Property if:

(a)   the Buyer:

(i)   creates, or attempts to create, over all or any part of the Charged Property a Security Interest without the prior written consent of the Seller; or

(ii)   disposes or attempts to dispose of all or any part of the Charged Property (other than property subject only to the floating charge while it remains uncrystallised which property may be disposed of in the ordinary course of business); or

(b)   a receiver is appointed over all or any of the Charged Property that is subject to the floating charge; or

(c)   any person levies or attempts to levy any distress, attachment, execution or other process against all or any part of the Charged Property; or

(d)   the Seller or the Seller's Administrators receive notice of the appointment of, or a proposal or an intention to appoint, an administrator of the Buyer.

3.3   Conversion of floating charge by notice

The Seller may in its sole discretion at any time by written notice to the Buyer convert the floating charge created under this debenture into a fixed charge as regards any part of the Charged Property specified by the Seller in that notice.

3.4 Assets acquired after any floating charge crystallisation

Any asset acquired by the Buyer after any crystallisation of the floating charge created under this debenture which but for such crystallisation would be subject to a floating charge shall (unless the Seller confirms in writing to the contrary) be charged to the Seller by way of first fixed charge.

3.5 Assignment

As a continuing security for the payment and discharge of the Secured Liabilities, the Buyer with full title guarantee assigns to the Seller absolutely, subject to a proviso for reassignment on irrevocable discharge in full of the Secured Liabilities:

(a) all its rights in each Insurance Policy, including all claims, the proceeds of all claims and all returns of premium in connection with each Insurance Policy; and

(b) the benefit of each Relevant Agreement and the benefit of any guarantee or security for the performance of a Relevant Agreement.

4. Liability of Buyer

4.1 Liability not discharged

The liability of the Buyer under this debenture in respect of any of the Secured Liabilities shall not be discharged, prejudiced or affected by:

(a) any security, guarantee, indemnity, remedy or other right held by or available to the Seller being or becoming wholly or partially illegal, void or unenforceable on any ground; or

(b) the Seller concurring in, accepting or varying any compromise, arrangement or settlement or omitting to claim or enforce payment from any other person; or

(c) any other act or omission which but for this provision might have discharged or otherwise prejudiced or affected the liability of the Buyer.

4.2 Immediate recourse

The Buyer waives any right it may have of requiring the Seller to enforce any security or other right or claim any payment from or otherwise proceed against any other person before enforcing this debenture against the Buyer.

5. Representations and warranties

5.1 Representations and warranties

The Buyer represents and warrants to the Seller in the terms set out in this clause 5.

5.2 Ownership of Charged Property

The Buyer is the legal and beneficial owner of the Charged Property.

5.3 No Security Interests

The Charged Property is free from any Security Interest other than the Security Interests created by this debenture.

5.4 Adverse claims

The Buyer has not received or acknowledged notice of any adverse claim by any person in respect of the Charged Property or any interest in it.

5.5 Adverse covenants

There are no covenants, agreements, reservations, conditions, interests, rights or other matters whatever, which materially adversely affect the Charged Property.

5.6 No breach of laws

There is no breach of any law or regulation, which materially and adversely affects the Charged Property.

5.7 No interference in enjoyment

No facility necessary for the enjoyment and use of the Charged Property is subject to terms entitling any person to terminate or curtail its use.

5.8 No overriding interests

Nothing has arisen or has been created or is subsisting, which would be an overriding interest in any Property.

5.9 Avoidance of security

No Security Interest expressed to be created by this debenture is liable to be avoided or otherwise set aside on the liquidation or administration of the Buyer or otherwise.

5.10 No prohibition or breaches

There is no prohibition on assignment in any Insurance Policy or Relevant Agreement and the entry into this debenture by the Buyer does not, and will not, constitute a breach of any Insurance Policy, Relevant Agreement or any other agreement or instrument binding on the Buyer or its assets.

5.11 Environmental compliance

The Buyer has at all times complied in all material respects with all applicable Environmental Law.

5.12 Enforceable security

This debenture constitutes and will constitute the legal, valid, binding and enforceable obligations of the Buyer, and is and will continue to be effective security over all and every part of the Charged Property in accordance with its terms.

5.13 Time for making representations and warranties

The representations and warranties set out in clauses 5.2 to 5.12 are made on the date of this debenture and shall be deemed to be made on each day of the Security Period with reference to the facts and circumstances then existing.

6. General covenants

6.1 Negative pledge and restrictions on disposal

The Buyer shall not at any time, except with the prior written consent of the Seller and the Seller's Administrators:

(a) create, purport to create or permit to exist any Security Interest on, or in relation to, any of the Charged Property other than the Security Interest created by this debenture;

(b) sell, assign, transfer, part with possession of, or otherwise dispose of in any manner (or purport to do so), all or any part of, or any interest in, the Charged Property (except in the ordinary course of business, such of the Charged Property that is only subject to an uncrystallised floating charge); or

(c) create or grant (or purport to create of grant) any interest in the Charged Property in favour of a third party.

6.2 Preservation of Charged Property

The Buyer shall not do, or permit to be done, any act or thing that would or might depreciate jeopardise or otherwise prejudice the security held by the Seller and the Seller's Administrators, or materially diminish the value of any of the Charged Property or the effectiveness of the security created by this debenture.

6.3 Compliance with laws and regulations

(a) The Buyer shall not, without the prior written consent of the Seller and the Seller's Administrators, use or permit the Charged Property to be used in any way contrary to law.

(b) The Buyer shall:

(i) comply with the requirements of any law and regulation relating to or affecting the Charged Property or the use of it or any part of it;

(ii) obtain, and promptly renew from time to time, and comply with the terms of all authorisations that are required in connection with the Charged Property or its use or that are necessary to preserve, maintain or renew any of the Charged Property; and

(iii) promptly effect any maintenance, modifications, alterations or repairs that are required by any law or regulation to be effected on or in connection with the Charged Property.

6.4 Enforcement of Rights

The Buyer shall use its best endeavours to:

(a) procure the prompt observance and performance of the covenants and other obligations imposed on the Buyer's counterparties (including each counterparty in respect of a Relevant Agreement and each insurer in respect of an Insurance Policy); and

(b) enforce any rights and institute, continue or defend any proceedings relating to any of the Charged Property with the Seller and/or the Seller's Administrators may require from time to time.

6.5 Notice of misrepresentation and breaches

The Buyer shall, promptly on becoming aware of any of the same, give the Seller and the Seller's Administrators notice in writing of:

(a) any representation or warranty set out in this debenture that is incorrect or misleading in any material respect when made or when deemed to be repeated; and

(b) any breach of covenant set out in this debenture.

6.6 Title documents

The Buyer shall on the execution of this debenture (or, if later, the date of acquisition of the relevant Charged Property) deposit with the Seller and the Seller shall during the continuance of this debenture be entitled to hold:

(a) all deeds and documents of title relating to the Charged Property which are in the possession or control of the Buyer (and, if not within the possession and/or control of the Buyer, the Buyer undertakes to obtain possession of all such deeds and documents of title);

(b) all Insurance Policies and any other insurance policies relating to the Charged Property that the Buyer is entitled to possess;

(c) all deeds and documents of title (if any) relating to the Book Debts as the Seller and/or the Seller's Administrators may specify from time to time; and

(d) copies of all the Relevant Agreements, certified to be true copies by either a director of the Buyer or by the Buyer's solicitors.

6.7 Insurance

(a) The Buyer shall insure and keep insured the Charged Property against:

(i) loss or damage by fire or terrorist acts;

(ii) other risk, perils and contingencies that would be insured against by reasonably prudent persons carrying on the same or a similar business as that carried on by the Buyer; and

(iii) all other risks, perils and contingencies as the Seller and/or the Seller's Administrators may reasonably require.

All such insurance must be with a reputable and responsible insurer or underwriters and on such terms as are reasonably acceptable to the Seller and the Seller's Administrators, and must not be for less than the replacement value of the Charged Property.

(b)   The Buyer shall procure that the interest of the Seller is noted on all such policies of insurance or that the Seller is named as co-insured with the Buyer in such manner as the Seller or the Seller's Administrators may in their absolute discretion require.

(c)   The Buyer shall not cancel any such insurance without giving at least 30 days prior written notice to the Seller and to the Seller's Administrators.

6.8   **Insurance Premiums**

The Buyer shall:

(a)   duly and punctually pay all premiums and any other monies necessary and do all other things necessary for maintaining its insurance in full force and effect; and

(b)   if the Seller or the Seller's Administrators so require, produce to or deposit with the Seller's Administrators the receipts for all premiums and other payments necessary for effecting and keeping up all insurance maintained by it or on its behalf.

6.9   **No invalidation of insurance**

The Buyer shall not do or omit to do, or permit to be done or omitted, any act or thing that may invalidate or otherwise prejudice any insurance policy maintained by it or on its behalf in relation to the Charged Property.

6.10   **Proceeds of insurance policies**

All monies received or receivable by the Buyer by virtue of any insurance of the whole or any part of the Charged Property at any time, whether or not this debenture has become enforceable shall:

(a)   immediately be paid to the Seller;

(b)   if they are not paid directly to the Seller by the insurers, be held by the Buyer as trustee of the same for the benefit of the Seller (and the Buyer shall account for them forthwith upon receipt to the Seller); and

(c)   at the option of the Seller and the Seller's Administrators be applied in making good or in recouping expenditure incurred in making good the loss or damage for which the monies were received or in or towards, discharge of the Secured Liabilities.

6.11   **Notices to be given**

The Buyer shall immediately on the execution of this debenture (or on the date of acquisition of any relevant asset which becomes Charged Property):

(a)   give notice to each insurer that it has assigned its rights and interest in and under each Insurance Policy to the Seller and procure that the insurer promptly provides to the Seller and the Seller's Administrators an acknowledgement of the notice of the Seller's interest;

(b)   give notice to each counterparty to a Relevant Agreement that it has assigned its rights and interest in and under that Relevant Agreement and procure that each addressee of any such notice promptly provides to the Seller and the Seller's Administrators an acknowledgement of the Seller's interest; and

(c)   give notice to any bank, financial institution or other person with whom it has an account that it has charged to the Seller its rights and interests under that account and procure that the bank, financial institution or other person promptly provides to the Seller and the Seller's Administrators an acknowledgement of the notice of the Seller's interest.

6.12 **Information**

The Buyer shall:

(a)   promptly provide to the Seller and/or the Seller's Administrators whatever information, documents or papers relating to the Charged Property as they may from time to time request, including (but not limited to) details concerning the location, condition, use and operation of the Charged Property;

(b)   permit any persons designated by the Seller or the Seller's Administrators to enter on its premises and examine any of the Charged Property, and the records relating to the Charged Property, at all reasonable times and on reasonable prior notice; and

(c)   promptly inform the Seller and the Seller's Administrators in writing of any action, claim or demand made by or against it in connection with the Charged Property or of any fact, matter or circumstance which may, with the passage of time, give rise to such an action, claim or demand, together in each case the Buyer's proposals for settling, liquidating, compounding or contesting any such action, claim or demand and shall, subject to the Seller's prior approval, implement those proposals at its own expense.

6.13 **Payment of outgoings**

The Buyer shall promptly pay all taxes, fees, licence duties, registration charges, insurance premiums and other outgoings in respect of the Charged Property and, on demand, produce evidence of payment to the Seller and to the Seller's Administrators.

6.14 **Waiver of set-off**

The Buyer waives any present or future right of set-off it may have in respect of the Secured Liabilities (including sums payable by the Buyer under this debenture).

7.   **Property covenants**

7.1   **Maintenance**

The Buyer shall keep all buildings and all fixtures on each Property in good and substantial repair and condition.

7.2 Preservation of Property, fixtures and Equipment

The Buyer shall not, without the prior written consent of the Seller and the Seller's Administrators:

(a) pull down or remove the whole, or any part of, any building forming part of any Property or permit the same to occur;

(b) make or permit any material alterations to any Property, or sever or remove, or permit to be severed or removed, any of its fixtures; or

(c) remove or make any material alterations to any of the Equipment belonging to, or in use by, the Buyer on any Property (except to effect necessary repairs or replace them with new or improved models or substitutes).

7.3 Conduct of business on Properties

The Buyer shall carry on its trade and business on those parts (if any) of the Properties as are used for the purposes of trade or business in accordance with the standards of good management from time to time current in that trade or business.

7.4 Planning information

The Buyer shall:

(a) give full particulars to the Seller and to the Seller's Administrators of any notice, order, direction, designation, resolution or proposal given or made by any planning authority or other public body or authority (**'Planning Notice'**) that specifically applies to any Property, or to the locality in which it is situated, within seven days after becoming aware of the relevant Planning Notice; and

(b) (if the Seller so requires) immediately, and at the cost of the Buyer, take all reasonable and necessary steps to comply with any Planning Notice, and make, or join with the Seller in making, any objections or representations in respect of that Planning Notice that the Seller or the Seller's Administrators may desire.

7.5 Compliance with covenants and payment of rent

The Buyer shall:

(a) observe and perform all covenants, stipulations and conditions to which each Property, or the use of it, is or may be subjected, and (if the Seller or the Seller's Administrators so require) produce evidence sufficient to satisfy the Seller and the Seller's Administrators that those covenants, stipulations and conditions have been observed and performed;

(b) diligently enforce all covenants, stipulations and conditions benefiting each Property and shall not (and shall not agree to) waive release or vary any of the same; and

(c) (without prejudice to the generality of the foregoing) where a Property, or part of it, is held under a lease, duly and punctually pay all rents due from time to time, and perform and observe all the tenant's covenants and conditions.

7.6 Payment of rent and outgoings

The Buyer shall:

(a) where a Property, or part of it, is held under a lease, duly and punctually pay all rents due from time to time; and

(b) pay (or procure payment of the same) when due all charges, rates, taxes, duties, assessments and other outgoings relating to or imposed on each Property or on its occupier.

7.7 Maintenance of interests in Properties

The Buyer shall not, without the prior written consent of the Seller and the Seller's Administrators:

(a) grant, or agree to grant, any licence or tenancy affecting the whole or any part of any Property, or exercise, or agree to exercise, the statutory powers of leasing or of accepting surrenders under sections 99 or 100 of the Law of Property Act 1925; or

(b) in any other way dispose of, surrender or create, or agree to dispose of surrender or create, any legal or equitable estate or interest in the whole or any part of any Property.

7.8 Registration restrictions

If the title to any Property is not registered at the Land Registry, the Buyer shall procure that no person (other than itself) shall be registered under the Land Registration Acts 1925 to 2002 as proprietor of all or any part of any Property without the prior written consent of the Seller and the Seller's Administrators. The Buyer shall be liable for the costs and expenses of the Seller in lodging cautions against the registration of the title to the whole or any part of any Property from time to time.

7.9 Development restrictions

The Buyer shall not, without the prior written consent of the Seller and the Seller's Administrators:

(a) make or, insofar as it is able, permit others to make any application for planning permission or development consent in respect of the Property; or

(b) carry out, or permit, or suffer to be carried out on any Property any development as defined in the Town and Country Planning Act 1990 and the Planning Act 2008, or change or permit or suffer to be changed the use of any Property.

7.10 Environment

The Buyer shall:

(a) comply with all the requirements of Environmental Law both in the conduct of its general business and in the management, possession or occupation of each Property; and

351

(b)   obtain and comply with all authorisations, permits and other types of licences necessary under Environmental Law.

7.11 No restrictive obligations

The Buyer shall not, without the prior written consent of the Seller and the Seller's Administrators, enter into any onerous or restrictive obligations affecting the whole or any part of any Property, or create or permit to arise any overriding interest, easement or right whatever in or over the whole or any part of any Property.

7.12 Proprietary rights

The Buyer shall procure that no person shall become entitled to assert any proprietary or other like right or interest over the whole or any part of any Property without the prior written consent of the Seller and the Seller's Administrators.

7.13 Inspection

The Buyer shall permit the Seller, the Seller's Administrators, any Receiver and any person appointed by any of them to enter on and inspect any Property on reasonable prior notice.

7.14 Property information

The Buyer shall inform the Seller and the Seller's Administrators promptly of any acquisition by the Buyer of, or contract made by the Buyer to acquire, any freehold, leasehold or other interest in any property.

7.15 VAT option to tax

The Buyer shall not, without the prior written consent of the Seller and the Seller's Administrators:

(a)   exercise any VAT option to tax in relation to any Property; or

(b)   revoke any VAT option to tax exercised, and disclosed to the Seller, before the date of this deed.

7.16 Registration at the Land Registry

The Buyer consents to an application being made by the Seller to the Land Registrar for the following restriction in Form P to be registered against its title to each Property:

> 'No disposition of the registered estate by the proprietor of the registered estate [or by the proprietor of any registered charge, not being a charge registered before the entry of this restriction] is to be registered without a written consent signed by the proprietor for the time being of the charge dated [DATE] in favour of [NAME OF PARTY] referred to in the charges register [or [their conveyancer or specify appropriate details]].'

8.   Investments covenants

8.1 Deposit of title documents

(a)   The Buyer shall:

(i) on the execution of this debenture, deposit with the Seller all stock or share certificates and other documents of title or evidence of ownership relating to any Investments owned by the Buyer at that time; and

(ii) on the purchase or acquisition by it of Investments after the date of this deed, deposit with the Seller all stock or share certificates and other documents of title or evidence of ownership relating to those Investments.

(b) At the same time as depositing documents with the Seller in accordance with clause 8.1(a) the Buyer shall also deposit with the Seller:

(i) stock transfer forms relating to the relevant Investments duly completed and executed by or on behalf of the Buyer, but with the name of the transferee, the consideration and the date left blank; and

(ii) any other documents (in each case duly completed and executed by or on behalf of the Buyer) that the Seller or the Seller's Administrators may request in order to enable the Seller or any of its nominees, or any purchaser or transferee, to be registered as the owner of, or otherwise obtain a legal title to, or to perfect its security interest in any of the relevant Investments,

so that the Seller may, at any time and without notice to the Buyer, complete and present those stock transfer forms and other documents to the issuer of the Investments for registration.

8.2 **Nominations**

(a) The Buyer shall terminate with immediate effect all nominations it may have made (including, without limitation, any nomination made under section 145 or section 146 of the Companies Act 2006) in respect of any Investments and, pending that termination, procure that any person so nominated:

(i) does not exercise any rights in respect of any Investments without the prior written approval of the Seller and the Seller's Administrators; and

(ii) immediately on receipt by it, forward to the Seller all communications or other information received by it in respect of any Investments for which it has been so nominated.

(b) The Buyer shall not, during the Security Period, exercise any rights (including, without limitation, any rights under sections 145 and 146 of the Companies Act 2006) to nominate any person in respect of any of the Investments.

8.3 **Additional registration obligations**

The Buyer shall:

(a) obtain all consents, waivers, approvals and permissions that are necessary, under the articles of association of any issuer that is not a public company or otherwise, for the transfer of the Investments to the Seller or its nominee, or to a purchaser on enforcement of this deed; and

(b) procure the amendment of the share transfer provisions (including, but not limited to, deletion of any pre-emption provisions) of the articles of association of each issuer that is not a public company in any manner that the Seller and/or the Seller's Administrators may require in order to permit such a transfer.

8.4 Dividends and voting rights before enforcement

(a) Before the security constituted by this debenture becomes enforceable, the Buyer may retain and apply for its own use all dividends, interest and other monies paid or payable in respect of the Investments and, if any are paid or payable to the Seller or any of its nominees, the Seller will hold all those dividends, interest and other monies received by it for the Buyer and will pay them to the Buyer promptly on request.

(b) Before the security constituted by this deed becomes enforceable, the Buyer may exercise all voting and other rights and powers in respect of the Investments or, if any of the same are exercisable by the Seller of any of its nominees, to direct in writing the exercise of those voting and other rights and powers provided that:

    (i) it shall not do so in any way that would breach any provision of the Agreement or this debenture or for any purpose inconsistent with the Agreement or this debenture; and

    (ii) the exercise of, or the failure to exercise, those voting rights or other rights and powers would not, in the Seller's opinion or the opinion of the Seller's Administrators, have an adverse effect on the value of the Investments or otherwise prejudice the Seller's security under this deed.

(c) The Buyer shall indemnify the Seller and the Seller's Administrators against any loss or liability incurred by the Seller or the Seller's Administrators as a consequence of the Seller (or its nominee) acting in respect of the Investments at the direction of the Buyer.

(d) The Seller shall not, by exercising or not exercising any voting rights or otherwise, be construed as permitting or agreeing to any variation or other change in the rights attaching to or conferred by any of the Investments that the Seller or the Seller's Administrators consider prejudicial to, or impairing the value of, the security created by this debenture.

8.5 Dividends and voting rights after enforcement

After the security constituted by this debenture has become enforceable:

(a) all dividends and other distributions paid in respect of the Investments and received by the Buyer shall be held by the Buyer on trust for the Seller and immediately paid into a Designated Account or, if received by the Seller, shall be retained by the Seller; and

(b) all voting and other rights and powers attaching to the Investments shall be exercised by, or at the direction of, the Seller or the Seller's Administrators and the Buyer shall, and shall procure that its nominees shall, comply with any directions the Seller or the Seller's Administrators may give, in their absolute discretion, concerning the exercise of those rights and powers.

8.6 Calls on Investments

The Buyer shall promptly pay all calls, instalments and other payments that may be or become due and payable in respect of all or any of the Investments. The Buyer acknowledges that the Seller and the Seller's Administrators shall not be under any liability in respect of any such calls, instalments or other payments.

8.7 No alteration of constitutional documents or rights attaching to Investments

The Buyer shall not, without the prior written consent of the Seller and the Seller's Administrators, amend, or agree to the amendment of:

(a) the memorandum or articles of association, or any other constitutional documents, of any issuer that is not a public company; or

(b) the rights or liabilities attaching to any of the Investments.

8.8 Preservation of Investments

The Buyer shall ensure (as far as it is able to by the exercise of all voting rights, powers of control and other means available to it) that any issuer that is not a public company shall not:

(a) consolidate or subdivide any of its Investments, or reduce or re-organise its share capital in any way;

(b) issue any new shares or stock; or

(c) refuse to register any transfer of any of its Investments that may be lodged for registration by, or on behalf of, the Seller or the Buyer in accordance with this debenture.

8.9 Investments information

The Buyer shall, promptly following receipt, send to the Seller and the Seller's Administrators copies of any notice, circular, report, accounts and any other document received by it that relates to the Investments.

9. Equipment covenants

9.1 Maintenance of Equipment

The Buyer shall:

(a) maintain the Equipment in good and serviceable condition (except for expected fair wear and tear) in compliance with all relevant manuals, handbooks, manufacturer's instructions and recommendations and maintenance or servicing schedules;

(b) at its own expense, renew and replace any parts of the Equipment when they become obsolete, worn out or damaged with parts of a similar quality and of equal or greater value; and

(c) not permit any Equipment to be:

    (i) used or handled other than by properly qualified and trained persons; or

    (ii) overloaded or used for any purpose for which it is not designed or reasonably suitable.

9.2 **Payment of Equipment taxes**

The Buyer shall promptly pay all taxes, fees, licence duties, registration charges, insurance premiums and other outgoings in respect of the Equipment and, on demand, produce evidence of such payment to the Seller and to the Seller's Administrators.

9.3 **Notice of charge**

The Buyer:

(a) shall, if so requested by the Seller or the Seller's Administrators, affix to and maintain on each item of Equipment in a conspicuous place, a clearly legible identification plate containing the following wording:

'NOTICE OF CHARGE

This [DESCRIBE ITEM] and all additions to it [and ancillary equipment] are subject to a fixed charge dated [DATE] in favour of [SELLER].';

(b) shall not, and shall not permit any person to, conceal, obscure, alter or remove any plate affixed in accordance with clause 9.3(a).

10. Book Debts covenants

10.1 **Realising Book Debts**

The Buyer shall:

(a) as an agent for the Seller, collect in and realise all Book Debts, pay the proceeds into a Designated Account immediately on receipt and, pending that payment, hold those proceeds in trust for the Seller;

(b) not, without the prior written consent of the Seller or the Seller's Administrators, withdraw any amounts standing to the credit of any Designated Account; and

(c) if called on to do so by the Seller or the Seller's Administrators, execute a legal assignment of the Book Debts to the Seller on such terms as the Seller or the Seller's Administrators may require and give notice of that assignment to the debtors from whom the Book Debts are due, owing or incurred.

10.2 Preservation of Book Debts

The Buyer shall not (except with the prior written consent of the Seller or the Seller's Administrators) release, exchange, compound, set-off, grant time or indulgence in respect of, or in any other manner deal with, all or any of the Book Debts.

11. Relevant Agreement covenants

11.1 Relevant Agreements

The Buyer shall, unless the Seller and the Seller's Administrators agree otherwise in writing:

(a)   comply with the terms of;

(b)   not amend or vary or agree to any change in, or waive any requirement of;

(c)   not settle, compromise, terminate, rescind of discharge (except by performance); and

(d)   not abandon, waive, dismiss, release or discharge any action, claim or proceedings against any counterparty to a Relevant Agreement or other person in connection with, any Relevant Agreement and any other document, agreement or arrangement comprising the Charged Property (other than the Insurance Policies).

12. Intellectual Property covenants

12.1 Preservation of rights

The Buyer shall take all necessary action to safeguard and maintain present and future rights in, or relating to, the Intellectual Property including (without limitation) by observing all covenants and stipulations relating to those rights, and by paying all applicable renewal fees, licence fees and other outgoings.

12.2 Registration of Intellectual Property

The Buyer shall use all reasonable efforts to register applications for the registration of any Intellectual Property, and shall keep the Seller and the Seller's Administrators informed of all matters relating to each such registration.

12.3 Maintenance of Intellectual Property

The Buyer shall not permit any Intellectual Property to be abandoned, cancelled or to lapse.

13. Powers of the Seller

13.1 Power to remedy

(a)   The Seller shall be entitled (but shall not be bound) to remedy a breach at any time by the Buyer of any of its obligations contained in this debenture.

(b) The Buyer irrevocably authorises the Seller and its agents to do all such things as are necessary or desirable for that purpose.

(c) Any monies expended by the Seller in remedying a breach by the Buyer of its obligations contained in this debenture shall be reimbursed by the Buyer to the Seller on a full indemnity basis and shall carry interest in accordance with clause 20.1.

13.2 Exercise of rights

The rights of the Seller under clause 13.1 are without prejudice to any other rights of the Seller under this debenture and the exercise of those rights shall not make the Seller liable to account as a mortgagee in possession.

13.3 Power to dispose of chattels

(a) At any time after the security constituted by this debenture shall have become enforceable, the Seller or any Receiver may dispose of any chattels or produce found on any Property as agent for the Buyer.

(b) Without prejudice to any obligation to account for the proceeds of any sale of such chattels or produce, the Buyer shall indemnify the Seller and any Receiver against any liability arising from such disposal.

13.4 Seller has Receiver's powers

To the extent permitted by law, any right, power or discretion conferred by this debenture on a Receiver may, after the security constituted by this debenture has become enforceable, be exercised by the Seller in relation to any of the Charged Property whether or not it has taken possession of any of the Charged Property and without first appointing a Receiver or not withstanding the appointment of a Receiver.

13.5 Conversion of currency

(a) For the purpose of or pending the discharge of any of the Secured Liabilities the Seller may convert any monies received, recovered or realised by the Seller under this debenture (including the proceeds of any previous conversion under this clause 13.5) from their existing currencies of denomination into such other currencies of denomination as the Seller may think fit.

(b) Any such conversion shall be effected at the Bank's then prevailing spot selling rate of exchange for such other currency against the existing currency.

(c) Each reference in this clause 13.5 to a currency extends to funds of that currency and, for the avoidance of doubt, funds of one currency may be converted into different funds of the same currency.

13.6 Indulgence

The Seller may in its discretion grant time or other indulgence or make any other arrangement, variation or release with any person or persons not being a party to this debenture (whether or not such person or persons are jointly liable with the Buyer) in respect of any of the Secured Liabilities or of any other security for them without prejudice either to this debenture or to the liability of the Buyer for the Secured Liabilities.

13.7 **Appointment of an Administrator**

(a)   The Seller may without notice to the Buyer appoint one or more persons to be an Administrator of the Buyer pursuant to paragraph 14 of Schedule B1 of the Insolvency Act 1986 if the security constituted by this debenture becomes enforceable.

(b)   Any appointment under this clause 13.7 shall:

(i)   be in writing by a duly authorised signatory of the Seller or by the Seller's Administrators; and

(ii)   take effect in accordance with paragraph 19 of Schedule B1 of the Insolvency act 1986.

(c)   The Seller may apply to the court for an order removing an Administrator from office and may by notice in writing in accordance with this clause 13.7 appoint a replacement for any Administrator who has died, resigned, been removed or who has vacated office upon ceasing to be qualified.

14.   Enforcement events

14.1 **Enforcement events**

The security constituted by this debenture shall be immediately enforceable in any of the circumstances set out in Schedule 3.

14.2 **Discretion**

After the security constituted by this debenture has become enforceable, the Seller may, in its absolute discretion, enforce all or any part of that security at the times and in the manner and on the terms it thinks fit, and take possession of and hold or dispose of all or any part of the Charged Property.

15.   Enforcement

15.1 **Statutory power of sale**

(a)   The power of sale and other powers conferred upon mortgagees under the LPA 1925 shall, as between the Seller and a purchaser from the Seller, arise on and be exercisable at any time after the execution of this debenture, but the Seller shall not exercise such power of sale until the security constituted by this debenture has become enforceable under clause 14.1.

(b)   Section 103 of the LPA 1925 does not apply to the security constituted by this debenture.

15.2 **Extension of statutory powers**

The statutory powers of sale, leasing and accepting surrenders conferred upon mortgagees under the LPA 1925 and/or by any other statute shall be exercisable by the Seller under this debenture and are extended so as to authorise the Seller whether in its own name or in that of the Buyer to:

(a) make any lease or agreement for lease;

(b) accept surrenders of leases; or

(c) grant any option of the whole or any part or parts of the Charged Property with whatever rights relating to other parts of it whether or not at a premium and containing whatever covenants on the part of the Buyer and generally on such terms and conditions (including the payment of money to a lessee or tenant on a surrender) and whether or not at a premium as the Seller or any Receiver thinks fit without the need to comply with any of the restrictions imposed by sections 99 and 100 of the LPA 1925.

15.3 **Access on enforcement**

(a) At any time after the Seller has demanded payment of the Secured Liabilities or if the Buyer defaults in the performance of its obligations under this debenture, the Buyer shall allow the Seller or the Seller's Administrators or any Receiver, without further notice or demand, immediately to exercise all of their rights, powers and remedies in particular (and without limitation) to take possession of any of the Charged Property and for that purpose to enter onto any premises where any of the Charged Property is situated (or where the seller or the Seller's Administrators or any Receiver reasonably believes the Charged Property to be situated) without incurring any liability to the Buyer for, or by reason of, that entry.

(b) At all times, the Buyer shall use its best endeavours to allow the Seller, the Seller's Administrators and/or any Receiver access to any premises for the purpose of clause 15.3(a), including obtaining any necessary consents or permits of other persons, and ensure that its employees and officers do the same.

15.4 **Prior Security Interests**

At any time after the security constituted by this debenture has become enforceable, or after any powers conferred by any Security Interest having priority to this deed shall have become exercisable, the Seller may:

(a) redeem that or any other prior Security Interest;

(b) procure the transfer of that Security Interest to it; and

(c) settle and pass any account of the holder of any prior Security Interest.

Any accounts so settled and passed shall be, in the absence of any manifest error, conclusive and binding on the Buyer. All monies paid by the Seller to an encumbrancer in settlement of any of those accounts shall, as from its payment by the Seller, be due from the Buyer to the Seller and shall bear interest and be secured as part of the Secured Liabilities.

15.5 Protection of third parties

No purchaser, mortgagee or other person dealing with the Seller or any Receiver shall be concerned:

(a) to enquire whether any of the Secured Liabilities have become due or payable or remain unpaid or undischarged, or whether the power the Seller or a Receiver is purporting to exercise has become exercisable; or

(b) to see to the application of any money paid to the Seller or any Receiver.

15.6 **Privileges**

Any and all Receivers and the Seller is entitled to all the rights, powers, privileges and immunities conferred by the LPA 1925 on mortgagees and receivers.

15.7 **No liability as mortgagee in possession**

Neither the Seller nor the Seller's Administrators nor any Receiver nor any Administrator shall be liable to account as mortgagee in possession in respect of all or any of the Charged Property nor shall any of them be liable for any loss upon realisation of, or for any neglect or default of any nature whatsoever in connection with, all or any of the Charged Property for which a mortgagee in possession might as such be liable.

15.8 **Conclusive discharge to purchasers**

The receipt of the Seller or any Receiver shall be a conclusive discharge to a purchaser and, in making any sale or other disposal of any of the Secured Assets or in making any acquisition in the exercise of their respective powers, the Seller and every Receiver may do so for any consideration, in any manner and on any terms that it or he thinks fit.

15.9 **Right of appropriation**

(a) To the extent that:

(i) the Charged Property constitutes Financial Collateral; and

(ii) this debenture and the obligations of the Buyer under it constitute a Security Financial Collateral Arrangement,

the Seller shall have the right, at any time after the security constituted by this debenture has become enforceable, to appropriate all or any of the Charged Property in or towards the payment or discharge of the Secured Liabilities in any order that the Seller or the Seller's Administrators may, in their absolute discretion, determine.

(b) The value of any Charged Property appropriated in accordance with this clause shall be the price of such of the Charged Property at the time the right of appropriation is exercised as listed on any recognised market index, or determined by any other method that the Seller or the Seller's Administrators may select (including independent valuation).

(c) The Buyer agrees that the methods of valuation provided for in this clause are commercially reasonable for the purposes of the Financial Collateral Regulations.

16. Receiver

16.1 Appointment

At any time after the security constituted by this debenture has become enforceable, or at the request of the Buyer, the Seller may without further notice appoint by deed or otherwise in writing under hand of a duly authorised officer of the Seller any one or more person or persons to be a receiver or a receiver and manager of all or any part of the Charged Property.

16.2 Removal

The Seller may, without further notice (subject to section 45 of the Insolvency Act 1986) from time to time by deed or otherwise in writing under hand of a duly authorised officer of the Seller remove any person appointed to be Receiver and may in like manner appoint a new Receiver in his place.

16.3 Remuneration

The Seller may fix the remuneration of any Receiver appointed by it without the restrictions contained in section 109 of the LPA 1925 and the remuneration of the Receiver shall be a debt secured by this debenture which shall be due and payable immediately upon its being paid by the Seller.

16.4 Power to appoint additional to statutory powers

The power to appoint a Receiver conferred by this debenture shall be in addition to all statutory and other powers of the Seller under the Insolvency Act 1986, the LPA 1925 or otherwise and shall be exercisable without the restrictions contained in sections 103 and 109 of the LPA 1925 or otherwise.

16.5 Power to appoint exercisable despite prior appointments

The power to appoint a Receiver (whether conferred by this debenture or by statute) shall be and remain exercisable by the Seller notwithstanding any prior appointment in respect of all or any part of the Charged Property.

16.6 Agent of the Buyer

Any Receiver appointed by the Seller under this debenture shall be the agent of the Buyer and the Buyer shall be solely responsible for the contracts, engagements, acts, omissions, defaults, losses and remuneration of the Receiver and for liabilities incurred by the Receiver. The agency of each Receiver shall continue until the Buyer goes into liquidation and after that the Receiver shall act as principal and shall not become agent of the Seller.

17. Powers of Receiver

17.1 General

(a) Any Receiver appointed by the Seller under this debenture shall in addition to the powers conferred on him by the LPA 1925 and the Insolvency Act 1986 have power to do all such acts and things as an absolute owner could do in the management of such of the Charged Property over which the Receiver is appointed and in particular the powers set out in this debenture.

(b) Where more than one person is appointed Receiver, each will have power to act separately (unless the appointment by the Seller specifies to the contrary).

(c) Any exercise by a Receiver of any of the powers given by clause 17 may be on behalf of the Buyer or himself.

17.2 To repair and develop Properties

A Receiver may undertake or complete any works of repair, building or development on the Properties and may apply for and maintain any planning permission, development consent, building regulation approval or other permission, consent or licence to carry out any of the same.

17.3 To surrender leases

A Receiver may grant or accept surrenders of any leases or tenancies affecting any Property upon such terms and subject to such conditions as he thinks fit.

17.4 To employ personnel and advisors

A Receiver may provide services and employ, or engage, such managers contractors workmen agents and other personnel and professional advisors upon such terms and subject to such conditions as he thinks fit. A Receiver may discharge any such person or persons appointed by the Buyer.

17.5 To make VAT elections

A Receiver may make, exercise or revoke such elections for value added tax purposes as he thinks fit.

17.6 To charge remuneration

A Receiver may charge and receive such sum by way of remuneration (in addition to all costs, charges and expenses incurred by him) as the Seller may prescribe or agree with him.

17.7 **To realise Charged Property**

A Receiver may collect and get in the Charged Property or any part of it in respect of which he is appointed or any part thereof and for that purpose make such demands and take any proceedings as may seem expedient and take possession of the Charged Property with like rights.

17.8 **To manage or reconstruct the Buyer's business**

A Receiver may carry on, manage, develop, reconstruct, amalgamate or diversify or concur in carrying on, managing, developing, reconstructing, amalgamating or diversifying the business of the Buyer.

17.9 **To dispose of Charged Property**

A Receiver may sell, exchange, convert into money and realise all or any part of the Charged Property in respect of which he is appointed in any manner (including without limitation by public auction or private sale) and generally on any terms and conditions as he thinks fit. Any such sale may be for such consideration as he shall think fit and he may promote or concur in promoting a company to purchase the Charged Property to be sold.

17.10 **To sever fixtures and fittings**

A Receiver may sever and sell separately any fixtures or fittings from any Property without the consent of the Buyer.

17.11 **To sell Book Debts**

A Receiver may sell and/or assign all or any of the Book Debts in respect of which he is appointed in any manner, and generally on any terms and conditions that he thinks fit.

17.12 **To give valid receipts**

A Receiver may give valid receipt for all monies and execute all assurances and things that may be proper or desirable for realising any of the Charged Property.

17.13 **To make settlements**

A Receiver may make any arrangement, settlement or compromise between the Buyer and any other person which he may think expedient.

17.14 **To bring proceedings**

A Receiver may bring, prosecute, enforce, defend and abandon all actions, suits and proceedings in relation to any of the Charged Property as he thinks fit.

17.15 **To improve the Equipment**

A Receiver may make substitutions of, or improvements to, the Equipment as he may think expedient.

17.16 **To make calls on Buyer members**

A Receiver may make calls conditionally or unconditionally on the members of the Buyer in respect of the uncalled capital with such and the same powers for that purpose and for the purpose of enforcing payments of any calls so made as are conferred by the articles of association of the Buyer on its directors in respect of calls authorised to be made by them.

17.17 To insure

A Receiver may, if he thinks fit, but without prejudice to the indemnity contained in clause 20, effect with any insurer any policy or policies of insurance either in lieu or satisfaction of, or in addition to, such insurance required to be maintained by the Buyer under this debenture.

17.18 LPA 1925

A Receiver may exercise all powers granted to a receiver in the LPA 1925 in the same way as if he had been duly appointed under the LPA 1925 and exercise all powers granted to an administrative receiver in Schedule 1 of the Insolvency Act 1986.

17.19 To borrow

A Receiver may for any of the purposes authorised by this clause 17 raise money by borrowing from any person on the security of all or any of the Charged Property in respect of which he is appointed upon such terms (including if the Seller shall consent to terms under which such security ranks in priority to this debenture) as he shall think fit.

17.20 To redeem prior Security Interests

A Receiver may redeem any prior Security Interest and settle and pass the accounts to which the Security Interest relates and any accounts so settled and passed shall be conclusive and binding on the Buyer and the monies so paid will be deemed to be an expense properly incurred by the Receiver.

17.21 To delegate

A Receiver may delegate his powers under this debenture.

17.22 Absolute beneficial owner

A Receiver may, in relation to all or any part of the Charged Property, exercise all powers, authorisations and rights he would be capable of exercising, and do all those acts and things, as an absolute beneficial owner could exercise or do in the ownership and management of the Charged Property.

17.23 Incidental powers

A Receiver may do all such other acts and things:

(a) as he may consider desirable or necessary for realising any of the Charged Property;

(b) that he may consider incidental or conducive to any of the rights or powers conferred on a Receiver under or by virtue of this debenture or law;

(c) that he may lawfully or can do as agent of the Buyer.

18. Delegation

18.1 Delegation

The Seller or the Seller's Administrators or any Receiver may delegate (either generally or specifically) by power of attorney or in any other manner to any person any right, power, authority or discretion conferred on them by this debenture (including the power of attorney granted under clause 22.1).

18.2 Terms

The Seller or the Seller's Administrators or any Receiver may make a delegation on the terms and conditions (including the power to sub-delegate) that they think fit.

18.3 Liability

Neither the Seller nor the Seller's Administrators nor any Receiver shall be in any way liable or responsible to the buyer for any loss or liability arising from any act, default, omission or misconduct on the part of any delegate.

19. Application of proceeds

19.1 Order of application of proceeds

All monies received by the Seller or a Receiver in the exercise of any enforcement powers conferred by this debenture shall (subject to any valid claims of any persons having prior rights) be applied:

(a) first in or towards payment of all unpaid fees, costs, charges and expenses or other liability incurred by or on behalf of the Seller (and any Receiver, attorney or agent appointed by it);

(b) second in paying the remuneration of any Receiver (as agreed between him and the Seller);

(c) third in or towards discharge of the Secured Liabilities in such order and manner as the Seller shall determine; and

(d) finally in paying any surplus to the Buyer or any other person entitled to it.

19.2 Appropriation

Neither the Seller nor any Receiver shall be bound (whether by virtue of section 109(8) of the LPA 1925, which is varied accordingly, or otherwise) to pay or appropriate any receipt or payment first towards interest rather than principal or otherwise in any particular order as between any of the Secured Liabilities.

19.3 Suspense account

All monies received by the Seller or a Receiver under this debenture:

(a) may, at the discretion of the Seller or Receiver, be credited to any suspense or securities realised account;

(b)　shall bear interest at such rate, if any, as may be agreed in writing between the Seller and the Buyer; and

(c)　may be held in such account for so long as the Seller or Receiver thinks fit.

20.　Costs and indemnity

20.1　Costs

The Buyer shall pay to or reimburse the Seller and the Seller's Administrators and any Receiver on demand, on a full indemnity basis, all Costs incurred by the Seller and/or the Seller's Administrators and/or any Receiver in relation to:

(a)　this debenture or the Charged Property; or

(b)　protecting, perfecting, preserving or enforcing (or attempting to do so) any of the Seller's or the Receiver's rights under this debenture; or

(c)　suing for, or recovering, any of the Secured Liabilities,

(including, without limitation, the Costs of any proceedings in relation to this debenture or the Secured Liabilities) together with interest on the amount due at the rate of interest and in the manner specified in the Agreement from the date on which the relevant Cost arose until payment of that Cost in full (whether before or after judgment, winding up or administration of the Buyer).

20.2　Indemnity

The Buyer shall indemnify the Seller, the Seller's Administrators and any Receiver and their respective employees and agents on a full indemnity basis out of the Charged Property in respect of all actions, liabilities and Costs incurred or suffered in or as a result of:

(a)　the exercise or purported exercise of any of the powers, authorities or discretions vested in them under this debenture; or

(b)　taking, holding, protecting, perfecting, preserving or enforcing (or attempting to do so) the security constituted by this debenture; or

(c)　any default or delay by the Buyer in performing any of its obligations under this debenture.

21.　Further assurance

21.1　Further assurance

The Buyer shall, at its own expense, take whatever action the Seller or the Seller's Administrators or any Receiver may reasonably require for:

(a)　creating, perfecting or protecting the security intended to be created by this debenture;

(b)　facilitating the realisation of any of the Charged Property; or

(c)   facilitating the exercise of any right, power, authority or discretion exercisable by the Seller or any Receiver in respect of any of the Charged Property,

including, without limitation (if the Seller or the Seller's Administrators or any Receiver thinks it expedient) the execution of any transfer, conveyance, assignment or assurance of all or any of the assets forming part of (or intended to form part of) the Charged Property (whether to the Seller or to its nominee) and the giving of any notice, order or direction and the making of any registration.

22.   Power of attorney

22.1   Appointment of attorneys

By way of security the Buyer irrevocably appoints the Seller and the Seller's Administrators and every Receiver separately to be the attorney of the Buyer and in its name and on its behalf and as its act and deed to execute any documents, and do any acts and things which:

(a)   the Buyer is required to execute and do under this debenture; and/or

(b)   any attorney may deem proper or desirable in exercising any of the rights, powers, authorities and discretions conferred by this debenture or by law on the Seller or any Receiver.

22.2   Ratification of acts of attorney

The Buyer ratifies and confirms and agrees to ratify and confirm anything which any of its attorneys may do in the proper and lawful exercise or purported exercise of all or any of the rights, powers, authorities and discretions referred to in clause 22.1.

23.   Release

23.1   Release

Subject to clause 25.3, upon the expiry of the Security Period (but not otherwise) the Seller and the Seller's Administrators shall, at the request and cost of the Buyer, take whatever action is reasonably necessary to release the Charged Property from the security constituted by this debenture and to reassign the Charged Property to the Buyer.

24.   Assignment

24.1   Assignment by Seller

(a)   The Seller and the Seller's Administrators may at any time, without the consent of the Buyer, assign or transfer the whole or any part of the Seller and the Seller's Administrators' rights and/or obligations under this debenture to any person.

(b)   The Seller and the Seller's Administrators may disclose to any actual or proposed assignee or transferee any information about the Buyer, the Charged Property and this debenture that the Seller or the Seller's Administrators consider appropriate.

24.2 Assignment by Buyer

The Buyer may not assign any of its rights or transfer any of its obligations under this debenture or enter into any transaction, which would result in any of those rights or obligations passing to another person.

25. Further provisions

25.1 Independent security

This debenture shall be in addition to and independent of every other security or guarantee which the Seller may at any time hold for any of the Secured Liabilities. No prior security held by the Seller over the whole or any part of the Charged Property shall merge in the security created by this debenture.

25.2 Continuing security

This debenture shall remain in full force and effect as a continuing security for the Secured Liabilities, notwithstanding any settlement of account or intermediate payment or other matter or thing whatsoever, unless and until the Seller and the Seller's Administrators discharge this debenture in writing.

25.3 Discharge conditional

Any release, discharge or settlement between the Buyer and the Seller shall be deemed conditional upon no payment or security received by the Seller in respect of the Secured Liabilities being avoided, reduced or ordered to be refunded pursuant to any law relating to insolvency, bankruptcy, winding up, administration, receivership or otherwise and, notwithstanding any such release, discharge or settlement:

(a)   the Seller or its nominee may retain this debenture and the security created by or pursuant to this debenture, including all certificates and documents relating to the whole or any part of the Charged Property, for such period as the Seller shall deem necessary to provide the Seller with security against any such avoidance, reduction or order for refund; and

(b)   the Seller shall be entitled to recover the value or amount of such security or payment from the Buyer subsequently as if such release, discharge or settlement had not occurred.

25.4 Certificates

A certificate or determination by the Seller or the Seller's Administrators as to any amount for the time being due to the Seller from the Buyer shall (in the absence of any manifest error) be conclusive evidence of the amount due.

25.5 Rights cumulative

The rights and remedies of the Seller and the Seller's Administrators conferred by this debenture are cumulative, may be exercised as often as the Seller and/or the Seller's Administrators consider appropriate, and are in addition to its or their rights and powers under the general law.

25.6 Waivers

Any waiver or variation of any right by the Seller or the Seller's Administrators (whether arising under this debenture or under the general law) shall only be effective if it is in writing and signed by the Seller (in respect of a waiver or variation on the part of the Seller) and (in any event) by the Seller's Administrators and applies only in the circumstances for which it was given and shall not prevent the Seller from subsequently relying on the relevant provision.

25.7 Further exercise of rights

No act or course of conduct or negotiation by or on behalf of the Seller or the Seller's Administrators shall in any way preclude the Seller or the Seller's Administrators from exercising any right or power under this debenture or constitute a suspension or variation of any such right or power.

25.8 Delay

No delay or failure to exercise any right or power under this debenture shall operate as a waiver.

25.9 Single or partial exercise

No single or partial exercise of any right under this debenture shall prevent any other or further exercise of that or any other such right.

25.10 Consolidation

The restriction on the right of consolidation contained in section 93 of the LPA 1925 shall not apply to this debenture.

25.11 Partial invalidity

The invalidity, unenforceability or illegality of any provision (or part of a provision) of this debenture under the laws of any jurisdiction shall not affect the validity, enforceability or legality of the other provisions. If any invalid, unenforceable or illegal provision would be valid, enforceable or legal if some part of it were deleted, the provision shall apply with any modification necessary to give effect to the commercial intention of the parties.

25.12 Counterparts

This debenture may be executed and delivered in any number of counterparts, each of which is an original and which together have the same effect as if each party had signed the same document.

25.13 **Perpetuity period**

If the rule against perpetuities applies to any trust created by this debenture, the perpetuity period shall be 125 years (as specified by section 5(1) of the Perpetuities and Accumulations Act 2009).

26.   Seller's Administrators

26.1 **Agency**

The Seller's Administrators act as agents of the Seller and neither they, their firm or agents will incur any personal liability under or by virtue of this debenture, nor in relation to any related documents, matters or claims whatsoever.

26.2 **Purpose**

The Seller's Administrators have entered into this debenture solely for the purpose of obtaining the benefit of the provisions of the debenture that are in the Seller's Administrators' favour.

27.   Notices

27.1 **Service**

Any notice or other communication given under or in connection with this debenture shall be:

(a)   in writing and shall be served by delivering it personally or by sending it by pre-paid first-class post or by fax; and

(b)   sent

   (i)   to the Buyer at:

   [ADDRESS]

   Fax: [NUMBER]

   Attention: [NAME]

   (ii)   to the Seller and to the Seller's Administrators at:

   [ADDRESS]

   Fax: [NUMBER]

   Attention: [NAME]

or to any other address or fax number as may be notified in writing from time to time by the relevant party to the other party.

27.2 **Receipt by the Buyer**

Receipt of any notice or other communication that the Seller or the Seller's Administrators give shall be deemed to have been received by the Buyer:

(a)   if delivered personally, at the time of delivery; or

(b)   in the case of pre-paid first-class letter, on the second Business Day from the date of posting; or

(c)   in the case of a fax, when received in legible form,

but if deemed receipt occurs:

    (i)   before 9:00 am on a Business Day, the notice shall be deemed to have been received at 9:00 am on that day; or

    (ii)   after 5:00 pm on a Business Day or on a day that is not a Business Day, the notice shall be deemed to have been received at 9:00 am on the next Business Day.

27.3 Receipt by the Seller or the Seller's Administrators

Any notice of communication given to the Seller or to the Seller's Administrators by the Buyer shall be deemed to have been received only on actual receipt.

27.4 E-mail invalid

Notice given under this debenture shall not be validly served if sent by e-mail.

28. Governing law and jurisdiction

28.1 Governing law

This debenture and any dispute or claim arising out of or in connection with it or its subject matter or formation (including non-contractual disputes or claims) shall be governed by and construed according to the law of England and Wales.

28.2 Jurisdiction

The parties to this debenture irrevocably agree that, subject as provided below, the courts of England and Wales shall have exclusive jurisdiction to settle any dispute or claim that arises out of or in connection with this debenture or its subject matter or formation (including non-contractual disputes or claims). Nothing in this clause shall limit the right of the Seller to take proceedings against the Buyer in any other court of competent jurisdiction, nor shall the taking of proceedings in any one or more jurisdictions preclude the taking of proceedings in any other jurisdictions, whether concurrently or not, to the extent permitted by the law of such other jurisdiction.

28.3 Other service

The Buyer irrevocably consents to any process in any proceedings being served on it in accordance with the provisions of this debenture relating to service of notices. Nothing contained in this debenture shall affect the right to serve process in any other manner permitted by law.

This document has been executed as a deed and is delivered and takes effect on the date stated at the beginning of it.

SCHEDULE 1: Property

Part 1 – Registered property

[DETAILS OF REGISTERED PROPERTY]

Part 2 – Unregistered property

[DETAILS OF UNREGISTERED PROPERTY]

SCHEDULE 2: Relevant Agreements

Type of agreement: [DESCRIBE CONTRACT]

Date: [DATE OF CONTRACT]

Parties: [SET OUT PARTIES TO THE CONTRACT]

SCHEDULE 3: Enforcement

Enforcement events

This debenture shall be enforceable if:

(a)   any of the Secured Liabilities shall not be paid or discharged when the same ought to be paid or discharged by the Buyer (whether on demand or at scheduled maturity or by acceleration or otherwise, as the case may be); or

(b)   the Buyer shall be in breach of any of its obligations under this debenture or the Agreement or under any other agreement between the Buyer, the Seller and the Seller's Administrators other than a failure to pay and that breach (if capable of remedy) has not been remedied to the satisfaction of the Seller or the Seller's Administrators within 14 days of notice by the Seller to the Buyer to remedy the breach; or

(c)   the Buyer:

    (i)   becomes unable to pay its debts as they fall due (and/or the value of the Buyer's assets is less than the amount of its liabilities, taking into account the Buyer's contingent and prospective liabilities); or

    (ii)   commences negotiations with any one or more of its creditors with a view to the general readjustment or rescheduling of its indebtedness; or

    (iii)   makes a general assignment for the benefit of, or a composition with, its creditors; or

(d)   the Buyer passes any resolution or takes any corporate action or a petition is presented or proceedings are commenced or any action is taken by any person for its winding up, dissolution, administration or reorganisation or for the appointment of a receiver, administrative receiver, administrator, trustee or similar officer of it or of any or all of its revenues and assets; or

(e)   a moratorium comes into being in respect of any liabilities of the Buyer; or

(f)   a distress, execution, attachment or other legal process is levied or enforced upon or sued against all or any part of the assets of the Buyer and remains undischarged for seven days; or

(g)   any event occurs in relation to the Buyer that is analogous to those set out in paragraphs 1(c) to 1(f) inclusive of this Schedule 3; or

(h)   the Buyer suspends or ceases to carry on (or threatens to suspend or cease to carry on) all or a material part of its business; or

(i)   any representation, warranty or statement made or deemed to be made by the Buyer under this debenture or under any other agreement between the Buyer, the Seller and the Seller's Administrators is or proves to have been incorrect or misleading in any material respect when made or deemed to be made; or

(j)   any security on or over any of the Buyer's assets becomes enforceable; or

(k)   the Buyer repudiates or evidences an intention to repudiate this debenture or any other agreement between the Buyer and the Seller; or

(l)   any event occurs (or circumstances exist) which, in the reasonable opinion of the Seller or the Seller's Administrators, has or is reasonably likely to have a Material Adverse Effect

and in any such event (whether or not the event is continuing), without prejudice to any other rights of the Seller or the Seller's Administrators, the powers of sale under the Law of Property Act 1925 shall immediately be exercisable and the Seller or teht Seller's Administrators may in its or their absolute discretion enforce all or any part of the security created by this debenture as they see fit.

Signed as a deed by .... **Limited**)   ....

in the presence of:)   Director

Signature of witness:

Name:

Address:

Occupation:

Signed as a deed by .... **Limited**)   ....

(in administration)   )   Administrator

acting by its administrator without)

personal liability pursuant to powers)

conferred under the Insolvency Act 1986)

in the presence of:)

Signature of witness:

Name:

Address:

Occupation:

Signed as a deed by ....)   ....

for and on behalf of the Administrators)   Administrator

in the presence of:)

Signature of witness:

Name:

Address:

Occupation:

F. Guarantee and indemnity[4]

DATED .... 20[   ]

(1)   XXXXXXXX
(2)   YYYYYYYY LIMITED (in administration)
(3)   A1 and A2 – ADMINISTRATORS

GUARANTEE AND INDEMNITY

DRAFT 1 .... 20[   ]

TO THE GUARANTOR:

BY ENTERING INTO THIS GUARANTEE AND INDEMNITY YOU MIGHT BECOME LIABLE TO PAY MONEYS INSTEAD OF OR AS WELL AS THE BUYER.

YOU SHOULD SEEK INDEPENDENT LEGAL ADVICE BEFORE ENTERING INTO THIS GUARANTEE.

DATE OF GUARANTEE: .... 20[   ]

PARTIES

(1)   **XXXXXXXX** of_____(**Guarantor**)

(2)   [   ] **Limited** (in administration) registered in England and Wales with company number: [   ] whose registered office is at [   ] (**'Seller'**) acting by the Administrators; and

(3)   [   ] and [   ] as joint administrators of the Seller both of [   ] (**'Administrators'**).

BACKGROUND

(A)   On the date of this guarantee the Seller and the Buyer and the Administrators entered into the Agreement.

---

[4]   Adapted from PLC's Guarantee and Indemnity precedent. For further information please visit http://uk.practicallaw.com/.

(B)   The Guarantor [is a director of the Buyer and] has agreed to enter into this guarantee for the purpose of providing security for the payment of all sums that are or may fall due for payment by the Buyer to the Seller and/or the Administrators under the terms of the Agreement.

1.   Definitions and interpretation

1.1   In this guarantee the following words and expressions shall have the following meanings:

'Agreement'	means a business sale agreement made on the date of this guarantee between (1) the Seller (2) the Buyer and (3) the Administrators under which the Buyer agreed to buy certain of the assets and the business of the Seller on the terms set out in the Agreement;
'Business Day'	means a day (other than a Saturday or a Sunday) on which banks are open for general business in London;
'Buyer'	means [NAME OF BUYER] registered in England and Wales with company number: [ ] whose registered office is at [ ];
'Guaranteed Obligations'	means all present and future payment obligations and liabilities of the Buyer due, owing or incurred under the Agreement to the Seller and/or the Administrators;
'Rights'	means any Security or other right or benefit whether arising by set-off, counterclaim, subrogation, indemnity, proof in liquidation or otherwise and whether from contribution or otherwise;
'Security'	means a mortgage, charge, pledge, lien or other security interest securing any obligation of any person, or any other agreement having a similar effect;
'Warranties'	means the representations and warranties set out in the Schedule.

1.2   The headings are included for convenience only and shall not affect the interpretation or construction of this Assignment.

1.3   References to **Clauses** or the **Schedule** are to clauses of or the schedule to this guarantee.

1.4   References to any of the **masculine, feminine and neuter genders** shall include the other genders and references to the singular number shall include the plural and vice versa.

1.5   References to a **document** are to that document as varied, supplemented or replaced from time to time.

1.6   References to **the Seller** and to **the Administrators** are references to any successor in title to any of them, including (but not limited to) any liquidators subsequently appointed to the Seller.

1.7   References to **writing** shall include any modes of reproducing words in a legible and non-transitory form but not email.

1.8 A reference to a statute or statutory provision is a reference to it as it is in force from time to time, taking account of any amendment, extension, or re-enactment and includes any statute, statutory provision or subordinate legislation which it amends or re-enacts.

1.9 A reference to a statute or statutory provision shall include any subordinate legislation made from time to time under that statute or statutory provision.

2. Guarantee and indemnity

2.1 In consideration of the Seller and the Administrators entering into the Agreement, the Guarantor guarantees to the Seller and the Administrators to pay on demand the Guaranteed Obligations.

2.2 If the Guaranteed Obligations are not recoverable from the Buyer by reason of illegality, incapacity, lack or exceeding of powers, ineffectiveness of execution or any other reason, the Guarantor shall remain liable under this guarantee for the Guaranteed Obligations as if he were a principal debtor.

2.3 The Guarantor as principal obligor and as a separate and independent obligation and liability from his obligations and liabilities under clause 2.1 agrees to indemnify and keep indemnified the Seller and the Administrators in full and on demand from and against all and any losses, costs, claims, liabilities, damages, demands and expenses suffered or incurred by the Seller and/or the Administrators arising out of, or in connection with, any failure of the Buyer to perform or discharge any of its obligations or liabilities in respect of the Guaranteed Obligations.

3. The Seller and the Administrators

3.1 This guarantee is and shall at all times be a continuing security and shall cover the entire balance from time to time owing to the Seller and/or the Administrators by the Buyer in respect of the Guaranteed Obligations.

3.2 The liability of the Guarantor under this guarantee shall not be reduced, discharged or otherwise adversely affected by:

3.2.1 any intermediate payment, settlement of account or discharge in whole or in part of the Guaranteed Obligations; or

3.2.2 any variation, extension, discharge, compromise, dealing with, exchange or renewal of any right or remedy which the Seller and/ or the Administrators may now or after the date of this guarantee have from or against any of the Buyer and any other person in connection with the Guaranteed Obligations; or

3.2.3 any act or omission by the Seller and/or the Administrators or any other person in taking up, perfecting or enforcing any Security, indemnity, or guarantee from or against the Buyer or any other person; or

3.2.4   any termination, amendment, variation, novation or supplement of or to any of the Guaranteed Obligations; or

3.2.5   any grant of time, indulgence, waiver or concession to the Buyer or any other person; or

3.2.6   any insolvency, bankruptcy, liquidation, administration, winding up, incapacity, limitation, disability, the discharge by operation of law, or any change in the constitution, name or style of the Buyer or any other person; or

3.2.7   any invalidity, illegality, unenforceability, irregularity or frustration of any actual or purported obligation of, or Security held from, the Buyer or any other person in connection with the Guaranteed Obligations; or

3.2.8   any claim or enforcement of payment from the Buyer or any other person; or

3.2.9   any act or omission which would not have discharged or affected the liability of the Guarantor had he been a principal debtor instead of a guarantor or indemnifier or by anything done or omitted by any person which, but for this provision, might operate to exonerate or discharge the Guarantor or otherwise reduce or extinguish his liability under this guarantee.

3.3   The Seller and the Administrators shall not be obliged before taking steps to enforce any of their rights and remedies under this Guarantee:

3.3.1   to take any action or obtain judgment in any court against the Buyer or any other person; or

3.3.2   to make or file any claim in a bankruptcy, liquidation, administration or insolvency of the Buyer or any other person; or

3.3.3   to make demand, enforce or seek to enforce any claim, right or remedy against the Buyer or any other person.

3.4   The Guarantor warrants to the Seller and the Administrators that he has not taken or received, and shall not take, exercise or receive the benefit of any Rights from or against the Buyer, its liquidator, an administrator, co-guarantor or any other person in connection with any liability of, or payment by, the Guarantor under this guarantee but:

3.4.1   if any of the Rights is taken, exercised or received by the Guarantor, those Rights and all monies at any time received or held in respect of those Rights shall be held by the Guarantor on trust for the Seller and the Administrators for application in or towards the discharge of the Guaranteed Obligations under this guarantee; and

3.4.2   on demand by the Seller and/or the Administrators, the Guarantor shall promptly transfer, assign or pay to the Seller and/or the Administrators all other Rights and all monies from time to time held on trust by the Guarantor under this clause 3.

3.5 This guarantee is in addition to and shall not affect nor be affected by or merge with any other judgment, Security, right or remedy obtained or held by the Seller and/or the Administrators from time to time for the discharge and performance by the Buyer of the Guaranteed Obligations.

4. Interest

4.1 The Guarantor shall pay interest to the Seller and the Administrators after as well as before judgment at the rate of 5 per cent above the base rate of [NAME OF BANK] on all sums demanded under this guarantee from the date of demand by the Seller and/or the Administrators or, if earlier, the date on which the relevant damages, losses, costs or expenses arose in respect of which the demand has been made, until, but excluding, the date of actual payment.

4.2 Interest under clause 4.1 shall accrue on a day-to-day basis calculated by the Seller and/or the Administrators upon such terms as the Seller and/or the Administrators may from time to time determine and shall be compounded quarterly.

4.3 The Seller and the Administrators shall not be entitled to recover any amount in respect of interest under both this guarantee and under any arrangements entered into between the Buyer and the Seller and/or the Administrators in respect of any failure by the Buyer to make any payment in respect of the Guaranteed Obligations.

5. Costs

The Guarantor shall on a full indemnity basis pay to the Seller and the Administrators on demand the amount of all costs and expenses (including legal and out-of-pocket expenses and any valued added tax on those costs and expenses) which the Seller and/or the Administrators incur in connection with:

5.1 the preparation, negotiation, execution and delivery of this guarantee;

5.2 any actual or proposed amendment, variation, supplement, waiver or consent under or in connection with this guarantee;

5.3 any discharge or release of this guarantee;

5.4 the preservation, or exercise and enforcement, of any rights under or in connection with this guarantee or any attempt so to do; and

5.5 any stamping or registration of this guarantee.

6. Representations and warranties

The Guarantor represents and warrants that the Warranties are true and correct on the date of this guarantee.

7. Suspense account

7.1 The Seller and/or the Administrators may place to the credit of a suspense account any monies received under or in connection with this guarantee in order to preserve the rights of the Seller and/or the Administrators to prove for the full amount of all its claims against the Buyer or any other person in respect of the Guaranteed Obligations.

7.2 The Seller and/or the Administrators may at any time and from time to time apply all or any monies held in any suspense account in or towards satisfaction of any of the monies, obligations and liabilities the subject of this guarantee as the Seller and/or the Administrators, in their absolute discretion, may conclusively determine.

8. Discharge conditional

8.1 Any release, discharge or settlement between the Guarantor and the Seller and/or the Administrators in relation to this guarantee shall be conditional on no Right, Security, disposition or payment to the Seller and/or the Administrators by the Guarantor, the Buyer or any other person in respect of the Guaranteed Obligations being avoided, set aside or ordered to be refunded pursuant to any enactment or law relating to breach of duty by any person, bankruptcy, liquidation, administration, protection from creditors generally or insolvency or for any other reason.

8.2 If any Right, Security, disposition or payment referred to in clause 8.1 is avoided, set aside or ordered to be refunded, the Seller and/or the Administrators shall be entitled subsequently to enforce this guarantee against the Guarantor as if such release, discharge or settlement had not occurred and any such right, Security, disposition or payment had not been given or made.

9. Payments

9.1 All sums payable by the Guarantor under this guarantee shall be paid in full to the Seller and/or the Administrators in the currency in which the Guaranteed Obligations are payable without any set-off, deduction, condition or counterclaim whatsoever.

9.2 The Guarantor shall not and may not direct the application by the Seller and/or the Administrators of any sums received by the Seller and/or the Administrators from the Guarantor under, or pursuant to, any of the terms of this guarantee.

10. Administrators

10.1 The Administrators act as agents of the Seller and neither they, their firm or agents will incur any personal liability under or by virtue of this deed, nor in relation to any related documents, matters or claims whatsoever.

10.2 The Administrators have entered into this guarantee solely for the purpose of obtaining the benefit of the provisions of the guarantee that are in the Administrators' favour.

11. Transfer

11.1 This guarantee is freely assignable or transferable by the Seller and the Administrators.

11.2 The Guarantor may not assign any of his rights and may not transfer any of his obligations under this guarantee or enter into any transaction which would result in any of those rights or obligations passing to another person.

12. Evidence of amounts and certificates

Any certificate, determination or notification by the Seller and/or the Administrators as to a rate or any amount payable under this guarantee is (in the absence of manifest error) conclusive evidence of the matter to which it relates and shall contain reasonable details of the basis of determination.

13. Remedies, waivers, amendments and consents

13.1 Any amendment to this guarantee shall be in writing and signed by or on behalf of each party.

13.2 Any waiver of any right or consent given under this guarantee is only effective if it is in writing and signed by the waiving or consenting party, and applies only in the circumstances for which it is given and shall not prevent the party giving it from subsequently relying on the relevant provision.

13.3 No delay or failure to exercise any right under this guarantee shall operate as a waiver of that right.

13.4 No single or partial exercise of any right under this guarantee shall prevent any further exercise of the same or any other right under this guarantee.

13.5 Rights and remedies under this guarantee are cumulative and not exclusive of any rights or remedies provided by law or otherwise.

14. Severance

14.1 The invalidity, unenforceability or illegality of any provision (or part of a provision) of this guarantee under the laws of any jurisdiction shall not affect the validity, enforceability or legality of the other provisions.

14.2 If any invalid, unenforceable or illegal provision would be valid, enforceable or legal if some part of it were deleted, the provision shall apply with whatever modification is necessary to give effect to the commercial intention of the parties.

15. Third party rights

Save for those third parties referred to in clause 10.1 above, a person who is not a party to this guarantee shall have no rights to enforce or enjoy the benefit of any term of this guarantee under the Contracts (Rights of Third Parties) Act 1999.

16. Counterparts

This guarantee may be executed and delivered in any number of counterparts, each of which is an original and which together have the same effect as if each party had signed the same document.

17. Notices

17.1 Every notice, request, demand, or other communication under this guarantee shall be:

17.1.1 in writing, delivered personally or sent by pre-paid first-class letter or fax (confirmed by letter); and

17.1.2 sent:

to the Guarantor at:

[ADDRESS]

Fax: [FAX NUMBER]

Attention: [NAME]

to the Seller and the Administrators at:

[ADDRESS]

Fax: [FAX NUMBER]

Attention: [NAME]

or to such other address or fax number notified in writing by one party to the other.

17.2 Any notice or other communication given by the Seller and/or the Administrators shall be deemed to have been received:

17.2.1 if sent by fax, with a confirmation of transmission, on the day on which it is transmitted;

17.2.2 if given by hand, on the day of actual delivery; and

17.2.3 if posted, on the second Business Day following the day on which it was dispatched by pre-paid first-class post,

provided that a notice given on a day which is not a Business Day (or after normal business hours in the place of receipt) shall be deemed to have been received on the next Business Day.

17.3 Any notice or other communication given to the Seller and/or the Administrators shall be deemed to have been given only on actual receipt by the Seller and/or the Administrators.

18. Governing law and jurisdiction

18.1 This guarantee and any dispute or claim arising out of or in connection with it or its subject matter or formation (including non-contractual disputes or claims) shall be governed by, and construed in accordance with, the law of England and Wales.

18.2 The parties to this guarantee irrevocably agree that, subject as provided below, the courts of England and Wales shall have exclusive jurisdiction to settle any dispute or claim that arises out of or in connection with this guarantee or its subject matter or formation (including non-contractual disputes or claims). Nothing in this clause shall limit the right of the Seller and/or the Administrators to take proceedings against the Guarantor in any other court of competent jurisdiction, nor shall the taking of proceedings in any one or more jurisdictions preclude the taking of proceedings in any other jurisdictions, whether concurrently or not, to the extent permitted by the law of such other jurisdiction.

18.3 The Guarantor irrevocably consents to any process in any proceedings under clause 18.1 being served on it in accordance with the provisions of this guarantee relating to service of notices. Nothing contained in this guarantee shall affect the right to serve process in any other manner permitted by law.

This document has been executed as a deed and is delivered and takes effect on the date stated at the beginning of it.

SCHEDULE

WARRANTIES

1. **Capacity**

   The Guarantor has the capacity to execute, deliver and perform his obligations under this guarantee and the transactions contemplated by them.

[2. **Director**

   The Guarantor is a director of the Buyer.]

3. **Non-contravention**

   The execution, delivery and performance of the obligations in, and transactions contemplated by, this guarantee does not and will not contravene any agreement or instrument binding on the Guarantor or his assets, or any applicable law or regulation.

4. **Authorisations**

   The Guarantor has taken all necessary action and obtained all required or desirable consents to enable him to execute, deliver and perform his obligations under this guarantee and to make this guarantee admissible in evidence in England and Wales. Any such authorisations are in full force and effect.

5. **Binding obligations**

   The Guarantor's obligations under this guarantee are, subject to any general principles of law limiting obligations, legal, valid, binding and enforceable.

6. **Litigation**

   No litigation, arbitration or administrative proceedings are taking place, pending or, to the Guarantor's knowledge, threatened against him or any of his assets.

7. **No default**

   No event or circumstance is outstanding which constitutes a default under any deed or instrument which is binding on the Guarantor, or to which his assets are subject, which might have a material adverse effect on the Guarantor's ability to perform his obligations under this guarantee.

8. **Ranking of obligations**

   The Guarantor's payment obligations under this guarantee rank at least pari passu with the claims of all his other unsecured and unsubordinated creditors, except for obligations mandatorily preferred by law generally.

BY ENTERING INTO THIS GUARANTEE AND INDEMNITY YOU MIGHT BECOME LIABLE TO PAY MONIES INSTEAD OF OR AS WELL AS THE BUYER.

YOU SHOULD SEEK INDEPENDENT LEGAL ADVICE BEFORE ENTERING INTO THIS GUARANTEE AND INDEMNITY.

Signed as a deed by ....   )   ....
in the presence of:)   Guarantor

Signature of witness:

Name:

Address:

Occupation: Solicitor

Signed as a deed by .... **Limited**)   ....
(in administration)   )   Administrator
acting by its administrator without   )
personal liability pursuant to powers   )
conferred under the Insolvency Act 1986)
in the presence of:)

Signature of witness:

Name:

Address:

Occupation:

Signed as a deed by ....   )   ....
for and on behalf of the Administrators)   Administrator
in the presence of:)

Signature of witness:

Name:

Address:

Occupation:

G.   Guaranteed Liabilities

'Guaranteed Liabilities' means all monies, debts and liabilities of any nature from time to time due, owing or incurred by the Buyer to the Seller and/or the Administrators under this Agreement, and including for the avoidance of doubt all of the costs and expenses of and incurred by the Seller or the Administrators as a result of or in connection with any default by the Buyer in compliance with the terms of this Agreement.

1.   Guarantee and indemnity

1.1   The Guarantor guarantees to the Seller and the Administrators to pay on demand the Guaranteed Liabilities.

1.2   If the Guaranteed Liabilities are not recoverable from the Buyer by reason of illegality, incapacity, lack or exceeding of powers, ineffectiveness of execution or any other reason, the Guarantor shall remain liable under this guarantee for the Guaranteed Liabilities as if it were a principal debtor.

1.3   The Guarantor as principal obligor and as a separate and independent obligation and liability from its obligations and liabilities under clause 1.1 agrees to indemnify and keep indemnified the Seller and the Administrators in full and on demand from and against all and any losses, costs, claims, liabilities, damages, demands and expenses suffered or incurred by the Seller and/or the Administrators arising out of, or in connection with, any failure of the Buyer to perform or discharge any of its obligations or liabilities in respect of the Guaranteed Liabilities.

1.4   The liability of the Guarantor under this clause 1 shall not be reduced, discharged or otherwise adversely affected by:

1.4.1   any intermediate payment, settlement of account or discharge in whole or in part of the Guaranteed Liabilities; or

1.4.2   any variation, extension, discharge, compromise, dealing with, exchange or renewal of any right or remedy which the Seller or the Administrators may have from or against the Buyer; or

1.4.3   any termination, amendment, variation, novation or supplement of or to any of the Guaranteed Liabilities; or

1.4.4   any grant of time, indulgence, waiver or concession to the Buyer; or

1.4.5   any insolvency, bankruptcy, liquidation, administration, winding up, incapacity, limitation, disability, the discharge by operation of law, or any change in the constitution, name or style of the Buyer; or

1.4.6   any invalidity, illegality, unenforceability, irregularity or frustration of any actual or purported obligation of the Buyer; or

1.4.7   any claim or enforcement of payment from the Buyer; or

1.4.8 any act or omission which would not have discharged or affected the liability of the Guarantor had it been a principal debtor instead of a guarantor, or indemnifier or by anything done or omitted by any person which but for this provision might operate to exonerate or discharge the Guarantor or otherwise reduce or extinguish his liability under this guarantee.

1.5 The Seller and/or the Administrators shall not be obliged before taking steps to enforce any of rights and remedies under this Guarantee:

1.5.1 to take any action or obtain judgment in any court against the Buyer; or

1.5.2 to make or file any claim in a bankruptcy, liquidation, administration or insolvency of the Buyer; or

1.5.3 to make demand, enforce or seek to enforce any claim, right or remedy against the Buyer.

Index

All references are to paragraph numbers

A

Accountants' report
due diligence, and, 4.37
Administration
applications, 1.17
appointment
company, by, 1.19
directors, by, 1.19–1.20
holder of floating charge, by,
1.18
capacity of seller, and, 4.14–4.15
commencement, 1.16
distress for rent arrears, 6.15
effect on directors, 1.23
introduction, 1.15
leasehold premises, and
assignment, and, 13.15
distress for rent, 6.15
generally, 13.2
moratorium, 1.22
pre-packs
appointment process, 2.7
benefits, 2.2
case law, 2.4
challenges, 2.12–2.17
criticisms, 2.3
definition, 2.1
employees, 2.8–2.9
future developments, 2.18
introduction, 2.1
landlords, 2.10
Statement of Insolvency Practice
(SIP13), 2.6
Statement of Insolvency Practice
(SIP16), 2.5
TUPE Regulations, 2.9
VAT, 2.11
purchasing vehicles and, 3.1
purpose, 1.21
secured creditors
position in transaction, 6.37
rights, 6.30
Administrative receivership
capacity of seller, and, 4.11
generally, 1.32

Advance payment
customers, and, 11.1
Anti-competitive agreements
customers, and, 11.1
Appointment
administration, and
company, by, 1.19
directors, by, 1.19–1.20
holder of floating charge, by, 1.18
leasehold premises, and
administrator, by, 13.15
company, by, 13.14
introduction, 13.13
liquidator, by, 13.16
procedure, 13.18
receiver, by, 13.17
terms, 13.18
pre-pack administrations, and, 2.7
Asset financing
raising cash, and, 5.19
Asset sales
generally, 3.2
method, 3.3
process, 3.4
Assignment
customer contracts, and, 11.7
security interests, and, 6.32
supplier contracts, and, 12.1

B

Bank guarantee
deferred consideration, and, 5.10
Bank overdrafts and loans
raising cash, and, 5.15
Banks
consents and approvals, and, 4.21
Bona vacantia
customers, and, 11.6
Book debts
charge, and, 6.2
excluded assets, and, 8.2
Books and records
company's, 8.3
officeholder's, 8.4